GARLAND STUDIES ON

# ASIAN AMERICANS

*edited by*

FRANKLIN NG
CALIFORNIA STATE UNIVERSITY,
FRESNO

A GARLAND SERIES

149690

# ASIAN AMERICANS AND THE MASS MEDIA

## A CONTENT ANALYSIS OF TWENTY UNITED STATES NEWSPAPERS AND A SURVEY OF ASIAN AMERICAN JOURNALISTS

VIRGINIA MANSFIELD-RICHARDSON

GARLAND PUBLISHING, Inc.
a member of the Taylor & Francis Group
New York & London/1999

Published in 2000 by
Garland Publishing Inc.
A Member of the Taylor & Francis Group
19 Union Square West
New York, NY 10003

10 9 8 7 6 5 4 3 2 1

Mansfield-Richardson, Virginia.
    Asian Americans and the mass media : a content analysis of
twenty United States' newspapers and a survey of Asian
American journalists / by Virginia Mansfield-Richardson.
        p. cm.
    Includes bibliographical references and index.
    ISBN - 0-8153-3476-1
    1. Asian Americans and mass media. 2. Asian American
mass media. 3. Mass Media surveys—United States. I. Title

P94.5.A75 M36 1999
302.23'089'95073–dc21
                                            99-046174

Printed on acid-free, 250-year-life paper
Manufactured in the United States of America

FOR MY HUSBAND BRIAN

# CONTENTS

# ACKNOWLEDGMENTS

There are many persons without whose support and guidance this book would not have been possible. My sincere appreciation is offered to Anne Cooper-Chen who oversaw the original dissertation research project that this book grew from. Other members of that dissertation committee also deserve sincere thanks, including Guido Stempel III, Harry Kaneshige, and Candice Thomas-Maddox for their expert advice and editing. Ralph Izard and the faculty and staff of the E.W. Scripps School of Journalism at Ohio University also deserve thanks for providing such a friendly and intellectually enriching environment for my doctoral studies. Terri Brooks and the faculty and staff of the College of Communications at Pennsylvania State University also provided a supportive atmosphere during my tenure as an associate professor there when I conducted much of the research for the project, and during the editing process for this book. The work of my research assistants, Nilanjana Bardhan and Dan Nicholson, was immensely helpful to this project. Of course, without the support of Lisa Chung and the members of the Asian Americans Journalists Association, much of the research in this book would not have been completed. Finally, I would also like to thank those persons at the newspapers that responded to my numerous inquiries during the data collection stages of this book.

# TABLES

# ASIAN AMERICANS
# AND THE MASS MEDIA

# CHAPTER 1

# INTRODUCTION

"We Can Always"
A television comedian says:
"Women are no longer bobbing
their hair because
they are slanting
their eyes"
and people laugh
A television comedian says:
"Hi! I'm Ruru,
fry me
to Florida"
and people laugh
A disc jockey says:
"You should know better
than to rob
a Chinese grocer
If you do
you will want to rob
again in another hour"
and people laugh
A newspaper columnist says:
"How come them heathen Chinee
are always observing New Year's
a month late?  When they gonna
get up to date?"
and if we can't laugh
at ourselves, we can always
go back.

—Nellie Wong,
*Dreams in Harrison Railroad Park*

# OVERVIEW

**Personal Experiences and Interesting Facts.** What does it mean to be an Asian American working in the mass media today? Here are a few examples of what some Asian Americans are experiencing in the newsrooms, television studios and radio stations across America:

> Once when I was pursuing an aggressive, slightly sneaky line of questioning with a county commissioner, he said, "Now, June, you're acting like Connie Chung now." It was a few days after the whole Connie Chung - Newt Gingrich's mom debacle. That same day, another source jokingly said to me, "So June, I hear you can't trust Oriental reporters anymore after the Connie Chung thing."
>
> > June Shih, former reporter for the Tampa Tribune

> A big negative experience that stands out in my mind is the time a tape editor called me a "f_ _ king gook" to my face, inside her edit room. At the time, I was a lowly production assistant, new to the industry and to the job, and I was devastated by this blatant, angry display of bigotry. I told some people in the newsroom about the incident (but no managers) and they all told me that this editor was known as a bigot and racist, and just to avoid her. Unfortunately, no one advised me to report the incident to managers, and I decided at the time that it wasn't worth "bothering" anyone with a complaint.
>
> > Female television reporter in New York City who asked not to be named

> One particular instance I remember happened about a year ago when I was following up on a shooting/gun possession arrest at a community I cover as a beat reporter. . . . I decided to visit the neighborhood to see what I could get from residents. Among my first stops while going door-to-door, I talked to a heavy-set, 30ish woman at home with her children. I identified myself and told her what I was looking for. After talking cordially for a few minutes and learning she knew very little, I thanked her and moved on. After finishing my canvas of the neighborhood I returned to the police station to see if the chief or a sergeant was around to con-

firm what I had gathered. The police dispatcher told me the woman had called, disbelieving my identity and supposing I was a member of some Asian gang looking to case her home or rob her. The dispatcher assured her I was a reporter and told her that she shouldn't worry. I didn't really think about it until afterwards and realized it was one of the most ridiculous things I'd ever experienced as a reporter. What did I do or say that made her think I was a gang member? My appearance was clean-cut and I was dressed professionally in a shirt, tie and shoes. I had a reporter's notebook in hand and pens in my pocket. I wrote notes about what little she said to me. She asked me for ID and I showed her my press card. The situation still puzzles me to this day.

> A male reporter at an East Coast newspaper who asked not to be named

Many negative experiences I've had stem from people's ignorance, and perhaps previous run-ins with other Asians. For example, while covering Memorial Day/Veteran's Day/Pearl Harbor commemoration stories, I'm often confronted with hostile veterans, friends, family members and widows who see me only as someone who 'looks like the enemy.' I've been denied access to certain ceremonies, causing my photographer to go alone to get video. I've also been outright snubbed verbally because I'm Asian.

> Victoria Lim, reporter for WWMT-TV in Kalamazoo, Michigan

One often-experienced phenomenon is being mistaken for Connie Chung when out on a shoot. For some reason, seeing an Asian woman with a camera crew brings out this odd assumption. We do not look anything alike, and I know many female Asian reporters encounter this syndrome.

> Susan Si-Lian Han, producer at KCTS/9 TV in Seattle

I have heard people say insensitive comments on the job—things such as mocking Indian accents or indicating that Indians have an accent, as if Americans don't. Once a colleague called a snake charmer a swami—who is a religious man, not a sidewalk entertainer—and laughed off the mis-

take. Another time, jokes were made about those Third
World people who worship animals.

> An Indian American who works as
> a reporter for a large metropolitan
> newspaper and asked not to be
> named.

Inclusion of Indian Americans under the umbrella of Asian
Americans may surprise some readers here, but as this book will
explain, the definition of just who is Asian American and the ethnic
origins of Asian Americans spans more than half the globe, from the
Pacific Islands to the Middle East—literally from Egypt to the
Hawaiian Islands. The breadth in defining Asian Americans is just
one of the many controversial issues facing this minority group today.

With that in mind, here are some more personal anecdotes of
Asian Americans working in the media, and problems they face
due to their ethnicity.

> When the Woody Allen scandal broke, and it came out that
> he was dating Mia Farrow's Korean-born adopted daughter,
> Soon-Yi, a very high profile anchorman yelled out the follow-
> ing joke across the newsroom: "What does Woody Allen
> have in common with Kodak film? The answer: they both
> come in little yellow boxes." I was typing in a cubicle, hid-
> den from others in the newsroom, when I heard this joke I
> remember being too embarrassed to come out for a long time
> after I heard people laughing. Being the only Asian American
> in the newsroom, and female, I remember just sitting in that
> cubicle, face flushed, hoping no one would see me there.

> > Female television reporter in New
> > York City who asked not to be
> > named.

Of course, talk to almost any Asian newswoman and you'll
find she's been called Connie Chung at least once. While I
am of mixed heritage, that doesn't come across to many
non-Asians. It drives me nuts that people, mostly whites,
are stupid enough to think we all look alike, even the "half-
breeds." I get called Connie all the time, either in jest or in
seriousness. I can't say this has hampered my news gathering because despite the Newt's-mom-affair, many people still
respect her. But I'm getting mighty sick of it.

> Female television reporter in New
> Jersey who asked not to be named.

I remember once getting on the elevator at the fifth floor
newsroom of The Washington Post and when the doors
closed a bunch of my colleagues, other reporters, started
making noises like "ching, chong, chink, chang." Yes, I was
hurt, but I never told anyone. Can you imagine, The
Washington Post, people would not think these kinds of attitudes exist, but they do. . . . I have experienced many racist
situations here (at The Washington Post) because I'm Asian,
yes, even from senior editors.

> Reporter of Asian ancestry who
> works at The Washington Post who
> asked not to be named.

I'm Iranian American, and I'm here to tell you I am not a
terrorist and neither are most Islamic people in this country.
. . This pervasive portrayal of Islamic people by the media
of this country is a real problem.

> Emilia Askari, a reporter for the
> Detroit Free Press, speaking at a
> panel on minorities and the media
> at the 1995 annual convention of
> the Association for Education in
> Journalism and Mass
> Communication.

I've been told on several occasions that the television market
where I have applied for a position 'is not ready for an
Asian sports anchor.' Obviously, the majority of television
news directors and general managers believe that Asians
can't anchor and report the sports news. How many Asian
sports anchors/reporters can you name? Not many, because
there aren't that many. I can go on and on about this topic.

> An Asian American man who
> works as a television sports anchor
> for a mid-sized station on the East
> Coast who asked not to be named.

After working at the *Chicago Tribune* for about a year, a
reporter asked how my first day went. She had confused me
with another Asian male who had started that day. This

guy is at least a foot taller than me, formally dressed, younger, didn't wear glasses at the time and otherwise looked completely different, sounded different and worked in a different department. I had gone on assignment with this reporter only a month previous, yet she still had me confused with a guy who'd only been there a day.

Also, and not surprisingly, throughout my time here, people consistently confuse me with the other Asian working on the picture desk, Jim. People call Jim, Eric. People call me Jim. Again, we don't look alike, talk alike. . . I wear glasses, he doesn't. Jim has worked here about five times longer than I have.

> Eric Chu, then assistant picture editor/one-year resident at the *Chicago Tribune.*

These disturbing first-hand accounts of Asian American journalists represent only a part of a larger problem in the United States concerning the treatment of and attitudes towards Asian Americans. Consider the following facts:

> As recently as 1988, President Ronald Reagan appointed Sherwin Chan as the first Asian American to serve on the U.S. Commission on Civil Rights, and the following year, in 1989, President George Bush appointed Sichan Siv as the first Asian American liaison to the White House and named Elaine Chao Deputy Secretary of Transportation, the highest office ever reached by an Asian American in the executive branch.

> Yen Le Espiritu, from the book Asian American Panethnicity

Japan Nips Creativity in the Bud

> Headline for an opinion column by James O. Goldsborough published in the San Diego Union-Tribune, February 6, 1992.

The U.S. Commission on Civil Rights concluded in a 1986 report that violence against Asians is a national problem. There have been scores of physical assaults over the past few years: beatings and harassment of Hmong refugees in Philadelphia; the assault on a Chinese immigrant by a Boston police officer; the arson of Cambodian families' homes in

Revere, Massachusetts; shots fired at Vietnamese fishermen in Texas and off the Northern California coast; the stabbing of a Chinese American in New York by teenagers shouting, "Let's get these Chinks out of here!"; the beating of two Japanese students at the University of Wisconsin by a group of drunken whites who uttered a racist remark; and the murder of Indian Americans in Jersey City, New Jersey, by a group called the "Dotbusters" whose sole aim was to terrorize the Indian community until they were forced to leave the Jersey City area for fear of their lives.

> From the Asian American Handbook, a media guide and joint project of the National Conference of Christians and Jews, and the Asian American Journalists Association.

In 1987, an article on the 100th Congress published in The New York Times described the U.S. Senate as "100 percent white," even though Sen. Daniel Inouye and Sen. Spark Matsunaga, who were both Democrats from Hawaii and both Japanese Americans, were serving at that time. In the same article, the U.S. House of Representatives was described as being "92 percent white, 5 percent black, and 3 percent Hispanic," which did not account for the members of Congress of Asian or Pacific Islander ancestry serving at that time: Rep. Daniel Akaka (Dem.-Hawaii), Rep. Robert Matsui (Dem.-California), Rep. Norman Mineta (Dem.-California), and the territorial delegates from Guam and American Samoa.

> The New York Times, January 5, 1987.

The May 4, 1984 cover of The National Review highlighted an article entitled "The Underhandedness of Affirmative Action" and featured as a graphic a list that read, in part, "two (2) Jews, one (1) cripple, one (1) Hispanic, one (1) Chink."

> The National Review, May 4, 1984.

If You're So Smart. . . Why Aren't You Japanese?

Headline on the cover of The
National Review, April 15, 1991.

Any time someone wanted to do a film in China or Hong
Kong, or about gangs in Chinatown, I was offered those. . .
the John Woo sort of stuff. That's the only area they feel
they can exploit. It's sad that what the American community knows about the Chinese is really bad.

Quote from Asian American film-
maker Wayne Wang, director of the
hit film, *The Joy Luck Club* in the
New York Times, September 5,
1993.

Asians in the U.S. were the targets of racially motivated
crimes nearly once a day on average in 1993, according to
the first such national assessment by community groups.

From an article in the San Francisco
Chronicle, April 24, 1994.

Most Americans find it hard to believe that Asian
Americans across the U.S. are afflicted with poverty, especially since 1990 figures show Asian- and Pacific-Americans
had a median household income of $36,000 a year.
However, Asians have a 14 percent poverty rate compared
to 9 percent for whites.

From an article in the *Houston
Chronicle*, July 30, 1994.

Just as anxiety about the growing economic strength of
Japan has resulted in an increase in Japan-bashing and violence against Asian Pacific Americans, in the first few weeks
of 1991—the beginnings of the air war in the Persian Gulf—
Arab Americans reported more incidents of harassment and
hate crimes than in all of 1990. In the first five weeks of
1991, the American-Arab Anti-Discrimination Committee
received reports of about 60 incidents from 25 states including nine each from California and Michigan and seven from
the District of Columbia.

The incidents ranged from threatening phone calls and vandalism to
beatings and bombings.

Some incidents recorded by the committee included two bombings at a Cincinnati grocery store owned by Arab Americans; vandalism of a Muslim school in Tulsa, Okla.; arson at a Los Angeles delicatessen owned by an Arab American; an attack on an Afghani American who was mistaken for an Arab American; and physical assaults on Arab Americans in Michigan, New York, New Jersey and the District of Columbia.

> From The Journalist's Guide to Middle Eastern Americans published by the Asian American Journalists Association, Detroit Chapter.

Another Penn State student has reported a racial slur written on her residence hall door. Penn State police said that at about 8 p.m. Friday, an Asian-American student living on the second floor of Thompson Hall told them someone had written a harassing racial message on the door to her room.

> From the Centre Daily Times, January 14, 1996, a Knight-Ridder newspaper that covers the Penn State University region.

It's very difficult for a normal South Asian person to come here [to the United States] and even if he is talented, make it. Unless he's willing to go through five to 10 years of agony. . . .If you're North Indian and lighter, then you have a better shot. At least you can play Spanish characters.

> Tennis star and actor Ashok Amritraj, discussing the difficulty of being an East Indian actor in the American film industry, in an article in the magazine Masala, September/October 1995.

Wallace Loh, dean of the University of Washington Law School, has been named president-elect of the Association of American Law Schools.

Loh, dean at UW since 1990, is the first and only Asian-American dean of an accredited U.S. law school and now

will be the first Asian-American to head the association in
its 95-year history.

> From an article in the Seattle Times,
> January 13, 1995.

A coalition of Asian lawyers criticized the Clinton administration yesterday, because there are no Asian Americans
among the president's first 50 nominees to federal judge-
ships across the country.

> From an article in the San Francisco
> Chronicle, March 2, 1994.

In a sport where no woman but of white, Northern
European birth or heritage has ever won the figs [figure
skating championship], the battle for the gold and all the
lucre it earns sets up a duel between two young women
named [Kristi] Yamaguchi and [Midori]Ito whose blood-
lines both stretch back, pure and simple, to the same soft,
cherry-blossom days on the one bold little island of Honshu.
. . .
It's a very funny thing, but (Tonya) Harding and Yamaguchi
are the two Americans and Ito and Yamaguchi are the two
Japanese, but Ito and Harding are the ones most alike. . . .
Certainly, deep within her, she [Kristi Yamaguchi] is still
Japanese—some of her must be—and if she should win it's
because, while the others have the triple axel, only she has
the best of both worlds.

> From the February 10, 1992, cover
> story in Newsweek, a profile on
> Olympic figure skater Kristi
> Yamaguchi,a fourth-generation
> Asian American.

No one ever insinuated that Dorothy Hamill would feel
some deep allegiance to whatever European countries her
ancestors were from.

> From a letter to the editor pub-
> lished in Newsweek the week fol-
> lowing the cover story on Kristi
> Yamaguchi, criticizing the racist
> tone of the article.

> A new line of greeting cards features bare-chested Asian male actors. The cards were created to debunk the stereotype of the sexless Asian male.
>
> From an article in the Los Angeles Times, February 23, 1995.

This unsettling list of facts relating to Asian Americans, and personal experiences of Asian Americans working in the media, is, unfortunately, only the tip of a larger iceberg that will be partially examined in this book. The broader picture of Asian Americans and their relationship with the U.S. media also includes many positive trends towards better coverage of the many ethnic communities that make up who is Asian American, as well as positive experiences within the workplace for Asian American journalists.

With all this in mind, this book is built on the basic premise that Asian Americans are an intricate part of all Americans' past, present, and future, and, consequently, Asian Americans are of vital importance to American media and American media scholarship.

**Statement of the Problem.** What role do Asian American journalists play in U.S. society? How are Asian Americans portrayed in the American media? Many Asian Americans will answer this last question by saying their communities and the issues affecting them are not given proper coverage in print, radio, television, and film media. Others claim that the number of Asian Americans hired in newsrooms is low in proportion to the nearly three percent of the U.S. population that Asian Americans now represent, according the 1990 U.S. Census (*U.S. Census - 1990* 1992, 323-325). Still others say that Asian Americans are wrongly stereotyped in the entertainment and news media. However, the real issue goes much deeper than these assertions. The fact is, no one really knows how Asian Americans are covered or portrayed in the media because there is a lack of research on these matters within the academic community, and there is only limited data on the number of Asian Americans employed in newspaper, radio and television newsrooms.

Jeffres and Hur wrote an article entitled "The Forgotten Media Consumer—The American Ethnic" in the spring 1980 edition of *Journalism Quarterly* that provided context to this book (Jeffres and Hur 1980). The article said that few studies had been conducted at that time on ethnic media and the uses of ethnic media. Jeffres and Hur gave supporting data that ethnic media "often fail to meet the needs of ethnics in order to maximize their [media organization's] profits" (11). If this is still the case with ethnic media, as studies cited in Chapter Three of this book will show, what questions does that pose about the mainstream media serving much larger markets? In fact, there is little data today on how the mainstream media meet the needs of Asian Americans, which is one issue this book will address.

Understanding the portrayal of Asian Americans in the media could affect Asian American consumers' decision to read a newspaper. Ignoring this fast-growing market could have implications for advertisers, as well as for media gatekeepers and, of course, for all media consumers, including Asian Americans.

To summarize, many stereotypes and much negative coverage of Asian Americans exists in newspapers, television, radio, and film today. Yet, there is also a great deal of positive coverage of Asian Americans, as this book will demonstrate. Unfortunately, as the related studies chapter of this book indicates, there were no recent content analyses published prior to this book that dealt solely with coverage of Asian Americans, and no ongoing documentation of how the media are portraying Asian Americans and the issues affecting them.

In the eleven years from 1982 to 1994, not a single doctoral book in mass communication has been written on any aspect of Asian Americans and the media (Wilhoit 1982-1987; Fowler 1988-1994). Also very few scholarly articles have been written recently on this important and fastest-growing minority in the United States.

The purpose, therefore, of this book will be to answer the broader question of how twenty of the largest newspapers in the country are actually covering Asian Americans and issues in their communities, and how Asian Americans, specifically Asian American journalists, perceive coverage of their minority in the American media. Many of the facts and studies referred to in this book deal with the time frame of the study, from 1994 to 1995, and are offered to help give context to the data collected.

It is important to study Asian Americans as a whole, compared to just studying the ethnic sub-groups of Asian Americans. Too often a study on one of the ethnic sub-groups of Asian

Americans—for example on Korean Americans or Chinese Americans—is wrongly translated to apply to all Asian Americans. While studying ethnic sub-groups of Asian Americans is valuable, it is just as important to study the vast and diverse group of Americans with Asian ethnic origins as a whole entity. Asian American is more broadly construed than Chinese, Japanese, Pacific Islander, or any other ethnic sub-group and it is extremely important to understand this reality, particularly when conducting scholarly research.

## DEFINITION OF TERMS

The terms "Asian Americans" and "Pacific Islanders" are used throughout this book. In many books and articles, as well as the U.S. Census, these terms are often listed separately to define the entire population of Asian Americans. This book defines the term "Asian Americans" as including Pacific Islanders. However, when referring to U.S. Census data, Pacific Islanders are occasionally listed separately from Asian Americans in this book to best explain the census categories.

Before coming up with a conceptual definition of Asian Americans for this book, several Asian American organizations were contacted to find out how they defined who Asian Americans are. As expected, nearly all of those group representatives contacted—which included the Asian American Studies Center at the University of California, Los Angeles—explained that they leave it up to their members to determine if they are Asian Americans.[1] Many Asian American groups, however, do not include Middle Eastern Americans. Yet, as will become evident in this book, no one organization, including various agencies of the U.S. government, has what can be considered a precise definition of who is an Asian American.

Since even the Asian American Journalists Association does not include Middle Eastern countries in their definition of the ethnic backgrounds of Asian Americans, and also since the U.S. Census does not include Middle Easterners as part of Asian Americans, Middle Eastern Americans have been included in part of the historical discussion of Asian Americans in this book and in other sections, but not included in the search keywords used for the content analysis. This will be explained in greater detail later.

There are nineteen ethnic sub-groups that are considered Asian Americans according to the Asian Americans Information Directory (Backus and Furtaw 1992, 11-12). [2] Several expansions and changes have been made in the race categories for the three most recent U.S. Censuses of 1990, 1980 and 1970. For example, the 1990 Census explains it was the first census "to undertake, on a 100-percent basis, an automated review, edit, and coding operation for written responses to the race item," so this represents the most thorough counting of Americans' ethnic identity in the history of the census (*U.S. Census: Social and Economic Characteristics* 1992, B-31). [3]

However, the determination of who is an Asian American is fraught with controversy. For example, scholar Paul Spickard argues that Asians and Pacific Islanders should be separated as he believes that their concerns and backgrounds are sufficiently different. It should be noted that if there is a separate "Pacific Islander" category in the census and governmental data, many Pacific Islanders fear Hawaiian hegemony over other Pacific Islanders such as Samoans, Fijians, Tongans, and Chamorros. The debate among scholars as to who constitutes an Asian American will be discussed further in section C of this chapter. There are some leading Asian American historians, such as Sucheng Chan, who refer to all Asians who worked in the United States prior to the 1960s as immigrants. [4] For the purpose of this book, however, that division in terminology was rejected.

The nineteen ethnic sub-groups now considered to be Asian Americans, according to the *Asian Americans Information Directory*, which differ from the ethnic sub-groups that fall under the U.S. Census classification for *Asian and Pacific Islander*, are (Backus and Furtaw 1992, 11-12):

| | |
|---|---|
| Bangladeshi Americans | Japanese Americans |
| Burmese Americans | Korean Americans |
| Cambodian Americans | Laotian Americans |
| Chinese Americans: | Malaysian Americans |
| (Hong Kong, Manchurians, | Nepalese Americans |
| Mongolians, Taiwanese, | Pacific Islanders |
| Tibetans) | Pakistani Americans |
| East Indian Americans | Singaporan Americans |
| Filipino Americans | Sri Lankan Americans |
| Hmong Americans | Thai Americans |
| Indonesian Americans | Vietnamese Americans |

The 1990 U.S. Census classification of Asian Americans includes most of these categories, but excludes some, and lists in more detail some of the ethnic sub-categories. Here is a breakdown of the ethnic sub-categories included in the U.S. Census under the umbrella classification of "Asian or Pacific Islander" (*U.S. Census 1990: Social and Economic Characteristics* 1993, B-30):

**Asian**
Chinese
Filipino
Japanese
Asian Indian
Korean
Vietnamese
Cambodian
Hmong
Laotian
Thai
Other Asian*
    Bangladeshi
    Bhutanese
    Borneo
    Burmese
    Celebesian
    Ceram
    Indochinese
    Indonesian
    Iwo-Jiman
    Javanese
    Malayan
    Maldivian
    Napali
    Okinawan
    Pakistani
    Sikkim
    Singaporean
    Sri Lankan
    Sumatran
Asian, not specified**

**Pacific Islander**
Hawaiian
Samoan
Guamanian
Other Pacific Islander*
    Carolinian
    Fijian
    Kosraean
    Melanesian***
    Micronesian***
    Northern Mariana Islander
    Palauan
    Papua New Guinean
    Ponapean (Pohnpeian)
    Polynesian***
    Solomon Islander
    Tahitian
    Tarawa Islander
    Tokelauan
    Tongan
    Trukese (Chuukese)
    Yapese
    Pacific Islander, not specified

\* In some data products, specified groups listed under "Other Asian" or "Other Pacific Islander" are shown separately. Groups not shown are tabulated as "All Other Asian" or "All Other Pacific Islander," respectively.

\*\* Includes entries such as Asian American, Asian, Asiatic, Ameriasian and Eurasian.

\*\*\*Polynesian, Micronesian, and Melanesian are Pacific Islander cultural groups.

For the purpose of this study the term "Asian Americans" will include all ethnic sub-groups listed in both the Asian American Information Directory for 1992, and by the U.S. Census for 1990. As stated, this book includes all Pacific Islander ethnic sub-groups when using the term "Asian Americans." There are, however, times when it is helpful to discuss Pacific Islanders separately from the whole of Asian Americans and in those cases throughout this book the term "Pacific Islander" refers to people whose ethnic origins are one or more of the ethnic sub-groups listed under "Pacific Islanders" in the 1990 U.S. Census.

As with all ethnic identities, there are many layers of those people who constitute this minority group in the United States. For the purpose of this book, the following ethnic backgrounds of persons, or combinations thereof, or classifications of citizenship of those persons are defined as being an Asian American:

1) Having an ethnic heritage with direct descent from any of the Asian American ethnic sub-groups listed in the 1990 U.S. Census or the 1992 *Asian American Information Directory*, and having United States citizenship. For example, a person whose ethnic lineage consists of only relatives of Japanese descent. This includes persons who are of full Asian ancestry and who are adopted by U.S. citizens of any race.

2) Having an ethnic heritage with direct descent from any two or more of the Asian American ethnic sub-groups, and having United States citizenship. For example, if a person's father is of Chinese descent and his or her mother is of Filipino descent.

3) Having an ethnic heritage with any one relative being of an Asian American ethnic sub-group as far back as three generations, and having United States citizenship. For example, this would include a person whose great-grandfather was Indonesian, but all other relatives since were Caucasian. Any person with a combination of mixed races with an Asian American ethnic sub-group going back three generations would be included in this category.

4) Immigrants (which includes refugees) with Asian or Pacific Islander heritage, or heritage that is included under numbers one, two or three of these definitions, who are living in the United States.

This final category—Asian immigrants living in the United States—might not seem to fit logically under the umbrella definition of Asian Americans. However, for the purpose of this study, often people who fall under one of the three categories defined above live under the same roof and are in the same family. People who would fall under definitions numbers one through three often socialize, own businesses, attend school, and mix in other ways with communities of Asian immigrants. Finally, it seems appropriate to argue that an Asian, Southeast Asian, Near Asian or Pacific Islander who has been living in the United States for several years (sometimes most of his or her life), but who has not changed his or her citizenship to that of a U.S. citizen, is very Americanized and has many of the same attitudes, personal identifications and experiences of prejudice as a person born in the United States of parents who are Asian, or some racial mix thereof which includes Asian heritage.

This last point was considered strongly in this book, particularly after interviewing numerous Asian Americans. Often it matters only that a person is perceived as being Asian by other people within a community which results in some form of insult or prejudice, whether intentional or not, against that person. Here lies one of the core problems studied in this book, particularly in the types of news articles published about Asian Americans or issues affecting Asian Americans.

Support for this last part of the definition of Asian American for this book includes the following facts. In 1991 six percent of hate crimes reported by approximately three thousand law enforcement agencies in thirty-two states were against Asian Americans (Gall and Gall 1993, 101). In a recent survey 18 percent of those interviewed said they would not want persons of Vietnamese heritage as neighbors, 14 percent said they would not want Koreans as neighbors and 15 percent said they would not want Pakistanis as neighbors, compared to 12 percent who said they would not want African Americans as neighbors and 16 percent who said they would not want Hispanics as neighbors (7). In the same survey, respondents were asked their attitudes of living in a neighborhood where 50 percent or more of the residents were of certain minorities. Of those responding, 29.5 percent said they strongly opposed Hispanics as neighbors, 28.7 percent strongly opposed African Americans as neighbors, and 26.3 percent strongly opposed Asian Americans as neighbors (8). Surveys such as these are alarming to many Asian Americans, and, indeed, to many other Americans as well who mistakenly assume Asian Americans receive more favorable treatment than other minorities in most areas of life. Often the true nature of attitudes towards Asian Americans, whether positive or negative, is not being properly conveyed in the American media.

The Asian American community is extremely multi-faceted, and, frankly, it is difficult to draw precise definitional boundaries for that population.⁵ Also, there were some cases where it was appropriate to mention an article or a quote that discussed Asian Canadians, Asian Mexicans, Asian Native Americans or Asians of other citizenships. This study includes the term "Asian Native Americans" as being Asian Americans, even though a person in this category might have been a member of a Native American tribal nation.⁶ The term "Asian Native Americans" is not widely used. Because of the time of their arrival thousands of years ago into the Americas, Native Americans should not be categorized as Asian Americans. The social and cultural definitions of Asian Americans and Asian countries are more appropriate for a much later point in time.

However, Asian Canadians, Asian Europeans, Asian Mexicans, Asian Africans or people of Asian ancestry living as citizens in a non-Asian or Pacific Island country, or who are not living in the United States, are not included in the official definition of "Asian American" in this book.

The term "Asian Indian" in this study refers to people whose ancestry comes from the Indian subcontinent. This term received official sanction in the 1980 U.S. Census to describe people of Asian descent from India. Asian Americans whose ancestry is from the Indian sub-continent are also referred to as East Indians, Hindus, and Hindustanis in some scholarly literature, but those terms will not be officially used as part of this book's definition of Asian Americans. The term "Asian Indian" also includes persons who are of Bengalese, Bharat, Dravidian, East Indian, or Goanese descent. However, persons of Bangladeshi, Pakistani, or Sri Lankan ancestry are not included in the Asian Indian classification in this book, in accordance to the U.S. Census definition of Asian Indian.

One point about transliterations used for Asian names in this book needs to be clarified. Ongoing debate as to the correct style for various Asian names is discussed later in this book. For clarification, however, for the names of authors cited in this study, this study honors the preferred style of each particular author or expert for his or her name. Otherwise, the style set by the *Chicago Manual of Style* for Chinese names, including the capitalization of and romanization of those names, has been used in this study.

## U.S. Census Data on Asian Americans

In a U.S. Census report, released December 8, 1995, the nation's Asian American and Pacific Islander population reached an all-time high of 8.8 million in 1994, up from nearly 7.3 million in 1990 (Associated Press, December 10, 1995). That same report said that Asian Americans and Pacific Islanders (combined) now comprise three percent of all Americans, and eight percent of all people living in the West, where six to 10 percent of all Asian Americans and Pacific Islanders live (Associated Press, December 10, 1995).

According to the 1990 U.S. Census there were approximately 7.2 million people living in the U.S. who are classified in the census as "Asian or Pacific Islanders." Table 1 is how the 1990 U.S. Census broke down that minority.

It is projected there will be more than 40 million Aisan Americans by 2050, up from nearly 5.5 million in 1990 (Gall and Gall 1993, 569). The spectacular 95 percent increase in the Asian American population from 1980 to 1990 far eclipsed any other ethnic minority group's growth during that decade, according to the U.S. Census (25). During that decade, the Asian American population explosion was followed by the Hispanic population in the United States which increased 52 percent during the same decade, and by the Native American population which increased 28 percent during that time (25). The African American population increased by 13 percent from 1980 to 1990, the non-Hispanic white population increased by 4 percent, the non-Hispanic other races actually decreased by 5.7 percent, and the total U.S. population grew by nearly 10 percent (9.8 percent) (25).

In certain states, mostly on the West Coast, the projected population increases of Asian Americans in the upcoming decades are even higher than the national figures. The *Seattle Times* reported in an April 1994 article that "the number of Asian and Pacific Islanders living in California is projected to more than double from 3.5 million in 1993 to 9.7 million in 2020" (*Seattle Times* April 21, 1994).

## 'East Coast Lens' of the Media

Deann Borshay, executive director of the National Asian American Telecommunications Association in 1994, addressed the

Table 1. Breakdown of Asian American or Pacific Islanders in the U.S. Census Compared to Other Minorities

| Race | Population |
|------|-----------|
| All persons | 248,709,873 |
| White | 199,827,064 |
| Black | 29,930,524 |
| American Indian, Eskimo or Aleut | 2,015,143 |
| American Indian | 1,937,391 |
| Eskimo | 55,674 |
| Aleut | 22,078 |
| Asian or Pacific Islander | 7,226,986 |
| Asian | 6,876,394 |
| Chinese | 1,648,696 |
| Filipino | 1,419,711 |
| Japanese | 866,160 |
| Korean | 797,304 |
| Asian Indian | 786,694 |
| Vietnamese | 593,213 |
| Cambodian | 149,047 |
| Laotian | 147,375 |
| Hmong | 94,439 |
| Thai | 91,360 |
| Other Asian | 282,395 |
| Pacific Islander | 350,592 |
| Hawaiian | 205,501 |
| Samoan | 57,679 |
| Guamanian | 47,754 |
| Other Pacific Islander | 39,658 |
| Other race | 9,710,157 |

SOURCE: 1990 U.S. Census, Social and Economic Characteristics, Table 4.

problem faced by the Asian American community of being so broadly defined, during a 1994 interview: "I think people don't like to be lumped into a huge category of who they are, but I think also people understand the necessary categorizing for the sake of measurement" (Borshay interview 1994). However, her organization believes that much of the media in America is seen through an "East Coast lens."

Borshay explained that "the East Coast lens is very narrow and portrays things very much in black and white (racially). . . . There's also a belief that there was no consciousness of racial oppression prior to the Civil Rights movement" in the 1960s (Borshay interview 1994). She explained this assault on the national media by saying, "The East Coast media understands there was slavery, there was a Civil War, and there was a Civil Rights movement. But other (minority) people fall into this gray area of oppression" (Borshay interview 1994).

Some of the research questions of this book will examine if Borshay's comments on the East Coast media are reflected in a difference of coverage of Asian Americans between the East Coast newspapers and the West Coast newspapers used in the content analysis. Several studies, however, indicate that the media have become much more responsible in reporting on minority groups, and providing a representative picture of society's constituent groups. Much of this expanded coverage stems from the 1947 Hutchins Commission report entitled *A Free and Responsible Press*. The Hutchins Commission, financed with a $200,000 grant in 1947 by Time magazine founder and publisher Henry Luce, was headed by Robert Maynard Hutchins and charged with studying the state of the American press (Vivian 1993, 97). The report of that commission said the press needed to become more socially responsible, and one of its many recommendations was for the press to provide a representative picture of society's constituent groups, including African Americans and other minorities (Commission for the Freedom of the Press 1947). Some media scholars think that the Hutchins Commission report marked the final shift from the libertarian view of the press to the social responsibility theory of the press which prevails in much of American media today. There has been much fairer and more comprehensive coverage of society's constituent groups, including Asian Americans, since the publication of the Hutchins

Commission report. However, as this study will demonstrate, in many respects the Hutchins Commission and its impact did not affect the coverage of Asian Americans to a great degree.

With that historical footnote in mind, consider that when Borshay speaks of an "East Coast media mentality," she is referring, upon her own admission, to most of the media in the United States outside of the West Coast. Since there are larger Asian American populations on the West Coast, with the exception of New York City on the East Coast, the West Coast media are more responsible in their coverage of Asian Americans, Borshay said.

Borshay added, "In terms of oppression, historically at least people and media on the West Coast are aware of the Chinese Exclusionary Act [of May 5, 1882], whereas the people and media on the East Coast [and the rest of the country] don't seem to have as much awareness of this" (Borshay interview 1994). So, Borshay alleges, there is a dual problem among the American media in explaining to media consumers 1) which ethnic groups constitute the broad category of Asian Americans, and, 2) in properly portraying the history of Asian American oppression and struggles. The results of this book will seek to find if these charges are true or not supported by the content analysis.

Lisa Chung, executive director of the Asian American Journalists Association in 1994, agreed that defining Asian Americans and covering all the ethnic sub-groups in that category is a problem for the American media. "The problem has to do with the awareness of society in general," Chung said, "Typically when you think of minorities, in general the American public thinks of Hispanics and blacks. By the time they get down to Asian American people, they just aren't that aware of who they [Asian Americans] are" (Chung interview 1994). Both Chung and Borshay believe much of this lack of understanding about who Asian Americans are and what their history is can be attributed to a national media that simply do not make it their job or agenda to educate the public on these matters (i.e., are not socially responsible). Chung agreed that there is a certain East Coast mentality to news coverage of Asian Americans. Again, this book will seek to find if there is merit to this assumption.

In the book *The State of Asian America, Activism and Resistance in the 1990s*, edited by Karin Aguilar-San Juan, another aspect of this problem of lumping so many ethnic groups in the category of Asian Americans is addressed. There is currently a movement afoot by native Hawaiians to petition the U.S. government to reclassify them as Native Americans, rather than Pacific Islanders, which is how they are presently classified by the U.S. Government, under the umbrella category Asian Americans/Pacific Islanders. In her book, Aguilar-San Juan explained the problem:

> In the title of this anthology the term Asian American is used to include U.S. citizens of Pacific Islander roots. Though convenient, this shorthand makes invisible the unique concerns of Pacific Islander Americans. Consequently, many writers within this book use the longer appellation, "Asian/Pacific Island American." Because our community is still growing and we are in the midst of defining our own experiences, no term is perfect—the fact that one contributor is Asian Canadian makes one wonder how accurate even the longer term can be (Aguilar-San Juan 1984, viii).

The very basic problem of determining who is an Asian American may be one obstacle that is preventing the media from correctly covering Asian Americans and Pacific Islanders. This assumption makes even more sense when considering the tendency by television and radio media to oversimplify the news in order to fit it into tight time spots and so as not to lose the very short attention spans of viewers and listeners.

## ASIAN AMERICANS' USE OF MEDIA

As will be shown in Chapter Three of this book, there is surprisingly little information on Asian Americans' use of the media. Two useful studies were conducted by Delener and Neelankavil and published in the *Journal of Advertising Research* in 1990. The 104 Asian respondents surveyed in both studies included Asian Americans and Asian immigrants living in New York City. One study compared media usage between the 104 Asian Americans and ninety-nine Hispanics, and found that there were two distinct groups of media consumers among the Asian Americans: educated younger Asians and older Asians (Delener and Neellankavil 1990, 45-52).

The study indicated that of the 104 Asian respondents, 77 percent regularly watched television, 57.7 percent regularly read newspapers, 56.7 percent regularly listened to the radio and 32.7 percent regularly read magazines (see Appendix 1) (Gall and Gall 1993, 33). The study also found that the Asian respondents preferred television (particularly feature and variety shows) and newspapers over radio and magazines, and that younger Asians preferred more upscale newspapers such as the *New York Times* and the *Wall Street Journal*, while older Asians read more Asian language daily newspapers (Delener and Neelankavil 1990, 45-52).

The second study, conducted in 1989, asked the 104 Asian American/Asian immigrant respondents what types of magazines they read regularly, listing a handful of magazines under each topic category (see Appendix 2) (Gall and Gall 1993, 32-33). For Asian respondents, general interest magazines such as *Newsweek*, *People*, and *Time*, were the most popular category among the magazine categories "Business/Trade," "Scientific," "Men's," "Women's," "Sports," General Interest," and "Ethnic: Chinese, Japanese and Spanish" (32-33). However, the magazine *Business Week* was read regularly by thirty-nine of Asian respondents, which ranked as one of the two most popular magazines among respondents with thirty-nine respondents saying they also regularly read *Time* magazine (32). Other than the general interest magazines mentioned above, other popular magazines among Asian respondents included *Fortune* with twenty-three of the respondents as regular readers, the women's magazine *Elle* with twenty-eight of the respondents as regular readers, and *GQ-Gentlemen's Quarterly* with twenty-one as regular readers (32-33).

Chaffee, Nass, and Yang conducted a study in 1991 that questioned 239 Korean American households in central California that examined correlations between trust in government and news media usage (Chaffee, Nass, and Yang 1991, 111-119). This study dealt with media usage by Korean Americans in a round-about manner. It found that respondents clearly differentiated between ethnic Korean newspapers and mainstream American newspapers, but not necessarily between the American press and the government, and that the perceived connection between a media bias favoring the U.S. government appeared to be a carry over from Korea to the United States. The study also found those respondents who received news solely from the Korean language press were no different from those who fell into the low-media-use group in differentiating press-government relationships in the United States than press-government relationships (ties) in Korea.

Chaffee, Nass, and Yang produced another article from a survey of Korean residents in the San Francisco area that indicated U.S. television news exposure ranked alongside American and Korean newspaper exposure in positively predicting respondents' knowledge about the American political structure and process, and among those respondents who had lived in the United States for the longest periods, the newspaper was the strongest predictor of political learning (Chaffee, Nass, and Yang 1990, 266-288). The study also indicated that for respondents who had lived in the United States the shortest amount of time, television news was the strongest predictor of political knowledge.

A 1990 study by Lee and Cho found that Korean housewives living in the United States preferred to rent videos of Korean soap operas over watching American soap operas, and discussed this audience preference in terms of the viewers' perceptions of Korean vs. American soap operas (Lee and Cho 1990, 30-44).

Shim and Salmon studied the Korean population in Seattle, Washington, to see if there was a relationship between community orientation and newspaper readership (Shim and Salmon 1990, 852-863). In fact, the research supported their hypothesis that Koreans who identified more with the Korean community were more likely to read ethnic Korean newspapers than those Koreans who identified more with the American community (these were more likely to be second and third generation Korean Americans) tended to read mainstream, English-language newspapers.

A few other studies on media use of Asian Americans will be mentioned in Chapter Two in a discussion of the histories of the various ethnic sub-groups. The review of literature for this book indicates that there have been more studies on Korean Americans and media use compared to other ethnic sub-groups of Asian Americans, which is why Koreans have been mentioned more in this sub-section. To generalize any of these surveys to the overall Asian American population would be incorrect and misleading. These studies do give some interesting insight into media preferences of Asian Americans, however.

A survey mentioned earlier conducted by the Republican National Committee in 1992 of five thousand Asian Americans living in California is helpful in understanding what media sources serve Asian Americans in seeking information on political issues (see Appendix 3) (21). Of the 1,149 Asian Americans who responded to the survey, 49.7 percent said newspapers were their major source of information about political issues, 39.3 percent said television was their major source, 5.8 percent said magazines were their major source, 4.4 percent said radio was the major source, and 0.3 percent said friends were their major source this type of information (21).

However, in looking at ethnic sub-group breakdowns of those surveyed, it becomes apparent that all the Asian Americans surveyed do not have the same media use habits when it comes to seeking information about political issues. For example, 61.3 percent of Asian Indians said newspapers were their major source for information on political issues, compared to 41.8 percent of Vietnamese, and 28.0 percent of those in the "Others" category (21). Another striking difference was that 13.9 percent of Korean Americans cited magazines as their major source, compared to 1.8 percent of Vietnamese, 4.9 percent of Japanese, 5.8 percent of Filipinos, 7.6 percent of Chinese, and 1.1 percent of others (21). More Asian Indians received their information on political issues primarily from radio (11.3 percent) than any other ethnic group in the survey, followed by Vietnamese (8.2 percent), others (4.3 percent), Chinese (4.15 percent), Japanese (3.3 percent), Filipino (1.7 percent), and Korean (1.3 percent) (21). Finally, the group that cited television the least as a primary source of information on political issues were Asian Indians (27.5 percent said television was their primary source), compared to 50 percent of Filipinos citing television, and 64.5 percent of others saying television was their primary source (21).

Much more research needs to be done in this area of how Asian Americans use media. These studies are useful for several reasons, however, especially in showing that all Asian Americans should not always be lumped together as a minority that thinks and acts alike. They also raise many good topics for future research, such as why do Asian Americans like certain types of magazines more than others, and why do certain ethnic sub-groups of Asian Americans prefer one medium over others?

# ASIAN AMERICANS IN THE MEDIA WORKFORCE

**Historical Overview.** Historically, small numbers of Asian Americans have entered media or communication professions. There are many reasons for this, however, one strong reason is that Asians have historically been oppressed and not allowed to be part of mainstream America, including being part of the dissemination of news or the process of communication. Asian American author Shirley Geok-lin Lim eloquently explains how this fact affected Asian Americans, in her essay entitled *The Ambivalent American: Asian American Literature on the Cusp*:

> But the condition of freedom constituted by our human access to language has another dimension; the freedom inherent in speech, even when accompanied by political freedom of speech, which is always and everywhere constrained, means nothing if access to an audience is absent. Thus the human birthright of speech can be made mute, silenced by sociopolitical structures. Language achieves little if it is denied listeners. One may express, create, discover, but how does one move, inform, persuade, protest without an audience? How can speech give the speakers access to social power without social permission? (Lim 1992, 14).

The point, of course, is a good one. The decades of discrimination against Asians and Asian Americans in the United States cannot be ignored as a factor contributing to the low numbers of Asian Americans working in the media today. For years Asians were not welcomed on newspaper staffs, and they were forced to start their own newspapers and magazines within their own communities. Some of the most famous of these publications are *Pacific Citizen, Asian Week, Little India, Hawaii Herald, Filipinas Magazine, Northwest Asian Weekly, Rafu Shimpo, Asian New Yorker, Hawaii Filipino Chronicle*, and the monthly English edition of *Korea Times*. More detail on the history and content of these publications is offered in Chapter Two. The voices of these publications' constituencies were not welcomed in mainstream media, so Asians and Asian Americans had no audience for their freedom of expression, which was guaranteed in the First Amendment of the U.S. Constitution. Of course, while an argument might be made by some people that immigrants had a language barrier that was difficult to overcome when expressing themselves in a language other than their native language, it does not apply to second-generation Asian Americans who speak English as their native language.

At the turn of the century, books such as the *Bibliography of the Chinese Question in the United States* were being compiled by the Library of Congress to warn people against "Japs" and the "Asiatic immigration and industrial menace," as well as to educate readers about organizations such as the Japanese and Korean Exclusion League or events such as the Chinese Exclusion Convention, which was held in San Francisco November 21 and 22, 1901 (Cowan and Dunlap [1909] 1980, 7 and 21).

The history of discrimination against and oppression of Asians and Asian Americans is lengthy and has continued from the first wave of Asian immigration in the early 1800s to the present. Many Asian Americans surveyed for this book said that historically, this discrimination has not been covered in the media, and Asian Americans, when covered, have often been portrayed negatively. However, at the time of this book's completion, there has not been a major academic study conducted to support or negate that claim.

However, even in the 1990s negative reporting of the diverse Asian American population persists in U.S. daily newspapers, and at radio and television stations, but no studies have attempted to determine the extent of negative, positive, or neutral coverage of Asian Americans. Chapter Six of this book gives some specific examples of stereotypes and negatively skewed reporting taken from articles studied in this content analysis.

Borshay explained her understanding of the problem: "Most people think that Asians have no problems, that they are just like white people, but that's not the case. . . .For the media to paint a picture that discrimination for Asian Americans does not exist anymore is wrong because, in fact, it does" (Borshay interview 1994). This book will seek to see if the media does, in fact, paint a rosy picture of life in the United States for Asian Americans as being relatively discrimination free, but only through the method of examing the types of articles published in twenty leading U.S. newspapers for a one-year period.

An article entitled "Southeast Asians Highly Dependent on Welfare in U.S.," published in the *New York Times*, March 19, 1994, is an example of negative reporting on Asian Americans. The article covered a report released by the Asian Pacific Public Policy Institute that discussed economic diversity of Asian Americans, and actually interpreted the report as supporting the 'model minority' stereotype of Asian Americans. The article stated:

> Indeed, the report showed, the (model minority) stereotype is true in many respects. Asian-Americans have the lowest divorce rate of any racial group (3 percent), the lowest rate of teen-age pregnancy (6 percent), the highest median family income ($35,000) and the lowest rate of unemployment (3.5 percent). The number of Asian-owned businesses skyrocketed by nearly 1,000 percent from 1972 to 1987 (Dunn *New York Times*, March 19, 1994).

The same article, however, also reported just a few paragraphs later:

> Asian-America has become a world of striking contrasts, the report said. For every Asian-America family with an annual income of $75,000 or more, there was roughly another making less than $10,000 a year. While more than a third of all Asian-Americans have at least a college degree, another 23 percent of those older than 25 had less than a high school diploma. For every Asian-American scientist or engineer, there was another making minimum wage (Dunn *New York Times*, March 19, 1994).

While this article went further than many stories to educate the public on the problems and diversity within the Asian American population, it also had a contradiction and said that the report, "in many respects," validated the 'model minority' stereotype. Yet, the *New York Times* article said the report claimed Asian Americans have much diversity and many social problems such as poverty and lack of education. If the *New York Times* was correct in interpreting the report as supporting the 'model minority' stereotype, why was one of the study's co-authors, Paul M. Ong, quoted as saying the stereotype of the 'model minority' and public ignorance of the diversity of Asian Americans had prevented the Asian American Public Policy Institute from being properly considered in national policy debates on issues like poverty, economic development and health care? It seems far more likely that the report was trying to disprove the 'model minority' stereotype rather than support it, as the *New York Times* incorrectly reported.

Borshay explained that problems of stereotyping Asian Americans and lack of roles available to Asian Americans is also rampant in the film industry. She pointed out that even though such recent strides for Asian Americans in films, with movies such as *The Joy Luck Club* having successful commercial runs have contributed to more widespread enlightenment in the entertainment business, Borshay warned, "I'd say it still as a very long way to go" (Borshay interview 1994).

Another example of how far Asian Americans have yet to go is in the scarcity of Asian faces seen on American television. Unfortunately, the scope of this book will not examine the number of roles on television played by Asian Americans, nor will it examine content of television programs for references to Asian American issues or discrimination against the minority.

Even the popular TV series *Kung Fu* had actor Keith Carradine, a Caucasian, made up to look like an Chinese man to portray the lead role. The casting of a white person was obviously preferred over casting an Asian actor by the series' producers. It was not until September 1994 that television had its first prime-time sitcom, *All-American Girl* (showcasing comedian Margaret Cho), which featured several Asian Americans in lead roles until it was cancelled. The only other program on television that has prominently featured Asians was the syndicated program *Vanishing Son*, according to an article entitled "Asians' 'All-American' Opportunity," published in *USA Today* September 13, 1994. In the content analysis of this book, an entire category in the second level of analysis is devoted to coverage of the series *All-American Girl* because such a large portion of the total coverage falling under the "entertainment" coding category in the twenty newspapers examined dealt with this television series.

This history of discrimination has also led to a history of fear of the media by Asian Americans, which has resulted in what some refer to as a 'silent minority' approach to facing up to the media by Asian Americans and a fear of demanding proper coverage. Consider that only one libel suit is cited in Hyung-chan Kim's book *Asian Americans and the Supreme Court*, A Documentary History (Kim 1992, 47-48). However, the lawsuit, argued before the Supreme Court on October 12, 1942, was filed by Kumezo Kawato against the ship *Rally* for lost wages after World War II began when Kawato worked on the ship, so this case had nothing to do with injury to reputation in the media.[7]

This means there have literally been no major libel or invasion of privacy law suits filed by Asian Americans to reach the U.S. Supreme Court. The history of libel cases in the media is relatively short, considering the first libel suit to reach the Supreme Court was New York Times v. Sullivan in 1964 (Overbeck 1994, 99). Also there have only been approximately fourteen libel suits and approximately ten invasion of privacy suits heard by the U.S. Supreme Court (100). So measuring the number of times Asian Americans may have been libeled in the media simply by examining the libel cases to have reached the Supreme Court is, admittedly, not a good one nor a comprehensive research method. This is mentioned merely to shed some light on how few libel cases have been filed by Asian Americans against the American media. There have been periods in communication law history, specifically from 1927 to 1943, when there were no major cases of litigation involving Asian Americans or Asian resident aliens in the United States, which is directly related to discrimination against Asians and Asian Americans during that time (Kim 1992, 48).

Another reason why so few Asian Americans have chosen to work in media jobs may be due to their cultural backgrounds, according to Lisa Chung of the Asian American Journalists Association. Jobs in the media, particularly at the entry level for recent college graduates, pay much less than professions such as doctors, lawyers, and engineers. Chung said that many Asian Americans' parents immigrated to the United States to provide a better life for their children. In Asian culture much of a family's resources go towards educating the children so that children can enter lucrative professions. "Asian American parents don't often come right out and say don't go into journalism, but when you've put all your resources into educating your child it doesn't take a genius to figure out that it would be better if your child became a doctor or a lawyer," Chung said (Chung interview 1994).

The hard sciences, which produce engineers and scientists, often have less discrimination against Asian Americans, Chung explained. "The hard sciences are more right or wrong. You don't have to explain an accent in the hard sciences, and they are not as subjective as to what your perspective is (Asian American vs. Caucasian majority America)," Chung said (Chung interview

1994). She added that Asian immigrants who come to America seeking jobs in the communications field are rare and are taking a very different path than the majority of Asian immigrants who have come to the U.S. in the past.

So the problem of low numbers of Asian Americans in the newsrooms and at television and radio stations may not be just one of a lack of desire to hire Asian Americans, but rather partially a reflection of cultural values that push Asian American children into higher paying professions or a desire by Asian Americans to chose a less subjective profession where their heritage is not constantly being questioned.

These examples from print, television, and film indicate that while there are most certainly many reasons yet unknown as to why few numbers of Asian Americans enter the media workforce, the history of discrimination against and stereotyping of Asian Americans in the media has greatly contributed to the reluctance on the part of many Asian Americans from entering the media as professionals. Also, other cultural factors, including parental pressure to enter higher paying professions, may have contributed to the low number of Asian Americans working as media professionals.

## ASIAN AMERICAN WORKFORCE AT NEWSPAPERS

This book looked specifically at the number of Asian Americans working in the nation's newsrooms during the time of the book's content analysis, 1994 to 1995. According to the American Society of Newspaper Editors (ASNE), which compiles an annual count of minorities in the newsrooms of newspapers across the country, 11.02 percent of the U.S. newsroom work forces in 1995 were minorities, or 6,100 people (American Society of Newspaper Editors 1996, 1). That figure represented an increase from 10.91 percent in 1994, or a 3.2 percent increase in minorities working in American newsrooms from 1994 to 1995 (1). The mid-1990s figures are shown here as they relate to the timeframe of the content analysis discussed in this book.

Of the 6,100 minorities working in newsrooms in 1995, 1,088 were Asian Americans, or 17.8 percent of all newsroom employees who were minorities (4). That figure represented an increase of only forty-four Asian Americans from the total of 1,044 Asian

Americans working in newsrooms in 1994, according to ASNE's annual survey for 1994 (American Society of Newspaper Editors 1995, 3). In 1994, of the 5,874 minorities working in newsrooms the 1,044 Asian Americans represented 17.7 percent of that total (3). So the number of Asian Americans working in newsrooms in the United States increased by 0.1 percent from 1994 to 1995. Here is a breakdown of the newsroom positions held by Asian Americans as of December 1995, according to the ASNE survey.

Table 3 lists the number of Asian Americans working in U.S. newsrooms in 1994.

While overall numbers indicate a slight increase in the number of Asian Americans working in newsrooms from 1994 to 1995, the number of Asian Americans holding supervisor positions actually fell by nine persons from 1994 to 1995, and the number of Asian American photographers increased by four from 1994 to 1995. The number of Asian American copy editors also showed only a minor increase in 1995 over the previous year.

In 1993, 10.49 percent of work forces in the U.S. newsrooms were minorities, or 5,365 people (American Society of Newspaper Editors 1994, 1-2). Of that figure, 983 were Asian Americans, or 18.3 percent of all minorities (3). So the percent of American newsroom employees who are Asian Americans has actually decreased since 1993. Table 4 gives a breakdown of the newsroom positions held by Asian Americans as of December 1993, according to the ASNE 1993 annual survey for that year.

According to Lisa Chung at the Asian American Journalists Association (AAJA), this is the most reliable data on the number of Asian Americans working at newspapers. So other than AAJA, which keeps some similar data, and the American Society of Newspaper Editors, there is no other national survey, or a more in-depth survey of Asian American journalists that is being regularly compiled. A representative of ASNE explained in November of 1994, "We don't do any detailed research on Asian Americans other than our annual newsroom employment census. We do some other research on blacks and Hispanics in the newsroom, but not on Asian Americans" (anonymous employee of ASNE interview 1994). By April of 1998, ASNE retreated from its longtime goal to have diversity in the nation's newsroom reflect the diversity of the U.S. population by the year 2000. According to an arti-

cle on the controversial decision, which ran April 6, 1998, in the
*New York Times*:

> About 6,300, or 11.4 percent of the nation's 54,700 news-
> paper reporters, photographers and editors are black, Asian,
> Hispanic or native American, according to a [ASNE] society
> survey. That is about triple the percentage in 1978, when
> the group set its goal. But gains have leveled off in recent
> years—with an increase of just one-tenth of 1 percent in the
> last year—while the country's minority population has
> grown far beyond the 15 percent the Society had projected
> for 2000. In 1994 nearly 26 percent of the nation's popula-
> tion were members of minorities (Barringer, *New York
> Times*, April 8, 1998).

Table 2. Asian Americans Working on U.S. Newspaper Staffs in 1995

| Position | No. | Percent of Total Asian Americans in Newsroom Work Force |
|---|---|---|
| Supervisors | 158 | 14 |
| Copy/Layout Editors | 235 | 22 |
| Reporters | 491 | 45 |
| Photographers | 204 | 19 |
| Total | 1,088 | |

SOURCE: American Society of Newspaper Editors, 1996.

In Chapter Five of this book, the number of Asian Americans
employed at several of the twenty newspapers used in the content
analysis will be presented. Comparisons with the total number of
Asian Americans working in newsrooms across the country are
made in that chapter also. While the number of minorities working on U.S. newspaper staffs has steadily increased from less than
2,000 in 1978 (or 3.95 percent of total newsroom employees
nationwide) to 6,100 in 1995 (11.02 percent of all newsroom
employees nationwide), and 11.4 percent in 1998, the percent of
Asian Americans in the U.S. newsroom workforce has actually
dropped since 1994 (American Society of Newspaper Editors
1996, 1). There remains a strong need for employment of more
Asian Americans at all levels of newsroom personnel.

Table 3. Asian Americans Working on U.S. Newspaper Staffs in 1994

| Position | No. | Percent of Total Asian Americans in Newsroom Work Force |
|----------|-----|--------------------------------------------------------|
| Supervisors | 167 | 16 |
| Copy Editors | 222 | 21 |
| Reporters | 446 | 43 |
| Photographers | 208 | 20 |
| Total | 1,044 | |

SOURCE: American Society of Newspaper Editors, 1995.

Table 4. Asian Americans Working on U.S. Newspaper Staffs in 1993

| Position | No. | Percent of Total Asian Americans in Newsroom Work Force |
|----------|-----|--------------------------------------------------------|
| Supervisors | 169 | 17 |
| Copy/Layout Editors | 207 | 21 |
| Reporters | 412 | 42 |
| Photographers | 195 | 20 |
| Total | 983 | |

SOURCE: American Society of Newspaper Editors.

## ASIAN AMERICAN WORKFORCE IN RADIO AND TELEVISION

There is even less precise data on the number of Asian Americans working at radio and television stations during the timeframe of the content analysis of this book. Both Chung and Borshay agree that some of the only figures available on how many Asian Americans work in radio and television comes from a 1993 survey by the Radio and Television News Directors Federation (RTNDF). The survey was conducted in 1992 and polled 411 television stations and 296 commercial radio stations nationwide with news operations. Of the stations polled, which were in all regions of the United States, there was an overall response rate of 55 percent for the television stations and 42 percent from the radio stations. So, while these are some of the only figures available on this segment of the Asian American work force, they are not widely representative of the business. The survey showed that minorities made up 18.5 percent of all television news personnel, 11.6 percent of radio news personnel, with minority employment highest in the large markets (Stone 1993, 68). There were approximately eight hundred Asian Americans working in television and radio news in 1992, the survey reported. Table 5 is a breakdown by gender of that figure:

Of course, an even more revealing statistic is the number of Asian Americans in management positions at radio and television news operations. The survey found only ten Asian Americans working as television news directors, and only fifty-one radio news directors. Here is a further breakdown of that information:

These figures clearly show a need for more Asian Americans in newsrooms, and at radio and television stations. Chung explained why it is important to have more Asian American representation in the media. She said the Asian American Journalists Association tries to "encourage the hiring of Asian Americans in the (media) business not simply to get more of us in there, but because of the belief that the more Asian Americans in the newsrooms, the more awareness there will be of Asian American issues" (Chung interview 1994). Chung added, "I also think the more diversity of people in decision-making and reporting roles, the greater the complexity of the coverage" (Chung interview 1994).

One way Asian Americans could offer better coverage of news is in the ability to cover multi-lingual communities. Many Asian Americans are either immigrants or have relatives who were immigrants, and who struggled to learn English as a second language. Consequently, these same people not only have a sensitivity to people who speak broken English, but they often are able to speak the

Table 5. Asian Americans Working in Broadcast News in 1992

|  | Television | | Radio | |
| --- | --- | --- | --- | --- |
|  | Estimated No. | Share* | Estimated No. | Share* |
| Asian Am. Men | 215 | .9 | 170 | 1.1 |
| Asian Am. Women | 260 | 1.1 | 170 | 1.1 |
| Total | 475 | 2.0 | 340 | 2.2 |

SOURCE: Stone, Vernon A. 1993. Good News, Bad News.
* Represents percentage share of the total television or radio work force, respectively, including Caucasians.

Table 6. Race and Sex of Asian American Broadcast News
Directors in 1992

| | Television | | Radio | |
|---|---|---|---|---|
| | Estimated No. | Share* | Estimated No. | Share* |
| Asian Am. Men | 5 | 0.7 | 17 | 0.3 |
| Asian Am. Women | 5 | 0.7 | 34 | 0.6 |
| Total | 10 | 1.4 | 51 | 0.9 |

SOURCE: Stone, Vernon A. 1993. Good News, Bad News.
* Represents percentage share of the total television or radio work force,
respectively, including Caucasians.

native language of people in the news. So newsrooms need to hire
more people who can speak Korean, Chinese, Japanese, and other
Asian languages, particularly if there is to be proper coverage of
Asian communities. Chung points out one of the most glaring
examples of this need. During the Los Angeles riots following the
verdict in the Rodney King beating by police, many Korean businesses in predominantly African American communities were van-
dalized or burned. Invariably, however, the news reports showed
frightened Korean shop owners on rooftops with guns and interviewed many Korean immigrants who could barely speak English.
As Chung points out, this was painted as a simplistic African
American/Korean race conflict in the news, with little effort given
to explaining the economic complexities that place Koreans and
many Arab immigrants in low income neighborhoods that just
happen to be predominately African American. There were many
instances of goodwill among neighbors of all races in these same
neighborhoods, but positive Korean/African American relations
don't often make the news.

Chung further stated that the Korean American community
was angry and very concerned about their image to the world, via
CNN and other news networks. Chung explained, "Since there
were no reporters who could speak Korean all the interviews were
done in English. . .Here are some people that are able to express
themselves with soul and depth and articulate clarity, but they
weren't able to because they weren't being interviewed in their
native language" (Chung interview 1994). She added, "The
Korean American community was very concerned about the power
of the image this projected to the world" (Chung interview 1994).

Like the Asian American Journalists Association, Borshay, of the National Asian American Telecommunications Association, said the reason her organization exists "is mainly because there was a lack of representation in mainstream media, and, secondly, because of the stereotypes of Asian Americans in the media. . .So our mission was really to try to address the lack of representation and the stereotypes by equipping the people in our community with the resources to produce films and other media to educate people" (Borshay interview 1994). Both Borshay and Chung acknowledge that much more needs to be done towards getting more Asian Americans to work in media professions.

The Asian American Journalists Association represents nearly 1,400 employees of news organizations, educators, and students. It was founded in 1981 and is the largest organization of Asian American journalists in the United States. The National Asian American Telecommunications Association was founded in 1980 and has more than three hundred members. It is the largest organization of Asian Americans in telecommunications in the United States.

## NOTES

[1] For example, Lisa Chung, former executive director of the Asian American Journalists Association, explained that her organization had no precise definition of who constitutes an Asian American. She said, however, that people from the Middle East are included as members in AAJA and that several Middle Eastern American members had been very active recently in writing pamphlets and other literature on biases in the American media during coverage of the Okalhoma City federal building bombing in 1995.

[2] This definition of who is Asian American has expanded greatly in the past one hundred years as explained later in this chapter.

[3] Also in the 1990 Census, in addition to the nine Asian or Pacific Islander categories given on the census questionnaire under the overall category of "Asian or Pacific Islander," respondents could also check the category "Other API" (For other Asian or Pacific Islander) and write in their ethnic sub-category.

[4] Some researchers adopt this approach since the Asian American movement in the United States developed in the late 1960s and early 1970s.

[5] This book's author found many instances where it is simply impossible to discern between who is an Asian American and who is not. For example, that determination could certainly not be made on whether a person's name "sounds" Asian for obvious reasons.

[6] Asian Native Americans are sometimes referred to as "Asian Indians" or "Asian American Indians," and should not be confused with "Asian East Indians" who are also referred to as "Asian Indians."

[7] This case reached the Supreme Court on October 12, 1942. Kumezo Kawato was born in Japan and came to the U.S. in 1905 were he worked on the ship *Rally*. Kawato filed the libel suit in order to claim wages he said he was entitled from his work on the ship. However, the owners of the ship filed a motion in the District Court for the Southern District of California to dismiss the libel action on the ground that Kawato had become an enemy alien due to that status given all Japanese living in the U.S. during World War II according to the Trading With the Enemy Act. The District Court granted the motion and Kawato appealed to the Circuit Court of Appeals to force the lower court to vacate its ruling. Justice Black delivered the Supreme Court's opinion which overruled the Circuit Court of Appeals. In his closing statement of the opinion, Black said, "the doors to our courts have not been shut to peaceful law-abiding aliens seeking to enforce rights growing out of legal occupations" (Kim 1992, 47).

# CHAPTER 2

# HISTORY OF ASIAN AMERICAN PUBLICATIONS

> What impelled me to write? The answer is—my
> grand dream of equality among men and freedom
> for all. To give literate voice to the voiceless one
> hundred thousand Filipinos in the United States,
> Hawaii, and Alaska. Above all and ultimately, to
> translate the desires and aspirations of the whole
> Filipino people in the Philippines and abroad in
> terms relevant to contemporary history.
>
> —Carlos Bulosan, *America is in the Heart*

The history of the newspapers, magazines, journals, and other media serving Asian Americans and earlier ethnic immigrant communities is as diverse as the histories of Asian Americans themselves. Unfortunately, there appear from the literature review for this book to be no books or major academic studies written to date on the history of Asian American media.

It should also be clarified that in this section a large portion of ethnic Asian and Asian American media will not be covered. This section is devoted mainly to print journalism as it relates to Asian Americans in keeping with the main focus of this book. Therefore, neither the numerous and rapidly growing television channels (particularly cable television channels) geared to Asian ethnic groups, nor the International Channel, are mentioned. Many magazines and nearly all ethnic Asian newsletters published in the United States are also not covered here. There are simply too many to attempt to cover in any detail and, like cable television channels catering to ethnic Asian populations in the United States, these magazines and newsletters are growing at exponential rates. Finally, this section does not cover computer on-line newsletters or other publications. Many computer Internet resources for Asian Americans are mentioned in Chapter Three (Ebihara 1995).

It is very likely that one of the next waves we will see is for on-line publications to begin to replace the scores of newsletters and other smaller-circulation publications published specifically for ethnic sub-groups of Asian Americans. Many of these publications are published in native Asian languages of recent immigrants (Ebihara 1995). One reason on-line publications will continue to flourish is because this new media can link Asians with persons in their countries of origin. Currently, Thai, Asian Indian, and Chinese communication groups are very active on the Internet (Ebihara 1995).

Since 1990, the creation of new ethnic newspapers serving Asian American communities has been phenomenal. These publications, closely tied to the communities they serve, survive because of active involvement. The *Northwest Asian Weekly*, for example, recently started a foundation for young people which also funds a summer educational program on Asian issues and leadership for the young Asian Americans in the Seattle area (Luna and Wong, *Northwest Asian Weekly*, December 1995-January 1996). The foundation also gives out scholarships and sponsors an annual art contest. The *Nguoi Viet* newspaper, which serves Vietnamese living in the Northwest United States, organizes an annual Moon Festival and a Lunar New Year's Festival that brings internationally known Vietnamese singers to the Seattle area (Luna and Wong, *Northwest Asian Weekly*, December 1995-January 1996). Ethnic newspaper-sponsored community programs such as these have been common in Asian American neighborhoods in many large U.S. cities since the early 1990s (Luna and Wong, *Northwest Asian Weekly*, December 1995-January 1996). In short, there are now major media markets of Asian Americans nationwide which have not gone unnoticed by mainstream as well as ethnic advertisers.

According to a July 1995 article in The *Christian Science Monitor*, the Asian-language media in the United States are growing at an explosive rate thanks to desktop publishing capabilities and increasing demand from thriving Asian ethnic communities.

Nationwide, the Asian-language media market includes more than three hundred newspapers (of which ninety-two are dailies), fifty radio stations, seventy-five television shows, and other miscellaneous media guides such as telephone directories (Trumbull, *Christian Science Monitor*, July 14, 1995). There are now approximately 580 Asian-oriented publications and broadcasts in the United States, according to Imada Wong Communications Group in Los Angeles (Trumbull, *Christian Science Monitor*, July 24, 1995). This boom in Asian-language media, as well as English-language media serving persons of Asian descent, is directly related to the population boom of Asian Americans. Many advertisers now see a growing market and are willing to place ads in ethnic media.

Industry officials see little end in sight, at least in the short run, according to the *Christian Science Monitor* article (Trumbull, *Christian Science Monitor*, July 24, 1995). For example, there is now an Orange County, California, radio station that broadcasts in Vietnamese for eighteen hours a day because the demand exists in that area (Trumbull, *Christian Science Monitor*, July 24, 1995). There is another radio station in southern California that broadcasts solely in Korean. However, the Trumbull article explains:

> Print publishers, for their part, have yet to make a resounding success of the pan-Asian, English-language market. One difficulty is bringing together many cultural backgrounds and ages. Since immigrants tend to read in their native language, these publications cater more to second- and third-generation Asian-Americans (Trumbull, *Christian Science Monitor*, July 24,1995).

As will be explained in this chapter, there has been a steadily growing pan-Asian market for publications since the late 1960s and early 1970s. Newspapers catering to Asian immigrants, on the other hand, have a nearly 150-year history in the United States. As mentioned in the beginning of Chapter One of this book, according to Jeffres and Hur, who conducted a study on American ethnic newspapers, the limited studies available on Chinese-language, African American newspapers and radio, Filipino American newspapers and Spanish-language newspapers, indicate that "the ethnic media often fail to meet the needs of ethnics in order to maximize their profits" (Jeffres and Hur 1980, 11). Some of this pattern can be seen when looking at the number of early publications, which eventually folded, that catered to the Asian immigrant and refugee populations.

However, ethnic newspapers have always served different needs in the communities they represent, particularly when compared to mainstream newspapers. A February 26, 1995, article in the *Seattle Times* discussed the recent explosive growth in ethnic newspapers, especially those serving Asian American ethnic subgroups:

> Language is just one connection ethnic newspapersmake
> with their readers. There is also the intimac of reporting on
> special community celebrations, important anniversaries,
> even birthdays. The ethnic press tends to view service in a
> very direct way: profiling people as role models for others;
> doing stories that help connect one generation with another;
> writing about places important to their community's sense
> of history. Uniting and uplifting a community may be as
> important to their mission as reporting about it (Colon,
> *Seattle Times*, Feb. 26, 1995).

The article explains that ethnic newspapers may bring together people who never knew each other in their home countries. These newspapers also provide services to readers that mainstream newspapers do not provide, for example, the *Hokubei Houchi* (the North American Post) published the names of all the victims of the Kobe, Japan, earthquake for its Japanese readers in America since many had relatives and friends living in Kobe (Colon, Seattle Times, Feb. 26, 1995). Da Le, editor of *The Vietnam Times*, published for the Vietnamese American community, explained his paper serves as a forum for the different factions that existed in Vietnam and continue to fight for political influence in the United States. "The newspaper is very much like a mediator to help solve community problems," Le explained (Colon, Seattle Times, Feb. 26, 1995).

There is also a recent growth in newspapers that aim to serve a cross section of Asian Americans, such as *The USAsians*, a tabloid published in Columbus, Ohio, which has separate editors for Japanese, Chinese, Asian Indian, and Korean cultures (Cho, *The USAsians*, Oct. 31, 1995). The newspaper offers a mix of news and features articles on all those Asian American ethnic sub-groups, as well as on Vietnamese, Cambodian and Laotian issues (Cho, *The USAsians*, Oct. 31, 1995).

Another such newspaper which aims at a broader audience of all Asian Americans is *Northwest Asian Weekly*, published by the Seattle Chinese Post, Inc., in Seattle since 1983. In its December 1995-January 1996 issue, that newspaper published a special edition on Asian community newspapers. Editor Deni Yamauchi Luna explained in the lead article of that special edition that in the Seattle area, where Asian Americans comprise 12 percent of the population, there are now more than thirty Asian Pacific newspapers, which represents a ten-fold increase since the early 1970s (Luna and Wong, *Northwest Asian Weekly*, December 1995-January 1996). Of the thirty Asian American ethnic newspapers currently published in Seattle, ten are Chinese, five are Korean, four are Vietnamese, and the remaining serve all Asian Americans (Luna and Wong, *Northwest Asian Weekly*, December 1995-January 1996). Luna, and reporter Dean Wong, explain the appeal of these newspapers:

> Today, 60 percent of Asian Pacific Americans are immigrants [this varies from U.S. Census figures]. This bilingual force still retains an interest in the homeland, while integrating full-forward into American life. For them, locally-produced newspapers in their native Asian language are an important resource (Luna and Wong, *Northwest Asian Weekly*, December 1995).

Like many other ethnic newspapers serving Asian Americans, *Northwest Asian Weekly* offers a mix of arts reviews, obituary notices of local Asian Americans, advertisements by local Asian American business persons and services for immigrants, and a guide of local restaurants serving Asian cuisine, as well as news and feature articles.

Some early newspapers serving the entire Asian American community in the Seattle region included the *Kapisanan* (meaning "brotherhood"), first published in 1970 by Filipino community leader Nemesio Domingo, who felt the Asian community needed a community-oriented newspaper (Luna and Wong, *Northwest Asian Weekly*, December 1995-January 1996). Soon thereafter, *Kapisanan* was restructured under new leadership and turned into *Asian Family Affair*. The newspaper, which has now folded, printed 500 to 600 copies per edition and covered issues, including racism in the media (Luna and Wong, *Northwest Asian Weekly*, December 1995-January 1996). *The International Examiner*, first published in Seattle in 1974 by businessman Lawrence Imamura, was more focused on business news of interest to Asian Americans (Luna and Wong, *Northwest Asian Weekly*, December 1995-January 1996).

The Chinese language *Seattle Chinese Post* began publishing in 1982 and is still published today (Luna and Wong, *Northwest Asian Weekly*, December 1995-January 1996). Seattle's first Korean language newspaper, *The Korea Times*, began publishing in 1977 and is an extension of a national newspaper in Korea which has branch offices in several cities, including New York, Los Angeles and Chicago (Luna and Wong, *Northwest Asian Weekly*, December 1995-January 1996). The Seattle edition of *The Korea Times* now employs twenty people and publishes a twenty-four-page daily newspaper, while the Los Angeles edition of *The Korea Times* is an eighty-to-ninety-page daily (Luna and Wong, *Northwest Asian Weekly*, December 1995-January 1996). Several English language newspapers serving Asian Americans have also sprung up nationwide. In Seattle, the *North American Post*, which serves the Asian American community there, began publishing the *Northwest Nikkei* in English to provide news specifically catered to the Japanese Americans in Seattle (Luna and Wong, *Northwest Asian Weekly*, December 1995-Janauary1996). There are similar examples of native language and English language publications that have been founded in the past twenty-five years to meet the demands of the explosion of Asian American communities, particularly since the influx of Asian immigrants during the post-Immigration Act of 1965 era.

These are just a few examples of the continuing growth and diversity represented in today's Asian American ethnic press. In some areas of the Asian American ethnic press readers are dropping off, as will be discussed in the next sections (Critser, *Christian Science Monitor*, April 27, 1983). However, with the growth of the Internet and desktop publishing capabilities, overall the Asian American ethnic press is rapidly growing. What follows are annotated histories of the publications for the major Asian American ethnic sub-groups.

## THE CHINESE PRESS

The first Asian American newspapers were started as early as April 1854, when Chinese immigrants living in San Francisco began publishing the *Kim-Shan Jit San-Luk*, which translated to English meant *Golden Hills' News* (Kim 1986, 424). This newspaper, published in Chinese, first came out twice weekly then as a weekly. Many newspapers, published either in Chinese, Japanese, or English, began to crop up in the West Coast Japanese and Chinese immigrant communities by the late 1800s. Other early Chinese newspapers were the *Oriental*, which began publishing in San Francisco in 1855, the *Chinese Daily News* published in Sacramento in 1856, *Chinese World* published in San Francisco in 1891, and New *China Daily News* published in Hawaii in 1900 (424). *Chinese World* became the first English/Chinese bilingual newspaper serving the Chinese community in the United States.

There have been numerous other newspapers that served the Chinese in America, which cannot all be mentioned here. Some more prominent newspapers included the *Chinese Daily News* and *Chinese Press* both published in New York, *Chinese Digest* published in San Francisco, and *Chinese Star*, which is just one of several historic Chinese newspapers published in Seattle.

Now there is a new wave of publications catering to Chinese Americans, such as *Chinese American Forum, A Cultural Bridge* (hereafter referred to as *Chinese American Forum*) which has been published quarterly since May 1984. It is published by the Chinese American Forum, Inc., which is based in Silver Spring, Maryland. This publication is less academic in approach than *Amerasia Journal* (discussed in a separate sub-section later in this chapter), but it is one of several publications for Chinese Americans that have cropped up in the past fifteen years.

A search of the issues in *Chinese American Forum* from May 1984 to April 1993 indicated there have been two articles published during that time that deal with Asian Americans and the media (Chiang et al. 1993, *Chinese American Forum*). Those two articles were, "American News Media and the Chinese," written by Oscar Chiang in the October 1985 issue, and "Journalism As a Profession - A Personal Experience," by Oscar Chiang in the March 1988 edition (Chiang 1985; Chiang 1988). So it is clear to see that even in this journal there appears to be few articles written on how Chinese Americans are covered by the media, or on Chinese Americans who work in the media.

This section would not be complete without some mention to *Sing Tao Daily*, the largest newspaper in the world serving Chinese living overseas. There are separate editions for Chinese who live in various parts of the world, including an edition for Chinese living in Southeast Asian countries, as well as for Chinese living in the United States. This highly successful newspaper, which publishes its U.S. editions out of Los Angeles, San Francisco, and New York, and offers news of interest to both Asian Americans and Chinese living in the United States. Most editions of *Sing Tao Daily* are published in Chinese. Advertising includes local-market businesses.

There are also several newspapers published in China, Taiwan, and Hong Kong that publish English-language editions which have broad readership among Chinese living in the United States.

One of the most successful newspapers published in China and read by Chinese living abroad is actually geared towards non-Chinese readers. The newspaper is *China Daily*, an English-language broadsheet that was founded in 1981 (Vanden Heuvel and Dennis 1993, 33). The newspaper is designed to appeal to foreign (non-Chinese) readers, and British and Australian journalists worked with Chinese journalists to help mold the newspaper to a more Western image when it was created (33). Here is how researchers at the Freedom Forum Media Studies Center described *China Daily*, in the publication *The Unfolding Lotus: East Asia's Changing Media*:

> *China Daily*, an English-language newspaper that most resembles Western-style journalism. . . . The eight-page broadsheet is transmitted via satellite to printers in Europe and North America. According to Huang Quing, deputy editor in chief of *China Daily*, the purpose of the paper is "to expose China's economic development to the rest of the world." Huang said that *China Daily* has recently launched a new English-language publication called Reports from China, and plans to begin an English-language paper in Shanghai, to be called the Shanghai Star. It is generally acknowledge that the Communist authorities grant *China Daily* a bit more latitude in covering events in China since most of its readers are non-Chinese (33).

Also, many of the newspapers published in those countries are readily available in America, particularly in Hawaii, on the West Coast, and in other large urban centers like New York, Washington, D.C., and Chicago. Some of the newspapers read by Chinese in America are *China Times*, *The China News* from Taiwan; the western edition of *People's Daily* from China; and *South China Morning Post* and *Hong Kong Standard* from Hong Kong (where there is a florishing newspaper market of more than 600 newspapers). Finally, there are now several newspapers published in those countries that are available to Chinese living in the United States.

The number of newspapers available to Chinese Americans as well as Chinese living in the United States has grown steadily in the past twenty years and reflects a long history of publications catering to Chinese in America. The newspapers reflect the diversity within this ethnic sub-group of Asian Americans, including the political, cultural, and economic differences between Taiwan, China, Hong Kong, and other countries with large populations of Chinese such as Singapore, Indonesia, and Malaysia. These newspapers also reflect the different interests of Chinese Americans whose families date back several generations on American soil and recent Chinese immigrants to the United States.

## THE JAPANESE PRESS

One of the first newspapers serving the Japanese American community was the *Nichi Bei Times*, which began publication in 1898 and is still published today. Other early newspapers serving the Japanese community in America were *North American Times*, *Japanese American Courier*, *Nippu Jiji*, and *Hawaii Hochi*. Other early Japanese newspapers were *Hawaii Choho*, *Hawaii Shimpo*, *Japan Times* and *Mail*, *Japan Weekly Mail*, the *Japanese American Courrier*, *Japanese American News*, and the *Nisei Democrat*. Another early publication was *Nichibei Nekan*, which translated to English was the Japanese American Yearbook. *Hawaii Herald* is an English-language newspaper which caters to Japanese Americans and which was an outgrowth of the Japanese-language newspaper *Hawaii Hochi*.

By the mid-1970s there were thirteen newspapers published by Japanese Americans, and that number has increased in the past twenty years. Many Japanese newspapers publish either bilingually in English/Japanese or have a Japanese section. *Gidra*, published in Los Angeles, was also a popular publication for Japanese Americans which should be mentioned here. It was one of the publications started as part of the panethnicity movement in the late 1960s and early 1970s, however, *Gidra* ceased publication several years ago and has never been revived or revamped into a publication with a different title.

Some of the leading Japanese American publications today are *Rafu Shimpo*, *Hokubei Mainichi*, *Chicago Simpo*, *Utah Nippo*, *New York Nichibei*, and *Pacific Citizen*. *Rafu Shimpo* has been highly successful and influential in the Japanese American community and is still published today, Mondays through Saturdays, in Los Angeles.

There are hundreds of newsletters and smaller ethnic Japanese newspapers that are published in the United States which will not be covered in this book. There are also specialized newspapers available which concentrate on Asian Pacific news, such as the *Nikkei Weekly*, a business newspaper focusing on the business in the Asia Pacific rim and published in New York. According to a flyer advertising subscriptions to *Nikkei Weekly*, the newspaper has sixty-three Japanese bureaus and thirty-six other bureaus throughout the world (*Nikkei Weekly* flyer 1995, 1). So much of its business coverage focuses on the Japanese markets.

Also popular among Japanese Americans and other Japanese living in America are newspapers and magazines published in Japan which are available in the United States, including the two largest dailies in Japan: *Yomiuri Shimbun* and *Asahi Shimbun* (Vanden Heuvel and Dennis 1993, 78). The circulations of these two newspapers are astronomical: *Yomiuri Shimbun* has a morning edition circulation of more than 9.7 million and an evening circulation of approximately 4.7 million, while *Asahi Shimbun* has a morning circulation of 8.2 million and an evening circulation of more than 4.7 million (78). It is no wonder why these two highly popular newspapers in Japan are also popular among Japanese Americans. These two newspapers' U.S. editions are most popular with Japanese business persons stationed in the United States and with first generation new Japanese U.S. immigrants, who are called shin Issei (translated it means "new first generation"). Japan has one of the largest newspaper markets in the world, and that passion for reading newspapers is also common among Japanese in the United States.

Kyodo, Japan's largest wire service, transmits twice daily in the form of a facsimile newspaper (Kyodo booklet 1995). The Japanese-language overseas service is transmitted twice a day to 3,000 Japanese ocean-going ships, fourteen Japanese-language newspapers, radio, or television stations in the United States and Latin American countries, and other Japanese media overseas (Kyodo booklet 1995). This facsimile newspaper, consisting of an average of 100,000 Japanese-language characters, is widely read by the Japanese community in these countries, according to a booklet about the service, because "it is the only Japanese-language print medium available overseas earliest each day" (Kyodo booklet 1995). As more publications go on-line, even more newspapers, magazines, and newsletters from Japan have become available to Japanese readers in the United States.

However, according to a 1983 article in the *Christian Science Monitor*, readership among Japanese Americans of the Japanese ethnic press in the United States is declining (Critser, *Christian Science Monitor*, April 27, 1983). According to Hiro Hishiki, publisher of the *Kashu Mainichi*, one of Los Angeles's two Japanese American daily newspapers, "The problem facing all the Japanese vernaculars is that the Issei (first-generation immigrants) who can read Japanese are almost all in their 80s" (Critser, *Christian Science Monitor*, April 27, 1983). The article added that unlike other ethnic newspapers in the United States that have benefited from large immigrations in the 1960s and 1970s, particularly Korean, Chinese, and Hispanic newspapers, Japanese American newspapers began experiencing declining circulations in the early 1980s due to "an ongoing decline in the number of readers who can understand the complex Japanese language" (Critser, *Christian Science Monitor*, April 27, 1983). Hishiki stressed in the article that most of the Nisei (second generation), Sansei (third generation), Yonsei (fourth generation), and now Gosei (fifth generation) Japanese Americans do not read Japanese.

The problem of declining readership of Japanese American newspapers is being faced throughout the nation. In 1982 the ninety-year-old *Hawaii Times* changed from a daily to a weekly newspaper, partially due to declining readership and also due to budget constraints (Critser, *Christian Science Monitor*, April 27, 1983). The article listed the three problems that faced the Japanese American press in the early 1980s. While some of those problems have been solved, such as conversion from older, costly printing methods to computerized equipment, some of the other problematic trends have not changed. Here is how the article described the three problems facing the Japanese American press:

1. Competition by Japanese-language television stations: "It's an affluent audience," says Pau Niedermeyer, station manager for KSCI-TV in Los Angeles, which broadcasts over 20 hours a week of Japanese-language programming. The station's most popular show is the news, Mr. Niedermeyer says, which is in the form of taped broadcasts from NHK, a large Japanese news network. He also notes that many of the station's advertisers are from the local ethnic community—the same restaurants and retail stores that usually advertise in the Japanese-American papers.

2. Antiquated production methods: Many Japanese-American papers operate with the same technology that their *issei* founders used. A walk into the Kashu's press room reveals a linotype operation reminiscent of those which dominated many American press rooms during the early part of this century. Breakdowns are common, parts are hard to find, and renovation is expensive. The Hawaii Hochi is one of the few to overcome this handicap, through capital and technology provided by the Chizuoka Shimbun, a Tokyo-based newspaper which purchased the Hochi in the mid-1950s.

3. Lack of new journalistic talent: Most Japanese-American papers are family operations. Mr. Hishiki took over the Kashu from his father-in-law in 1954. The Rafu Shimpo, Los Angeles's other Japanese-American daily, is run by the third-generation of the Komai family (Critser April 27,1983, *Christian Science Monitor*).

According to Harry Kitano, a sociology professor who specializes in Asian American studies at the University of California - Los Angeles and the author of the book *Asian Americans, Emerging Minorities*, young Japanese American journalists often start off at Japanese ethnic newspapers, but they do not stay long due to low salaries (Critser, Christian Science Monitor, April 27, 1983). This trend of an inability to match higher salaries paid at larger newspapers has not been rectified by the Japanese American press, and is faced by other small Asian American ethnic newspapers. Kitano said that the flight away from the Japanese American press by younger generations is symbolic of the preoccupation with becoming assimilated into American culture and is further evidence of the breakup of the once tightly knit Japanese American family (Critser, Christian Science Monitor, April 27, 1983).

The Japanese American ethnic press continues to flourish as newer, more broad-based publications draw readers from the traditional Japanese-language newspapers which catered to once tightly knit Japanese American communities. Many newsletters focusing on special interests have cropped up in the past fifteen years among Japanese American readers. Also popular are Japanese-language newspapers published in Japan, as well as newspapers that report on world business markets and other international events. The traditional Japanese American ethnic press survives today, but has faced problems of dropping circulations in recent years as the Japanese American community shifts with the times.

## THE KOREAN PRESS

Early Korean immigrants in the United States started their first newspaper with the *Korean Times*, published in Honolulu from June 10, 1905, to September 1906 (Kim 1986, 424). The first Korean newspaper published in the mainland United States was *Kongnip Sinmum* (in English, *Korean News*), first printed in San Francisco in 1905 (Hundley Jr. 1976, 150). That newspaper stayed in publication until 1910, when it was absorbed by *Sin-Han Minbo* (in English, *New Korea*), which is still published today in Los Angeles and remains probably the oldest Korean newspaper published in the United States (150). *New Korea* is an organ of the Korean National Association of North America.

Two years after the first two Korean newspapers were published in Hawaii, the *New Korean World* was started in San Francisco on April 16, 1907, but later folded (Kim 1986, 424). The oldest Korean magazine published in what is now the United States was *Korean Pacific Weekly*, which was first printed as a weekly magazine in 1913 (Hundley Jr. 1976, 150). Other early newspapers for Korean immigrants, which all eventually folded, were *United Korean News*, which was published from 1907 to 1968 in various forms, the *United Korean Weekly, New Korean News, Korea Review* and *Great United Information*. Only the early newspaper *New Korea* survives today and is published under the same name in Los Angeles (424).

Nearly all these early Korean newspapers were political in nature. As historians Lee Houchins and Chang-su Houchins explain:

> Both news content and editorial policy [in the early Korean newspapers] were designed to instill in the immigrant reader a sense of Korean nationalism. The most frequently reported topics and editorial themes centered on the Korean independence movement in Korea proper and overseas, the spirt of aeguk chongsin (patriotism), and the dream of *kwangbok* (restoration of Korean independence. In addition to the publications of various Korean student associations, there were several distinctive, special-purpose Korean language periodicals (Hundley Jr. 1976, 150).

The special-purpose periodicals were also largely political in nature and usually associated with a political party or movement. For example, the *Tansan Sibo* (in English, *Korean Report*) was first published in 1925 by a Korean communist group in Honolulu, and the publication *Tongmu* (*Comrades in English*) was published in 1921 by the Korean Socialist-Labor party in Los Angeles (151). Houchins and Houchins (1976) explain that "the overseas Korean periodicals that survived probably did so because the subsidizing political organizations required subscriptions as a condition of membership" (151).

One of the most successful ethnic newspapers catering to Koreans today is *The Korea Times*, which has a northwest edition published out of Seattle with a circulation of approximately 50,000. The newspaper targets first-generation Koreans who find it easier to read in their native Korean, explained Andrew Cho, editor of the northwest edition, in a recent *Seattle Times* article (Colon, *Seattle Times*, Feb. 26, 1995). *KoreAm Journal*, published in Gardena, California, is another highly successful publication serving Korean Americans for the past several years.

One of the most famous Korean American journalists is K.W. Lee, who was referred to as the "godfather of Asian American journalism" in a recent edition of *Northwest Asian Weekly* (Park, *Northwest Asian Weekly*, December 1995-January 1996). Lee was the publisher of *Koreatown Weekly*, a short-lived but important newspaper which published from 1979 until it folded in 1982. It has been called "the cutting edge of ethnic journalism" because it presented a unique view of the lives of Korean Americans and Korean immigrants which was not being reported in the mainstream press (Park, *Northwest Asian Weekly*, December 1995-January 1996).

However, it was the investigative journalism of Lee while he was working as a reporter for the *Sacramento Union* that forced much national attention on what is now called the Chol Soo Lee movement. Once Lee began publishing *Koreatown Weekly*, he continued to force attention on the issue by publishing updates on Chol Soo Lee each week. Here is how the *Northwest Asian Weekly* profile on Lee explained this important event in Korean American journalism history:

> In his long career as a print journalist, he (Lee) has brought many fascinating stories to light, highlighting the plight of the underdogs of American society, as well as exposing political graft. In the late seventies, Lee's investigative reporting sparked the first national pan-Asian movement to fight for the freedom of a wrongly convicted Korean American—Chol Soo Lee —on death row for a murder he did not commit.

> The Chol Soo Lee movement sprung up among the emerging Korean immigrant communities across the country after K.W. Lee broke the story of Chol Soo's plight in the *Sacramento Union*. It became clear to veteran newsmen that Korean Americans were sorely lacking a voice with which to broadcast miscarriage of justice (Park, *Northwest Asian Weekly*, December 1995-January 1996).

The history of the Korean ethnic press in the United States is long and rich. There are numerous other publications today that cater to Korean Americans, and the demand for these publications has steadily grown along with the Korean American population over the past fifty years.

## THE FILIPINO PRESS

There have been more than twenty newspapers geared towards Filipino Americans or Filipino immigrants in the past seventy years in the United States. One of the first such newspapers was *Kauai Filipino News*, which changed its name to *Filipino News* in 1931. Some of the other early successful Filipino newspapers were *Commonwealth Courier* founded in 1931, the *Philippine Advocate* first published in 1934, the *Philippine Herald* published in 1920, and the *Philippines Mail*, published beginning November 3, 1930, which was the successor to the first newspaper for Filipinos in the continental United States, the *Philippine Independent News*. Another early newspaper published by Filipinos living in the United States was the *Evening Pajaronian*.

Many of these newspapers began reporting news of the labor disputes and labor union movement which Filipino immigrants were so closely involved with. The *Manila Times*, published in the Philippines, has always been popular with Filipino Americans as a good source of news from the Philippines and issues affecting Filipinos.

Today there are a few publications, like *Filipinas* magazine published in New York, which cater to second- and third-generation, young Filipino Americans. Filipinas magazine is now four years old (it began publishing in May 1992), but it has a steadily growing circulation and it reflects the newest demands of Filipino media consumers. This book, as stated earlier, cannot begin to survey anything but newspapers. *Filipinas* is mentioned here because its editorial mission statement partially explains these new demands, by stating:

> *Filipinas* enhances the Filipino community's visibility by highlighting achievers and role models and providing a balanced treatment of the community's trials, controversies and triumps (*Filipinas* May 1995).

In many respects this editorial statement also reflects what other Asian American ethnic groups want in newspapers and magazines published specifically for them—positive role models that do not reflect incorrect stereotypes, intellectual discussions and reporting of issues or controversies facing the various ethnic groups, and some light-hearted features.

Filipino Americans have some options for ethnic newspapers and magazines available to them as this century draws to a close, but there is certainly a need and a demand for more publications to cater to this important audience. It is possible that as Filipino American ethnic publications, such as *Filipinas* magazine, grow in circulation that other publications targeting Filipino Americans will be born as a result of these existing communication outlets.

## THE VIETNAMESE, CAMBODIAN AND LAOTIAN PRESS

It has only been in the past twenty years that there has been any development in publications serving the Vietnamese, Cambodian, and Laotian refugees who flooded American shores after the Vietnam War. Most newspapers serving these communities have only been founded in the past five to ten years as those communities have layed down roots and grown.

"Vietnamese people like to read. For them, it's like a hobby," explained Kim Pham, publisher of the Vietnamese language newspaper *Nguoi Viet* (which means *Northwest Vietnamese Weekly News* in English) (Luna and Wong, *Northwest Asian Weekly*, December 1995-January 1996). Pham is typical of many new publishers serving Vietnamese communities in major U.S. cities. Pham has a network of forty-five full-time, part-time, and freelance employees who span several geographic regions of the United States to offer the best coverage available of the nationwide community of Vietnamese Americans.

One of the problems facing these Southeast Asian American ethnic newspapers are that Iu-Mien and Hmong immigrants are often preliterate and, therefore, have no use for native-language newspapers. Also, many people who immigrated to the United States from Vietnam, Cambodia, and Laos following the Vietnam War are now returning to their homelands (Mydans, *New York Times*, April 17, 1996). While some Southeast Asian refugees are returning back to their former homelands, the number is balanced, and probably surpassed, by those who are arriving to join relatives in the United States. So this already diverse population of Asian Americans who hail from Vietnam, Cambodia, and Laos continues to face divisions and changes that make it difficult to fully represent through ethnic newspapers. However, not enough studies have been conducted on this segment of the Asian American population concerning their newspaper-reading habits, which makes it difficult to properly determine why ethnic newspaper trends in these communities are occurring.

As the communities of Vietnamese, Laotians, and Cambodians become more acculturated, and as their children produce third and fourth generations of these ethnic groups, the demand for newspapers serving these people will most likely be the fastest growing of all Asian American ethnic media in the next twenty years.

## THE ASIAN INDIAN PRESS

While there have not been as many publications historically which catered to Asian Indians in America, the early newspapers for these immigrants were impressive efforts. Like the early Korean publications, the first Asian Indian publications were also political in nature. In 1908, political activity among West Coast Asian Indians revolved to a great extent around the publication *Free Hindustan*, which was first published that year by Taraknath Das, a student at the University of Washington who had fled India a few years earlier to avoid punishment for his political activism (Hundley Jr. 1976, 166). By 1911 a similar political publication, Ghadr (which means "revolution" or "mutiny") was published in English as the organ of the political movement by the same name led by Har Dayal, a former student at Oxford (166).

One of the only studies published on the Asian Indian ethnic press in the United States was written by Mohammed Siddiqui and published in the academic journal *Gazette* in 1987. In the article, Siddiqui explains that while the majority of East Indian immigrants have arrived in the United States since the late 1960s, the Indian ethnic press is thriving with forty-one publications, although none represents a daily newspaper. Four of the leading Indian ethnic news weeklies, as of 1987 and according to the study, were: *India Abroad*, founded in 1970 and published in New York (circulation 32,000), *India News*, founded in 1970 and published in Washington, D.C. (circulation 10,000), *India Tribune*, founded in 1970 and published in Chicago (circulation 15,000), and *The Overseas Times*, founded in 1977 and published in Jersey City, New Jersey (circulation 18,000).

*India Abroad* remains one of the most popular ethnic newspapers for Asian Indian Americans. In addition to its New York edition, it also publishes editions in Atlanta, Chicago, Dallas, Los Angeles and Toronto. It claims to be "the oldest Indian newspaper in North America and the largest outside India" (*India Abroad*, March 1, 1996).

Another newspaper popular among Asian Indian Americans is *News India-Times*, founded in 1975 and published in New York. *Masala* magazine, founded in 1994 and published in New York, was a popular magazine among Asian Indian Americans before going out of print [note to editors: I need to check this fact].. The magazine covered South Asians in general, with particular emphasis to East Indians, explained editor Dilip Massand in a 1995 telephone interview (Massand interview, November 1995). *Onward* magazine, launched in June 1994 and edited by co-founder Sazro Mahambrey, caters to the fast-growing second generation of Indian Americans; its circulation has grown steadily in the past two years.

These are just a few examples of the ever-increasing number of publications meeting the demands of the diverse East Indian American community. There is a need, however, in the scholarly community to conduct more research on the Asian Indian ethnic press.

## THE PACIFIC ISLANDER PRESS

Newspapers have been published in the Pacific Islands for more than 250 years, and the press in these islands continues to thrive. According to Suzanna Layton's 1990 Markham Award winning paper entitled "The Contemporary Pacific Islands Press," presented at the 1990 annual conference of the Association for Education in Journalism and Mass Communication, the total number of periodicals published in the Pacific Islands, excluding Hawaii, increased nearly two and a half times from 1973, when there were sixty-nine total publications, to 1989, when 156 total publications were found in the Pacific Islands (see Appendix 4) (Layton, 11). The total circulations of these periodicals jumped from 320,017 in 1973 to 682,998 in 1989, and circulation of daily newspapers rose by 56 percent in the same time, from 81,637 in 1973 to 127,426 in 1989 (13).

Unfortunately, this success in newspaper readership is not evident in the mainland United States among communities of Pacific Islander Americans and immigrants. There were few newspapers and magazine which cater to ethnic Pacific Islander communities in the United States that were uncovered in this book's research.

*Hale Pai*, a newspaper published for native Hawaiians living in the mainland United States, is one such publication designed specifically for a segment of the Pacific Islander population. Other publications for Pacific Islanders that sprung up in the late 1960s and early 1970s as a result of the Asian American pan-ethnicity movement, were the journals *Hawaiian Ethnos*, published in Honolulu, *Hawaii Free People's Press*, published quarterly in Haleiwa, Hawaii, *Hawaii Pono Journal*, published quarterly in Honolulu (which ceased publication many years ago), and *Kalayaan International*, published in San Francisco.

There are most likely several smaller publications serving Pacific Islanders, but they don't receive a great deal of media coverage. This may be partially due to the smaller numbers of Pacific Islanders compared to other ethnic Asian sub-groups in the United States, and due to the fact that Pacific Islanders are more widespread throughout the United States, compared to other Asian ethnic populations.

Pila Laronal, publisher of *Hale Pai*, explains that Pacific Islanders suffer from incorrect media stereotypes, but they are different from other Asian American media stereotypes:

> When newspapers talk about the gang situation among Samoans, a good piece could talk about how 95 percent of the parents migrate and it's a shock to them [living in the United States]. They don't have the opportunities or resources. They don't understand the system. Samoans are smashed by the media all the time. Samoans are portrayed as either in a gang or athletics. There's nothing inbetween. What about their education? Do reporters know that there is a Samoan church, with the largest religious figure, right here in Seattle? (Luna and Wong December 1995-January 1996, *Northwest Asian Weekly*)

The history of the native Hawaiian press is different. There were several early publications which specifically served native Hawaiians. However, as assimilation with Caucasians increased throughout this century, and once Hawaii became the fiftieth state, most newspapers and magazines designed for Hawaiian audiences represent a mix of native Hawaiians and other Americans. One of the earlier newspapers in Hawaii was the *Hawaiian Star*. Other historically influential newspapers which have, in general, given fair treatment to Asian immigrants and Asian Americans, have been the *Honolulu Star Bulletin* and the *Kauai Garden Island*. Some of the Japanese, Chinese, and Filipino newspapers published in Hawaii, as mentioned earlier, were also influential in the coverage of issues facing Pacific Islanders.

The Pacific Islander ethnic press represents some of the oldest Asian American ethnic newspapers in existence. However, research indicates there is a strong need for more ethnic newspapers in the mainland United States which serve Pacific Islanders.

## LEADING TWENTY ASIAN ETHNIC PUBLICATIONS

This historic overview would not be complete without some mention of the leading publications serving ethnic sub-groups of Asian Americans during the mid-1990s, which is the timeframe of the content analysis section of this book. Unfortunately, there is no one single resource that lists these publications, other than the ethnic publications listed in the *Asian Americans Information Directory* (Backus and Furtaw 1992). To search these publications for their content on media-related articles was too time consuming for this book's timetable. Also, it was difficult to assess the importance in terms of community impact and circulation of the top Asian American ethnic publications. Therefore, a professional researcher was hired to determine the top twenty Asian American ethnic publications in the United States based on the following criteria: 1) stability of circulation, 2) representation of the community and/or communities to which each publication targets, and 3) coverage of topics and issues reflective of the targeted group/s.

Before setting the criteria for the search, Marjorie Lee, librarian of the Reading Room of the Asian American Studies Center at the University of California - Los Angeles, was consulted by telephone interview. Lee recommended the criteria set since, she explained, the size of a publication's circulation does not always indicate its impact on a segment of the Asian American community. Following an extensive search, Lee produced a list of the leading academic journals, magazines and newspapers that serve Asian Americans and ethnic sub-groups of Asian Americans.[8] The list of those leading publications can be found in Appendix 5.

As part of the research for this book, editors from each of those twenty publications, as well as the editor of *Chinese American Forum*, were sent letters requesting their opinions on the state of coverage of Asian American events in the U.S. media and for historical information on each of their publications.

## PUBLICATIONS OF THE ASIAN AMERICAN PANETHNICITY MOVEMENT

As the Asian American panethnicity movement developed in the late 1960s and 1970s, there was also a growth in Asian American periodicals. Espiritu explains that until the late 1960s, "most of the Asian newspapers and periodicals [published in the United States] were concerned primarily with local and single-ethnic issues" (Espiritu 1992, 38). The new breed of Asian American publications that cropped up in the late 1960s and early 1970s dealt more with concerns of the Asian American community as a whole. Until that time, most of the Asian American newspapers and periodicals concentrated on local issues or issues relating to a single Asian American ethnic sub-group. Table 7 is a partial listing of those periodicals that began publishing in the 1960s and 1970s as an out-growth of the Asian American panethnicity movement.

Other journals to grow out of the pan-ethnicity movement were: *Asian Women's Journal*, published in Berkeley, California, and *Getting Together*, published in New York Many of the panethnicity movement publications grew out of Asian student movements on college campuses. As Espiritu explained:

> While the traditional ethnic press continued to be important, its neglect and disdain of such political issues as civil rights, the Vietnam war, and ethnic studies prompted young dissidents to launch their own publications. Much of their journalism was committed to the empowerment of the Asian American people (Espiritu 1992, 40).

Some of these publications were short-lived, like the publication *Gidra*, which was born when five UCLA students each contributed $100 to start the publication (40). It was published for only five years, but *Gidra* became the first and most widely circu-

Table 7. Partial Listing of Asian American Periodicals, 1960s to Early 1970s

| Publication | Place of Publication |
| --- | --- |
| AACTION | Philadelphia, Pa. |
| AASA | California State University, Northridge |
| AASA | Cornell University, Ithaca, N.Y. |
| Aion | San Francisco |
| Amerasia Journal | Yale University, New Haven, Connecticut (now at UCLA) |
| Ameri-Asia News | Forest City, Florida |
| Asian American for Equal Employment Newspaper | New York City |
| Asian Expression | California State University at Dominguez Hills |
| Asian Family Affair | Seattle, Washington |
| Asian Spotlight | College of San Mateo, California |
| Asian Student, The | Berkeley, California |
| Asian Student | City College of New York |
| Asian Student Voice | San Francisco State University |
| Bridge: An Asian American Perspective | New York City |
| Crosscurrents | Los Angeles |
| East Wind | Los Angeles |
| Eastern Wind | Washington, D.C. |
| Getting Together | New York City Chinatown |
| Gidra | Los Angeles |
| Jade: The Asian American Magazine | Los Angeles |
| Pacific Ties | Los Angeles |
| Rice Paper | Madison, Wisconsin |
| Rodan | San Francisco |

SOURCE: Espiritu, Yen Le. 1992. *Asian American Panethnicity.* Philadelphia: Temple University Press, 39.

lated pan-Asian publication. As Asian American activist Rocky Chin said during the heyday of *Gidra*, "If there is an 'Asian-American Movement' publication, it is *Gidra*, the most widely circulated Asian American newspaper-magazine in the country" (Wei 1993, 103). Asian American scholar William Wei described, in part, the impact of *Gidra*:

> It [*Gidra*] was prominent and creditable enough to be included in the Federal Bureau of Investigation's counterintelligence program. The FBI's Los Angeles field office described the paper as "mildly militant (and sometimes obscene) in nature and espouses all yellow power issues. It

reports regularly on Asian American activities on the
California campuses as well as other areas of the country
and has proved to be a wealth of information concerning
the identities of organizations and individuals devoted to
these causes" (103).

According to Wei, the three most important publications that
started the Asian American Alternative press movement, and
which represented the Asian American pan-ethnicity movement,
were *Gidra*, *Bridge*, and Amerasia Journal. *Bridge* had many
changes since it first started publishing in 1970 and catered more
to Chinese Americans than any other Asian ethnic group.
However, that all changed in the mid-1970s as *Bridge* took up
where Gildra left off as a leading publication of the Asian
American movement. The publication survived many philosophical changes as the Asian American community changed, and survived several financial challenges. However, *Bridge* eventually
ceased publication several years ago and was never to be revived,
like some of the other popular publications to come out of the
panethnicity movement.

One of the most important of all the Asian American movement publications has been *Amerasia Journal*, which has now
grown into a widely respected journal within the academic community as well as the Asian American community. In 1971 the
Yale Asian American Students Association started publishing
*Amerasia Journal* (which is now published at UCLA), which
became the first and only national scholarly publication at that
time devoted entirely to the experiences of Asians living in America
(Wei 1993, 40). *Amerasia Journal* remains one of the leading
Asian American publications today.

*Amerasia Journal* was orginally published quarterly, but,
beginning with Volume Two, which was published in the fall of
1973, the University of California at Los Angeles agreed to co-
sponsor the journal, and at that time it became a bi-annual publication. For a few years in the mid-1970s it published only one
issue per year. It was expanded to three issues per year in the late
1980s; however, the journal still occasionally publishes only two
issues per year. Its inaugural issue was in March of 1971, and was
published by members of the Yale University Asian American
Students Association. Here is how the journal's mission was
explained in that first issue:

> *Amerasia Journal* is not our journal. It belongs to our readers. We exist as a journal to collect and publish the best and most provocative material we can find on Asians in America. . . . For in the end, it will be our readership that sustains or deserts us. Unless we or our goals are relevant to their needs, concerns, and aspirations, we're simply shouting loud and listening to the echoes of our own voices in a closed room. We'd like Amerasia Journal to be more than a soliloquy, and we need your assistance. (Leong et al. 1971, 2).

Three goals were also set in that initial edition, which were:

1) to accurately assess our past,
2) to obtain a clear knowledge of our present situation,
3) to pose plausible, well-defined visions of our future (Leong et al. 1988b, 10).

Since its inception, the journal's publishing headquarters were subsequently (in 1974) moved from Yale University to the Asian American Studies Center at the University of California - Los Angeles. It has had several editors over the years, including Lowell Chun-Hoon, the first editor, and Megumi Dick Osumi and Carolyn Yee. Since the fall of 1977 Russell C. Leong has been the editor.

There have been several single-topic editions to help address issues pertaining to specific segments of the Asian American community. For example, there was an entire issue, in 1986-87, devoted to presenting, as the journal stated, an "alternative" interpretation of the internment of Japanese Americans during World War II (Leong 1986-87). Other special topic issues have been devoted to the Filipino American experience, as well as Vietnamese Americans.

The *Amerasia Journal* is widely recognized among Asian American scholars as the leading academic journal on Asian American issues. According to the *Dictionary of Asian American History*, the journal "is the only publication devoted exclusively to Asian American history as well as to the contemporary issues and problems facing Asian Americans and their communities" (Kim 1986, 131). Some people may dispute this since there are several newer publications since that dictionary was published in 1986 that deal with more specific subjects of interest to Asian

Americans, but the importance of Amerasia Journal to Asian American scholarship is evident.

Another publication, *Asian Quilt*, started in 1993 by Vassar College students, represents "the only undergraduates in the country publishing a nationally distributed Asian American literary journal" (no author cited,*Vassar Quarterly* Spring 1996, 5). It approaches the Asian American experience through fiction, nonfiction, poetry, photography, and artwork of Asian American students.

The importance of scholarly journals that examine issues within the Asian American community has grown steadily since the panethnicity movement of the late 1960s and early 1970s. One of the leading journals of Asian American scholarship today is *Amerasia Journal.*

## NOTES

[8] The search was conducted for a fee of $75 and using the resources of the UCLA Asian American Studies Center.

# CHAPTER 3

# RELATED STUDIES

> I still continually find false ideas in America con-
> cerning Chinese customs, manners, and institu-
> tions. Small blame to the people at large, who
> have no means of learning the truth, except
> through newspapers or accounts of travellers who
> do not understand what they see. . .
>
> —Lee Yan Phou
> *When I Was a Boy in China*

## THEORETICAL FOUNDATIONS OF THE BOOK

In 1947 the press was sharply criticized by the Hutchins
Commission for not providing representative coverage of society's
constituent groups, including minorities (Commission on the
Freedom of the Press 1947; Vivian 1993, 97-98). Since the rivet-
ing report of that commission, which was formally known as the
Commission of Freedom of the Press, the social responsibility theory of the media has replaced much of the libertarian theoretical
foundations of the press that prevailed during the previous century and on into the early part of this century. Twenty-one years
later another landmark commission gathered to study the media.
The Kerner Commission, formally known at the National
Advisory Commission on Civil Disorders, used the social responsibility groundwork of the Hutchins Commission to examine how
the media covered race relations (National Advisory Commission
on Civil Disorders 1968). Some of the key recommendations to

come out of the Kerner Commission report were: 1) that the media needed to include more minority perspectives in its news coverage, 2) that coverage of minority communities needed to be expanded, 3) that reporters needed to be permanently assigned to cover minority communities, and, 4) that more minority reporters should be hired in media institutions (National Advisory Commission on Civil Disorders 1968). Likewise, mass communication scholars have studied how well the media is meeting this social responsibility of giving fair and adequate coverage to society's constituent groups, which includes racial and ethnic minorities, handicapped persons, the poor, religious minorities, and numerous others.

As this review of related studies will demonstrate, there have been few studies by media scholars examining how the entire Asian American population, which this book classifies as one of society's constituent groups, is represented and covered in the media. So, as stated in Chapter One, while there is a lot of knowledge and research about the Asian American population in social, economic, and other scholarly arenas, there is a lack of knowledge on how Asian Americans and issues facing Asian Americans are covered in the press and on how Asian Americans, specifically journalists, perceive the Asian American community is being covered.

That is where the need for this book arises.

This book represents the only content analysis ever conducted, according to this review of literature, that specifically examines coverage of all Asian Americans in the press, as compared to only examining one of the ethnic sub-groups of Asian Americans. It also is one of the largest surveys ever conducted of Asian American journalists on their job experiences, job satisfaction, and their perceptions of how the mass media covers Asian Americans and issues affecting Asian Americans. Finally, it gives a bit more insight than previously known into the number of Asian Americans who work at the twenty newspapers used in the content analysis, as well as providing more knowledge of the editorial policies, or lack thereof, on covering Asian Americans at those same twenty newspapers. So there is a three-fold approach to the comprehensive scope of this book's topic, and those three areas of research are inter-connected, as explained in Chapter One.

**Agenda Setting Hypothesis.** One theoretical basis for this book's research is the agenda setting hypothesis, which states that if the media choose to emphasize coverage of an issue or an area of the news, then the public will deem that issue or area of news as important, and the public will, in turn, get excited about those issues (McCombs and Shaw 1972; McCombs and Shaw 1993). This book's research only studies half of the agenda setting hypothesis, however. The content analysis indicates the agenda set for coverage of Asian Americans and ethnic sub-groups of Asian Americans by the twenty newspapers examined, but whether the public deems that agenda to be valid is not studied in this book. To determine the public's perception of newspapers' agenda for news coverage of Asian Americans, a broad survey needs to be conducted, and that was not done as part of this book.

However, the agenda setting hypothesis, which many researchers say is a theory, is a crucial theoretical basis for the content analysis. This hypothesis was forced into the forefront of mass communication research in 1972 when McCombs and Shaw published their landmark article that said news gatekeepers play an extremely important role in determining what issues become important in the minds of news consumers during political campaigns (McCombs and Shaw 1972). Here is how they described the intricate relationship between media gatekeepers and media consumers, according to the agenda setting hypothesis:

> In choosing and displaying news, editors, newsroom staff, and broadcasters play an important part in shaping political reality. Readers learn not only about a given issue, but also how much importance to attach to that issue from the amount of information in a news story and its position. In reflecting what candidates are saying during a campaign, the mass media may well determine the important issues— that is, the media may set the "agenda" of the campaign (176).

Since this important article was published, numerous mass media scholars have studied how the agenda setting hypothesis applies to other areas of establishing the public's agenda on issues. There are some studies, however, which claim the agenda setting hypothesis is not valid, and thus, also claim to disprove the theory.

Unfortunately, no study has examined how the agenda setting hypothesis applies to the public's perception of Asian Americans and issues facing Asian Americans. This fact becomes even more unsettling when considering that Rogers, Dearing, and Bregman in 1993 found more than two hundred articles on agenda setting in social science journals and other scholarly literature since the publication of the 1972 McCombs and Shaw article (Rogers, Dearing, and Bregman 1993).

Therefore, some other important studies on agenda setting contributed to this theoretical foundation of the book and should be mentioned. By 1977, McCombs and Shaw were working on an expansion to the first level of the original agenda setting hypothesis by looking at contingent conditions that enhance or limit media agenda setting (McCombs and Shaw 1993, 59). At approximately the same time, during the 1976 presidential campaign, agenda setting entered a third phase when Weaver, Graber, McCombs, and Eyal looked at the two new areas of agenda setting, which were: 1) how the agenda of candidate characteristics reported in the news was learned by media consumers, and 2) examining the broad spectrum of all aspects of politics and how it was reflected in the news through mention of personal concerns of voters (59).

In a 1993 article that traced the twenty-five-year history of research on agenda setting, McCombs and Shaw cited these first three phases of the evolution of agenda setting, and said the fourth phase of research in this area, which has occurred since 1980, "focused on the sources of the *media agenda*" (59). In other words, as McCombs and Shaw explained:

> While the opening phases of agenda-setting research concentrated on the question "Who sets the public agenda—and under what conditions?", the most recent phase of work has shifted its attention to the question "Who sets the media agenda?" The question has linked agenda-setting research to a number of social science, communication, and journalism subfields (60).

This is certainly relevant in seeking to find the sources of the media agenda of news about Asian Americans and issues affecting Asian Americans. The subfields of sociology and psychology play a significant role in the most recent phase of agenda setting research.

Other important agenda setting studies examined for this book's theoretical foundations include Benton and Frazier's 1976 article, which said people who read newspapers rely on newspapers to help them determine their agenda of what is news, and that people who are television dependent for getting their news rely on television for their news agenda setting (Benton and Frazier 1976). Another important article on agenda setting that has strong influence on this book's theoretical foundations is McCombs and Weaver's article that linked the spiral of silence theory to agenda setting through the concept of the readers' need for orientation in establishing their news agenda (McCombs and Weaver 1985).

This linking of the spiral of silence theory to agenda setting is particularly important to minority populations since the spiral of silence theory states members of society's constituent groups fall into a downward spiral of silence because they perceive themselves to be less important within a society due to the lack of coverage they receive in the media's agenda (McCombs and Weaver 1985; Noelle-Neumann 1984). Noelle-Neumann explained in her book *The Spiral of Silence*, that the media give little attention to minorities and that members of minority groups look to the media to find out what the agenda is for them, so they, therefore, conclude they have very little power in society due to the lack of news coverage on minorities (Noelle-Neumann 1984). So linking spiral of silence theory to agenda setting was important in relation to this book's goals. Finally, another key study on agenda setting was Shoemaker and Reese's look at how the different ideologies of journalists affect the overall agenda set within a given media organization (Shoemaker and Reese 1991).

One interesting agenda setting study dealt with how newspapers cover race issues in political campaigns. Grainey, Pollack, and Kusmierek conducted a content analysis of three Chicago daily newspapers during the 1983 Chicago general election and looked at the way the three newspapers presented racial issues (Grainey, Pollack, and Kusmierek 1984). All issues of the *Chicago Sun-Times*, the *Defender*, and the *Chicago Tribune* for a two-month period (February to April 1983) were analyzed for content. The study showed that although all three newspapers frequently carried stories where people interviewed insisted race should not become an issue in the campaign, that since so much space was devoted to discussing it race became an issue in the campaign (Grainey, Pollack, and Kusmierek 1984).

McCombs and Shaw summed up both the importance of agenda setting and the importance of how the hypothesis has evolved, by stating:

> Bernard Cohen's (1963) classic summation of agenda setting—the media may not tell us what to think, but they are stunningly successful in telling us what to think about—has been turned inside out. New research exploring the consequences of agenda setting and media framing suggest that the media not only tell us what to think about, but also how to think about it, and, consequently, what to think (McCombs and Shaw 1993, 65).

This discussion of related studies later cites a handful of other journal articles and conference papers that study ethnic sub-groups of Asian Americans, such as Pacific Islanders, and certain relationships those groups have with the media, but none was a comprehensive content analysis of how all Asian Americans are covered in the media.

The agenda setting hypothesis states that the mass media set the agenda for what is news, as opposed to mass media consumers determining their own agenda for what is news. In other words, media consumers accept the news agenda set by the media. Thus, issues about Asian Americans reported in the media may influence public perceptions of Asian Americans even though very little research has been done to confirm this relationship. But this theoretical foundation can also be linked to how minorities perceive themselves and their role in society. So it is an important theory base when studying the agenda set by leading newspapers in coverage of Asian Americans and issues affecting Asian Americans. This book will not use survey research to track influences of topics, but will attempt to determine what the media agenda is for Asian Americans.

Stereotypes. The role of stereotypes portrayed in whatever agenda is set by the media in covering Asian Americans is crucial to the theoretical foundation of the research in the content analysis portion of this book, just as it is to most studies that examine the media agenda for covering minorities and other constituency groups.

Several studies were found to support the theory that minorities are stereotyped, usually negatively, in the mass media. Simon and Alexander studied 110 years of U.S. magazine coverage of immigrants, from 1880 to 1990, and found the most important messages that the majority of the magazines communicated were the desire to reduce sharply overall numbers of immigrants arriving on U.S. shores, and to exclude persons from certain regions of the world from entering the United States (Simon and Alexander 1993). Miller edited an in-depth, comprehensive book on how ethnic minorities are stereotyped in American film and television (Miller 1978). The book, *Ethnic Images in American Film and Television*, looked at the role of television and film in perpetuating stereotypes of Puerto Ricans, Jews, Italian Americans, and German Americans. However, most relevant to this book was the final chapter of that book which discusses the strong, negative psychological implications of Asian stereotypes in film and television and their relation to the Asian American experience in the United States.

The Jeffres and Hur study mentioned earlier in this book also has implications for stereotypes of minorities (Jeffres and Hur 1980). While this study does not focus on stereotyping directly, it does conclude that ethnic newspapers and radio programs portray minorities in a more positive light, which could be translated to positive images (or stereotypes) of minorities, and, therefore, minority readers and listeners develop a positive relationship with their use of those minority news mediums (13-16). Another study that looked at stereotypes presented in ethnic media was Downing's 1990 article on minority radio stations in the United States (Downing 1990, 135-148). The article provided an overview of ethnic minority broadcasting in the United States, and looked specifically at several African American radio stations as well as a Native American radio station. In this sweeping examination of minority broadcasting, Downing also concludes that these radio stations tend to portray minorities in more positive images when compared to mainstream radio programs (140). So from these two studies we can see that stereotypes exist within minorities' media, but those stereotypes are usually positive in nature.

In 1988, Raub published a study that examined how stereotypes of ethnicity and non-Caucasian minorities have changed from 1950 to 1984 in *National Geographic* (Raub 1988). This study is significant in that it found while the stereotypes of ethnic minorities portrayed in the magazine have changed significantly during that twenty-four-year period, the magazine continued to portray ethnic minorities in such stereotypes as citizens from developing nations being exotic, and that seldom are local customs of these people explained adequately to dispel these stereotypes. The article also found that *National Geographic* tends to portray persons from countries other than the United States in a context that makes them appealing to American tourists (369). So this study helps to demonstrate the often subtle nature of stereotyping ethnic minorities in media images.

Winkel's look at how minorities are portrayed in news articles on crime also is important to theoretical foundation of stereotyping in the media (Winkel 1990). In this study Winkel found that ethnic references in newspaper headlines on crime stories resulted in a reader bias against ethnic minorities due to association with a negative stereotype of the minority listed in the story. The article also found serious negative stereotyping of ethnic minorities in newspaper crime coverage. Winkel concludes his article by arguing all references to ethnic minorities should be dropped from newspaper coverage of crime due to the negative stereotypes such references perpetuate among readership (99-100). This study is relevant to Asian Americans and the content analysis portion of this book, since stories have been coded to see which ethnic subgroups of Asian Americans are mentioned in crime stories.

Yum and Park's article on the effects of stereotyping added greatly to the literature on this topic (Yum and Park 1990). That article confirmed the hypothesis that it is harder to change a definite (strong) stereotype of an ethnic minority, as opposed to changing a person's attitude when that person has a less definite stereotypical image of an ethnic minority. This is an important finding when considering stereotypes portrayed in the media since it confirms the difficulty in overcoming stereotype images the stronger, or more definite, those images are portrayed in the media.

Guitierrez's study of racial stereotypes portrayed in advertising drew similar conclusions about the impact of negative stereotypes (Guitierrez 1990). The article confirms that negative images of racial minorities in advertisements reinforce racial, social, cultural, and linguistic differences in the United States.

Other supporting studies that served as stereotype theoretical foundations for this book's research included Martindale's survey of the *New York Times, Boston Globe, Chicago Tribune,* and *Atlanta Constitution* on changes in images of African Americans in news coverage (Martindale 1990). She found stereotypes of African Americans as criminals and entertainment/sports figures predominated in the 1950s, and dropped to less than six percent of coverage on African Americans in the civil rights era of the 1960s in all the newspapers except the *Chicago Tribune* (Martindale 1990). In another content analysis of coverage in the *New York Times* of America's largest minority groups from 1934 to 1994, Martindale found the stereotype of criminal activities linked to minorities to be strong (Martindale, unpublished paper, 1995). This stereotype received the largest percent of total column inches of coverage for Asian Americans (23 percent), and Latinos (38 percent), and the second largest percent of total column inches of coverage for African Americans (11 percent) (Martindale, unpublished paper, 1995).

Finally, Pease's long-term study of minority news coverage in the *Columbus Dispatch* contributed significantly to understanding the types of minority images, and stereotypes, portrayed in that news coverage examined (Pease 1989). The study analyzed the minority-related news content in several two-week periods in 1965, before the violence leading up to the riots in 1967, and for two-week periods in 1987. A total of 138 stories in twenty-four editions of the newspaper were examined, and Pease found that minority-related coverage became less "bad" and more "good" between 1965 and 1987, even though there wasn't much more news about minorities in the newspaper in 1987 (30-35). Pease also found significant changes in the *Dispatch's* coverage of social issues between 1965 and 1987. Clearly there is a need for more studies of this type on representation of minorities in the media.

Barna has done a great deal of research in intercultural communication, including studies on the effects of stereotyping of individuals. He describes stereotypes as one of the six "stumbling blocks of communication" (Samovar and Porter 1991, 349). Here is how he describes stereotyping:

> The fourth stumbling block (of communication) is the presence of *preconceptions* and *stereotypes*. If the label "inscrutable" has preceded the Japanese guest, few try to understand his "strange" behavior, including the constant and seemingly inappropriate smile. . . . A professor who expects everyone from Indonesia, Mexico, and many other countries to "bargain" may unfairly interpret a hesitation or request from an international student as a move to manipulate preferential treatment. Stereotypes help do what Ernest Becker says the anxiety-prone human race must do—reduce the threat of the unknown by making the world predictable. Indeed, this is one of the basic functions of culture: to lay out a predictable world in which the individual is firmly oriented. Stereotypes are generalize, second-hand beliefs that provide conceptual bases from which we "make sense" out of what goes on around us, whether or not they are accurate or fit the circumstance (349).

Part of this book's research will be to show, through the content analysis, the types of stereotypes and stereotypical coverage, or lack thereof, that occurs in the mainstream press.

There are many more important studies on the impact of stereotyping of ethnic minorities in the media. Unfortunately, as we will see later in this chapter, few studies have looked specifically at stereotyping of Asian Americans in print, radio, or television media.

Coorientation. This book first asks what stereotypes, agendas, and other media messages (or lack thereof) are presented in the twenty newspapers of the content analysis. Then, through the survey of five hundred Asian American journalists, this book seeks to find out their perceptions of how Asian Americans are covered in the mainstream media, as well as seeking information about job experience and job satisfaction. It is this second research method of the survey that utilizes coorientation as one of its theoretical foundations.

Beyond indicating what agenda the newspapers are setting in covering Asian Americans, or indicating where Asian Americans and issues facing Asian Americans fall in the overall news agenda, the results will also determine if those Asian American journalists surveyed are over-estimating or under-estimating the news agenda on Asian Americans. Unfortunately, to determine if the agenda set by those twenty newspapers in coverage of Asian Americans is accepted by the public at large, a much broader survey would need to be conducted.

In an overall sense, coorientation theory states that people become human by observing how others interact. This relationship is also called symbolic interaction, which is a term brought about through the various studies of famed anthropologist Margaret Mead. The crucial part of coorientation theory, as it relates to mass media, states that part of that symbolic interaction comes about when people use media and observe messages in the media (Culbertson 1975/76; Chaffee and McLeod 1968). So coorientation theory is often involved with studying people's perception of news coverage. This is an important theoretical foundation for this book in looking at Asian American journalists' perceptions of how the media portrays Asian Americans.

The literature on coorientation is vast and complex, and only a few key studies will be mentioned here. The concept of coorientation was first proposed by the social psychologist Theodore Newcomb in 1953 (Newcomb 1953). In 1968, Chaffee and McLeod's research design, in an article on contamination effect in media sensationalism, drew a great deal of attention from media scholars and carried coorientation theory into a new phase by applying it to communication (Chaffee and McLeod 1968). This article also drew attention to the importance of communication dyads, which was later a building block for studying relationships between viewer-news commentator dyads. The summary in that article set the stage for encouragement of other coorientation studies:

> In the absence of direct evidence that communication is the intervening process that produces Accuracy [*sic*] and Understanding [*sic*], of course, further conjecture is pointless. Studies are needed that examine the kinds of communication that best effect improvements in these coorientational criterion variables. Studies where the content of communication is either coded or systematically varied would help to specify the nature of the coorientation process (669).

By the early 1970s , research in coorientation entered a new phase with the publication of Pearce and Stamm's landmark article which further applied coorientation to interpersonal communication (Pearce and Stamm 1973).

Certainly Culbertson has contributed greatly to the study of coorientation. His article on gatekeeper coorientation gave much more insight into using the coorientation model in analysis of the types of job orientations that exist among gatekeepers and how those various orientations affect what ultimately becomes news (Culbertson 1975/76). Culbertson continued this line of research in 1981 by studying differences in perspectives held by reporters and editors (Culbertson 1981).

Two years later, in 1983, Culbertson published a major piece of research on coorientation and print media which was published as a monograph (Culbertson 1983). Finally, in 1989 Culbertson applied coorientation methods to studying whether journalists should take a lead role in agenda setting, or whether the direction of news agendas should come from audiences (Culbertson 1989). The jury appears to still be out in this constantly changing area of coorientation theory, but it remains a topic that continues to captivate researchers today.

Underwood and Stamm also conducted a key study in coorientation, published in 1992, that applied the theory to trends of newsroom policies becoming more reader oriented (Underwood and Stamm 1992). A decade earlier, however, Atkin, Burgoon, and Burgoon did an in-depth coorientation study on journalists' perception of their audience and how they reach that perception (Atkin, Burgoon, and Burgoon 1983). Buddenbaum's 1987 article that applied coorientation theory to religious news coverage also gained a great deal of attention from media researchers and became a major building block in the evolution of coorientation theory (Buddenbaum 1987).

Another relevant study is Tillinghast's article on perceptions of news sources and how they judge facts reported in news articles (Tillinghast 1983). Some of the comments made by Asian American journalists in answering this book's survey questions make references to source perceptions that may relate to the journalists' ethnic status as Asian Americans.

Korzenny et al. published another relevant article on coorientation which studied cultural identification as a predictor of media preferences in Chicano and Mexican children (Korzenny et al. 1983). Along a similar vein, Faber, O'Guinn, and Meyer looked at differing ethnic perceptions of television portrayals of Hispanics (Faber, O'Guinn, and Meyer 1987). This study is important to the book since the survey of five hundred journalists examines perceptions of Asian Americans who work in the media concerning news coverage of that minority.

Likewise, Lichter and Lichter found that television plays a role in shaping ethnic images for some ethnic minorities, but not for others (Lichter and Lichter 1988). Jewish students who participated in the study were least likely to be influenced by television in shaping their images of ethnic minorities, while African American students surveyed were the most likely to be influenced by television images of minorities. A correlation was found between heavy television viewing and TV's ability to shape a test participant's image of ethnic minorities.

One of the most important studies dealing with cooreintation theory and minorities, as it relates to this book's research, was Pease and Smith's monograph looking at job satisfaction and the impact of racial diversity at U.S. newspapers (Pease and Smith 1991). That study is discussed in the latter part of this chapter.

The long evolution of coorientation theory is an important theoretical underpinning for this book. Many research studies have shed light on the importance of the mutual perceptions and relationships among media gatekeepers, media messages, and media consumers. This book hopes to give even more understanding to the importance of Asian Americans journalists' perceptions of how they are covered in the mainstream media.

**Spiral of Silence Theory and the Theory of Hegemony.** As explained earlier, the spiral of silence theory states that society's constituent groups, particularly minorities, develop a perception of their role in society through the agenda set for them in the news media (Noelle-Neumann 1984, 4-12). The second half of the theory says that since minorities receive less coverage than whites in the news, and since the coverage of minorities often concentrates on negative images and stereotypes—such as minorities being associated with crime—then members of society's constituent groups perceive themselves as being less important, less politically influential, and, in general, a silent, unheard segment of society as a whole (4-12). The final part of the theory states that minorities accept the agenda set for them by the media, and because of the negative image it creates within the member of a societal minority, those persons spiral into a silent role within society (4-12).

Noelle-Neumann has written two landmark books on the spiral of silence theory, which she states dates back to 1965 when a member of a minority political faction in the former West Germany readily accepted his group's loss in a national election, thus choosing to remain passive (silent) rather than to be outraged or even mildly angry (1). It was from this event that Noelle-Neumann began her research on the spiral of silence. It is clear to see why this is an important theory base for this book's research, since it is examining the coverage of Asian Americans in the mainstream press, as well as perceptions by Asian American journalists of news coverage about Asian Americans.

Here is how Noelle-Neumann explains part of the dynamics of the spiral of silence theory:

> The fear of isolation seems to be the force that sets the spiral of silence in motion. To run with the pack is a relatively happy state of affairs; but if you can't, because you won't share publicly in what seems to be a universally acclaimed conviction, you can at least remain silent, as a second choice, so that others can put up with you (6).

These comments seem almost ironic when considering some of the comments made by Asian American journalists in the first pages of this book, and the full text of their comments which are presented in appendices of Chapter Five. It is also uncanny to consider that Asian Americans are actually stereotyped as being the "model minority," which includes a gross stereotype of Asian submissiveness and quietude.

Noelle-Neumann's research on the spiral of silence theory is vast and valuable. There are, however, several other studies that have contributed to this important theory as it applies to minorities and the media. One such study is Tierney's 1979 article which suggests another rung to the spiral of silence theory by looking at research that states that minorities, or subcultures, which do not have regular access to mainstream media gradually begin to perceive themselves as "illegitimate" (Tierney 1979, 176-177). Tierney looked at how factors of mobility outside the ethnic environment affects members of minorities and their perceptions of themselves as illegitimate.

Gist's 1990 study on minorities in newsrooms and minority representation in newspaper content argued that the lack of opportunities for minorities in newsrooms coupled with poor images of minorities in the press literally has a cognitive effect on minorities in that they "learn" what they cannot achieve in life (Gist 1991). This study emphasized that this negative cognitive effect is particularly strong on minority youths in that they see only limited roles for themselves in society both through the lack of minorities in newsrooms and the lack of broad coverage of minorities in society.

Yum looked at how communication patterns and the type of media used by Korean immigrants Hawaii affected their perceptions of themselves in her study which looked more broadly at cognitive patterns of Korean immigrant media consumers (Yum 1982). Yum found that more diverse media use and overall communication patterns than previously assumed by researchers were being utilized by the immigrants, and this, in turn, affected their self-images.

Tan's 1983 study on media use and political orientations of ethnic groups examined the positive effects hypothesis, which is closely related to the spiral of silence theory. The positive effects hypothesis is based on the assumption that the mainstream media reflect the what is normal in society's political and social hierarchy by increasing that "normal" status among all audiences, particularly among minority audiences (Tan 1983). This study found that the positive effects hypothesis is strongest among newspaper readers, and that Mexican Americans participating in the study readily accepted the normative status of social and political hierachies in the United States which placed that ethnic group at low ends of the hierarchies. So, in effect, this study helps to explain from another angle how minority media consumers begin their spiral of silence.

These represent some of the key studies on the spiral of silence theory conducted in the past twenty years. This remains a vigorous area of mass communication research and certainly the spiral of silence theory will become even more relevant as minorities, like Asian Americans, grow in population and in their contributions to mass communication.

The theory of hegemony states that mass media messages are the primary conduits through which constituent groups, particularly minorities, in society are taught dominant values and philosophies since the mass media reflects the values and philosophies of the majority within a given society (Gitlin 1979; Tuchman 1978).

Both of these theories served as foundations for the survey of Asian American journalists in the book, which was used to determine how Asian Americans perceive they are covered in the media. Again, there were no existing studies found in this review of literature that specifically surveyed Asian Americans in this regard. However, there were some useful studies that helped to serve as models, and which supported this theoretical basis for the survey portion of the book.

As early as 1978 Carter showed that African Americans favored television programs that featured African American actors, and that most African Americans in the study relied heavily on television for information and to formulate their perceptions of the world (Carter 1978). Gandy and Matabane found that television images of African Americans and Hispanics affected racial attitudes and self esteem by members of those two minority groups (Asanate and Gudykunst 1989). Tan examined African Americans' and Mexican Americans' evaluations of television and newspaper portrayals of their respective ethnic groups and found both groups were generally negative in their perceptions of the media's coverage of their group (Tan 1978). In both ethnic groups, those surveyed who were most critical in their assessment of how the media portrayed them tended to be highly educated and young.

Some studies, such as Allen and Clarke's look at demographic variables relationship to media exposure in African Americans and Latinos, further emphasize the importance of the theory of hegemony (Allen and Clarke 1980). In the Allen and Clarke study, certain demographic factors such as age and sex indicated even stronger impacts of media messages on the two minorities studied.

The spiral of silence theory and the theory of hegemony, combined, provide a significant theoretical base to this book's research. These two theories indicate both the psychological impact of the media on minorities and the ability for media messages to sway minorities towards mainstream beliefs and perceptions of the world.

**Communicator Analysis and Work Satisfaction.** This final theoretical foundation for the book research is not often categorized as a formal theory of mass communication. However, several studies support the importance of examining communicator analysis and work satisfaction. Specifically, there are four studies that did not relate to the spiral of silence theory or to the theory of hegemony, but which served as models of the two questions on the survey of Asian American journalists concerning their roles in the workplace, and which supported the section of the book which examines the number of minority journalists employed at newspapers.

Shafer conducted a study of seventy-two Hispanic and African American journalists in 1993 which identified constraints those journalists perceived existed to full newsroom equality due to racial discrimination on the job (Shafer 1993). This study was particularly helpful in that, the study found, African American journalists identified three prevailing race-related problems on their newsroom staffs: 1) tokenism, or filling slots simply due to their racial status, 2) pigeonholing, or being required to focus on coverage of minority issues and events, and 3) demands for a performance to a higher standard than white colleagues to achieve equal professional status within a newsroom (Shafer 1993). In fact, the Asian American journalists surveyed for this book often cited those exact problems in their respective newsrooms.

Bramlett-Solomon conducted a survey of Hispanic and African American journalists to find out what job appeal factors they ranked as important and found that the overall level of job satisfaction tended to be positive with 23 percent of respondents as very satisfied, 48 percent were fairly satisfied, while 23 percent were somewhat dissatisfied, and only 6 percent were very dissatisfied with their newsroom jobs (Bramlett-Solomon 1993). This book did not attempt to measure job satisfaction; however, research such as Bramlett-Solomon's survey was useful in the conceptual stage of the book's survey.

Stone found in analyzing newsroom hiring records of the Radio Television News Directors Association (RTNDA) from 1976 to 1986 that women have made considerable gains while African Americans have lagged markedly (Stone 1988). Finally, Haws found that:

> Since the American Society of Newspaper Editors set minority hiring goals in 1978, the number of minorities working in newsrooms has crept up from about 4 percent to nearly 8 percent by 1990. But the goal of racial 'equivalency' to be

met by year 2000 finds the minority community growing so fast that gains are being wiped out. . . . Daily newspapers that achieve minimum minority hiring goals are in communities with, proportionately speaking, small numbers of minorities. When communities have minorities of at least 15 %, newspapers, whetherlarge or small, cannot seem to match that percentage on news staffs (Haws 1991, 764).

This was a particularly enlightening study in view of the fact that all the newspapers used in the content analysis for this book had very large circulations, and since many of the Asian American journalists surveyed hailed from cities with large Asian American populations.

Pease surveyed the effects of roles of African Americans, specifically the activism of the civil rights movement, on the type of coverage of the African American community in Columbus, Ohio, and changes in coverage of African Americans in the *Columbus Dispatch* from a two-week period in 1965 to the same time period in 1987 (Pease 1989). Pease found that the role of African Americans within society affected the amount and type of coverage that minority group received in the newspaper studied. This is a significant study because it draws attention to the larger role of minorities within society and the effect that role has on media coverage and, ultimately, media images of minorities.

Finally, in 1990 Pease and Stempel published a significant study on job satisfaction among minority newspaper executives (Pease and Stempel 1990). Of forty-five minority newspaper executives surveyed in the study, thirty-six (or 85.7 percent) said they had found some racism or a great deal of racism at their place of employment (71). There was also a consensus among those interviewed that as minorities in a newsroom environment they had to maintain a higher standard of professionalism compared to their white counterparts in order to succeed in the newspaper industry. This study is relevant to the survey of Asian American journalists for this book, particularly in how the Asian Americans perceive their roles within newsrooms and what they feel they must do in order to succeed.

Theories relating to communicator analysis and the role of work satisfaction on minorities in the media are the final theoretical foundation for this book's research. This area of research is particularly important when analyzing the survey of five hundred Asian

American journalists as to their work satisfaction and their perceptions of how Asian Americans and covered in the media today.

**Summary of Theoretical Foundations.** With this background in mind, we shall now look at what research has been conducted on Asian Americans and ethnic sub-groups of Asian Americans by communication scholars. After understanding the cumulative research on this topic, as of the mid-1990s, research questions examined in this book will be formulated in the final section of this chapter.

## PREVIOUS STUDIES ON ASIAN AMERICANS THAT RELATE TO THE THEORETICAL FOUNDATIONS

Despite an exhaustive search of studies on Asian Americans (Mansfield-Richardson 1996, 545-639), few studies were found in the five theoretical areas that specifically relate to Asian Americans.

Eight areas were examined for this search of literature, and the search yielded the following relevant studies for this book: 1) five articles in scholarly journals on mass communication (including one monograph), 2) no articles in scholarly journals on communication from all the social sciences, 3) three masters' theses and one doctoral book in mass communication written from 1963 to 1994[9], 4) one doctoral book in the social sciences other than mass communication, 5) three research papers presented at recent annual conferences of the International Communication Association, and, 6) one paper presented at recent annual conference of the Association for Journalism and Mass Communication, and, 7) one paper presented at a recent regional conference on mass communication.

This lack of attention to the Asian American population in the United States by leading American and international scholars can be put in better perspective by looking at the mass media research being done on other minorities. First, consider again that the Asian American community is the fastest growing minority group in the U.S. population (*U.S. Census-1990* 1992, 323-325). The number of persons of Asian descent in the U.S. more than doubled between 1970 and 1980, from 1.5 million to 3.7 million (Backus and Furtaw 1992, vii). The 1990 U.S. Census shows nearly another 100 percent increase in size of the Asian American population between 1980 to 1990 to 7.2 million Asian Americans, or nearly three percent of the total U.S. population (*U.S. Census-1990* 1992, 323-325). The largest minority group in the United States is African Americans, who make up 12.1 percent of the population, followed by people of Hispanic origin, who make up nine percent of the population, with the next largest minority group being Asian Americans and Pacific Islanders who make up 2.9 percent of the population (*U.S. Census-1990* 1992, 323-325). Native Americans are one of the smallest minorities in the U.S., consisting of 1.8 million people, or less than one percent (.8 percent) of the population (*U.S. Census-1990* 1992, 323-325).

Research on all minority groups and media treatment of those people is long overdue and extremely valuable. This book in no way intends to criticize research conducted on other minorities; rather, part of its purpose is to encourage such research. However, for the sake of comparison, consider that in the thirty-five leading mass communication journals from 1988 to 1993, there were ten articles on Asian Americans, nine on Native North Americans (U.S. and Canada), nine on people of Hispanic origin, and fifty-five on African Americans (*Index to Journals in Mass Communication* 1989 to 1994). This means that there were nearly as many articles published on Native Americans and the media as there were on Asian Americans, yet there are 7.2 million Asian Americans and Pacific Islanders compared to 1.8 million Native Americans (*U.S. Census-1990* 1992, 323-325). Certainly, research on people of Hispanic origin is even more under-represented in these statistics than the research on Asian Americans, when making population percentage comparisons.

To further put this data in perspective, it is helpful to know that the number of articles classified under "Minorities/Minority Media" by the *Index to Journals in Mass Communication* has jumped considerably since 1988, when there were only a total of fourteen articles listed under that category (*Index to Journals in Mass Communication* 1989, 37). In 1989 that number increased to eighteen, in 1990 to thirty, in 1991 it dropped to twenty-three, in 1992 it rose again to twenty-seven, and in 1993 it jumped to forty-nine (*Index to Journals in Mass Communication* 1990 to 1994). That index was converted to a computer database in 1995 for articles published in 1994 and the classification of "minorities/minority media" no longer exists. When searched for articles published in 1994 the computer data base of *Index to Journals in Mass Communication* yields only one article on minorities. That article, by Jane W. Licata and Abhijit Biswas, was entitled "Representation, Roles, and Occupational Status of Black Models in Television Advertisements," and was published in *Journalism Quarterly* in the Winter 1994 edition (Licata and Biswas 1994). So there were no articles published in the thirty-five journals that dealt with Asian Americans or any ethnic sub-group of Asian Americans.

Other than articles on African Americans, people of Hispanic origin, Asian Americans and Pacific Islanders, and Native Americans, the articles under the classification of "minorities/minority media" also cover gays and lesbians, women, ethnic groups in other countries, as well as more comprehensive articles on minorities in general. One of the more obscure minorities that has received nearly as much attention by media scholars as Asian Americans are aborigine populations, mostly in Australia and Canada. From 1988 to 1993 there were eight articles published on aborigines and the media (*Index to Journals in Mass Communication* 1990 to 1994).

With this perspective of research in mind, what follows are the results from each of the areas studied in the review of literature, organized according to the five key theoretical areas relevant to this book.

**Agenda Setting Hypothesis.** First, several studies were found which looked at editorial content in newspapers as it related to the internment of Japanese Americans during World War II, and indirectly with how those editorials affect readers' news agendas. However, this book did not consider editorials in its content analysis, so these studies do not relate directly to this book's research. Overall, two masters' theses and one conference paper contributed to the research of this book's topic as it relates the theoretical foundation of agenda setting.

One of the few studies which dealt specifically with agenda setting was a master's thesis by Jennifer Mu at the University of Texas at Austin, which looked at the news agendas set in coverage of Chinese Americans in the *New York Times* from 1900 to 1980 (Mu 1982). Mu found that while certain images of Chinese Americans, and news agendas, have shifted drastically from reporting mostly on immigrant problems and relations in the early part of this century to a much broader range of topics during the latter half, a few areas of coverage have not changed that drastically. This includes articles which continue to perpetuate stereotypes of Chinese Americans, as well as a lack of news coverage in other areas, and, therefore, a lack of a broad news agenda being set for Chinese Americans.

Another master's thesis, entitled "The Treatment of Chinese Americans and Chinatown in Three American Newspapers," also looked at agenda setting as it related to Chinese Americans, as well as examined stereotypes of Chinese Americans in newspaper coverage (Wang 1983). So this thesis acutally falls under two theoretical areas of this book. The study found that Chinese Americans receive low coverage and often are the subjects of "routine" articles on Chinese New Year and rarely are the subjects of innovative enterprise articles. The remainder of the thesis looked extensively at how press images helped to determine news agendas among readership.

Finally, Martindale wrote a study on how several minority groups have been covered in the *New York Times*, from 1934 to 1994 (Martindale 1995, unpublished paper presented at an AEJMC annual conference). The study dealt both with agenda setting and stereotyping as these theories relate to news coverage of Asian Americans in the *New York Times*. Martindale found that, in general, there was little coverage of Asian Americans during most of the time frame studied, which translated to an agenda that Asian Americans and issues facing them were not a high news priority for the newspaper and therefore, not a high priority for readers. Of course, this paper has elements of three theory bases of this book: agenda setting, stereotyping, and the spiral of silence theory. Martindale also found that for much of the period studied, the newspaper tended to cover "model minority" stories, as well as stories on Asian gang violence. However, in the final decade of the study the *New York Times* broadened its coverage of Asian Americans, and, thus, began setting a different news agenda for that minority.

**Stereotyping.** Beyond the two studies mentioned under agenda setting which also studied stereotyping, there were five studies which contributed to the theory base of stereotyping as it relates to the focus of this book. Auman found that "news coverage of Chinese Americans is tied to the history of immigration of Chinese into the United States, the later exclusion of immigrants, and the rising voice of second generation Chinese," with initially most news coverage portraying Chinese almost exclusively in their immigrant status, and in the later time period portraying Chinese Americans in a "model minority" stereotype (Auman 1995, unpublished media conference paper). Fong traced the origins of the "model minority" stereotype of Chinese Americans to depictions of that ethnic sub-group in numerous popular U.S. magazines (Fong 1989, book). This exhaustive research project contributed greatly to the understanding of the origins of that stereotype being linked to the strong work ethic of Chinese immigrants that was passed on to future generations of Chinese Americans. Several magazine articles which perpetuated this stereotype are cited in the study. Nakayama also wrote a study on how the media reinforces the "model minority" image of Asian Americans, and the history of that stereotype (Nakayama 1988). This article helped to expand the understanding of historical roots to this stereotype that is often linked to Asian Americans.

Two other studies were particularly helpful in supporting the need to study overall coverage of Asian Americans in leading U.S. newspapers. Ma and Hildebrandt found that the Chinese community in Canada is receiving rapidly increasing attention from the press in the past decade (1980 to 1990) for the first time since the early waves of Chinese immigration in the late 1880's (Ma and Hildebrandt 1993). Their study looked specifically at coverage of Chinese communities in the *Toronto Star* and *Vancouver Sun*. While this book deals solely with the twenty newspapers of the content analysis, the Ma and Hildebrant article offered useful information about the theory base of stereotyping as it relates to mass media news coverage. Finally, in 1979, Sang-Chul Lee, a doctoral student in mass communication at the University of Minnesota, wrote a book entitled "The Japanese Image Projected in Four U.S. Dailies Over a Sixty-Seven Year Period," which helped to show the various types of stereotypes and other images of Japanese and Japanese Americans in the four major newspapers studied (Lee 1979, book). This was the only doctoral book in mass communication written since 1963 that this book's review of literature found which dealt with any of the five theoretical foundations of this book as they related to Asian Americans and the media.

Coorientation. As mentioned earlier in this chapter, one of the most relevant studies on coorientation for this book's topic was Pease and Smith's monograph which studied job satisfaction and the impact of racial diversity at twenty-seven newspapers in the United States (Pease and Smith 1991). It deals with coorientation in that it is based on a premise that supervisors assume Asian American employees are satisfied with their jobs, but this study finds that many Asian Americans, in fact, are not satisfied with their work at newspapers. This important study surveyed 1,328 minority journalists, including 130 Asian Americans (sixty-three men and sixty-seven women) (11). Part of the study looked at the journalists' judgment of their newspapers' coverage of minority issues. Of the Asian American respondents, only 29 percent of the men and 26.9 percent of the women said their newspaper was doing "very/pretty well" at covering minority issues, while 71 percent of the men and 73.1 percent of the women said their newspaper was only doing a "marginal/poor" job at the coverage (25). This is one of the few, and largest, studies ever conducted to look at news perceptions and job satisfaction issues as they relate to minority journalists, and with specific references to Asian American journalists employed at newspapers. It is also the only study on coorientation uncovered in this review of literature that specifically looked at Asian Americans. Pease and Smith also found that minority journalists are much more likely to switch jobs than are white journalists, but that minority journalists are not necessarily flocking to leave the media profession (15-16). Overall, this study was one of the closest to this book in both theoretical foundations and research design. Much more on the Pease and Smith monograph is outlined later in this chapter in the theory section on communicator analysis and job satisfaction. The Pease and Smith monograph was also the only relevant study which related directly to that theoretical foundation in this book's research.

Spiral of Silence Theory and the Theory of Hegemony. Dongshin Lee, a student at California State University—Northridge, wrote a masters' thesis entitled "The Media Habits of Korean-Americans in the Los Angeles Area" in 1981 which discussed the tendency of Korean Americans to gravitate to media which cater specifically to immigrant Korean communities, as well as to use other mainstream media for attaining news (Lee 1981). The study linked this tendency for Korean Americans to use ethnic media, in part, to both the spiral of silence theory and the theory of hegemony. Korean Americans are not routinely covered in mainstream media, and they gain a better perspective of their role in society by reading ethnic newspapers, part of the study explained. In fact, Lee argued, Korean Americans turn to ethnic media in part because they become convinced they have little role in mainstream society after using mainstream media and, thus, find ethnic media to be a strong source for establishing their perceptions of how they fit with more meaning into society even though the "society" becomes a much smaller ethnic community on the periphery of a larger mainstream society.

Another study that touched upon the spiral of silence theory as it relates to media use by Asian Americans, particularly among Asian immigrants, was Wang and Kincaid's examination of the types of news of interest to immigrants in Hawaii (Wang and Kincaid 1982). Again, these scholars found ethnic media play a role in the spiral of silence theory in much the same capacity as Lee described in his thesis. Shim presented a paper at the 1995 national convention of the International Communication Association entitled "The Media Coverage of Korean-Black Tensions and its Social-Level Effects on Ethnic Newcomers Before the 1992 Los Angeles Riots" which also looked at the spiral of silence theory as it related to media images of these two ethnic groups and effects on Korean immigrants (Shim 1995, unpublished ICA paper). He found marked differences in immigrants' images of their place in society from the pre-riot era to the post-riot era of intensive media coverage of crime-related articles on race tensions between blacks and Korean Americans. Another research paper presented at the 1991 annual conference of ICA also looked at the spiral of silence theory in relation to how Korean Americans from various social classes developed images of their role in society from mass mediated messages (Messaris and Woo 1991, unpublished ICA paper).

Shiramizu's study of the Japanese press in Hawaii had as a theoretical base, although not mentioned in the article, the theory of hegemony (Shiramizu 1991). Instead of mainstream media setting the stage for Japanese immigrants' understanding of their dominant values and philosophies, this study emphasized the importance of the role of the ethnic press to the theory of hegemony and instilling those values and philosophies in Japanese immigrant readers.

Finally, studies which dealt solely with Asian language media and the two theories outlined in this section are not mentioned here since this book deals with mainstream, English-language newspapers and coverage of Asian Americans and issues facing Asian Americans.

**Communicator Analysis and Work Satisfaction.** The Pease and Smith monograph, discussed in section B3 of this chapter, also dealt with job satisfaction (Pease and Smith 1991). In fact, an entire section of that study dealt with issues relating to job satisfaction among minorities who worked at twenty-seven newspapers, including Asian Americans, and it was the only study found in this review of literature which dealt specifically with job satisfaction issues as they relate to Asian American journalists, as this book will also study.

Pease and Smith found that 85.7 percent of the Asian American men surveyed, and 77.6 percent of the Asian American women surveyed, felt it was very likely or likely they would still be in newspaper journalism in five years, and only 14.3 percent of the men and 22.4 percent of the women thought it unlikely or very unlikely they would remain in print journalism after five years (15). The authors also asked if the survey respondents did leave their print media job, what the single most important factor influencing the decision would be. Of the Asian American respondents, 14.8 percent of the men and 15.2 percent of the women cited better advancement opportunities outside of their present newspaper position (16). The respondents were also asked about job aspirations within the newspaper of their employment. Of the Asian American respondents, the largest percentage of men, 23.8 percent, said they aspired to middle management (20.9 percent of the women aspired to this level), while the largest percent of women, 32.8 percent, said they wanted a better beat (12.7 percent of the men wanted a better beat) (17).

When asked if the environment for minorities would be better if their newspaper adopted a policy of mainstreaming, of the Asian American respondents, 71 percent of the men and 71.4 percent of the women said yes, and 29 percent of the men and 28.6 percent of the women said no (27). The respondents were also asked what they thought the biggest obstacle to their career advancement in newspapers was, and the responses were bundled under the topics of "lack of experience," "lack of training," "race," "gender," "competition," and "other." Of the Asian American respondents, 19.9 percent of the men and 16.7 percent of the women cited race as the number one obstacle in their advancing in the newspaper profession (20). It was also interesting that a smaller percentage (compared to the race answer to this question) of the Asian American women, 16.7 percent, cited gender as the top obstacle to their advancement (20). The question of whether a "glass ceiling" barring minorities and women from upper management existed at the respondent's newspaper was also raised in the study. Of the Asian Americans, 53.2 percent of the men and 74.2 percent of the women said yes, while 46.8 percent of the men and 25.8 percent of the women said no (28). There were several other relevant questions asked of the journalists surveyed, and some of the Asian American responses will be given in Chapter Five of this book to offer context to the results reported in that chapter.

The Pease and Smith monograph offered the best insights on how Asian American journalists feel about job satisfaction, racism in newsrooms, and advancement opportunities. No other relevant articles or other types of research were found that related to Asian Americans, or any ethnic sub-group of Asian Americans, and this theory base.

While there are many important studies on Asian Americans as they relate to the five theory bases of this book, the overall volume of literature on this topic is still low. This look at related studies indicates a strong need for more research such as this book's look into newspaper coverage of Asian Americans, and how Asian American journalists perceive media coverage of that minority, as well as their views on their own job satisfaction and other issues relating to being an Asian American in the media workforce. There is a particular need for more studies in coorientation, communicator analysis and job satisfaction, and the theory of hegemony as these theories relate to media coverage of Asian Americans, impacts of media images on Asian Americans, and levels of job satisfaction among Asian Americans who are media professionals.

## RESEARCH QUESTIONS OF THE BOOK

The research questions of this book fall into three sections reflecting the three inter-related research approaches, as explained in Chapter One. Those sections are: 1) the content analysis of twenty leading newspapers in the United States, 2) the survey of five hundred Asian American journalists, and data collected from the editors of the twenty newspapers of the content analysis, 3) studies of various U.S. Census data, as well as data received on the number of minorities working in newsrooms of the twenty newspapers used in the content analysis. Finally, as explained in earlier sections of this chapter, the five theoretical foundations of this book apply to specific research approaches of the content analysis, survey of Asian American journalists, and examination of U.S. Census data and data on employment of Asian Americans at the twenty newspapers of the content analysis. With this structure established what follows are this book's research questions (listed in bold type).

**Content Analysis.** Research questions one to four are based on studies in agenda setting and stereotyping of Asian Americans and ethnic sub-groups of Asian Americans.

1. What newspapers carry the most stories onAsian Americans?
2. Which ethnic sub-groups are the most covered by each newspaper?
3. Which story topics are the most covered by each newspaper?
4. What thematic stereotypes are presented in each newspaper?

**Survey.** Research questions five to seven are based on studies in coorientation and communicator analysis (looking at job satisfaction) and will be answered ustilizing data from the survey of five hundred Asian American journalists.

5. How many Asian Americans are employed in the mainstream media?
6. How do Asian Americans working in the mainstream media assess coverage of Asian Americans? How do editors of Asian American publications assess coverage?

7. How do Asian Americans working in the mainstream media feel about their jobs in terms of positive and negative experiences?Census and Survey Data.

**Census and Survey Data.** Research questions eight to ten are based on studies in spiral of silence theory and the theory of hegemony, and will be answered utilizing U.S. Census data, information on minority members of newsrooms staffs provided from the editors or human resouces managers of the the twenty newspapers used in the content analysis.

8. How does the percentage of Asian Americans living in a city correlate with the amount of coverage of Asian Americans?

9. How does the percentage of Asian Americans working in a newsroom correlate with the amount ove coverage of Asian Americans?

10. How does the percentage of Asian Americans living in a city correlate with the percentage of Asian Americans working in a newsroom of a newspaper covering that city?

## SUMMARY

Other media theories that could apply to this book are discussed in Chapter Six. However, it should now be clear after learning of this extensive review of literature and of studies which relate to the book's five theoretical foundations, that those theories of agenda setting, stereotyping, communicator analysis, coorientation, and spiral of silence and hegemony best serve as a framework for this study. Finally, now that the research questions of the book have been formulated, it is necessary to understand full details of the book's research design before presenting the results of those questions and offering an anaylsis of the results. The research design is explained fully in the next chapter on method.

## NOTES

[9] Journalism Abstracts, a record of all masters' theses and doctoral books written annually in the discipline of mass communication, had not been published for theses and books published in 1995 at the time of this study's completion. *Journalism Abstracts* was first published in 1963 by the Association for Education in Journalism.

# CHAPTER 4

# METHOD

> The greatest evil the papers do is not with their
> reporting, but that they tell us what we ought to
> think of this and that, about our high chiefs or the
> high chiefs of other lands, about what other people
> do and what happens to them. They want to fash-
> ion every mind to the same pattern, which is
> against my beliefs.
>
> —Samoan Chief Tuiavi'i,
> circa 1910

## OPERATIONAL PLAN

This book's research encompasses three building blocks. First, is
a content analytical study of the amount and types of news coverage Asian Americans received in twenty of the nation's largest
newspapers. The results of the content analysis will be examined
to see what agendas are being set by each newspaper, and in the
aggregate of all twenty newspapers, concerning coverage of
Asian Americans. The second building block of this book is a
survey on job satisfaction as it relates to being an Asian
American journalist, and how respondents believe Asian
Americans are being covered in the media. The third and final
building block is a survey of the executive edtiors or newsroom
human resources managers of the twenty newspapers used in the
content analysis of the book to find out how many Asian
Americans were employed on those staffs, and to assess the edi-

torial policies relating coverage of Asian Americans at those newspapers. So two research tools have been used in this book: 1) the content analysis, and 2) the survey.

**Content Analysis.** Certainly the content analysis method of research was the best choice to assess how much and what types of coverage has been given to Asian Americans in the twenty newspapers examined. There are several reasons for this.

First, as Berelson explained, "content analysis is a research technique for the objective, systematic, and quantitative description of the manifest content of communication" (Stempel and Westley 1989, 125). Since one of the goals of this book was to conduct an objective, systematic, and quantitative description of the content of articles covering Asian Americans and issues affecting Asian Americans in twenty leading U.S. newspapers, the content analysis was the perfect research tool to achieve that goal. Also, as Stempel explains, one should not assume that because a content analysis is quantitative in design that it cannot also be qualitative (126). As will be seen in the method design of the content analysis of this book's research, results achieved will be both quantitative and qualitative.

Content analyses also produce a great deal of information, if designed and carried out correctly, for a minimal amount of time invested. As Babbie points out, "probably the greatest advantage of content analysis is its economy in terms of both time and money" (Babbie 1995, 320). So using this research tool was also a viable option for a single researcher who was only able to hire one or two assistants to help with article selection and coding. Another appeal of content analyzing the Asian American news in the twenty newspapers was the preciseness of coding categories created to examine if stereotypes or particular types of stories were being given more coverage than others.

Since this author was looking for several different variables, for example how much coverage was given to specific ethnic groups, or how much coverage was given to festivals or gangs, it seemed the flexibility of the content analysis as a research tool was the perfect choice in reaching my desired goals.

**Self-Administered Survey.** The survey is a useful tool to reach the ends attained in this research. Babbie explained that "the advantages of a self-administered questionnaire over an interview survey are economy, speed, lack of interviewer bias, and the possibility of anonymity and privacy to encourage more candid responses on sensitive issues" (Babbie 1995, 277). This last point of encouraging anonymity and privacy is particularly relevant to the survey of Asian American journalists conducted for this research. In fact, without the option of guaranteed privacy, many of the most telling and relevant comments received most likely would not have been forthcoming. Also, it is unlikely that a telephone interview format would have drawn out some of the shocking anecdotes and passionate commentaries.

Babbie adds that survey research in general has advantages "in terms of economy and the amount of data that can be collected. The standardization of the data collected represents another special strength of survey research" (277). This book aims to solicit as much information as possible on job experiences, as well as opinions of news coverage of Asian Americans, and the self-administered questionnaire seemed the best approach to meet this goal.

Shoemaker and McCombs also stressed that self-administered surveys "avoid biases due to interviewers, ensure standardized presentation of questions, give respondents more privacy (important for sensitive questions), and may increase the validity of responses that required the respondent to check information or to think about his or her answer" (Stempel and Westley 1989, 155). Much of the information sought from Asian American journalists was so sensitive that they might have been unwilling to go on the record with their answers due to politically sensitive situations at their workplaces or simply for fear of losing their jobs. The possibility for an increase in validity over telephone interviews was also appealing and affected the choice for a self-administered survey.

However, as Shoemaker and McCombs also pointed out, the response rate on self-administered surveys is often lower than on telephone interviews. This was an acceptable drawback, and which held less weight than the necessity to offer anonymity and a setting of privacy in answering the survey to the respondents.

Now that it is clear why the dual approach of a content analysis and self-administered surveys was used in this book, each building block of the research will be addressed in order: the content analysis; the survey letter sent to editors of the twenty leading Asian American publications; the survey of the five hundred Asian

American journalists; and the survey letter sent to the editors or human resource managers of the twenty newspapers of the content analysis.

## CONTENT ANALYSIS OF TWENTY LEADING NEWS-PAPERS

As explained in Chapter Three, the content analysis is designed to answer research questions one through four:

1. What newspapers carry the most articles on Asian Americans?
2. Which ethnic sub-groups are the most covered by each newspaper?
3. Which story topics are the most covered by each newspaper?
4. What thematic stereotypes are presented in each newspaper?

The theoretical basis for this portion of the book research is: 1) the agenda setting hypothesis, in examining topics covered in the newspapers concerning Asian Americans and issues facing Asian Americans, and, 2) stereotyping, in the newspapers' portrayals of ethnic subgroups of Asian Americans.

**Computer Data Base Searches.** All of the twenty newspapers used in the content analysis, except for the *Seattle Times,* were searched via the computer data base "Newspaper Abstracts." The *Seattle Times* was not available on that data base, so it was searched, using the same method, on the computer data base "Nexis." All the articles published for those twenty newspapers used in the content analysis were searched for the one-year period from March 1, 1994 to February 28, 1995. The twenty newspapers searched are listed below. Note that the *Atlanta Constitution, Atlanta Journal,* and *Atlanta Journal-Constitution,* which all have the same editor and are all published by cox Enterprises, Inc., are counted as one newspaper in the content analysis and listed in Chapter Five under the name *Atlanta Journal-Constitution. The Detroit News, Detroit Free Press,* and *Detroit News* and *Free Press,* are counted as two newspapers (and in some parts of Chapter Five are counted as three newspapers), since the *Detroit News* and the *Detroit*

*Free Press* have separate editors and ownership, while the *Detroit News* and *Free Press* is the Sunday edition of the *Detroit News* and *Detroit Free Press* and is published jointly by Knight-Ridder, Inc., and Gannett Company.

Here is some specific information, taken from 1994, on the newspapers used in the 1994-1995 content analysis (Anderson 1994, I-87 and I-72):

**Atlanta Constitution:** Published Mondays through Fridays (morning newspaper); circulation 299,669; published by Cox Enterprises Inc.; Dennis Berry, publisher; Ron Martin, editor.

**Atlanta Journal:** Published Mondays through Fridays (evening newspaper); circulation 142,635; published by Cox Enterprises Inc.; Dennis Berry, publisher; Ron Martin, editor.

**Atlanta Journal-Constitution:** Published Sundays; circulation 708,560 (Sundays); published by Cox Enterprises Inc.; Dennis Berry, publisher; Ron Martin, editor.

Boston Globe: Published daily; circulation 507,647 (weekdays) 814,036 (Sundays); published by The *New York Times* Co.; William O. Taylor, publisher; Matthew V. Storin, editor.

**Christian Science Monitor:** Published Mondays through Fridays; circulation 92,076; published by The *Christian Science Monitor*; Al Carnesciali, general manager; Richard J. Cattani, editor.

**Chicago Tribune:** Published daily; circulation 629,063 (weekdays) 1,101,863 (Sundays); published by Tribune Company; John W. Madigan, publisher; Howard A. Tyner, editor.

**Denver Post:** Published daily; circulation 284,542 (weekdays) 440,148 (Sundays); published by Media News; Ryan McKibben, president/publisher; Neil Westergaard, editor.

**Detroit Free Press:** Published weekdays (morning newspaper); circulation 871,890; published by Knight-Ridder Inc.; Neal Shine, publisher; Heath J. Meriwether, editor.

**Detroit News:** Published weekdays (evening newspaper); circulation 366,988; published by Gannett Co.; Robert H. Giles, editor/publisher.

*Detroit News and Free Press*: Published Sundays; circulation 1,186,116; published jointly by Knight-Ridder Inc. and Gannett Co.

*Houston Chronicle*: Published daily; circulation 413,448 (Mondays through Saturdays) 606,525 (Sundays); published by the *Houston Chronicle*; Richard J.V. Johnson, chairman/publisher; Jack Loftis, editor.

*Houston Post*: Published daily (the paper shut down in April 1996); circulation 284,220 (Mondays through Saturdays) 320,975 (Sundays); formerly published by Media News; Ike Massey, publisher/CEO; Gerald Garcia, vice president/executive editor.

*Los Angeles Times*: Published daily; circulation 1,012,880 (Mondays through Saturdays) 1,448,484 (Sundays); published by the Times Mirror Co.; Richard Schlosberg III, publisher/CEO; Shelby Coffey III, editor.

*New York Times*: Published daily; circulation 995,308 (Mondays through Saturdays) 1,756,635 (Sundays); published by the *New York Times* Co.; Arthur Sulzberger Jr., publisher; Joseph Lelyveld, executive editor.

*St. Louis Post-Dispatch*: Published daily; circulation 322,535 (Mondays through Saturdays) 559,223 (Sundays); published by the St. Lousi Post-Dispatch; Nicholas G. Penniman IV, publisher; Cole Campbell, editor (Note: William F. Woo, editor of the St. Louis Post-Dispatch for nearly ten years and a leading Asian American journalist, resigned as editor of the St. Louis Post-Dispatch in the summer of 1996.)

*San Francisco Chronicle*: Published daily; circulation 518,125 (Mondays through Saturdays) 702,067 (Sundays); published by the San Francisco Chronicle; Richard T. Thieriot, publisher/editor.

*Seattle Times*: Published daily; circulation 225,339 (Mondays through Saturdays) 504,458 (Sundays); published by the *Seattle Times*; F.A. Blethen, publisher; Michael R. Fancher, vice president and executive editor.

*The Times-Picayune*: Published daily; circulation 250,507 (Mondays through Saturdays) 320,385 (Sundays); published by Newhouse Newspapers; Ashton Phelps Jr., publisher; Jim Amoss, editor.

*USA Today*: Published weekdays; circulation 1,904,844; published by Gannett Co.; Thomas Curley, publisher; Peter Prichard, editor.

*Wall Street Journal*: Published weekdays; circulation 1,818,562; published by Dow Jones & Co.; Peter R. Kann, CEP/publisher; Robert L. Bartley, editor.

*Washington Post*: Published daily; circulation 761,253 (Mondays through Saturdays) 1,138,877 (Sundays); published by The Washington Post Co.; Donald Graham, publisher; Leonard Downie, editor.

*Washington Times*: Published daily; circulation 71,665 (Mondays through Saturdays) 65,002 (Sundays); published by The Washington Times; Dong Moon Joo, president; Wesley Pruden, editor.

**Keyword Searches.** The keywords used in the search were "Asian," "American," and "Americans," as well as all the ethnic sub-classifications of Asian Americans listed in the 1992 Asian Americans Information Directory and the 1990 U.S. Census. However, for the larger ethnic sub-groups, both the name of the group and the words "American" and "Americans" were entered as keywords for a single search. For example, for the sub-classification of Hmong Americans the keywords "Hmong," "American," and "Americans" were entered into the computer. All the articles with only the word "Hmong" as well as articles with the words "Hmong" and "American" or "Hmong" and "Americans" came up in the search. The word "Americans" was used in the "Newspaper Abstracts" searches in addition to the singular "American" since many more articles came up using the plural "Americans," however, a few different articles appeared when a specific keyword, combined with the singular "American" was entered into the database. For the "Nexis" search of the *Seattle Times* only the singular "American" needed to be entered in combination with various keyword searchers to bring up all the entries, including those with the singular word "American."

However, in both database searches ("Newspaper Abstracts" and "Nexis") a distinction in the search keywords entered was made between the ethnic sub-groups that represented the largest segments of the Asian American population, compared to smaller segments of the Asian American population. For the larger ethnic groups both the keyword representing a particular group and the keyword "American" (for "Nexis") or the keywords "Americans" and "American" (for "Newspaper Abstracts") were entered for a full search.

With most of the smaller groups two or three searches were done: 1) ethnic group title and "American" and "Americans" as keywords (example, "Samoan" and "American" and "Samoan" and "Americans"), 2) ethnic group title only as a keyword (example, "Samoan"), and, 3) name of country/island origin of ethnic group as a keyword (example, "Samoa"). The determination of what constituted a larger ethnic sub-group compared to a small ethnic sub-group was made from the breakdown of Asian American ethnic groups in the 1990 U.S. Census (See Table 1 in Chapter One). All of the Asian American ethnic sub-groups broken out in the census were searched by the three keywords (name of ethnic sub-group and the words "American" and "Americans"). This means the following fourteen ethnic sub-groups were searched in that manner:

| | |
|---|---|
| Chinese | Hmong |
| Filipino | Laotian |
| Japanese | Thai |
| Indian | Pacific Islander |
| Korean | Hawaiian |
| Vietnamese | Samoan |
| Cambodian | Guamanian |

Any other ethnic sub-group not listed was searched both by the keyword for that ethnic group alone, and again using the two keywords. For some of the ethnic sub-groups from small islands or countries the name of the island or country was also entered in as a separate search. In most of these cases where three separate searches were used for one ethnic sub-group either no articles came up in the computer or the same articles came up in all three searches.

Appendix 7 is a list of the 193 individual searches entered into the computer data bases for the content analysis search. Keywords that were added from the two listings of Asian American ethnic sub-groups are listed in bold. Those keywords were added due to different spellings that might be used by newspapers.

**Keyword Searches by Names of Prominent Asian Americans.** Other keywords representing the names of famous or otherwise prominent Asian Americans were also entered into the computer search for the content analysis. Since an article on a famous Asian American may not use any of the 193 keywords listed in Appendix 7, it seemed valid to include certain names. For the purpose of this book, an article that devotes 40 percent or more of its space to discussing the work, art, sport, life, or other matters of an Asian American is defined as having Asian American content. This meant that reviews of art exhibits or performances of Asian American artists were included in the content analysis.

However, since the determination of most articles was made from an abstract of that article, if the Asian American personality being searched by name was described in the abstract as the subject of the article, then that article was counted and coded as covering an Asian American. If the Asian American personality being searched was mentioned in a headline then that article was included in the content analysis.

Other names of famous Asian Americans were also selected from listings in the *Dictionary of Asian American History* of noted persons who died within the twentieth century and those who are still living. Names were also selected from the *1995 U.S. Congressional Directory, 104th Congress* of Asian Americans who serve as U.S. senators or members of the House of Representatives, as well from the directory *Who's Who in America*, 49th Edition of famous Asian Americans. Names of the highest ranking Asian American, active duty U.S. military officers as of 1992 were listed from the book *Statistical Record of Asian Americans.* (Gall and Gall 1993, 559). Finally, some names of well-known Asian Americans that were not found in any of those directories but who were familiar to this author, for example, Yoko Ono, an artist and the wife of slain musician John Lennon, were also added to the list of names to use as keywords. Some personalities, such as former news anchor Connie Chung, were only known by their nickname. In these cases the formal name (for example, Constance Chung) was first entered as keywords, followed by the better known nickname (Connie Chung).

From these four methods of selecting names of famous Asian Americans, the list of names—as seen in Appendix 8—was also entered as keywords in the computer search for the content analysis representing prominent Asian Americans. It should be noted, however, that no list of famous Asian Americans is not without unintentional omissions since a definition of "most prominent" Asian Americans is often a matter of some subjectivity. For some names, full names were entered first (including the middle name), and if nothing appeared, then last names only were entered, and finally first and last names only were entered as keywords. See Appendix 8 for the 123 names searched.

Only those articles dealing with Asian American and Pacific Islander issues and/or personalities were included in the content analysis. Therefore, articles that dealt solely with U.S. relations with Asian, Southeast Asian, Near East or Pacific Island countries were not be included in the content analysis. Articles about dignitaries from Asian countries (or other countries that came up from the keywords) who were visiting the United States were also excluded from the content analysis. Many of the ethnic sub-classifications, when entered in a search of "Newspaper Abstracts" and "Nexis," were found in articles that did not deal with Asian Americans, so those articles were not considered in the content analysis.

In general, when keywords were entered into the computer for a search, articles came up that did not discuss Asian Americans as defined in Chapter One of this book; further, if the articles did not deal with an issue relevant to the Asian American community, then they were discarded from the search. However, if it was unclear whether an article dealt with Asian Americans or an ethnic subgroup, such as an article dealing with Hawaiians, then it was classified as covering Asian Americans. This example is offered because so many Hawaiian citizens are members of ethnic subgroups of Asian Americans that it is often impossible to tell if an article is addressing Caucasians, African Americans, native Hawaiians or other Pacific Islanders who are living in Hawaii. Hawaii is somewhat unique compared to other states that were datelines of articles used in the content analysis.

The same 193 searches by ethnic identities and 123 searches of Asian American names of personalities were used in the content analysis computer search in the data base "Nexis" of the *Seattle Times*. The same time period used for the search of the nineteen newspapers in the data base "Newspaper Abstracts" also served as the boundaries of the *Seattle Times* "Nexis" search. Those time boundaries meant that any article that was published after March 1, 1995, and any article published prior to February 28, 1994, was not included in the content analysis.

**Coding.** A copy of the abstract for each article referenced in the content analysis was made. The coding for these article abstracts was based on two studies. The first was Deutschmann's ten categories for a newspaper content analysis described in his book *News-Page Content of Twelve Metropolitan Dailies* (Deutschmann 1959, 58-62). Those ten categories, which were refined from the fifty basic news categories of Freyschlag, are:

1) politics and government acts
2) war, rebellion and defense
3) economic activity, transportation and travel
4) crime
5) public moral problems
6) public health and welfare
7) accidents and disasters
8) science and invention
9) education, classic arts, and popular amusements
10) general human interest

Stempel's fourteen news categories that are an elaboration of Deutschmann's categories, as published in the 1985 *Journalism Quarterly* article on gatekeeping, were also a basis for the categories used to code this content analysis (Stempel 1985, 791-796). Those categories are (793):

1) government and politics
2) war and defense
3) diplomacy and foreign relations
4) economic activity
5) agriculture
6) transportation and travel
7) crime
8) public moral problems
9) accidents and disasters
10) science and invention
11) public health and welfare
12) education and classic arts
13) popular amusements
14) general human interest

From these two studies the following coding categories were defined for this content analysis. Most of the definitions were either taken directly from those in the Stempel (1985) article, or slightly modified from that article (793).

1) *Politics and Government Acts* —Government acts and politics at local, state, national, or international level.
2) *War and Defense* —War, defense, rebellion, military use of space. This includes any articles on Asian Americans serving in the military in any capacity. It also includes

any articles relating to the internment of Japanese by the U.S. government during World War II.

3) *Economic Activity*—General economic activity, prices, money, labor, wages and natural resources. This does not include success stories of Asian America or Asian immigrant mom and pop stores.

4) *Crime*—All crime stories including criminal proceedings in court. This includes all stories on Asian gangs.

5) *Public Moral Problems* —Human relations and moral problems including alcohol, divorce, sex, race relations and civil court proceedings. This includes stories on human rights, and racism.

6) *Accidents and Disasters* —Includes both man-made accidents and natural disasters. It includes all stories on the earthquake that occurred in Kobe, Japan, in early 1995.

7) *Science and Invention*—Science other than defense related and other than health and medicine.

8) *Classic Arts* —Classic arts includes classical music, opera, classic painting and other traditional art forms of the East and West. Tae Kwan Do and Tai Chi Chuan is included as a classic art form. Any stories on museums (except films shown at museums) and museum exhibits are included in this category.

9) *Popular Amusements*—Entertainment and amusements, sports, television, radio, and other media. This also includes restaurant reviews of establishments that feature foods of the various Asian American ethnic sub-groups listed above where Asian American patrons are mentioned. It also includes stories on films shown at museums.

10) *Public Health and Welfare* —Health, public welfare, social and safety measures, welfare of children and marriage and marriage relations. This category includes all stories on issues of poverty.

11) *Education*—Any stories on education, including stories discussion affirmative action issues at universities.

12) *General Human Interest*—Human interest, weather, obits, animals, cute children and juvenile interest. Success stories of Asian Americans in business, including mom and pop stores run by Asian immigrants, are included in this category. Any articles dealing with religion and philanthropy are included in this category.

13) *Other*—Any article that does not fit into the first twelve categories.

All articles on the television series *All-American Girl* were coded under the category of "popular amusements," as well as sub-coded as having content of the television series. This was so those articles could later be counted separately to indicate how much media attention was given to this new program, which may be interpreted as having skewed the "popular amusements" category of the year searched. So the reader can see, in the final analysis, the difference in number of articles in the category with the All American Girl articles included and when they were excluded.

Research conducted for the book proposal indicated that a great deal of media coverage was given to this television situation comedy. Since the year being researched for the content analysis was also the year that saw the first television program with Asian Americans in lead roles, it is likely a higher number of articles on Asian Americans ran in U.S. dailies that year compared to the previous year. In other words, the creation of *All-American Girl* and subsequent media coverage on the program, may skew the counts in categories such as "popular amusements" for the coverage of Asian American issues in the twenty newspapers researched.

There were two other events that occurred during the year coded that had to be taken into account. First, the flap between news woman Connie Chung and the mother of Congressman Newt Gingrich received a lot of coverage. None of those articles were included in the content analysis since the main topic was the controversial interview in which Chung asked Gingrich's mother to whisper what she really thought of Hillary Clinton. Chung promised confidentiality, but then announced on air what Gingrich's mother said. Since the subject of these articles was not Chung, but rather the controversy, they were not included in the content analysis.

Also during the year searched, the deadly earthquake occurred in Kobe, Japan. Consequently, it was expected that many stories would relate to this story and that any articles dealing with how the Asian American community in the United States was dealing with the tragedy would be kept in the content analysis. Any stories that dealt with Kobe, Japan, were also sub-coded.

There were other sub-codes assigned to stories so that certain types of stories could be seen in the overall assessment of a particular category, or in the overall results of the content analysis. Some of the sub-codes were applied to see how many stories dealt with stereotypes of Asian Americans or Asian American news, as perceived by the five hundred Asian American journalists surveyed. Those sub-codings were for: 1) any story relating to Asian gangs, 2) any story relating to racism and Asian Americans, 3) any story about Chinese New Year celebrations or about other Asian festivals, and 4) and article that discussed success stories of Asian Americans or which dealt with the "model minority" stereotype of Asians.

Also, stories that discussed the Japanese internment during World War II were sub-coded to see what percentage of news coverage of Japanese Americans is devoted to articles concerning this topic. In addition, many of the classic arts stories dealt with cellist Yo Yo Ma, so those stories were also sub-coded to see what percent was represented by coverage of his performances. Finally, if a story was written by a journalist with an Asian-sounding name, as defined earlier in this chapter, then that story was sub-coded as having an Asian American author.

Editorials were not included in the content analysis since they represent opinions and not necessarily news coverage. A coding sheet was filled out for each abstract to highlight the following information:

1) Newspaper
2) Issue date
3) Section/page placement
4) Length of article
5) Headline
6) Author
7) Coding category of article/sub-coding of article
8) Main Asian American ethnic sub-group mentioned
9) Keywords used in obtaining the article from the data base

If an exact length could not be determined for the article in terms of inches, then a ranking of short, medium or long was recorded if such a ranking was given in the abstract. In general, a short article was determined to be six inches or less, a medium-length article was six to eighteen inches, and a long article is anything longer than eighteen inches. The Seattle Times' abstracts listed article lengths in number of words. So for those articles a short article was 250 words or less, a medium article was 250 to 750 words, and a long article was anything over 750 words.

In coding for article placement, the only two categories used were for the front, or A, section, and for all other sections. This was done since it was impossible to tell from the abstracts what subjects correlated to what sections, other than the front section. In other words, it was impossible to tell if a story that fell on page D12 was in a sports section or an entertainment section. All articles in the *Christian Science Monitor* were coded for the front section since that newspaper is a tabloid size with only one section. Finally, sections were not given in the abstracts for the *Boston Globe*, so that portion of the coding sheets were left blank for that particular newspaper.

The ethnic sub-groups coded for number eight of the coding sheet were: 1) all Asian Americans, 2) Chinese, 3) Japanese, 4) Koreans, 5) Filipinos, 6) Asian Indians, 7) Pakistani Americans, 8) Vietnamese, 9) Hmong, 10) Laotian, 11) Cambodian, 12) Thai, 13) Hawaiian, 14) other Pacific Islander, 15) other Asian American, and 16) Asian American prominent personality. This final coding category was established so since some articles were devoted entirely to a prominent Asian American whose ethnic identity could not be determined solely on the name of that person.

**Rankings of Newspaper Coverage of Asian Americans.** Once the total number of articles on Asian Americans are counted for each newspaper, the newspapers will be ranked according to the number of articles which ran on Asian Americans. Newspapers will then be placed in one of the following six ranks, according to the total number of articles which ran on Asian Americans during the year of the content analysis:

| | |
|---|---|
| Extremely High Volume Coverage: | 200 or more articles |
| High Volume Coverage: | 100 to 199 articles |
| Medium Volume Coverage: | 50 to 99 articles |
| Low Volume Coverage: | 10 to 49 articles |
| Extremely Low Volume Coverage: | 1 to 9 articles |
| No Coverage: | zero articles |

**Reliability Tests.** To ensure that the author's judgments of the coding were not biased, a doctoral student in Ohio University's E.W. Scripps School of Journalism, Nilanjana Bardhan, was hired to conduct a coding of a portion of the articles, beginning with deciding which articles should be pulled from the computer search by following the descriptions in this method section. She was paid $5 an hour for the time she spent on this partial coding. For both the author and Ms. Bardhan, if there was a question of how to code an article in reading just the abstract, then the full text of the article was read. If a decision on how to code an article could not be made even after reading the full text, then that article was to be coded as "neutral."

A second coder reliability test was conducted by Dan Nicholson, a graduate student in mass communication at Pennsylvania State University, who helped with the content analysis coding. Mr. Nicholson was not paid by the author directly for his work, but was paid by a university stipend. The same procedures were followed by Mr. Nicholson as those followed by Ms. Bardhan.

The inter-coder reliability of the three tests indicated no inconsistencies among the three researchers. The Holsti formula, a useful tool of researchers for determing inter-coder reliability, was used for the three tests.[10]

Each coder independently coded fifty articles randomly selected from the keyword search using the words "Asian" and "Americans." All three coders gave the same codes to the fifty articles, with the exception of two articles coded by Mr. Nicholson. Both of those articles dealt vaguely with racism, and he coded them under the "neutral" category, while Ms. Bardham and the author coded the articles under "public moral problems." The inter-coder reliability tests results were 1.0, or 100 percent agreement, for Ms. Bardham and the author; and 0.96, or 96 percent agreement, for Ms. Bardham and Mr. Nicholson, as well as for the author and Mr. Nicholson. So, overall, there were no serious inconsistencies with inter-coder reliability.

## SURVEY OF FIVE HUNDRED ASIAN AMERICAN JOURNALISTS

This section of the book's research answered research questions five, six, and seven:

> 5. How many Asian Americans are employed in the mainstream media?

6. How do Asian Americans working in the mainstream media assess coverage of Asian Americans? How do editors of Asian American publications assess coverage?
7. How do Asian Americans working in the mainstream media feel about their jobs in terms of positive and negative experiences?

To answer resesarch questions five, six, and seven a survey of four questions was sent to five hundred Asian American journalists working at mostly mainstream newspapers, radio stations, and television stations throughout the United States to seek their opinions and experiences on being Asian Americans in the media workforce. These letters asked the journalists to answer the following four survey questions:

1) Have you ever had any negative experiences on the job that you feel were related to your ethnic status as an Asian American?
2) Have you ever had any positive experiences on the job that you feel were related to your ethnic status as an Asian American?
3) In your opinion, what is being done right in the media today in covering Asian Americans and issues affecting Asian Americans?
4) In your opinion, what is being done wrong in the media today in covering Asian Americans and issues facing Asian Americans?

The first two questions sought to find out about job satisfaction among the Asian Americans journalists. The last two questions are based on co-orientation theory, and deal with the Asian Americans predictions of news coverage on Asian Americans and issues facing Asian Americans.

To answer research question five, the number of Asian Americans employed in the mainstream media will be assessed from the mailing list used for this broad survey, as well as from responses from some of these journalists, and from the survey of newsroom personnel sent to the editors or human resource managers of the twenty newspapers used in the content analysis.

To answer research question six, the responses to survey questions three and four were examined and analyzed both qualitatively and quanitatively. The quanitative analysis was from a content analysis of the responses, as explained in this chapter.

To answer research question seven, the responses to survey questions one and two will be examined and analyzed both qualitatively and quanitatively. The quanitative analysis will again be from a content analysis, as explained in this chapter. With these approaches to answering research questions five, six, and seven, the details of that methodology will now be explained.

An initial letter was sent to five hundred members of the Asian American Journalists Association on September 18, 1995. A follow-up letter was mailed on November 1, 1995, to the approximately 440 persons who had not responded to the initial survey letter as of that same date. Both letters had publication permission/consent forms and self-addressed, stamped return envelopes enclosed.

**Selection of Asian American Journalists.** A few of the journalists were selected either by their prominence as a reporter, such as Connie Chung, former news anchor for CBS News, or by their byline if it turned up in research for this book. However, as it turned out, those journalists selected due to their prominence or byline were also members of the Asian American Journalists Association, and it was from the AAJA mailing list that five hundred names were eventually selected for the survey mailing. So the names of prominent Asian American journalists were the first to be selected from the AAJA list to be survey respondents.

Lisa Chung, the executive director of AAJA in 1994, agreed to supply the mailing list for her organization to be used for this book's survey after she reviewed a sample survey letter. She said she only releases the AAJA mailing list, which consists of 1,392 names and addresses, if it is being used for academic, non-commercial purposes.

To select which five hundred members of AAJA out of the nearly 1,400-person list would be sent surveys, several criteria were used. First, the names of prominent journalists or journalists whose bylines came up in the content analysis were selected to be included in the survey. This amounted to approximately twenty people. Then the names of members whose addresses were that of a university or high school were eliminated since it was assumed many of these people were scholars, students or researchers and not working journalists. This process omitted 283 names from the list.

Next the names of journalists who worked as foreign correspondents in the United States for Asian or Middle Eastern newspapers were dropped from the questionnaire mailing list since it was assumed these people may be foreign nationals living in the United States and, therefore, not Asian Americans. Also, AAJA members who worked for news organizations outside the United States were eliminated from the list since it was assumed they were not dealing with attitudes in the United States on a daily basis. These two cuts eliminated nearly fifty more names from the list.

Next, members with addresses at private homes were dropped as potential survey respondents since it was unclear from the address if they were journalists or working in some other capacity. This cut amounted to 126 names. It is true that some potential valid respondents may have been omitted in this cut, but since there were plenty of members with addresses that indicated what type of media organization they worked for, it seemed better to stick to those names. In the results, and later in this section, a breakdown of the respondents' media organizations was given to show that a solid mix of radio, print, and television journalists was surveyed.

Finally, AAJA members with corporate addresses, or government addresses—including law firms, non-profit organizations, museums, and federal, state and local government offices—were dropped from the pool since it was assumed they may not be working journalists. This cut amounted to 114 names being dropped from the pool.

After making those eliminations, 850 names remained. The list for the survey was created using the following criteria. First, only those persons were selected with names that sounded as if their heritage was of an ethnic sub-group of Asian Americans. This may be the most questionable part of the selection process since many Asian Americans have names that might be described as Western sounding. So someone with a last name of Wong or Yamamoto, for example, or a first name of Indira or Putri, was selected over a name like Mary Smith. There were several women with hyphenated last names where one of the names was Western and the other Asian. These people were kept in the pool. If any portion of a name sounded Asian, such as John In-wah Doe, that person was kept in the pool of names for the survey. The Asian

American Journalists Association has several members who are not Asian American. To be fair, a handful of questionnaires were sent to persons with Western sounding names in case they were Asian Americans—for example, a person of Korean heritage who was adopted by an American family and given a Western first and last name. Of the 520 surveys sent out (including the twenty sent to the editors of leading Asian American publications) only two were returned with notes that the respondents were not Asian Americans.

Finally, a fairly even mix of print, radio, and television journalists, along with a balance of men and women in relation to the

Table 8. Gender of the Asian American Journalists Surveyed

| Gender | Number | Percent of Total |
|---|---|---|
| Women | 308 | 61.6 % |
| Men | 175 | 35.0 % |
| Name did not reveal the sex | 17 | 3.4 % |
| Total surveyed | 500 | |

number of men and women members of AAJA, was selected from the remaining names in the pool. There are nearly twice as many women members of AAJA as men. In sheer numbers, that translates to approximately 850 women members of AAJA compared to approximately 485 men who are members (and approximately sixty persons whose names are not clearly identifyable as a man or a woman), so the mailing list for the book's survey included more women than men. In Chapter Six of this book there is a discussion on why, throughout all media positions, there are generally many more Asian American women employed in media compared to Asian American men.

Also, as much as could be determined, a balance of people were selected with names of various ethnic origins, including Chinese, Japanese, Filipino, Korean, Vietnamese, Indian, Hawaiian or other Pacific Islanders, and Middle Eastern. Finally, AAJA members were selected for the survey from the states that had members, with more members selected from states with high Asian American populations.

Tables 8 and 9 are breakdowns of the demographics and gender of the five hundred persons surveyed from the AAJA mailing list.

Table 9. Medium of Employment of Asian American
Journalists Surveyed

| Medium of Employment | Number | Percent of Total |
|---|---|---|
| Print | 327 | 65.4 % |
| Radio | 35 | 7.0 % |
| Television | 138 | 27.6 % |
| Total surveyed | 500 | |

These numbers roughly reflect the many more print journalists who are members of AAJA, compared to television journalists, and the much smaller number of radio broadcasters compared to the first two categories of journalists. Most of those surveyed work for mainstream media organizations (small, mid-sized, and large), as opposed to small, ethnic-focused media organizations.

Below is a breakdown of the number of persons surveyed from each state. There are many more members of AAJA who come from the states of California, Washington, New York, Hawaii, and the District of Columbia.

| | | | | | |
|---|---|---|---|---|---|
| 1) | Alabama | 0 | 27) | Montana | 0 |
| 2) | Alaska | 1 | 28) | Nebraska | 0 |
| 3) | Arizona | 4 | 29) | Nevada | 7 |
| 4) | Arkansas | 1 | 30) | New Hamp. | 0 |
| 5) | California | 126 | 31) | New Jersey | 9 |
| 6) | Colorado | 1 | 32) | New Mexico | 1 |
| 7) | Connecticut | 5 | 33) | New York | 99 |
| 8) | Delaware | 1 | 34) | N. Carolina | 3 |
| 9) | Dis. of Columbia | 21 | 35) | North Dakota | 0 |
| 10) | Florida | 11 | 36) | Ohio | 3 |
| 11) | Georgia | 12 | 37) | Okalahoma | 1 |
| 12) | Hawaii | 32 | 38) | Oregon | 13 |
| 13) | Idaho | 1 | 39) | Pennsylvania | 12 |
| 14) | Illinois | 17 | 40) | Rhode Is. | 2 |
| 15) | Indiana | 1 | 41) | S. Carolina | 1 |
| 16) | Iowa | 0 | 42) | S. Dakota | 0 |
| 17) | Kansas | 2 | 43) | Tennessee | 1 |
| 18) | Kentucky | 1 | 44) | Texas | 15 |
| 19) | Louisiana | 1 | 45) | Utah | 2 |
| 20) | Maine | 0 | 46) | Vermont | 2 |
| 21) | Maryland | 8 | 47) | Virginia | 12 |
| 22) | Massachusetts | 15 | 48) | Washington | 26 |
| 23) | Michigan | 9 | 49) | W. Virginia | 0 |
| 24) | Minnesota | 12 | 50) | Wisconsin | 6 |
| 25) | Mississippi | 0 | 51) | Wyoming | 0 |
| 26) | Missouri | 4 | | | |

Most of the states with no persons receiving survey letters had no AAJA members. Also, some states, such as Alaska, had only one AAJA member working in the media, and that person was sent a survey to gain the broadest representation of journalists working throughout the United States.

Content Analysis of the Survey Responses. After collecting all the survey responses of both Asian American journalists and editors of Asian American publications, an informal content analysis will be conducted to see how many persons responded "yes," "no," and "not sure," to the first two survey questions of whether they had had negative or positive experiences in the work place that they felt were due to their status. The responses will be coded as "yes," "no," or "not sure." If a respondent answers the first survey question with "yes and no," but gives an example of a "yes" answer, then the response will be coded as "yes." Similarly, if a respondent answers "yes and no" to question two, but then gives an example of a positive experience at the work-force that that answer will be coded as a "yes."

Three categories of coding will be established for answers to the third survey question about "what is being done right in the media today in covering Asian Americans and issues affecting Asian Americans." Those categories will be "very little is being done right," "some coverage done right," and "not sure." So, if a respondent gives an example or examples of balanced, fair or positive coverage, or who specifically states that some things are being done right or better to cover Asian Americans, then that response would be coded under "some coverage done right." Multiple coding will be allowed.

For the final question—"what is being done wrong in the media today in covering Asian Americans and issues facing Asian Americans"—the coding categories will be "too many stereotypes in coverage," "too much negative coverage," "nothing is seriously wrong" and "not sure." If a respondent says there is too much stereotyping in coverage of Asian Americans, and says there is too much negative coverage, then that response will be marked in both coding categories. Thus totals will equal more than the number of actual responses.

The results of the content analysis will be presented in numbers of responses per coding category only. Chi square values will be calculated on the data for survey questions one through three, but not for the responses to survey question four since there are several coding categories which should not be collapsed in a chi square calculation to fit at least five responses per cell. The comparison of the sets of responses will address the research questions six and seven.

Reporting of Survey Results From Asian American Journalists and Editors of Asian American Publications. The actual responses from the journalists and editors will also be presented either through direct quotes, chiefly from those who did not request anonimity, or paraphrasing the response. These responses will be given for each question, with some general analysis offered.

## SURVEY OF THE EDITORS OF THE TWENTY LEADING ASIAN AMERICAN PUBLICATIONS

This portion of the book research will answer the second half of research question six:

6. How do editors of Asian American publications assess coverage?

To answer the second half of research question six, a survey letter was sent to editors of the twenty leading publications serving Asian Americans and/or covering Asian American issues on October 7, 1995. (See Appendix 5 for a list of those twenty Asian American publications.) A follow-up letter was sent on November 10, 1995, to those editors who had not responded within a month. These letters asked the editors to answer the same four survey questions as posed to the five hundred Asian American journalists working in mainstream media, as explained in the previous section of this chapter. However, the letters sent to the editors of the twenty leading Asian American publications also asked for information about the editor's specific publication, particularly any content analysis or other documentation they may have kept on the number of articles published in his or her publication that dealt with Asian Americans and the media.

The survey questions were phrased rather broad so as to seek anecdotes or other stories of positive and negative experiences these people may have experienced on the job due to their ethnic status as Asian Americans. The final two survey questions were designed to assess what predictions the editors of these leading

Asian American publications had on how Asian Americans and issues affecting Asian Americans were being covered, or not covered, in the mainstream U.S. press.

Also enclosed in both letters was a publication permission/consent form and a self-addressed, stamped return envelope. The form not only asked for permission to publish the editors' responses in a doctoral dissertation and any subsequent publications to come from the dissertation (including this book), but also allowed the editors to request anonymity from their responses. As explained earlier, this was a key element in the choice to conduct a self-administered survey.

## CENSUS DATA

Table 10 is a breakdown of the Asian American population for the circulation areas of the newspapers used in the content analysis.

These figures show that the largest percentages of Asian Americans to the total population are in the metropolitan areas of the circulation areas of the three West Coast newspapers included in the content analysis—Los Angeles, San Francisco and Seattle—with the exception of New York. This U.S. Census data will be the basis for answering research questions eight and ten.

To answer research question eight, this census data will be compared to the amount of coverage of Asian Americans within the circulation area of each newspaper in the content analysis. A rank-correlation (Spearman's rho) will be calculated on the data. Research question eight is:

Table 10. Populations of Cities of Newspapers in the Content Analysis

| Metropolitan Area | Total Population | Total Asian American* | Percent Asian American* |
|---|---|---|---|
| Atlanta, Georgia | 2,833,511 | 49,965 | 1.8 % |
| Boston, Mass. | 4,171,747 | 119,949 | 2.9 |
| Chicago, Ill. | 8,065,633 | 255,621 | 3.2 |
| Denver, Colo. | 1,848,319 | 42,279 | 2.3 |
| Detroit, Mich. | 4,665,236 | 67,886 | 1.5 |
| Houston, Texas | 3,711,043 | 130,225 | 3.5 |
| Los Angeles, Calif. | 14,531,529 | 1,339,990 | 9.2 |
| New Orleans, La. | 1,238,816 | 20,976 | 1.7 |
| New York, N.Y. | 18,087,251 | 866,394 | 4.8 |
| San Francisco, Calif. | 6,253,311 | 928,026 | 14.8 |
| Seattle, Wash. | 2,559,164 | 164,386 | 6.4 |
| St. Louis, Mo. | 2,444,099 | 22,808 | 0.9 |
| Washington, D.C. | 3,928,574 | 201,502 | 5.1 |

SOURCE: U.S. Census, 1990: Social and Economic Characteristics.
* Includes Pacific Islander population.

8. How does the percentage of Asian Americans living in a city correlate with the amount of coverage of Asian Americans?

To answer research question ten, this census data will be compared to the information on the number of Asian Americans working in each newsroom of the content analysis, as collected by the survey of newspaper editors or human resource managers. A rank-correlation (Spearman's rho) will be calculated on the data. Research question ten is:

10. How does the percentage of Asian Americans living in a city correlate with the percentage of Asian Americans working in a newsroom of a newspaper covering that city?

## PERSONNEL SURVEY OF THE EDITORS OF THE TWENTY MAINSTREAM NEWSPAPERS IN THE CONTENT ANALYSIS

This final survey was conducted to answer research questions nine and ten. The editor-in-chief of each of the twenty mainstream newspapers researched in the content analysis was contacted by a letter sent on October 7, 1995, asking for the number of Asian Americans, African Americans, Native Americans, and Hispanics employed in the newsroom of that newspaper. The letter also asked if there were any editorial policies in that particular newsroom for covering Asian Americans and issues affecting Asian Americans. A copy of the style manual used by each newspaper was also requested.

A follow-up letter was sent on November 16, 1995, to those editors who had not responded by that date. Both letters said the editor could refer the letter to the personnel/human resources manager of the newsroom for a response, and both letters had a self-addressed, stamped return envelope enclosed for respondents to use to send information. Finally, the editor was invited to make any comments on the study's topic. If an editor or newsroom personnel director did not respond to the follow-up letter, a telephone call was placed with the editor or that person's administrative assistant, and a phone interview conducted seeking the information requested in the two letters.

The responses on minority newsroom personnel from these letters and telephone calls will be presented in a table as a percentage of total newsroom employees. Any responses on newsroom policies, or any comments from editors or newsroom personnel directors, will be simply quoted or paraphrased and analyzed. Finally, policies on Asian names or any other style points from the various style manuals of the newspapers will be presented in appendices. The results presented from this section, while representing the first building block of the book's research, will answer the final two research questions, numbers nine and ten. The method for ansering research question ten has been explained. Research question nine asks:

9. How does the percentage of Asian Americans working in a newsroom correlate with the coverage of Asian Americans?

To answer this question, the information on the number of Asian Americans working in the newsrooms of the newspapers used in the content analysis will be compared to the number of articles on Asian Americans in the year studied published by each of those newspapers, and a rank-correlation (Spearman's rho) will be conducted on the data.

## NOTES

[10] The Holsti formula for inter-coder reliability is:
$2m \div (N_1 + N_2) = \text{Reliability}.$

[11] Where M = number of decisions agreed, and N1 and N2 are the number of decisions for judge one and judge two.

# Chapter 5

# RESULTS AND DISCUSSION

> Usually only sensational news—such as gang vio-
> lence, Chinatown sweatshops, or the massive influx
> of immigrants and refugees—arouses curiosity or
> attracts the attention of the predominately white
> media establishment.
>
> —Editorial, *East/West*

## OVERVIEW

The results from all the segments of this book's research will be
presented in the order of the ten research questions, which reflect
the methodological building blocks of the book: 1) content analysis, 2) surveys of Asian American journalists, editors of twenty
leading Asian American publications, and the editors of the newspapers used in the content analysis, and, 3) census and survey data
analysis. Therefore, the results will be presented for each research
question, followed by a discussion of those results for each question. The discussion will compare the present study's results with
previous research where any exists.

## CONTENT ANALYSIS

The content analysis of twenty leading mainstream newspapers in the United States reflects the theoretical foundations of

agenda setting and stereotyping. This portion of the research served to answer research questions one through four.

**Research Question One.** Research question one asks:

1) What newspapers carry the most articles on Asian Americans?

A total of 635 articles—after removal of all duplicates and articles that turned up but that did not deal with Asian Americans—was the final result of the content analysis search of the twenty newspapers in the one-year period of March 1, 1994, to February 28, 1995. The reader should remember that "article" could mean anything from in-depth local enterprise feature about the newspaper's "own" Asian Americans to a wire story about a one-shot event, such as the death of a prominent Asian American.

The *Seattle Times* stands head and shoulders above the other nineteen; its 215 articles totalled more than the next three papers combined. It's in a class by itself. Sadly, three newspapers—the *Detroit Free Press*, the *Michigan Chronicle*, and the *Washington Times*— had no stories on Asian Americans or issues affecting Asian Americans (according to the coding guidelines) for this time frame.

Some other newspapers had relatively few articles. For example, nine of the twenty newspapers had twenty or fewer article for the year studied: the *Detroit News* and *Free Press* (a newspaper published only on Sundays and which is a separate newspaper from the *Detroit Free Press*) had one article, the *St. Louis Post-Dispatch* had four, the *Christian Science Monitor* had six, the *Detroit News* had seven, the *Wall Street Journal* had eight, the *Denver Post* had ten, the *Houston Post* had fifteen, the *Times-Picayune* had sixteen, *USA Today* had nineteen, and the *Washington Post* had twenty. By contrast, other newspapers had significant coverage of Asian Americans. Table 11 lists the total articles on Asian Americans (under all keywords searched) for each newspaper, with the rankings outlined in Chapter Four. As explained in Chapter Four, the *Detroit News*, *Detroit Free Press*, and *Detroit News* and *Free Press* will be counted as three newspapers when necessary in reporting results of the content analysis, although for the overall study they were counted as two newspapers for reasons explained in the last chapter.

The only other newspapers with a significant volume of coverage of Asian Americans were all on either the East Coast—the

*Boston Globe* and the *New York Times*—or on the West Coast—the *San Francisco Chronicle*, and the *Los Angeles Times*. The *Seattle Times*, as noted, stands in a class by itself. With the exception of the *Seattle Times*, all the newspapers provided little cover-

Table 11. Articles on Asian Americans in Eighteen Newspapers,
1994–1995

| Newspaper | Number of Articles | Ranking |
|---|---|---|
| Seattle Times | 215 | Extremely High Volume |
| Los Angeles Times | 73 | |
| San Francisco Chronicle | 70 | |
| New York Times | 54 | Medium Volume |
| Boston Globe | 52 | |
| Atlanta Journal-Constitution * | 28 | |
| Chicago Tribune | 25 | |
| Washington Post | 20 | |
| USA Today | 19 | Low Volume |
| Times-Picayune (New Orleans) | 16 | |
| Houston Post | 15 | |
| Houston Chronicle | 12 | |
| Denver Post | 10 | |
| Wall Street Journal | 8 | |
| Detroit News | 7 | |
| Christian Science Monitor | 6 | Extremely Low Volume |
| St. Louis Post Dispatch | 4 | |
| Detroit News and Free Press | 1 | |
| Detroit Free Press | 0 | |
| Michigan Chronicle | 0 | No Coverage |
| Washington Times | 0 | |
| Total Articles | 635 | |

\* Includes the Atlanta Constitution (morning edition of the Atlanta Journal),
the Atlanta Journal, and the Atlanta Journal-Constitution (Sunday edition).

age of Asian Americans and issues facing Asian Americans. Excluding the three newspapers with no articles on Asian Americans, the remaining newspapers break down into four groups and will be discussed as such. A Spearman rank-correlation later in this chapter will show how volume related to local Asian populations.

*Research Question Two.* Research question two asks:

2) Which ethnic sub-groups are the most covered by each newspaper?

**All Newspapers.** The results of research questions two through four will be given by presenting each newspaper after first presenting the cumulative results for all newspapers. In all the results, the ethnic breakdown of "Asian Americans" indicates those articles dealt with Asian Americans as a group and, therefore, did not discuss a specific ethnic sub-group of Asian Americans. Also, the category of "Well-Known Persons" means those of undetermined ethnicity for reasons explained in the previous chapter.

Table 12 gives the breakdown of all 635 articles by ethnic subgroup topic. The articles are listed with the *Seattle Times* articles in a separate column to show how much of a difference those 215 articles made to the overall counts. For example, of the six articles on Pakistani Americans, five were published in the *Seattle Times*.

Table 12. Ethnicity of Asian Americans Covered in Articles in Eighteen Newspapers, 1994–1995

| Ethnic Group | Seattle Times No. Articles | Other Newspapers No. Articles | All Newspapers No. Articles/ Rank Order |
|---|---|---|---|
| Chinese Americans | 22 | 36 | 58 (3)⁻ |
| Japanese Americans | 20 | 33 | 53 (4) |
| Vietnamese Americans | 6 | 46 | 52 (5) |
| Korean Americans | 10 | 37 | 47 (6) |
| Filipino Americans | 14 | 10 | 24 (7) |
| Asian Indians | 5 | 7 | 12 (8) |
| Hawaiian Americans | 6 | 5 | 11 (9) |
| Pacific Islander Americans | 9 | 2 | 11(10) |
| Cambodian Americans | 0 | 9 | 9(11) |
| Hmong Americans | 4 | 3 | 7(12) |
| Pakistani Americans | 5 | 1 | 6(13) |
| Thai Americans | 5 | 1 | 6(14) |
| Laotian Americans | 2 | 1 | 3(15) |
| Other Asian Americans (2-Indonesians, 1-Burmese) | 1 | 2 | 3(15) |
| Well-Known Persons | 8 | 69 | 77 (2) |
| Asian Americans | 98 | 158 | 256 (1) |
| Totals | 215 | 420 | 635 |

NOTE: Only one main group was coded for each article.

Overall, stories that concentrated on Asian American personalities received the most coverage over all ethnic sub-groups of Asian Americans. The rank-correlation (Spearman's rho) for Table 12 (newspapers v. ethnicity) is .93, which represents a very strong correlation between the rankings of each ethnic sub-group for total news coverage and all newspapers combined. The biggest percentage of all the articles published on Asian Americans dealt with the Asian American population as a whole and did not address specific ethnic sub-groups of Asian Americans.

Of the Asian American ethnic sub-groups, Chinese Americans received the most coverage with seventy-six articles, followed by Japanese Americans and Vietnamese Americans, which had fifty-three and fifty-two articles, respectively. Notably, the second largest group of Asian Americans—Filipino Americans—came in sixth and had only twenty-four articles. It is equally notable that Asian Indians, Hawaiian Americans, and other Pacific Islanders received so few articles. Finally, those groups with ten or fewer articles published on them in all the twenty newspapers have a legitimate complaint that these important ethnic groups of Asian Americans are receiving scant coverage in the American press.

Just as the total coverage for Asian Americans in the newspapers examined could be ranked from extremely high volume coverage to extremely low volume coverage, a similar ranking should be given to the coverage of the ethnic sub-groups. Receiving a total of forty or more articles were: Chinese Americans, Japanese Americans, Vietnamese Americans, and Korean Americans. The next level was twenty to thirty-nine articles, which had only Filipino Americans with twenty-four articles. The next level was ten to twenty articles, which represented Asian Indians, Hawaiian Americans, and Pacific Islander Americans. Finally, there was the level with the lowest coverage of nine articles or less, which had five ethnic sub-groups: Cambodian Americans, Hmong Americans, Pakistani Americans, Thai Americans, and Laotian Americans. So, from this type of classification of the data, we see some interesting patterns. We know from Table 1 in Chapter One that the order—from largest to sixth largest—ethnic sub-groups of Asian Americans are: Chinese Americans, Filipino Americans, Japanese Americans, Korean Americans, Asian Indian Americans, and Vietnamese Americans. Those six groups are also the sixth most covered groups according to the rank order findings of this book. So there is a strong .93 correlation between the population of the six largest Asian American ethnic sub-groups and amount of coverage each receives in the newspapers examined.

Beyond that observation, it is notable that Pacific Islanders and Hawaiian Americans received precisely the same amount of coverage with eleven articles each, or a perfect rank-correlation of 1.0 (Spearman's rho). The last grouping one sees is the number of Southeast Asian ethnic sub-groups which fall into the least-covered category of nine articles or less, including Cambodian Americans, Hmong Americans, Thai Americans, and Laotian Americans.

It is also important to note that the majority of stories on certain ethnic sub-groups of Asian Americans came from the *Seattle Times*. This is true of the following ethnic sub-groups: Laotian Americans, Pakistani Americans, Thai Americans, Hmong Americans, Hawaiian Americans, Pacific Islander Americans, and Filipino Americans. This is a very important fact to come out of this book's research, and the overall lack of coverage for many ethnic sub-groups of Asian Americans needs to be researched further.

Looking at the actual numbers of articles published by each newspaper provides a more micro analysis of this data. What follows is a breakdown by newspaper of the ethnic groups covered in articles on Asian Americans for the one-year period of the content analysis. The newspapers will be presented in order of the four rankings, as outlined in Chapter Four, which represent various levels of coverage of Asian Americans: 1) extremely high volume, 2) medium volume, 3) low volume, and, 4) extremely low volume. None of the newspapers had high volume coverage of Asian Americans, which was defined in Chapter Four as one hundred to 199 articles on Asian Americans published in one year.

**Extremely High Volume Coverage of Asian Americans.** Only one newspaper, the *Seattle Times*, had extremely high volume coverage of Asian Americans, or more than two hundred articles on Asian Americans published during the year studied.

1) *Seattle Times*. Table 13 is a breakdown by ethnic subgroup of the 215 articles on Asian Americans that ran in the *Seattle Times*.

The Northwest United States is one of the fastest growing regions of the country, according to recent news reports and U.S.

Census data. It is also a region with a fast-growing and diverse Asian American population. Of Seattle's 2.5 million residents, more than 164,000, or 6.4 percent, are Asian Americans (*U.S. Census 1990*). The 215 articles on this thriving group of Seattle

Table 13. Ethnicity of Asian Americans Covered in Articles in the *Seattle Times*, 1994–1995

| Ethnic Group | Number of Articles |
| --- | --- |
| Asian Americans | 98 |
| Chinese Americans | 22 |
| Japanese Americans | 20 |
| Filipino Americans | 14 |
| Korean Americans | 10 |
| Pacific Islander Americans | 9 |
| Hawaiian Americans | 6 |
| Vietnamese Americans | 6 |
| Pakistani Americans | 5 |
| Thai Americans | 5 |
| Asian Indians | 5 |
| Hmong Americans | 4 |
| Laotian Americans | 2 |
| Other Asian Americans (Burmese) | 1 |
| Well-Known Persons | 8 |
| Total | 215 |

NOTE: Only one main group was coded for each article.

residents represents the highest coverage of any of the twenty newspapers researched for the content analysis. Beyond the sheer number of articles published on Asian Americans, the number of ethnic sub-groups of Asian Americans covered is also impressive. The one article coded as other Asian Americans was on a Burmese American woman (the former Burma is now Myanmar) living in Seattle who had become a leading scientific researcher in the United States.

It is interesting that the *Seattle Times* gave a nearly even split of coverage in number of articles between Chinese Americans and Japanese Americans. It also offered the most comprehensive coverage of Pacific Islander Americans of the twenty newspapers researched. While fourteen articles on Filipino Americans is not a great deal, it also represents the most coverage by any newspaper on the second largest ethnic sub-group of Asian Americans.

Overall, the coverage of Asian Americans in the *Seattle Times* is by far the best of any newspaper in the content analysis. On the average, the articles in the *Seattle Times* were also longer than articles in the other newspapers studied. Finally, the *Seattle Times* gave coverage to thirteen ethnic sub-groups of Asian Americans, which is five more than the newspaper with coverage of the second most ethnic sub-groups of Asian Americans—the *New York Times* —which had stories on eight ethnic sub-groups. Some ethnic sub-groups, like Asian Indians, still received only brief coverage of their communities. However, in general, the *Seattle Times* is the best example of the twenty newspapers examined for how to give comprehensive coverage to Asian Americans.

**Medium Volume Coverage of Asian Americans.** Four newspapers had medium volume coverage of Asian Americans, which was defined in Chapter Four as fifty to ninety-nine articles published on Asian Americans during the year studied. Those newspapers were: the Los Angeles Times with seventy-three articles, the *San Francisco Chronicle* with seventy articles, the *New York Times* with fifty-four articles, and the *Boston Globe* with fifty-two articles.

    1) *Los Angeles Times.* Table 14 is a breakdown by ethnic sub-group of the seventy-three articles on Asian Americans that ran in the *Los Angeles Times*.

Table 14.  Ethnicity of Asian Americans Covered in Articles in the
*Los Angeles Times*, 1994–1995

| Ethnic Group | Number of Articles |
| --- | --- |
| Asian Americans | 17 |
| Korean Americans | 13 |
| Vietnamese Americans | 12 |
| Japanese Americans | 9 |
| Chinese Americans | 6 |
| Cambodian Americans | 2 |
| Hmong Americans | 1 |
| Other Asian Americans (Indonesians) | 1 |
| Well-Known Persons | 12 |
| Total | 73 |

NOTE:  Only one main group was coded for each article.

While this may appear on the surface, when compared with other newspapers' coverage of Asian Americans, to be high volume coverage of the Asian American community in Los Angeles, in fact it is not. The reason is that 9.2 percent of the 14.5 million people living in Los Angeles are Asian Americans, or 1.3 million people—a higher absolute and percentage figures than Seattle (U.S. Census 1990). A total of seventy-three articles on 1.3 million persons and more than 9 percent of a city's population does not necessarily translate into high volume coverage of the Asian American community in Los Angeles and issues, both national and local, affecting that community and thereby all Angelenos, Asian American or not.

The article on Indonesian Americans was about a small community of Indonesians who have opened shops in the Hollywood area on Sunset Boulevard. It represented one of only two articles on Indonesian Americans of the entire 635 articles on Asian Americans found in the content analysis. The other article on Indonesian Americans was published in the *San Francisco Chronicle*. Several of the articles on Korean Americans dealt with the efforts of that community to rebuild businesses following the 1992 riots there.

2) *San Francisco Chronicle*. Table 15 is a breakdown by ethnic sub-group of the seventy articles on Asian Americans that ran in the *San Francisco Chronicle*.

Table 15. Ethnicity of Asian Americans Covered in Articles in the *San Francisco Chronicle*, 1994–1995

| Ethnic Group | Number of Articles |
|---|---|
| Asian Americans | 31 |
| Chinese Americans | 11 |
| Filipino Americans | 9 |
| Japanese Americans | 8 |
| Korean Americans | 2 |
| Asian Indians | 1 |
| Vietnamese Americans | 1 |
| Other Asian Americans (Indonesians) | 1 |
| Well-Known Persons | 6 |
| Total | 70 |

NOTE: Only one main group was coded for each article.

Like the *New York Times* and *Los Angeles Times*, the large number of article in the *San Francisco Chronicle* on first appearance
seems high. However, it acutally represents low coverage of Asian
Americans among the newspapers examined because nearly 15
percent of San Francisco's population is Asian American, or more
than 928,000 people. The city has the second largest Asian
American population of any city in the United States, surpassed
only by Los Angeles with 1.3 million Asian Americans (*U.S.
Census 1990*). Seventy news articles for a year's worth of news
about nearly one million Asian Americans, as well as state and
national issues affecting that community, actually represents low
coverage.

It is also notable that so few ethnic sub-groups of Asian
Americans are represented in this breakdown of news coverage.
There are large Vietnamese American, Japanese American, Chinese
American, Filipino Amerian, and many other ethnic groups of
Asian Americans living in San Franciso. Most of these communi-
ties are receiving low to no coverage in the *San Francisco
Chronicle*. This newspaper does have the third highest number of
stories published on Asian Americans in the one-year period of the
twenty newspapers examined.

   3) *New York Times.* Table 16 is a breakdown by ethnic sub-
group of the fifty-four articles on Asian Americans that ran
in the *New York Times*.

Table 16. Ethnicity of Asian Americans Covered in Articles in the
*New York Times*, 1994–1995

| Ethnic Group | Number of Articles |
|---|---|
| Asian Americans | 13 |
| Chinese Americans | 8 |
| Japanese Americans | 4 |
| Vietnamese Americans | 4 |
| Hawaiian Americans | 2 |
| Hmong Americans | 2 |
| Korean Americans | 2 |
| Asian Indians | 1 |
| Pacific Islander Americans | 1 |
| Well-Known Persons | 17 |
| Total | 54 |

NOTE: Only one main group was coded for each article.

The nearly 900,000 Asian Americans living in New York City comprise 4.8 percent of the city's population (U.S. Census 1990). These population figures may not have much significance for the New York Times' coverage of Asian Americans since it is a national newspaper with most of its local news coverage being in the metropolitan section. While the number of stories is the fourth highest of the twenty newspapers researched for the content analysis, fifty-four articles on Asian Americans and local, state and national issues facing Asian Americans for a one-year period represents low coverage.

Some of the same patterns of coverage already seen in the newspapers mentioned are also seen with the *New York Times*. For example, there are many ethnic sub-groups of Asian Americans not represented in the coverage for this one-year period, yet New York City is known for its diverse immigrant population and people all ethnic sub-groups of Asian Americans live in that city.

4) *Boston Globe.* Table 17 is a breakdown by ethnic sub-group of the fifty-two articles on Asian Americans that ran in the *Boston Globe.*

Table 17. Ethnicity of Asian Americans Covered in Articles in the *Boston Globe*, 1994–1995

| Ethnic Group | Number of Articles |
|---|---|
| Asian Americans | 22 |
| Chinese Americans | 8 |
| Cambodian Americans | 4 |
| Korean Americans | 3 |
| Asian Indians | 2 |
| Hawaiian Americans | 1 |
| Japanese Americans | 1 |
| Laotian Americans | 1 |
| Vietnamese Americans | 1 |
| Well-Known Persons | 9 |
| Total | 52 |

NOTE: Only one main group was coded for each article.

The *Boston Globe* gives significant coverage to the nearly 120,000 Asian Americans who live in that city and who represent nearly 3 percent of the city's population (*U.S. Census 1990*). Boston has approximately 80,000 fewer Asian Americans than Washington, D.C., yet the *Boston Globe* published thirty-two more articles on Asian Americans than the *Washington Post* did during the one-year period of the content analysis.

Japanese Americans had just one article, and Filipino Americans had no coverage. Vietnamese Americans also received very little coverage, as did Asian Indians.

**Low Volume Coverage of Asian Americans.** Eight newspapers had low volume coverage of Asian Americans, which was defined in Chapter Four as any newspaper having ten to forty-nine articles on Asian Americans during the year studied. Those newspapers were: the *Atlanta Journal-Constitution* with twenty-eight articles, the *Chicago Tribune* with twenty-five, the *Washington Post* with twenty, *USA Today* with nineteen, the *Times-Picayune* with sixteen, the Houston Post with fifteen, the *Houston Chronicle* with twelve, and the Denver Post with ten.

1) *Atlanta Journal-Constitution.* Table 18 shows the break down by Asian American ethnic sub-group of the twenty-eight articles that appeared in the *Atlanta Journal-Constitution.*

Table 18. Ethnicity of Asian Americans Covered in Articles in the *Atlanta Journal-Constitution*, 1994–1995

| Ethnic Group | Number of Articles |
|---|---|
| Asian Americans | 10 |
| Korean Americans | 6 |
| Vietnamese Americans | 4 |
| Japanese Americans | 2 |
| Asian Indians | 1 |
| Chinese Americans | 1 |
| Well-Known Persons | 4 |
| Total | 28 |

NOTE: Only one main group was coded for each article.

Considering there are nearly 50,000 Asian Americans living in Atlanta the number represents low coverage of that community (*U.S. Census 1990*).

2) *Chicago Tribune.* Table 19 is a breakdown by ethnic sub-group of the twenty-five articles on Asian Americans that ran in the *Chicago Tribune*.

Table 19. Ethnicity of Asian Americans Covered in Articles in the *Chicago Tribune*, 1994–1995

| Ethnic Group | Number of Articles |
|---|---|
| Asian Americans | 6 |
| Vietnamese Americans | 4 |
| Korean Americans | 3 |
| Hawaiian Americans | 2 |
| Japanese Americans | 2 |
| Well-Known Persons | 8 |
| Total | 25 |

NOTE: Only one main group was coded for each article.

For the approximately 256,000 Asian Americans living in Chicago, or 3.2 percent of that city's 1.8 million citizens, this represents low coverage of Asian Americans, locally and nationally, and issues facing Asian Americans (U.S. Census 1990). There was not a single article written about Chinese Americans specifically for the entire one-year period of the content analysis. The total of three articles on Korean Americans and two articles on Japanese Americans also represents low coverage of these important ethnic sub-groups of Asian Americans.

3) *Washington Post.* Table 20 is a breakdown by ethnic sub-group of the twenty articles on Asian Americans which ran in the *Washington Post*.

More than 5 percent of Washington, D.C.'s 3.9 million residents are Asian American, so twenty articles in one year represent very low coverage of this important segment of the nation's capital and the local, state, and national issues affecting them (*U.S. Census 1990*). This also represents little to no coverage of most ethnic sub-groups of Asian Americans. In fact, only nine articles were published in the *Washington Post* which dealt with ethnic sub-groups, during the year examined in the content analysis.

Table 20. Ethnicity of Asian Americans Covered in Articles in the *Washington Post*, 1994–1995

| Ethnic Group | Number of Articles |
|---|---|
| Asian Americans | 10 |
| Japanese Americans | 4 |
| Korean Americans | 2 |
| Cambodian Americans | 1 |
| Filipino Americans | 1 |
| Pacific Islander Americans | 1 |
| Well-Known Persons | 1 |
| Total | 20 |

NOTE: Only one main group was coded for each article.

4) *USA Today.* Table 21 is a breakdown by ethnic sub-group of the nineteen articles on Asian Americans that ran in *USA Today*.

Table 21. Ethnicity of Asian Americans Covered in Articles in *USA Today*, 1994–1995

| Ethnic Group | Number of Articles |
|---|---|
| Asian Americans | 10 |
| Vietnamese Americans | 2 |
| Japanese Americans | 1 |
| Well-Known Persons | 6 |
| Total | 19 |

NOTE: Only one main group was coded for each article.

As mentioned earlier, *USA Today* is a national newspaper which has been a unique and ground-breaking experiment in American journalism. Many of the articles in *USA Today* are shorter in length than articles in other newspapers, and they usually are not jumped to other pages. However, USA Tdoay's ability to, therefore, often offer more articles which are shorter in length did not translate into high coverage of Asian Americans and issues facing Asian Americans. One article on Japanese Americans and two on Vietnamese Americans, in a one-year time frame, translates into virtually little to no coverage of most ethnic subgroups of Asian Americans. *USA Today* devoted nearly a third of its coverage to Asian American personalities in the news that usually ran in that newspaper's Life section, which includes entertainment news. In general, for a national newspaper, nineteen articles on Asian Americans represents low coverage of the fastest growing minority in the United States.

5) *Times-Picayune*. Table 22 is a breakdown by ethnic subgroup of the sixteen articles on Asian Americans that ran in the New Orleans newspaper, the *Times-Picayune*.

Table 22. Ethnicity of Asian Americans Covered in Articles in the *Times-Picyune*, 1994–1995

| Ethnic Group | Number of Articles |
|---|---|
| Vietnamese Americans | 11 |
| Asian Americans | 5 |
| Total | 16 |

NOTE: Only one main group was coded for each article.

There are many more ethnic sub-groups of Asian Americans living in New Orleans, a city with nearly 21,000 Asian Americans, than just Vietnamese Americans (*U.S. Census 1990*). Sixteen articles in a one-year time period is very low coverage of Asian Americans and local, state, and national issues facing Asian Americans living in New Orleans, who represent 1.7 percent of that city's more than 1.2 million residents (*U.S. Census 1990*). The *Times-Picayune* represents the lowest coverage of ethnic subgroups of Asian Americans of any of the twenty newspapers in the content analysis, with the exception of those newspapers with no articles on Asian Americans or just one article.

6) *Houston Post*. Table 23 is a breakdown by ethnic subgroup of the fifteen articles on Asian Americans that ran in the Houston Post.

The *Houston Post* published just three more articles on Asian

Table 23.  Ethnicity of Asian Americans Covered in Articles in the
*Houston Post*, 1994–1995

| Ethnic Group | Number of Articles |
|---|---|
| Asian Americans | 10 |
| Korean Americans | 3 |
| Vietnamese Americans | 2 |
| Total | 15 |

NOTE: Only one main group was coded for each article.
The Houston Post ceased publication in April 1996.

Americans compared to its competitor, the Houston Chronicle. This represents very low coverage of the Asian Americans living in the Houston area and the issues facing them. There was some coverage, like a review of a photographic exhibit on Asian Americans which was featured at the Houston Center for Photography, which the *Houston Post* offered readers and which the *Houston Chronicle* did not.

7) *Houston Chronicle.* Table 24, on the next page, is a breakdown by ethnic sub-group of the twelve articles on Asian Americans that ran in the *Houston Chronicle.*

Table 24.  Ethnicity of Asian Americans Covered in Articles in the
*Houston Chronicle*, 1994–1995

| Ethnic Group | Number of Articles |
|---|---|
| Asian Americans | 9 |
| Vietnamese Americans | 1 |
| Well-Known Persons | 2 |
| Total | 12 |

NOTE: Only one main group was coded for each article.

Houston's Asian American population represents more than 130,000 persons (U.S. Census 1990). So these twelve articles represent very low coverage of that important segment of Houston's overall population of 3.7 million people, and the local, state, and national issues affecting them (U.S. Census 1990).    Asian

Americans make up 3.5 percent of the Houston population, yet they only received twelve articles of news coverage in the *Houston Chronicle* over a year's time. This was also the same year that the first primetime television program with an all-Asian cast premiered, but there was only one article—a profile of the program's lead actress Margaret Cho—in the entertainment news of the Houston Chronicle. Of the nine articles on Asian Americans, five dealt with racism, poverty, or other negative aspects of the Asian American community.

8) *Denver Post.* Table 25 is a breakdown by ethnic sub-group of the ten articles on Asian Americans that ran in the *Denver Post.*

Table 25. Ethnicity of Asian Americans Covered in Articles in the
*Denver Post*, 1994–1995

| Ethnic Group | Number of Articles |
|---|---|
| Vietnamese Americans | 3 |
| Asian Americans | 2 |
| Japanese Americans | 2 |
| Korean Americans | 2 |
| Cambodian Americans | 1 |
| Total | 10 |

NOTE: Only one main group was coded for each article.

Denver's Asian American community of more than 42,200 is 7,600 fewer than Atlanta's Asian American community, yet the *Atlanta Journal Constitution* has nearly two-thirds more articles on Asian Americans compared to the Denver Post (U.S. Census 1990). There are many other ways to make comparisons to coverage of Asian Americans by the *Denver Post.* There is no coverage of most ethnic sub-groups of Asian Americans represented in the ten articles. This was also one of the few newspapers of the twenty studied that had no articles on Asian American personalities in the news (which would fall under the "Well-Known Persons" coding category). Overall, this represents low coverage of Asian Americans living in Denver and local and national issues of interest to that community.

**Extremely Low Volume Coverage of Asian Americans.** Five newspapers had extremely low coverage of Asian Americans, which was defined in Chapter Four as any newspaper which published a total of one to nine articles on Asian Americans during the year studied. Those newspapers with extremely low coverage of Asian Americans are: the *Wall Street Journal* with eight articles, the *Detroit News* with seven, the *Christian Science Monitor* with six, the St. Louis Post-Dispatch with four, and the *Detroit News* and *Free Press* with one.

    1) *Wall Street Journal.* Table 26 is a breakdown by ethnic subgroup of the eight articles on Asian Americans that ran in the *Wall Street Journal.*

Table 26.  Ethnicity of Asian Americans Covered in Articles in the *Wall Street Journal*, 1994–1995

| Ethnic Group | Number of Articles |
|---|---|
| Asian Americans | 2 |
| Asian Indians | 1 |
| Cambodian Americans | 1 |
| Chinese Americans | 1 |
| Well-Known Persons | 3 |
| Total | 8 |

NOTE: Only one main group was coded for each article.

    The Wall Street Journal is not only a national newspaper, but it is also specialized to give in-depth coverage of business news. Therefore, it is not unexpected that Asian Americans and issues facing Asian Americans received so little coverage in the one-year period studied. Many economic stories concerning the state of affairs on a national level for various ethnic sub-groups of Asian Americans such as Hmong Americans and Asian Indians were not covered in the Wall Street Journal. The economic impact of Asian Indians in the hotel management industry also received no coverage in the Wall Street Journal during the year studied. So there are many stories concerning the Asian American community which were not covered in the Wall Street Journal, even though this newspaper has a different focus from the other nineteen newspapers of the content analysis.

2) *Detroit News.* Table 27 is a breakdown by ethnic sub-group of the seven articles on Asian Americans that ran in the *Detroit News.*

Table 27. Ethnicity of Asian Americans Covered in Articles in the *Detroit News*, 1994–1995

| Ethnic Group | Number of Articles |
|---|---|
| Asian Americans | 5 |
| Asian Indians | 1 |
| Chinese Americans | 1 |
| Total | 7 |

NOTE: Only one main group was coded for each article.

Some people might argue that since the *Detroit Free Press* had no articles on Asian Americans, that the *Detroit News* should be recognized for at least writing seven articles on the nearly 68,000 Asian Americans living in Detroit. However, seven articles published on a community that represents 1.5 percent of a city's population, as well as representing the fastest growing minority in the United States, is low coverage (U.S. Census 1990). Needless to say, most ethnic sub-groups of Asian Americans received no coverage in the *Detroit News* during the one-year period studied.

3) *Christian Science Monitor.* Table 28 is a breakdown by ethnic sub-group of the six articles on Asian Americans that ran in the *Christian Science Monitor.*

The *Christian Science Monitor* is similar to *USA Today* and the *Wall Street Journal* in that it does not cover a local community and, instead, caters to a national audience. It is a twenty-page tabloid not comparable to the two other newspapers mentioned above, which are both broadsheets and which can run to many more pages. It is interesting, however, that this is the only newspaper of the twenty researched, other than the *Seattle Times*, to run an article on Pakistani Americans. Again, we see no coverage of Chinese Americans, Filipino Americans, and Japanese Americans.

Table 28. Ethnicity of Asian Americans Covered in Articles in the *Christian Science Monitor*, 1994–1995

| Ethnic Group | Number of Articles |
|---|---|
| Asian Americans | 3 |
| Korean Americans | 1 |
| Pakistani Americans | 1 |
| Well-Known Persons | 1 |
| Total | 6 |

NOTE: Only one main group was coded for each article.

4) *St. Louis Post-Dispatch.* Table 29 is a breakdown by ethnic sub-group of the four articles on Asian Americans that ran in the *St. Louis Post-Dispatch*.

Table 29. Ethnicity of Asian Americans Covered in Articles in the *St. Louis Post-Dispatch*, 1994–1995

| Ethnic Group | Number of Articles |
|---|---|
| Asian Americans | 2 |
| Thai Americans | 1 |
| Vietnamese Americans | 1 |
| Total | 4 |

NOTE: Only one main group was coded for each article.

Of the thirteen cities covered by the twenty newspapers of the content analysis, St. Louis has the smallest percentage of Asian Americans. Just under one percent of that city's 2.4 million residents are Asian Americans, or 22,808 persons (U.S. Census 1990). However, even with this information in mind, four articles is extremely low as the total one-year coverage of any segment of a community and local, state, and national issues affecting that community. It is interesting that the only article found in the content analysis on Thai Americans published in a newspaper other than the *Seattle Times* was an article on Thai religious temple in Florissant, Mo., published in the *St. Louis Post-Dispatch*.

5) *Detroit News* and *Free Press*. The one article which ran in the *Detroit News* and *Free Press* dealt with Asian Americans and did not discuss a specific ethnic sub-group of Asian Americans. This newspaper is the Sunday edition of two separate newspapers, the *Detroit News* and the *Detroit Free Press*. So it was unique among the twenty newspapers surveyed for the content analysis in that it was the only Sunday edition which was examined separately. However, when combining the results of the three newspapers mentioned here, there were only a total of eight articles on Asian Americans for the year of the content analysis (the *Detroit News* had seven articles, and the *Detroit Free Press* did not have any articles).

These three Detroit Newspapers are similar to the *Atlanta Journal, Atlanta Constitution*, and the *Atlanta Journal-Constitution*, but different because the Atlanta newspapers represent three editions of the same newspaper published by the same publisher. The *Detroit News* and *Detroit Free Press* have different publishers. However, while populations of cities covered in the content analysis will be discussed in the results presentation to research question eight, it is worth mentioning here that 1.5 percent of Detroit's 4.6 million population are Asian American, and 1.8 percent of Atlanta's 2.8 million population are Asian American, yet the combined three Detroit Newspapers have more than two-thirds fewer articles on Asian Americans for the year surveyed (U.S. Census 1990).

In summary, the results of research question two indicate that, with the exception of the *Seattle Times*, all newspapers in the content analysis gave low coverage of Asian Americans or issues facing Asian Americans in each of the circulation areas, or on a national level for those newspapers serving national audiences. Some newspapers gave sparse coverage to this important and fast-growing minority group. In general, Chinese Americans, Japanese Americans, Vietnamese Americans, and Korean Americans received the most coverage of the ethnic sub-groups of Asian Americans. Laotian Americans, Pakistani Americans, Thai Americans, Hmong Americans, Cambodian Americans, Hawaiian Americans, Pacific Islander Americans, Filipino Americans (the second largest ethnic sub-group), and Asian Indians received the least coverage of the ethnic sub-groups of Asian Americans. Also, there were many more articles published in the twenty newspapers on Asian American persons in the news (under the coding category of "Well-Known Persons") than on each of the ethnic sub-groups of Asian Americans.

**Research Question Three.** Research question three asks:
  3) Which story topics are the most covered by each newspaper?

Table 30 gives the breakdown of all 635 articles of the content analysis by type of story. Again, the articles which ran in the *Seattle Times* are broken out to demonstrate how these figures may have influenced the total results of all newspapers articles. In all of the tables, labels for data to answer research question three, are abbreviated for space purposes.

Table 30. Topics of Articles on Asian Americans in Eighteen Newspapers, 1994–1995

| Type of Article | Seattle Times | Other Newspapers | All Newspapers |
|---|---|---|---|
| Entertainment | 62 | 94 | 156 |
| Human Interest | 40 | 91 | 131 |
| Crime | 35 | 44 | 79 |
| Classic Arts | 26 | 52 | 78 |
| Politics | 21 | 46 | 67 |
| Moral | 8 | 37 | 45 |
| Health and Welfare | 13 | 22 | 35 |
| Education | 4 | 8 | 12 |
| Economic | 2 | 8 | 10 |
| Accidents | 3 | 7 | 10 |
| Defense | 1 | 6 | 7 |
| Other | 0 | 4 | 4 |
| Science | 0 | 1 | 1 |
| Total | 215 | 420 | 635 |

Here are the translations of those abbreviations, which refer to the coding categories in Chapter Four:

Politics—articles dealing with politics and government acts
Defense—war and defense articles

Economic—articles on economic activity

Crime—crime articles

Moral—articles on public moral problems and human relations (includes articles on racism)

Accidents—articles dealing with accidents and disasters

Science—Articles on science and invention

Classic Arts—Articles on the classic arts, including Tai Kwan Do and Tai Chi Quan

Entertainment—Articles on popular amusements

Human Interest—general human interest articles

Health and Welfare —public health and welfare articles

Education—Articles on education

Other—Articles that did not fall into one of the above categories

Articles dealing with popular amusements, which includes performance reviews, sports, television, magazine and other media articles, as well as articles on Chinese New Year and other ethnic Asian festivals, constituted nearly one-fourth of the total coverage on Asian Americans in the twenty newspapers for the year examined. The human interest articles included stories on successes of Asian immigrants, 'model minority' articles about successful Asian Americans, as well as articles on religion, philanthropy and various human interest pieces. These types of articles received nearly one-fifth of the total coverage on Asian Americans for that year. The third most common type of article dealt with crime and Asian Americans, which tends to support complaints by Asian Americans who say too many negative articles are published in newspapers which associate Asian Americans with crime, particularly gang violence. The coverage of gang violence examined in the content analysis will be discussed in the next section on research question four. Some of the complaints about too much coverage of Asian Americans and crime came from the five hundred Asian American journalists surveyed for this book. Those comments will also be presented later in this chapter.

In many of the categories, the articles in the *Seattle Times* sharply increased the total coverage in all newspapers for a particular type of story. This phenomenon was most striking with stories about politics, moral issues, and human interest. It is also noteworthy that there was only one article about Asian Americans and the sciences, even though there are numerous Asian Americans who work as scientists and who teach and conduct research in scientific fields in the United States.

It appears that the topics of war and defense, economics, natural disasters and other accidents, and education are rarely associated with the Asian American population in newspaper coverage, according to the results of this content analysis. Even with the earthquake in Kobe, Japan, having occurred during the year studied for the content analysis, few articles were written concerning Asian Americans and their association with that disaster. Table 31 presents the data on article type by each coded category for all the newspapers.

Table 31. Top Article Types in Eighteen Newspapers, 1994–1995

| Article Type/Newspaper | Number of Articles | Percent of Total Articles |
|---|---|---|
| **Human Interest** | | |
| Times-Picayune | 9 | 56 % |
| Detroit News | 3 | 43 % |
| Denver Post | 4 | 40 % |
| Houston Post | 6 | 40 % |
| Christian Science Monitor | 2 | 33 % |
| Atlanta Journal-Constitution | 7 | 25 % |
| San Francisco Chronicle | 17 | 24 % |
| **Entertainment** | | |
| USA Today | 13 | 68 % |
| Wall Street Journal | 4 | 50 % |
| Detroit News | 3 | 43 % |
| Washington Post | 7 | 35 % |
| Houston Chronicle | 4 | 33 % |
| Seattle Times | 62 | 29 % |
| Los Angeles Times | 16 | 22 % |
| **Crime** | | |
| Denver Post | 4 | 40 % |
| Christian Science Monitor | 2 | 33 % |
| Boston Globe | 10 | 19 % |
| **Classic Arts** | | |
| Chicago Tribune | 9 | 36 % |
| New York Times | 12 | 22 % |
| Boston Globe | 10 | 19 % |
| **Moral** | | |
| St. Louis Post-Dispatch | 2 | 50 % |

NOTE: Includes ties for top article type category. Omits Detroit News and Free Press.

It is useful to analyze the data by looking at the actual numbers for each newspaper. That information is what follows, as presented by each newspaper in alphabetical order.

*Atlanta Journal-Constitution.* Table 32 shows the breakdown by type of story for the twenty-eight articles on Asian Americans that appeared in the *Atlanta Journal-Constitution* during the year studied.

Table 32. Article Types in the *Atlanta Journal-Constitution*, 1994–1995

| Type of Article | Number of Articles | Percent of Total |
|---|---|---|
| Human Interest | 7 | 25 % |
| Moral | 5 | 18 % |
| Entertainment | 5 | 18 % |
| Politics | 4 | 14 % |
| Crime | 4 | 14 % |
| Classic Arts | 1 | 4 % |
| Education | 1 | 4 % |
| Health and Welfare | 1 | 4 % |
| Total | 28 | |

Most of the entertainment articles involved profiles of prominent Asian Americans such as tennis player Michael Chang, ice skater Michelle Kwan, and actress Margaret Cho. The general human interest articles are the largest category with the help of a "Chinatown Mall" which opened in Atlanta during the year of the content analysis, the usual Chinese New Year article, as well as an article on a Korean bank scheduled to open in Atlanta. Atlanta has an active Korean American community, and there is a substantial Southeast Asian American community in the Atlanta region. Many of the twenty-eight articles reflect coverage of these two communities.

*Boston Globe.* Table 33 shows the breakdown by type of story for the fifty-two articles on Asian Americans that appeared in the *Boston Globe* during the year studied.

Nearly all the crime articles published in the *Boston Globe* dealt with Asian Americans and racism. It is interesting that one of the political articles discussed Asian Americans as the fastest growing minority group in Massachusetts, making up approximately 3 percent of the state's population. The *Boston Globe* had extremely low coverage in certain topic areas such as education,

Table 33. Article Types in the *Boston Globe*, 1994–1995

| Type of Article | Number of Articles | Percent of Total |
|---|---|---|
| Crime | 10 | 19 % |
| Human Interest | 9 | 17 % |
| Entertainment | 7 | 13 % |
| Politics | 6 | 12 % |
| Moral | 5 | 10 % |
| Health and Welfare | 2 | 4 % |
| Economic | 1 | 2 % |
| Education | 1 | 2 % |
| Other | 1 | 2 % |
| Total | 52 | |

economics, and health and welfare issues. The article which was coded "other" dealt with the fears of an estimated 70,000 Korean Americans who lived in Flushing, New York, who feared American efforts to impose sanctions on North Korea could lead to war.

*Chicago Tribune.* Table 34 shows the breakdown by type of story for the twenty-five articles on Asian Americans that appeared in the *Chicago Tribune* during the year studied.

Table 34. Article Types in the *Chicago Tribune*, 1994–1995

| Type of Article | Number of Articles | Percent of Total |
|---|---|---|
| Classic Arts | 9 | 36 % |
| Crime | 3 | 12 % |
| Entertainment | 3 | 12 % |
| Human Interest | 3 | 12 % |
| Politics | 3 | 12 % |
| Economic | 2 | 8 % |
| Education | 1 | 4 % |
| Moral | 1 | 4 % |
| Total | 25 | |

As mentioned earlier, this is low coverage of Asian Americans for one year in a newspaper the size of the *Chicago Tribune*. The entertainment and classic arts articles nearly all involved prominent Asian Americans, including tennis star Michael Chang, ice skater Michelle Kwan, actress Margaret Cho, cellist Yo Yo Ma (who was the subject of six of the nine articles coded classic arts), and conductor Zubin Mehta.   Finally, racism was the topic of many of the non-entertainment/classic arts articles.

*Christian Science Monitor.* Table 35 shows the breakdown by type of story for the six articles on Asian Americans that appeared in the *Christian Science Monitor* during the year studied.

Table 35.  Article Types in the *Christian Science Monitor*, 1994–1995

| Type of Article | Number of Articles | Percent of Total |
|---|---|---|
| Human Interest | 2 | 33 % |
| Crime | 2 | 33 % |
| Education | 1 | 17 % |
| Entertainment | 1 | 17 % |
| Total | 6 | |

Of the two crime articles, one dealt with Asian gangs and the other dealt with Korean Americans rebuilding their businesses following the Los Angeles riots.   In general, the subjects of the remaining four articles were more unique than some of the other newspaper's coverage of Asian Americans.   For example, the television program *All-American Girl* was not covered, but the philanthropy of a Pakistani American woman was featured.   Another article discussed the myth of the model minority image of Asian Americans.   This is precisely the type of articles many of the Asian American journalists surveyed for this book said needs to be covered in newspapers.

*Denver Post.* Table 36 shows the breakdown by type of story for the ten articles on Asian Americans that appeared in the *Denver Post* during the year studied.

Table 36.  Article Types in the *Denver Post*. 1994–1995

| Type of Article | Number of Articles | Percent of Total |
|---|---|---|
| Crime | 4 | 40 % |
| Human Interest | 4 | 40 % |
| Defense | 1 | 10 % |
| Politics | 1 | 10 % |
| Total | 10 | |

The *Denver Post*'s defense article was one of only seven defense-related articles on Asian Americans published in all twenty newspapers for the year examined. The article was on first-hand experiences of Japanese Americans imprisoned at the Manzanar internment camp in Independence, Calif., during World War II. Two of the four crime articles dealt with racism, and the political article looked at the opinion among Colorado's Japanese Americans concerning a visit by Japanese Emperor Akihito.

*Detroit News.* Table 37 shows the breakdown by type of story for the seven articles on Asian Americans that appeared in the *Detroit News* during the year studied.

Table 37.  Article Types in the *Detroit News*, 1994–1995

| Type of Article | Number of Articles | Percent of Total |
|---|---|---|
| Entertainment | 3 | 43 % |
| Human Interest | 3 | 43 % |
| Crime | 1 | 14 % |
| Total | 7 | |

This coverage of Asian Americans represents two articles on the television show *All-American Girl*, one article on Chinese New Year, and an article on the book "Who's Who Among Asian Americans" which received coverage because it was published by a Detroit publishing house, a story about an Asian immigrant business that was robbed, and two other human interest articles. One has to wonder what type of coverage the large Asian American population in Detroit would have received if there had not been a television show with an all Asian cast premiering that year, a book not published locally, a couple robbed, and the obligatory Chinese New Year article.

*Detroit News* and *Free Press.* The one article that ran in the *Detroit News* and *Free Press* dealt with general human interest about the economic status of all Asian Americans. It was a long (more than eighteen inches), in-depth article which ran on the front page of the newspaper in April of 1994. It was also a locally written enterprise article, as opposed to a national wire story.

*Houston Chronicle.* Table 38 shows the breakdown by type of story for the twelve articles on Asian Americans that appeared in the *Houston Chronicle* during the year studied.

Table 38. Article Types in the *Houston Chronicle*, 1994–1995

| Type of Article | Number of Articles | Percent of Total |
|---|---|---|
| Entertainment | 4 | 33 % |
| Human Interest | 2 | 17 % |
| Moral | 2 | 17 % |
| Health and Welfare | 2 | 17 % |
| Politics | 2 | 17 % |
| Total | 12 | |

The two political articles dealt with prominent Asian Americans in Houston: Councilwoman Martha Wong and lawyer Harry Gee, Jr., who was the first Asian American to sit on a local transportation board. Two of the entertainment articles dealt with personalities: actress Margaret Cho and ice skater Kristi Yamaguchi. One article dispelled the model minority myth by taking an in-depth look at poverty among Asian Americans nationwide.

*Houston Post.* Table 39 shows the breakdown by type of story for the fifteen articles on Asian Americans that appeared in the Houston Post during the year studied (NOTE: The Houston Post ceased publication in April 1996).

Table 39. Article Types in the *Houston Post*, 1994–1995

| Type of Article | Number of Articles | Percent of Total |
|---|---|---|
| Human Interest | 6 | 40 % |
| Entertainment | 3 | 20 % |
| Politics | 3 | 20 % |
| Crime | 1 | 7 % |
| Health and Welfare | 1 | 7 % |
| Moral | 1 | 7 % |
| Total | 15 | |

This coverage was somewhat unusual in that the largest number of articles fell into the human interest category, and since there was only one article on Asian Americans and crime. Two of the political articles dealt with City Councilwoman Martha Wong. Coverage included an article on a 310-page report issued by the state government on the large numbers of Vietnamese Americans living in Texan cities, which, notably, was not covered in the *Houston Chronicle*.

*Los Angeles Times*. Table 40 shows the breakdown by type of story for the seventy-three articles on Asian Americans that appeared in the *Los Angeles Times* during the year studied.

Table 40. Article Types in *Los Angeles Times*, 1994–1995

| Type of Article | Number of Articles | Percent of Total |
| --- | --- | --- |
| Entertainment | 16 | 22 % |
| Human Interest | 13 | 18 % |
| Classic Arts | 12 | 16 % |
| Politics | 12 | 16 % |
| Moral | 7 | 10 % |
| Crime | 4 | 5 % |
| Defense | 3 | 4 % |
| Accidents | 2 | 3 % |
| Economics | 2 | 3 % |
| Health and Welfare | 2 | 3 % |
| Total | 73 | |

It comes as little surprise that the largest story category for the *Los Angeles Times* in this content analysis is entertainment, considering it is one of leading newspapers in the world for coverage of the entertainment industry. This is also one of the few newspapers in the content analysis to run articles related to accidents. In this case, the two accident articles dealt with the earthquake in Kobe, Japan. It is also interesting that crime related articles are few in number and that human interest, political, and articles dealing with moral issues were more abundant than crime articles. Some Asian American journalists surveyed said too many articles have run in the media overall on crimes committed against Korean Americans during the Los Angeles riots, and follow-up articles on racial tensions in that city, particularly between African Americans and Korean Americans. In the next section on sub-topics of the content analysis, this accusation will be further addressed. However, in looking at the article topics for the *Los Angeles Times*, there does not appear to be high coverage of Asian Americans and crime, but without knowing the actual number of crimes being committed in Los Angeles that involved Asian Americans during the year studied, as well as the nature and severity of the crimes, this becomes a somewhat mute point.

The political articles ranged in coverage of ethnic sub-groups of Asian Americans, including the reactions of Japanese Americans to a visit by Japan's emperor to political activism by Cambodian Americans and Vietnamese Americans. The economic and defense articles also represented a range of topics, as opposed to coverage in one area or of one ethnic sub-group.

*New York Times.* Table 41 shows the breakdown by type of story for the fifty-four articles on Asian Americans that appeared in the *New York Times* during the year studied.

Table 41. Article Types in the *New York Times*, 1994–1995

| Type of Article | Number of Articles | Percent of Total |
|---|---|---|
| Classic Arts | 12 | 22 % |
| Entertainment | 11 | 20 % |
| Human Interest | 9 | 17 % |
| Crime | 7 | 13 % |
| Politics | 4 | 7 % |
| Accidents | 3 | 6 % |
| Economic | 2 | 4 % |
| Health and Welfare | 2 | 4 % |
| Defense | 1 | 2 % |
| Education | 1 | 2 % |
| Moral | 1 | 2 % |
| Other | 1 | 2 % |
| Total | 54 | |

The *New York Times*' coverage of Asian Americans is similar to that in the *Los Angeles Times* when looking at story type as both newspaper gave the most coverage in the areas of entertainment, classic arts and human interest. Both of the accident articles dealt with the earthquake in Kobe, Japan, and the defense article concerned the internment of Japanese Americans in World War II. The one article that did not fall into a specific topic coding category was about Asian-born professionals who were moving back to their native countries due to increased job opportunities in those countries.

*St. Louis Post-Dispatch.* Table 42 shows the breakdown by type of story for the four articles on Asian Americans that appeared in the St. Louis Post-Dispatch during the year studied.

Table 42. Article Types in the *St. Louis Post-Dispatch*, 1994–1995

| Type of Article | Number of Articles of | Percent Total |
|---|---|---|
| Moral | 2 | 50 % |
| Crime | 1 | 25 % |
| Entertainment | 1 | 25 % |
| Total | 4 | |

With only four articles written on Asian Americans for a one-year period, it seems hardly pertinent to discuss the story type. However, the one entertainment story was also one of the few articles in the study to be on Thai Americans. Both of the stories in the moral category dealt with racism against Asian Americans, and the crime article dealt with a Vietnamese gang. One of the moral stories dealt with both Asian Americans and Native Americans, so it was not solely on an issue relating to Asian Americans.

*San Francisco Chronicle.* Table 43 shows the breakdown by type of story for the seventy articles on Asian Americans that appeared in the *San Francisco Chronicle* during the year studied.

San Francisco has by far the highest percentage of Asian Americans—14.8 percent of its 6.2 million residents—of any city served by a newspaper in the content analysis. So the breakdown by topic of the articles in the *San Francisco Chronicle* is particularly interesting in what it says about covering a large Asian American population. However, like the *Los Angeles Times* and *New York Times*, the *San Francisco Chronicle* had human interest and entertainment articles in the top three most covered topic areas. However, the *San Francisco Chronicle* gave the most coverage to human interest articles. The *San Francisco Chronicle*

Table 43. Article Types in the *San Francisco Chronicle*, 1994–1995

| Type of Article | Number of Articles of | Percent Total |
|---|---|---|
| Human Interest | 17 | 24 % |
| Entertainment | 14 | 20 % |
| Health and Welfare | 11 | 16 % |
| Moral | 9 | 13 % |
| Politics | 8 | 11 % |
| Classic Arts | 4 | 6 % |
| Crime | 3 | 4 % |
| Education | 2 | 3 % |
| Accidents | 1 | 1 % |
| Economic | 1 | 1 % |
| Total | 70 | |

devoted more stories to this topic area than any other newspaper in the content analysis other than the *Seattle Times*.

It is also notable that the *San Francisco Chronicle* devoted so few stories to crime and Asian Americans, which may or may not reflect an effort on that newspaper's part to not over-report on Asian gangs and other crimes. Again, without knowing the actual volume, type, and intensity of crimes involving Asian Americans which occurred in San Francisco during the year studied, it is impossible to draw concrete conclusions about the crime coverage. The one accident article dealt with the Kobe earthquake, and the one economic story discussed the economic hardships faced by Filipino American veterans of World War II. The eight political articles reflect the political involvement of Asian Americans in the San Francisco area at local, state, and national levels.

Finally, in looking at the range of articles in categories such as moral issues, the *San Francisco Chronicle* offered a variety of coverage both in actual story subjects and for the various ethnic subgroups of Asian Americans living in San Francisco.

*Seattle Times.* Table 44 shows the breakdown by type of story for the 215 articles on Asian Americans that appeared in the *Seattle Times* during the year studied.

Beyond the immense coverage of Asian Americans found in the *Seattle Times* in this content analysis, the variety of coverage within the various topic areas is also most impressive. Unfortunately, there is not enough space to fully describe the

Table 44. Article Types in the *Seattle Times*, 1994–1995

| Type of Article | Number of Articles of | Percent Total |
|---|---|---|
| Entertainment | 62 | 29 % |
| Human Interest | 40 | 19 % |
| Crime | 35 | 16 % |
| Classic Arts | 26 | 12 % |
| Politics | 21 | 10 % |
| Health and Welfare | 13 | 6 % |
| Moral | 8 | 4 % |
| Education | 4 | 2 % |
| Accidents | 3 | 1.4 % |
| Economic | 2 | 0.9 % |
| Defense | 1 | 0.5 % |
| Total | 215 | |

numerous types of stories within each topic area, particularly as compared to other newspapers. However, the *Seattle Times* gave the most coverage to what might be considered more obscure topics and/or ethnic groups compared to the other newspapers. For example, the *Seattle Times* covered art exhibits and performances representing lesser covered ethnic groups, such as Pacific Islanders and Filipino Americans. It is interesting that 41 percent of the total coverage of Asian Americans in the *Seattle Times* was related to entertainment or the classic arts.

As with the other accident articles, two of the three which appeared in the *Seattle Times* were about the Kobe, Japan, earthquake. The high number of political articles reflects the political participation and activism of Asian Americans living in Seattle. It also reflected what turned out to be a crisis concerning Washington state apple exports to Japan, which occurred during the year of the study. The *Seattle Times* had a relatively low volume of economic stories. This is a particularly relevant considering that city's importance to trade with Asia and the number of Asian business persons who have important contacts and dealings with the Asian American community in Seattle. So it is worth noting the low volume of articles covering that aspect of Seattle and its role as a key economic and business link between the United States and Asia.

Finally, Asian American crime-related articles received a lot of space in the *Seattle Times* during the year examined. As will be seen in the next section answering research question four, many of these articles reflect racial tensions in Seattle between Asian Americans and other minority groups and with Caucasians. During the year examined, a handful of racial incidents required continual coverage as communities dealt with raising awareness of the racial problems and how to prevent future racial tensions. Overall, the *Seattle Times* gave the highest coverage of Asian Americans for any newspaper in the content analysis, both in quantity and quality.

*Times-Picayune.* Table 45 shows the breakdown by type of story for the sixteen articles on Asian Americans that appeared in the *Times-Picayune* during the year studied.

Table 45. Article Types in the *Times-Picayune*, 1994–1995

| Type of Article | Number of Articles | Percent of Total |
|---|---|---|
| Human Interest | 9 | 56 % |
| Crime | 2 | 13 % |
| Entertainment | 2 | 13 % |
| Moral | 2 | 13 % |
| Other | 1 | 6 % |
| Total | 16 | |

More than half of the coverage of Asian Americans, as well as local, state, and national issues facing Asian Americans in the New Orleans area by the Times-Picayune was devoted to human interest articles. As will be seen in the next section of this chapter, most of the human interest articles were devoted to the active Vietnamese American community in New Orleans. The one article which did not appear to fall into a specific topic area dealt with a rife between Vietnamese gardeners and their landlord, and how that issue was being resolved.

*USA Today.* Table 46 shows the breakdown by type of story for the nineteen articles on Asian Americans that appeared in *USA Today* during the year studied.

This breakdown of story types for USA Today does not present many surprise results when considering the entertainment and soft news slant of this national newspaper. The only aspect that

Table 46.  Article Types in *USA Today*, 1994–1995

| Type of Article | Number of Articles | Percent of Total |
|---|---|---|
| Entertainment | 13 | 68 % |
| Classic Arts | 2 | 11 % |
| Accidents | 1 | 5 % |
| Education | 1 | 5 % |
| Human Interest | 1 | 5 % |
| Other | 1 | 5 % |
| Total | 19 | |

might be notable is just how much of the total coverage, more than three-fourths, is devoted to entertainment and classic arts. The accident article dealt with the Kobe earthquake, and the education article was a "model minority" piece about a Vietnamese immigrant who built a successful life in the United States.

*Wall Street Journal.* Table 47 shows the breakdown by type of story for the eight articles on Asian Americans that appeared in the *Wall Street Journal* during the year studied.

Table 47.  Article Types in the *Wall Street Journal*, 1994–1995

| Type of Article | Number of Articles | Percent of Total |
|---|---|---|
| Entertainment | 4 | 50 % |
| Human Interest | 3 | 38 % |
| Classic Arts | 1 | 13 % |
| Total | 8 | |

When analyzing these few articles which ran in the *Wall Street Journal* during a one-year period, it is crucial to consider this newspaper as one of the leading financial publications in the United States as well as internationally. Therefore, it is worth noting that there were no articles on Asian Americans which dealt specifically with Asian Americans and economic or financial topics. Two of the human interest articles were on economically oriented topics: one dealt with the monopoly Cambodian Americans have on the doughnut shops in California, and the other discussed that financial service firms are finally starting to target Hispanics and Asian Americans after years of ignoring minority groups. However, there were no articles on the immense contribution Asian Americans make as business leaders and in contributing to the strength of the American economy.

*Washington Post.* Table 48 shows the breakdown by type of story for the twenty articles on Asian Americans that appeared in the *Washington Post* during the year studied.

Table 48. Article Types in the *Washington Post*, 1994–1995

| Type of Article | Number of Articles | Percent of Total |
|---|---|---|
| Entertainment | 7 | 35 % |
| Politics | 3 | 15 % |
| Crime | 2 | 10 % |
| Human Interest | 2 | 10 % |
| Moral | 2 | 10 % |
| Classic Arts | 1 | 5 % |
| Defense | 1 | 5 % |
| Health and Welfare | 1 | 5 % |
| Science | 1 | 5 % |
| Total | 20 | |

The only science article relating to Asian Americans to be found in the entire 635 articles of the content analysis ran in the Washington Post. It dealt with a research project at the National Institutes of Health by an Asian American scientist. Also worth noting is that articles of a political nature received the second highest amount of coverage in the largest newspaper serving the nation's capital, but it is interesting that in a year's span the Washington Post found just three news items to cover on Asian Americans and politics, at local, state, and national levels.

In summary, in examining the coverage of Asian Americans by story topic, we see that this important minority group receives more soft news coverage in the form of entertainment articles than other types of articles. The types of stories to receive low coverage tend to be science and defense oriented. There is also low coverage devoted to economic news as it relates to Asian Americans. In general, the majority of newspapers in the content analysis did not offer a variety of story topics that reflected the numerous facets of Asian Americans and issues affecting Asian Americans.

**Research Question Four.** Research question four asks:

4) What thematic stereotypes are presented in each newspaper?

To answer this final research question related to content, the data were compared—using two variables in each comparison—in three different ways: 1) newspaper by article sub-topic, 2) type of story by Asian American ethnic sub-group, and, 3) Asian American ethnic sub-group by article sub-topic. The reason for the first analysis was to see if certain types of articles, such as stories on gang violence, appear consistency in a particular newspaper, which would reinforce a stereotype associated with Asian Americans. The second form of analysis was conducted to see if certain types of stories, such as entertainment articles, appear regularly in a newspaper with regard to a specific Asian American ethnic sub-group/s. The third analysis was done to see if certain sub-topics regularly appear in articles about specific ethnic sub-groups, thus reinforcing stereotypes about a particular ethnic sub-group, such as a pattern of gang violence articles on Vietnamese Americans. These results will first be presented for all newspapers, and then in the form of three tables (representing the three forms of comparison analysis) for each newspaper. Comments will follow each trio of tables.

As explained in Chapter Three, all 635 articles of the content analysis were coded for thematic sub-topics to see the amount of certain types of articles. Here are the abbreviated terms used in the upcoming tables (with some variations due to space constraints for certain tables) for those thematic sub-topics:

**All American Girl**—articles which discussed the television program *All-American Girl*, which was the first TV program with an all Asian cast of leading actors

**Festivals**—articles on an Asian festival such as Tet or Chinese New Year

**Gangs**— articles on Asian gangs

**Internment**—articles dealing with the internment of Japanese Americans during World War II

**Kobe**—articles associated with the earthquake in Kobe, Japan

**Model Minority**—articles with stereotypes associated with this term of Asian Americans as successful, unassuming, intelligent people

**Racism**—articles about racial issues and Asian Americans

**Yo Yo Ma**—articles about cellist Yo Yo Ma

**None**—articles with none of the thematic sub-topics listed above

Table 49 gives the breakdown of thematic sub-topics for all 635 articles in the content analysis. The articles which ran in the *Seattle Times* are broken out to demonstrate how those figures may have influenced the totals for each thematic sub-topic.

Table 49. Thematic Sub-Topics of Articles on Asian Americans in Eighteen Newspapers, 1994–1995

| Sub-Topic | Seattle Times | Other Newspapers | All Newspaper | Per-scent |
|---|---|---|---|---|
| None | 170 | 266 | 436 | 68.6 % |
| Racism | 19 | 41 | 60 | 9.4 % |
| All American Girl | 4 | 25 | 29 | 4.5 % |
| Festivals | 5 | 20 | 25 | 3.9 % |
| Gangs | 6 | 18 | 24 | 3.7 % |
| Yo Yo Ma | 2 | 22 | 24 | 3.7 % |
| Model Minority | 5 | 14 | 19 | 2.9 % |
| Internment | 2 | 7 | 9 | 1.4 % |
| Kobe | 2 | 7 | 9 | 1.4 % |
| Total ☐☐☐ | 215 | 420 | 635 | |

These results indicate that the majority of the content analysis articles had no thematic stereotypes or sub-topics, and the leading thematic sub-topic was articles on racism and Asian Americans. In fact, 9 percent of all articles on Asian Americans published in the newspapers for the year studied dealt with topics of racism. However, 69 percent of the total articles had no specific thematic sub-topic which could be translated into supporting stereotypes about Asian Americans. This result is interesting since the press is often accused of reinforcing stereotypes of minorities, including Asian Americans, via the types of stories they choose to cover.

Smaller chunks of articles dealt with the *All-American Girl* television program and Asian festivals, as well as discussing Yo Yo

Ma or articles on Asian gangs. It should be noted that articles on Yo Yo Ma were not considered "model minority" articles. One thematic sub-topic which was a complaint of many of the Asian American journalists surveyed—that too much media coverage reinforces the model minority stereotype of Asian Americans— cannot be seen in these results since only nineteen of the 635 articles, or 3 percent of the total articles, dealt with model minority subjects. Cellist Yo Yo Ma received more coverage than articles on the Asian American model minority stereotype.

It is interesting that topics related to the internment of Japanese Americans, fifty years prior to the time frame of the content analysis, continue to be the topic of newspaper articles. This observation is not meant to imply that covering news associated with such a dark period of American history is not important. In fact, it may surprise and disappoint many people that only nine articles were written in twenty of the largest newspapers in America in one year on issues relating to the Japanese internment, at the fifty-year anniversary marking the end of World War II. It would be interesting to compare articles on that historic event with articles on other historical events in the United States which resulted in extreme harm to a group of individuals.

Table 50 gives the second analysis made to answer research question four: breakdown of type of story for each ethnic sub-group of Asian Americans, as coded in the content analysis. This table is presented in two tiers due to space constraints.

The largest number of crime-related articles for any ethnic sub-group is with Vietnamese Americans, while many other groups have little to no crime articles. Vietnamese Americans also had a high number of entertainment articles and human interest articles. Chinese Americans and Japanese Americans were the only other ethnic sub-groups with more than ten entertainment articles. However, Chinese Americans and Vietnamese Americans had nearly twice an many human interest articles as Japanese Americans. Korean Americans also had a high number of human interest articles compared to the other ethnic sub-groups. What is most interesting for Korean Americans is that this group has the most political articles of any group, and with the exception of Chinese Americans with eleven political articles, most groups have very few to no articles which were political in nature. Most of the classic arts and entertainment articles, with the exception of those

Table 50. Types of Articles by Asian American Ethnic Sub-Group,
1994–1995

| Sub-Topic | AA | AI | CA | CAM | FA | HA | HAW | JA | KA | LA |
|---|---|---|---|---|---|---|---|---|---|---|
| None | 162 | 10 | 45 | 7 | 15 | 5 | 10 | 29 | 39 | 2 |
| Racism | 40 | 0 | 5 | 0 | 3 | 0 | 0 | 4 | 4 | 0 |
| AA Girl | 29 | 0 | 0 | 0 | 0 | 0 | 0 | 0 | 0 | 0 |
| Festivals | 8 | 0 | 4 | 0 | 3 | 1 | 1 | 1 | 1 | 0 |
| Gangs | 12 | 0 | 2 | 1 | 3 | 0 | 0 | 0 | 0 | 0 |
| Yo Yo Ma | 0 | 0 | 0 | 0 | 0 | 0 | 0 | 0 | 0 | 0 |
| Model Min. | 5 | 2 | 2 | 1 | 0 | 1 | 0 | 1 | 3 | 1 |
| Internment | 0 | 0 | 0 | 0 | 0 | 0 | 0 | 9 | 0 | 0 |
| Kobe | 0 | 0 | 0 | 0 | 0 | 0 | 0 | 9 | 0 | 0 |
| Totals | 256 | 12 | 58 | 9 | 24 | 7 | 11 | 53 | 47 | 3 |

| Sub-Topic | PA | PIA | TA | VA | Name | Other | Total |
|---|---|---|---|---|---|---|---|
| None | 6 | 10 | 6 | 36 | 52 | 24 | 36 |
| Racism | 0 | 1 | 0 | 3 | 0 | 0 | 60 |
| AA Girl | 0 | 0 | 0 | 0 | 0 | 0 | 29 |
| Festivals | 0 | 0 | 0 | 6 | 0 | 0 | 25 |
| Gangs | 0 | 0 | 0 | 6 | 0 | 0 | 24 |
| Yo Yo Ma | 0 | 0 | 0 | 0 | 24 | 0 | 24 |
| Model Min. | 0 | 0 | 0 | 2 | 0 | 1 | 19 |
| Internment | 0 | 0 | 0 | 0 | 0 | 0 | 9 |
| Kobe | 0 | 0 | 0 | 0 | 0 | 0 | 9 |
| Totals | 6 | 11 | 6 | 53 | 76 | 36 | 35 |

NOTE: Ethnic sub-groups have the following abbreviations: AA - Asian Americans as a whole, AI - Asian Indian, CA - Chinese Americans, CAM - Cambodian Americans, FA - Filipino Americans, HA - Hmong Americans, HAW - Hawaiian Americans, JA - Japanese Americans, KA - Korean Americans, LA - Laotian Americans, PA - Pakistani Americans, PIA - Pacific Islander Americans (except Hawaiians), TA - Thai Americans, VA - Vietnamese Americans, Name - main topic of story was on a prominent Asian American.

dealing with Asian Americans as a whole, fell into the name category. This is because many entertainment articles focused on a particular Asian American of prominence.

The five crime-related articles on Pakistani Americans were also a surprise, as were the six articles on Thai Americans, considering the low number of total articles published on these two ethnic sub-groups. It appears that without coverage of conductor Zubin Mehta, Asian Indians would not have had a single article published the entire year in any of the newspapers dealing with classic arts. Also, it should be noted that seven of the twelve articles on Asian Indians, or just more than half, were human interest stories.

Table 51 represents the final comparison made to answer research question four. It is a breakdown of thematic sub-topics for each ethnic sub-group of Asian Americans, as coded in the content analysis.

Table 51.  Thematic Sub-Topics in Eighteen Newspapers' Articles and
Asian American Ethnic Sub-Groups, 1994–1995

| Topic | AA | AI | CA | CAM | FA | HA | HAW | JA | KA | LA |
|---|---|---|---|---|---|---|---|---|---|---|
| Entertain. | 60 | 2 | 16 | 0 | 3 | 1 | 5 | 17 | 5 | 0 |
| Human Int. | 50 | 7 | 15 | 4 | 8 | 3 | 4 | 8 | 10 | 0 |
| Crime | 42 | 1 | 5 | 2 | 3 | 1 | 0 | 0 | 5 | 1 |
| Classic Arts | 17 | 2 | 4 | 0 | 0 | 0 | 0 | 5 | 1 | 0 |
| Politics | 26 | 0 | 11 | 1 | 3 | 0 | 1 | 4 | 13 | 0 |
| Moral | 24 | 0 | 4 | 0 | 4 | 0 | 0 | 4 | 7 | 0 |
| Health, Wel. | 24 | 0 | 2 | 2 | 0 | 2 | 0 | 0 | 1 | 1 |
| Education | 6 | 0 | 1 | 0 | 1 | 0 | 0 | 1 | 1 | 1 |
| Accidents | 0 | 0 | 0 | 0 | 0 | 0 | 0 | 9 | 1 | 0 |
| Economic | 4 | 0 | 0 | 0 | 2 | 0 | 1 | 0 | 2 | 0 |
| Defense | 1 | 0 | 0 | 0 | 0 | 0 | 0 | 5 | 0 | 0 |
| Other | 1 | 0 | 0 | 0 | 0 | 0 | 0 | 0 | 1 | 0 |
| Science | 1 | 0 | 0 | 0 | 0 | 0 | 0 | 0 | 0 | 0 |
| Totals | 256 | 12 | 58 | 9 | 24 | 7 | 11 | 53 | 47 | 3 |

| Topic | PA | PIA | TA | VA | Name | Other | Total |
|---|---|---|---|---|---|---|---|
| Entertainment | 0 | 3 | 6 | 11 | 27 | 0 | 156 |
| Human Interest | 1 | 2 | 0 | 16 | 1 | 2 | 131 |
| Crime | 5 | 3 | 0 | 10 | 0 | 1 | 79 |
| Classic Arts | 0 | 1 | 0 | 2 | 46 | 0 | 78 |
| Politics | 0 | 1 | 0 | 6 | 1 | 0 | 67 |
| Moral | 0 | 1 | 0 | 1 | 0 | 0 | 45 |
| Health & Welfare | 0 | 0 | 0 | 3 | 0 | 0 | 35 |
| Education | 0 | 0 | 0 | 1 | 0 | 0 | 12 |
| Accidents | 0 | 0 | 0 | 0 | 0 | 0 | 10 |
| Economic | 0 | 0 | 0 | 1 | 0 | 0 | 10 |
| Defense | 0 | 0 | 0 | 1 | 0 | 0 | 7 |
| Other | 0 | 0 | 0 | 1 | 1 | 0 | 4 |
| Science | 0 | 0 | 0 | 0 | 0 | 0 | 1 |
| Totals | 6 | 11 | 6 | 53 | 76 | 3 | 635 |

NOTE: Ethnic sub-groups have the following abbreviations: AA - Asian Americans as a whole, AI - Asian Indian, CA - Chinese Americans, CAM - Cambodian Americans, FA - Filipino Americans, HA - Hmong Americans, HAW - Hawaiian Americans, JA - Japanese Americans, KA - Korean Americans, LA - Laotian Americans, PA - Pakistani Americans, PIA - Pacific Islander Americans (except Hawaiians), TA - Thai Americans, VA - Vietnamese Americans, Name - main topic of story was on a prominent Asian American.

First, note that the majority of articles for all ethnic sub-groups did not have a sub-topic. The sub-topics—particularly in the cases of festivals, model minority, gangs, and racism—were coded to see if there was a pattern of articles with these stereotypes of Asian Americans. The sub-topic category with the most articles was racism, as mentioned earlier. These articles, however, were fairly evenly spread among the following ethnic sub-groups: Chinese Americans, Filipino Americans, Japanese Americans, Korean Americans, and Vietnamese Americans. Yet, for Filipino Americans the three articles dealing with racism represented 12.5 percent of the total twenty-four articles on Filipino Americans, compared to the four racism articles on Chinese Americans which represented 6.8 percent of the total fifty-eight articles on that group.

These data do not support the complaint from many of the Asian Americans surveyed that too much newspaper coverage is devoted to the stereotypical Chinese New Year stories and not much beyond that. In fact, Vietnamese Americans has the most festival articles, usually on the Tet celebrations, which is not a holiday recognized only by Vietnamese Americans—yet the media usually associate this festival with Vietnamese. Surprisingly, Filipino Americans had just one fewer festival article than Chinese Americans, and Japanese Americans, Hmong Americans, Hawaiian Americans, and Korean Americans all had just one festival-related article each.

Coding articles on cellist Yo Yo Ma in a sub-topic category proved useful, as 32 percent of the total seventy-six articles in the name category were on this one Asian American, which certainly raises a legitimate question: What type and magnitude of coverage would Asian Americans receive in terms of personality profiles if Yo Yo Ma decided to end his impressive performance career? Japanese Americans should also have a serious concern over coverage of that ethnic group since these data indicates 34 percent of the total fifty-three articles on Japanese Americans dealt with the World War II internment and the Kobe earthquake. Without these two events the coverage of Japanese Americans would drop of significantly, yet this large and diverse ethnic sub-group certainly has many more facets to their news which deserve coverage.

Since the *Seattle Times* alone had enough stories to see certain patterns in an 11 X 15 table (165 cells), we will display results only for that newspaper in Tables 52 and 53. Results for all other newspapers are in Appendix 9.

Of course, the mix of story topics as well as the number of Asian ethnic sub-groups covered is most impressive here. Fourteen ethnic sub-groups are represented in this year's worth of news coverage. The highest concentration of articles was, as stated earlier, entertainment and classic arts. There were also heavy coverage of crime, human interest, and political articles. It is interesting that Japanese Americans had eleven entertainment articles, and Korean Americans, as well as Filipino Americans had no entertainment articles. In fact, Thai Americans and Vietnamese Americans received more coverage in that category than nine other ethnic sub-

Table 52.　Type of Article and Asian American Ethnic Sub-Group in the *Seattle Times*, 1994–1995

| Article Topic | AA | AI | CA | FA | HA | HAW | JA | KA | LA |
|---|---|---|---|---|---|---|---|---|---|
| Accidents | 0 | 0 | 0 | 0 | 0 | 0 | 2 | 1 | 0 |
| Classic Arts | 15 | 1 | 4 | 0 | 0 | 0 | 2 | 0 | 0 |
| Crime | 19 | 1 | 0 | 3 | 0 | 0 | 0 | 2 | 1 |
| Defense | 0 | 0 | 0 | 0 | 0 | 0 | 1 | 0 | 0 |
| Economic | 0 | 0 | 0 | 1 | 0 | 0 | 0 | 1 | 0 |
| Education | 3 | 0 | 0 | 1 | 0 | 0 | 0 | 0 | 0 |
| Entertainment | 22 | 1 | 8 | 0 | 1 | 2 | 11 | 0 | 0 |
| Human Interest | 12 | 2 | 6 | 6 | 3 | 4 | 3 | 1 | 0 |
| Moral | 6 | 0 | 0 | 1 | 0 | 0 | 0 | 0 | 0 |
| Health & Welfare | 11 | 0 | 1 | 0 | 0 | 0 | 0 | 0 | 1 |
| Politics | 10 | 0 | 3 | 2 | 0 | 0 | 1 | 5 | 0 |
| Totals | 98 | 5 | 22 | 14 | 4 | 6 | 20 | 10 | 2 |

| Article Topic | PA | PIA | TA | VA | Other* | Name | Total |
|---|---|---|---|---|---|---|---|
| Accidents | 0 | 0 | 0 | 0 | 0 | 0 | 3 |
| Classic Arts | 0 | 1 | 0 | 0 | 0 | 3 | 26 |
| Crime | 5 | 3 | 0 | 1 | 0 | 0 | 35 |
| Defense | 0 | 0 | 0 | 0 | 0 | 0 | 1 |
| Economic | 0 | 0 | 0 | 0 | 0 | 0 | 2 |
| Education | 0 | 0 | 0 | 0 | 0 | 0 | 4 |
| Entertainment | 0 | 2 | 5 | 5 | 0 | 5 | 62 |
| Human Interest | 0 | 2 | 0 | 0 | 1 | 0 | 40 |
| Moral | 0 | 1 | 0 | 0 | 0 | 0 | 8 |
| Health & Welfare | 0 | 0 | 0 | 0 | 0 | 0 | 13 |
| Politics | 0 | 0 | 0 | 0 | 0 | 0 | 21 |
| Totals | 5 | 9 | 5 | 6 | 1 | 8 | 215 |

\* Burmese/Myanmarian Americans

Table 53.　Article Sub-Topics and Asian American Ethnic Sub-Grouips in the *Seattle Times*, 1994–1995

| Sub-Topic | AA | AI | CA | FA | HA | HAW | JA | KA | LA |
|---|---|---|---|---|---|---|---|---|---|
| All American Girl | 4 | 0 | 0 | 0 | 0 | 0 | 0 | 0 | 0 |
| Festivals | 0 | 0 | 1 | 2 | 1 | 1 | 0 | 0 | 0 |
| Gangs | 3 | 0 | 0 | 3 | 0 | 0 | 0 | 0 | 0 |
| Japanese Intern. | 0 | 0 | 0 | 0 | 0 | 0 | 2 | 0 | 0 |
| Kobe | 0 | 0 | 0 | 0 | 0 | 0 | 2 | 0 | 0 |
| Model Minority | 1 | 0 | 0 | 0 | 1 | 0 | 1 | 1 | 0 |
| Racism | 16 | 0 | 0 | 1 | 0 | 0 | 1 | 0 | 0 |
| Yo Yo Ma | 0 | 0 | 0 | 0 | 0 | 0 | 0 | 0 | 0 |
| None | 74 | 5 | 21 | 8 | 2 | 5 | 14 | 9 | 2 |
| Totals | 98 | 5 | 22 | 14 | 4 | 6 | 20 | 10 | 2 |

| Sub-Topic | PA | PIA | TA | VA | Other* | Name | Total |
|---|---|---|---|---|---|---|---|
| All American Girl | 0 | 0 | 0 | 0 | 0 | 0 | 4 |
| Festivals | 0 | 0 | 0 | 0 | 0 | 0 | 5 |
| Gangs | 0 | 0 | 0 | 0 | 0 | 0 | 6 |
| Japanese Intern. | 0 | 0 | 0 | 0 | 0 | 0 | 2 |
| Kobe | 0 | 0 | 0 | 0 | 0 | 0 | 2 |
| Model Minority | 0 | 0 | 0 | 0 | 1 | 0 | 5 |
| Racism | 0 | 1 | 0 | 0 | 0 | 0 | 19 |
| Yo Yo Ma | 0 | 0 | 0 | 0 | 0 | 2 | 2 |
| None | 5 | 8 | 5 | 6 | 0 | 6 | 170 |
| Totals | 5 | 9 | 5 | 6 | 1 | 8 | 215 |

\* Burmese/Myanmarian Americans

groups. The next table provides a futher breakdown of thematic stereotypes.

It is interesting that half of the gang-related articles deal with Filipino Americans and, unlike many other newspapers in the content analysis, none deals with Vietnamese Americans. Otherwise, there appear to be no strong concentrations of articles with thematic stereotypes for any specific Asian American ethnic sub-group. Overall, a large number of articles deal with Asian Americans and racism, but no other type of article sub-topic is strongly represented here. In fact, nearly 80 percent of the total 215 articles do not fall into a thematic stereotype category. This lack of thematic stereotypes in the *Seattle Times* says a great deal about a newspaper which gives a lot of coverage, and a variety of coverage, to the local Asian American community. It appears that the *Seattle Times* attempts to avoid writing stereotypical articles on Asian Americans, or avoid coverage which reinforces stereotypes of that minority group.

In summary, most of the newspapers in the content analysis did not give coverage of Asian Americans which fell into thematic stereotypes such as stories on Asians as the model minority. While there was not a clear pattern of associated gang violence with Vietnamese Americans, there were more articles on gangs which dealt with Vietnamese than with any other Asian American ethnic sub-group. There were no indications that newspapers in the content analysis were giving too much coverage to Chinese New Year and other Asian festivals. In some newspapers, ethnic sub-groups other than Chinese Americans received more coverage of festivals than did Chinese Americans. There was support that numerous articles dealt with Asian Americans and racism, which could be considered a thematic stereotype. Also, more than half the newspapers gave high coverage of Asian Americans to entertainment and classic arts stories. Overall, however, nearly 70 percent of the total 635 articles had no thematic stereotypes of Asian Americans.

## SURVEY

**Research Question Five.** Research question five asks:

5) How many Asian Americans are employed in the mainstream media?

To answer this question, results of the 1994 and 1995 American Society of Newspaper Editors' annual newsroom employment census of the nation's newspapers will first be presented, followed by the responses from the editors of each of the twenty mainstream newspapers searched in the content analysis for this book, listed in alphabetical order of newspaper title. These editors were asked for the number of Asian Americans working in their newsrooms and any editorial policies held by that newspaper concerning coverage of Asian Americans. Most newspaper editors who responded did not have a specific editorial policy concerning coverage of Asian Americans, other than their overall policies for fair, unbiased coverage of minorities in general. None of the style manuals for the newspapers in the study had specific entries on how to cover Asian Americans, or even the proper style on the term Asian American (i.e., for example, if the two words should be hyphenated).[11]

Overall, just over 50 percent of the newspaper editors (or representatives responding on an editor's behalf), or eleven, responded to the letters requesting newsroom policies, if any, concerning coverage of Asian Americans, as well as the number of minorities working in the newsrooms. The newspapers of editors who did not respond to the two letters and follow-up telephone messages were: 1) *Christian Science Monitor*, 2) *Denver Post*, 3) *Detroit News*, 4) *Detroit Free Press/Detroit News* and *Free Press*, 5) *Houston Post*, 6) *Michigan Chronicle*, 7) *Times-Picayune*, 8) *USA Today*, and, 9) *Washington Times*. All of the letter responses except one came from representatives of the editors. Only William F. Woo, former editor of the *St. Louis Post-Dispatch*, gave a personal response to the letter. Woo, a member of the Asian American Journalists Association, was also the only Asian American among the editors of the twenty mainstream newspapers surveyed. Woo resigned as editor of the *St. Louis Post-Dispatch* in the summer of 1996, after serving at the helm of that newspaper for nearly a decade and with a total of thirty-four years as a journalist at that newspaper (Fitzgerald, Editor & Publisher, Sept. 21, 1996).

Tables 54 through 57 give the results of the 1996 and 1995 American Society of Newspaper Editors' annual newsroom employment census of the nation's newspapers. All tables are presented in two tiers due to space constraints, and the percentages

Table 54. 1996 Annual Newsroom Employment Census of the American Society of Newspaper Editors for Minority Employees

| Job Category | Asian Americans No. | Percent | African Americans No. | Percent |
|---|---|---|---|---|
| Supervisors | 158 | 14 % | 562 | 19 % |
| Copy/Layout Eds. | 235 | 22 % | 459 | 15 % |
| Reporters | 491 | 45 % | 1,692 | 57 % |
| Photographers | 204 | 19 % | 268 | 9 % |
| Totals | 1,088 | | 2,980 | |

| Job Category | Hispanics No. | Percent | Native Americans No. | Percent |
|---|---|---|---|---|
| Supervisors | 324 | 18 % | 61 | 27 % |
| Copy/Layout Eds. | 272 | 15 % | 29 | 13 % |
| Reporters | 883 | 50 % | 95 | 42 % |
| Photographers | 289 | 16 % | 39 | 17 % |
| Totals | 1,768 | | 224 | |

SOURCE: American Society of Newspaper Editors.

represent the percent of the total of the minority group listed working in a specific job category (Tables 64 and 66) or the percent of the total of all minorities or whites within a specific job category (Tables 55 and 57).

Table 55. 1996 Annual Newsroom Employment Census of the American Society of Newspaper Editors for all Employees

| Job Category | Total Work Force | Minorities No. | Percent | Whites No. | Percent |
|---|---|---|---|---|---|
| Supervisors | 13,165 | 1,104 | 8.4 % | 12,061 | 91.6 % |
| Copy/Layout Eds. | 10,262 | 996 | 9.7 % | 9,266 | 90.3 % |
| Reporters | 25,774 | 3,161 | 12.3 % | 22,613 | 87.7 % |
| Photographers | 5,777 | 800 | 13.8 % | 4,977 | 86.2 % |
| Totals | 54,978 | 6,061 | | 48,916 | |

SOURCE: American Society of Newspaper Editors.

Table 56. 1995 Annual Newsroom Employment Census of the American Society of Newspaper Editors for Minority Employees

| Job Category | Asian Americans | | African Americans | |
| | No. | Percent | No. | Percent |
| --- | --- | --- | --- | --- |
| Supervisors | 167 | 16 % | 527 | 18 % |
| Copy/Layout Eds. | 222 | 21 % | 475 | 16 % |
| Reporters | 446 | 43 % | 1,680 | 57 % |
| Photographers | 208 | 20 % | 285 | 10 % |
| Totals | 1,044 | | 2,967 | |

| Job Category | Hispanics | | Native Americans | |
| | No. | Percent | No. | Percent |
| --- | --- | --- | --- | --- |
| Supervisors | 302 | 18 % | 53 | 27 % |
| Copy/Layout Eds. | 270 | 16 % | 29 | 15 % |
| Reporters | 822 | 49 % | 89 | 45 % |
| Photographers | 274 | 16 % | 25 | 13 % |
| Totals | 1,667 | | 196 | |

SOURCE: American Society of Newspaper Editors.

Table 57. 1995 Annual Newsroom Employment Census of the American Society of Newspaper Editors for all Employees

| Job Category | Total Work Force | Minorities | | Whites | |
| | | No. | Percent | No. | Percent |
| --- | --- | --- | --- | --- | --- |
| Supervisors | 12,817 | 1,049 | 8.2 % | 11,768 | 91.8 % |
| Copy/Layout Eds. | 9,832 | 996 | 10.1 % | 8,836 | 89.9 % |
| Reporters | 25,444 | 3,037 | 11.9 % | 22,407 | 88.1 % |
| Photographers | 5,747 | 792 | 13.8 % | 4,955 | 86.2 % |
| Totals | 53,840 | 5,874 | | 47,966 | |

SOURCE: American Society of Newspaper Editors.

This indicates that other than Native Americans, Asian Americans have the lowest number of any minority group surveyed working in the nation's newsrooms; just under five hundred total Asian Americans work as reporters across the country. Overall, in 1996 the 1,088 total Asian Americans made up only 1.98 percent of the total newsroom workforce, African Americans made up 5.42 percent (2,980 total African American journalists), Hispanics made up 3.22 percent (1,768 journalists), and Native Americans made up 0.41 percent (224 journalists) (ASNE news release, April 1996). Even though total minority newsroom employment has increased from 3.95 percent of all newsroom employees in 1978 to 11.02 percent in 1996, these percentages remain very low in comparison to the percent of the U.S. population these minorities represent and to the number of whites working in newsrooms (ASNE news release, April 1996). These numbers have more significance when one looks at the total newsroom census for 1996, as presented in Table 55.

With these figures, the need for the voice of more minorities to enter print journalism, including Asian Americans, becomes more evident. Note that as the level of responsibility and, in most cases, income increases (i.e., copy editors/layout editors and supervisors) the percentage of minorities holding these positions decreases and the percentage of whites increases. Tables 56 and 57 give this same data, which was collected by ASNE for 1995.

The number of Asian Americans in the print journalism workforce increased by forty-four from 1995 to 1996. However, the number of Asian American supervisors dropped by nine persons, and the number of photographers dropped by four persons from 1995 to 1996. Table 57 gives the overall number of minorities working in newsrooms as compared to whites in 1995.

The number of minorities in all job categories increased from 1995 to 1996, with the exception of the number of copy/layout editors, which remained at 996 for both years. The percentage of total minorities working in the print news profession took a bigger leap when compared to the percentage of whites, but that is largely due to the larger number of whites working in the news business during both years. Overall, this numbers support the need for more Asian Americans and other minorities to join the ranks in the print newspaper business.

What follows is a more macro look at the number of Asian Americans employed in the twenty newspapers of the content analysis. As mentioned earlier, only those newspapers which responded to the survey letter are listed, or an explanation of the response refusing to release the information in a letter is given. Newsroom personnel figures were provided in various formats, so these figures are not consistent for all newspapers responding and not all information provided by some newspapers is listed.

*Atlanta Journal-Constitution.* James Mallory, news personnel manager of the *Atlanta Journal and Constitution* responded on behalf of Editor Ron Martin (Mallory 1995, Letter to author). Table 58 is the breakdown of newsroom employees he provided, which were for 1994.

Table 58.  Ethnicity of Full-Time Newsroom Employees at the
*Atlanta Journal-Constitution* for 1994

| Minority | Number Employed |
|---|---|
| African Americans | 72 |
| Hispanics | 7 |
| Asian Americans | 7 |
| Native Americans | 1 |
| Total Minorities | 87 |
| Total professional staff | 467 |

Mallory explained the figures do not include copy messengers, secretaries, or librarians, except for the library director, who is considered a supervisor.

Out of a total of 467 employees on the professional staff of that newsroom, only seven are Asian American, which represents 1.5 percent of the total professional staff, compared to the 1.8 percent of Asian Americans who make up the population of Atlanta, Georgia. (See Table 20 in Chapter 4 of this book for all demographic percentages of Asian Americans living in the circulation areas of the twenty newspapers surveyed.)

**Boston Globe.**  Louisa Williams, assistant managing editor of the *Boston Globe*, responded on behalf of Editor Matt Storin (Williams 1995, Letter to author).  The newsroom personnel figures below do not include part-time staff members, and copy aide positions at the *Boston Globe* are usually filled as part-time positions using local college students, according to Williams.  These figures include the following job categories: supervisors; reporters; editors; photographers; and artists (including cartoonists and graphic artists), and do not include librarians or secretaries.  Table 59 lists the number of full-time employees of the *Boston Globe*'s newsroom as of November 1, 1995.

Table 59.  Ethnicity of Full-Time Employees at
the *Boston Globe* for 1995

| Minority | Number Employed |
|---|---|
| African Americans | 42 |
| Asian Americans | 18 |
| Hispanic Americans | 10 |
| Native Americans | 0 |
| Total Minorities | 70 |

Unfortunately, the letter did not specify the total number of newsroom personnel. However, of the seventy minority employees in that newsroom, eighteen are Asian American, or 25.7 percent of the total number of minorities who work in the *Boston Globe* newsroom. The portion of Asian Americans who make up the 4.1 million population of the Boston area is 2.9 percent.

**Chicago Tribune.** George Langford, public editor of the *Chicago Tribune*, responded on behalf of Editor Howard A. Tyner (Langford 1995, Letter to author). The figures in Table 60, which lists the minority employees in the *Chicago Tribune* newsroom for 1995, do not include copy aides.

Table 60. Ethnicity of Newsroom Employees at
the *Chicago Tribune* for 1995

| Minority | Number Employed |
| --- | --- |
| Supervisors: | |
|     Asian Americans | 1 |
|     African Americans | 7 |
|     Hispanics | 2 |
|     Native Americans | 1 |
|     Whites | 105 |
| Reporters/Writers: | |
|     Asian Americans | 1 |
|     African Americans | 24 |
|     Hispanics | 4 |
|     Native Americans | 1 |
|     East Indian | 1 |
|     Whites | 204 |
| Copy/Layout Editors: | |
|     Asian Americans | 5 |
|     African Americans | 24 |
|     Hispanics | 3 |
|     Native Americans | 0 |
|     East Indian | 1 |
|     Whites | 115 |
| Photographers/Artists: | |
|     Asian Americans | 4 |
|     African Americans | 4 |
|     Hispanics | 5 |
|     Native Americans | 0 |
|     Whites | 78 |
| Total Minorities | 88 |
| Total Professional Staff | 590 |

These figures indicate that out of the total 590 newsroom personnel, only thirteen are Asian Americans (which includes the two East Indians), or 2.2 percent of the total newsroom staff, and only two of the thirteen Asian Americans are supervisors. The portion of Asian Americans which lives in the Chicago area is 3.2 percent of the eight million total population there.

**Houston Chronicle.** Fernando Dovalina, assistant managing editor of the *Houston Chronicle*, responded on behalf of editor Jack Loftis (Dovalina 1995, Letter to author). The newsroom personnel figures provided were from the 1994 ASNE survey, and they do not include copy aides, secretaries, or librarians, except for the library director, who is considered a supervisor, or secretaries. The figures in Table 61 are for full-time reporters/writers, copy/design/wire editors, photographers/artists and supervisors who worked at the *Houston Chronicle* in 1994.

Table 61. Ethnicity of Newsroom Employees at
the *Houston Chronicle* in 1994

| Minority | Number Employed |
|---|---|
| Supervisors: | |
|     Asian Americans | 0 |
|     African Americans | 2 |
|     Hispanics | 3 |
|     Native Americans | 0 |
|     Whites | 47 |
| Reporters/Writers: | |
|     Asian Americans | 3 |
|     African Americans | 5 |
|     Hispanics | 8 |
|     Native Americans | 1 |
|     Whites | 113 |
| Copy/Layout Editors: | |
|     Asian Americans | 1 |
|     African Americans | 4 |
|     Hispanics | 4 |
|     Native Americans | 1 |
|     Whites | 50 |
| Photographers/Artists: | |
|     Asian Americans | 1 |
|     African Americans | 0 |
|     Hispanics | 2 |
|     Native Americans | 0 |
|     Whites | 31 |
| Total Minorities | 35 |
| Total Professional Staff | 276 |

According to the personnel figures, of the 276 newsroom employees accounted for, only five are Asian Americans, or 1.8 percent of the total newsroom employees, and none of those five Asian Americans are supervisors. In the Houston area, 3.5 percent of the total population of 3.7 million are Asian Americans.

**Los Angeles Times.** Susan Denley, director of editorial hiring and development, responded to the request on behalf of editor Shelby Coffey (Denley 1995, Letter to author). The figures listed below are for full-time professional staff, which includes reporters, editors, photographers, artists and designers. Table 62 gives the minority breakdown of the *Los Angeles Times* full-time newsroom staff for 1995. These figures do not include copy aides, secretaries, and other clerks.

Table 62. Ethnicity of Full-Time Employees at
the *Los Angeles Times* for 1995

| Minority | Number Employed |
|---|---|
| Hispanics | 60 |
| Asian Americans | 53 |
| African Americans | 42 |
| Native Americans | 1 |
| Total Minorities | 156 |

The total number of newsroom personnel was not provided in this letter. However, of the 156 minorities who work in the newsroom, fifty-three are Asian Americans or 34 percent of the total minorities who work in the newsroom. This represents the second largest ethnic/minority group in the *Los Angeles Times'* newsroom surpassed only by the sixty Latinos who work there. Asian Americans make up 9.2 percent of the total 14.5 million population of Los Angeles.

**New York Times.** Dennis Stern, associate managing editor of the *New York Times*, responded on behalf of Executive Editor Joseph Lelyveld (Stern 1995, Letter to author). Stern explained that "the number of minorities on our staff is information that we only use internally. We have a longstanding policy of not making such information public" (Stern 1994, Letter to author). Unfortunately, newsroom personnel figures for the *New York Times* were not available through any other source. However, 4.8 percent of New York City's 18 million population are Asian

Americans. This may be a somewhat irrelevant comparison since the *New York Times* has a widespread national and international readership.

**St. Louis Post-Dispatch.** William F. Woo, who resigned as editor of the St. Louis Post-Dispatch in the summer of 1996, was the only editor-in-chief of the twenty newspapers surveyed who personally responded to the letter (Woo 1995, Letter to author). Table 63 gives the 1995 personnel figures for that newspaper, which does not include part-time employees.

Table 63. Ethnicity of Full-Time Employees at
the *St. Louis Post Dispatch* for 1995

| Minority | Number Employed |
| --- | --- |
| African Americans | 27 |
| Asian Americans | 5 |
| Hispanics | 0 |
| Native Americans | 0 |
| Total Minorities | 32 |
| Total Full-Time Professionals | 260 |

So, 1.9 percent of the 260 total full-time newsroom personnel of the St. Louis Post-Dispatch are Asian Americans. This represents a higher percentage of Asian Americans in the newsroom when compared to the 0.9 percent of Asian Americans who make up the 2.4 million population of St. Louis.

**San Francisco Chronicle.** Marianne Chin, director of editorial hiring and development at the *San Francisco Chronicle*, responded on behalf of Publisher/Editor Richard T. Thieriot (Chin 1995, Correspondence to author). Table 64 is the personnel data she provided for all employees in that newspaper's newsroom for 1995.

Table 64. Ethnicity of Newsroom Employees,
*San Francisco Chronicle* for 1995

| Minority | Number Employed |
| --- | --- |
| Senior Managers: | |
|     Asian Americans | 2 |
|     African Americans | 0 |
|     Hispanics | 1 |
|     Native Americans | 0 |
|     Whites | 18 |

Continued on next page

## Table 64 continued

Assistant Editors:
| | |
|---|---|
| Asian Americans | 2 |
| African Americans | 1 |
| Hispanics | 1 |
| Native Americans | 0 |
| Whites | 15 |

Reporters:
| | |
|---|---|
| Asian Americans | 5 |
| African Americans | 7 |
| Hispanics | 5 |
| Native Americans | 1 |
| Whites | 103 |

Copy Editors:
| | |
|---|---|
| Asian Americans | 8 |
| African Americans | 6 |
| Hispanics | 0 |
| Native Americans | 0 |
| Whites | 57 |

Photographers/Artists:
| | |
|---|---|
| Asian Americans | 6 |
| African Americans | 1 |
| Hispanics | 1 |
| Native Americans | 0 |
| Whites | 24 |

Librarians:
| | |
|---|---|
| Asian Americans | 0 |
| African Americans | 4 |
| Hispanics | 0 |
| Native Americans | 0 |
| Whites | 11 |

Systems Technicians:
| | |
|---|---|
| Asian Americans | 1 |
| African Americans | 0 |
| Hispanics | 1 |
| Native Americans | 0 |
| Whites | 4 |

Editorial Assistants:
| | |
|---|---|
| Asian Americans | 3 |
| African Americans | 3 |
| Hispanics | 3 |
| Native Americans | 1 |
| Whites | 30 |

Copy Clerks:
| | |
|---|---|
| Asian Americans | 1 |
| African Americans | 3 |
| Hispanics | 1 |
| Native Americans | 0 |
| Whites | 4 |

Secretarial:
| | |
|---|---|
| Asian Americans | 1 |
| African Americans | 0 |
| Hispanics | 0 |
| Native Americans | 0 |
| Whites | 3 |
| Total Minorities | 69 |
| Total Professional Staff | 338 |

These figures indicate of the 338 total newsroom employees, twenty-nine are Asian Americans, or 8.6 percent of the newsroom staff. This represents the largest percentage of Asian Americans employed in a newsroom staff of those newspapers for which complete personnel data was provided. However, it is lower in proportion to the 14.8 percent of Asian Americans of the total 6.2 million population of the San Francisco area.

*Seattle Times.* Administrative assistant Belinda Mathers responded on behalf of the *Seattle Times'* vice president and executive editor Michael R. Fancher (Mathers 1995, Letter to author). Table 65 are the newsroom personnel figures she provided for 1995.

Table 65. Ethnicity of Newsroom Employees at
the *Seattle Times* for 1995

| Minority | Number Employed |
|---|---|
| Asian Americans | 24 |
| African Americans | 14 |
| Hispanics | 10 |
| Native Americans | 0 |
| Total Minorities | 48 |
| Total Newsroom Employees | 300 |

Asian Americans make up the largest minority/ethnic group in this newsroom. Of the three hundred newsroom employees at the *Seattle Times*, twenty-four are Asian Americans, which represents 8 percent of the total newsroom staff. This is higher than the proportion of Asian Americans in the 2.5 million Seattle area. Of that population, 6.4 percent are Asian Americans.

*Wall Street Journal.* Administrative Assistant Patricia Broderick responded on behalf of Robert L. Bartley, editor of the *Wall Street Journal* (Broderick 1995, Letter to author). The newsroom personnel figures for the *Wall Street Journal* include those who work in the Editorial Department, which, for budget purposes, is completely separate from the News Department.

According to Carolyn Phillips, assistant managing editor for the newspaper, "The same editors who decide hiring for newsroom positions have zero sway on responsibility for what the editorial page is doing. For the Journal that makes a difference because we end up folding twenty-seven news [Editorial Department] positions that don't reflect the same diversity the News Department has. We are probably one of the few newspapers in the country who are set up this way" (Phillips 1996, Telephone interview with the author). Table 66 gives the full-time newsroom personnel figures for 1995 for the *Wall Street Journal*.

Table 66. Ethnicity of Full-Time Newsroom Employees at the *Wall Street Journal* for 1995

| Minority | Number Employed |
|---|---|
| Supervisors: | |
| Asian Americans | 2 |
| African Americans | 8 |
| Hispanics | 3 |
| Native Americans | 0 |
| Whites | 104 |
| Reporters/Writers: | |
| Asian Americans | 15 |
| African Americans | 13 |
| Hispanics | 9 |
| Native Americans | 0 |
| Whites | 169 |
| Copy/Layout Editors: | |
| Asian Americans | 6 |
| African Americans | 6 |
| Hispanics | 8 |
| Native Americans | 0 |
| Whites | 65 |
| Photographers/Artists: | |
| Asian Americans | 0 |
| African Americans | 1 |
| Hispanics | 0 |
| Native Americans | 0 |
| Whites | 10 |
| Total Minorities | 71 |
| Total Professional Staff | 419 |

It is interesting that the *Wall Street Journal* employs the most Asian American reporters of any newspaper responding to this survey. Like the *New York Times*, the *Wall Street Journal* does not serve a single city so no population portions of Asian Americans should be offered here.

**Washington Post.** Jana Long, assistant to the director of recruiting and hiring, responded on behalf of *Washington Post* editor Leonard Downie (Long 1995, Letter to author). Table 67 gives the newsroom personnel figures for the *Washington Post* for 1995, as provided by Long. In the table the professional staff includes: managing editors, assignment editors, copy editors, reporters, directors of recruiting, training and research, photographers, and artists. The administrative and technical support staff includes: news systems employees, assistant librarians, confidential secretaries, administrative aides, editorial aides, news aides, and copy aides.

Table 67. Ethnicity of Full-Time Newsroom Employees at the *Washington Post* for 1995

| Minority or other Classification | Number Employed |
|---|---|
| Total Newsroom Employees: | 665 |
| Total Newsroom by Minorities | |
| Asian Americans: | 22 |
| African Americans: | 96 |
| Hispanics: | 14 |
| Native Americans: | 2 |
| Whites: | 531 |
| Total Newsroom by Type of Job | |
| Professionals: | 562 |
| Administrative Support: | 103 |
| Professional Staff: | |
| Whites: | 445 |
| Minorities : | 107 |
| Asian Americans: | 16 |
| African Americans: | 76 |
| Hispanics: | 13 |
| Native Americans: | 2 |
| Administrative and Technical Support Staff: | |
| Whites: | 76 |
| Minorities: | 27 |
| Asian Americans: | 6 |
| African Americans: | 20 |
| Hispanics: | 1 |
| Native Americans: | 0 |

These figures indicate of the 665 total newsroom employees, twenty-two, or 3.3 percent, are Asian Americans. This is lower than the overall proportion of Asian Americans to the Washington, D.C.'s, population of 3.9 million. Approximately 5.1 percent of those residents are Asian Americans.

In summary, while efforts to hire more Asian Americans in the past twenty years have increased the number of Asian Americans in newsrooms, this fastest growing minority group in the United States is still under represented in comparison to the nearly 3 percent of the U.S. population now made up by Asian Americans. Nearly all the newspapers responding to the survey indicated that the number of Asian Americans working in their newsrooms is a smaller proportion of the total newsroom staff compared to the proportion of Asian Americans living in the circulation area of the respective newspaper. Some newspapers have poor records of hiring Asian Americans and other minority groups. Other newspapers, such as the *Seattle Times* and the *San Francisco Chronicle*, have much better records of strong hiring of Asian Americans in their newsrooms. Overall, however, much more hiring of Asian Americans needs to occur on the staffs of newspapers if it is to match representations in the general population.

*Research Question Six.* Research question six is actually two questions which will be addressed separately. The entire question asks:

6) How do Asian Americans working in the mainstream media assess coverage of Asian Americans? How do editors of Asian American publications assess coverage?

The first half of research question six will be answered by studying the results of questions three and four from the survey of five hundred Asian American journalists, while the second half will be answered by studying the survey responses from the editors of the twenty leading Asian American publications discussed in Chapters 3 and 4. What follows are the responses to the first half of research question six, preceded by an overview of the overall survey responses.

*Overview of Survey Responses.* Of the five hundred Asian American journalists who were surveyed, ninety-six responded to the survey, three respondents said they were not Asian Americans and therefore could not answer the survey, eighteen sent letters to explain that they either could not respond to the survey or requested telephone interviews, three surveys were returned due to address changes with no forwarding addresses, and one survey was returned with a note from an employee that the addressee no longer worked at that place of employment. Therefore, there were a total of 121 responses of some sort to the original five hundred survey letters (and the follow-up letters sent to those who did not respond to the first survey request).

After subtracting out the three responses from persons who said they were not Asian Americans, as well as the three unopened surveys returned for addresses no longer in use, and the letter explaining that a respondent no longer worked at the media organization to which the survey was sent, there remained 114 responses. However, eighteen of those respondents either said they could not respond to the survey (usually with no explanation of why), or they requested a telephone interview with the book's author. In the sample original survey letter sent to the respondents, the option for a telephone interview with the book author was offered if the journalists were too busy to write out their survey responses. However, after that letter was sent out, and after the follow-up letter was sent, it was determined that to mix written responses and responses received over the telephone represented two very different methods of seeking responses and that those two types of responses should not be mixed together in the analysis. Appendix 10 gives breakdowns by sex, occupation, and state of employment of those eighteen persons who responded to the survey with a letter, but who did not actually answer the four survey questions.

Both Babbie and Stempel warn against mixing methods of seeking responses within the same survey and they attempting to analyze those responses together (Babbie 1995; Stempel and Westley 1989). Therefore, no telephone surveys were conducted by the author and those journalists requesting telephone interviews were contacted and asked to send their responses in writing. So, after subtracting those eighteen letters from respondents who did not answer the survey, ninety-six surveys remained to be analyzed, both quantitatively and qualitatively.

However, added to the ninety-six responses was the survey response from one of the editors of the leading twenty Asian American publications (who asked to remain anonymous), as well as the survey response from Dean Wong, Editor of the *International Examiner*. Therefore, the final number of responses that were analyzied was ninety-eight. Of that total, forty-five respondents, or 45.9 percent of the total, agreed to give their name and occupation (including Wong), while fifty-three respondents, or 54.1 percent of the total, requested anonymity (including the editor of a leading Asian American publication just mentioned).

So this represented an overall response rate of ninety-six out of five hundred (without the two additional responses from the previous section added into the total), or a 19.2 percent response rate, and a response rate (when adding in those last two responses of the two Asian American publication editors) of ninety-eight out of 502, or a 19.5 percent response rate. This is a relatively poor response rate for a survey, so the results should be considered in the context of this low overall response rate.

The response represents a fairly even split between those who requested anonymity (54.1 percent of the total ninety-eight respondents) and those who did not (45.9 percent of the total respondents). The split between men and women respondents was thirty-six men, or 37.7 precent of all respondents, and sixty-two women, or 63.3 percent of respondents. This was a fairly good reflection of the gender breakdown of the total five hundred surveyed (which was 61.6 percent women, or 308; 35.0 percent men, or 175; and 3.4 percent where sex could not be determined by the name, or seventeen). The sex of all ninety-eight total survey respondents was able to be determined by the name or salutation in the AAJA address list.

The breakdown by medium for the place of work of survey respondents indicated different proportions from the medium breakdown of the original five hundred surveyed (which was 65.4 percent in print journalism, or 327; 27.6 percent in television, or 138; and 7.0 percent in radio, or 35 persons). Of the ninety-eight survey respondents, most work in print (58.2 percent or fifty-seven persons), followed by those who work in television (38.8 percent or thirty-eight persons), and only three respondents, or 3.1 percent of the total ninety-eight respondents, work in radio.

Table 68. Sex and Occupation of Asian American Journalists: Survey Respondents

| Sex | | Number | Percent Total |
|---|---|---|---|
| Men: | | 36 | 37.7 % |
| Print: | 24 | | |
| Television: | 12 | | |
| Radio: | 0 | | |
| Women: | | 62 | 63.3 % |
| Print: | 33 | | |
| Television: | 26 | | |
| Radio: | 3 | | |

Table 69.  Media Occupation of Asian American Journalists: Survey
Respondents

| Media Occupation | Number | Percent of Total |
|---|---|---|
| Print | 57 | 58.2 % |
| Television | 38 | 38.8 % |
| Radio | 3 | 3.1 % |
| Total | 98 | |

Table 70.  States Where Asian American Journalists Work:
Survey espondents

| State | Number of Respondents |
|---|---|
| California | 21 |
| New York | 13 |
| Washington | 8 |
| Massachusettes | 5 |
| Pennsylvania | 5 |
| Washington, D.C. | 5 |
| Illinois | 4 |
| Oregon | 4 |
| Texas | 4 |
| Florida | 3 |
| Michigan | 3 |
| New Jersey | 3 |
| Virginia | 3 |
| Hawaii | 2 |
| Missouri | 2 |
| Arizona | 1 |
| Idaho | 1 |
| Kansas | 1 |
| Kentucky | 1 |
| Louisiana | 1 |
| Nevada | 1 |
| North Carolina | 1 |
| Ohio | 1 |
| Rhode Island | 1 |
| South Dakota | 1 |
| Vermont | 1 |
| Wisconsin | 1 |
| Total Respondents | 98 |

Tables 68 to 70 give a complete breakdown of the total
respondents to the survey by sex, media occupation, and state
where the respondents work.

What follows is a look at how survey questions three and four
were answered by the respondents. Each question will be restated

at the beginning of the corresponding sub-section for the reader's convenience.

*Statistical Analysis of the Responses to Question Three.* Survey question three asked respondents:

> In your opinion, what is being done right in the media today in covering Asian Americans and issues affecting Asian Americans?

As explained in Chapter Four, the answers to this open-ended question were coded in one of the following categories: 1) very little, 2) some right, or 3) not sure. The overall response to this question was fairly evenly split between "very little," which received forty-three answers, or 43.9 percent of respondents, and "some things are being done right" (hereafter called "some right"), as indicated in Table 71. Only seven respondents, or 7.1 percent, said they were "not sure."

Table 71. Positive Media Efforts: Responses to Survey of Asian American Journalists

| Answer | Number of Answers | Percent of Total |
|---|---|---|
| Very Little | 43 | 43.9 % |
| Some Right | 48 | 49.0 % |
| Not sure | 7 | 7.1 % |
| Total | 98 | |

A chi square analysis was done for the answers "very little" and "some right," but not for the answer "not sure" due to the small number of answers in that category. The chi square value at the 0.05 level for one degree of freedom is 3.84. The value of the first two answers is .754, which is larger than 3.84. Therefore, the difference between the answers for "very little" and "some right" is a real difference and did not occur by chance.

Table 72 gives a breakdown by media profession of the respondents for each answer category.

Table 72. Positive Media Efforts: Percent by Media Profession of Survey respondents

| Response | Number Responding | Percent of Total in Each Media Profession |
|---|---|---|
| Print Journalists: | | |
| Very Little | 22 | 39 % |
| Some Right | 33 | 58 % |

Continued on next page

Table 72 continued

| | | |
|---|---|---|
| Not Sure | 2 | 3 % |
| Total Print | 57 | |
| Television Journalists: | | |
| Very Little | 19 | 50 % |
| Some Right | 14 | 37 % |
| Not Sure | 5 | 13 % |
| Total TV | 38 | |
| Radio Journalists: | | |
| Very Little | 2 | 67 % |
| Some Right | 1 | 33 % |
| Not Sure | 0 | 0 % |
| Total Radio | 3 | |

While this information is interesting, it has little statistical significance given the sampling error between print journalists and broadcast journalists of 21 percent.

The Pease and Smith study of minority journalists mentioned in Chapter Three offers a barometer for comparison for the results to this research question (Pease and Smith 1991). In their study, Pease and Smith asked respondents "How well do you think your newspaper covers minority communities and issues within your coverage area?" (25). The question is framed differently from this research question, but the overall information sought is related. The Pease and Smith survey found that of the 130 Asian American respondents, the following results for answer categories, as presented in Table 73.

Table 73. Results of 1991 Study Asking Asian American Journalists How Well They Thought Their Newspaper Covered Minority Issues

| | Percent of Total 130 Asian Americans | |
|---|---|---|
| Answer | Men | Women |
| Very well | 1.8 % | 1.5 % |
| Pretty well | 24.2 % | 25.4 % |
| Marginally | 50.0 % | 59.7 % |
| Poorly | 21.0 % | 13.4 % |

SOURCE: Pease and Smith 1991, Ohio Journalism Monographs, 25.

In contrast, the respondents to this book's survey question three, there was closer to a fifty-fifty split between respondents who said "very little" is being done right in the media today in covering Asian Americans, and those who responded that some things were being done right. The Pease and Smith study in 1991 found much more pessimism—close to 75 percent saying their newspaper was doing a marginal to poor job covering minority issues, and approximately 25 percent saying their newspaper was doing very well to pretty well. Because of this survey's low response rate, it is hard to tell if Asian Americans were really feeling better in 1995 about coverage.

**Qualitative Analysis of the Responses to Question Three.** Interestingly, many of the responses to this question were twisted into critiquing what is not being done right in covering Asian Americans and issues facing Asian Americans (see Appendix 11). Many respondents complained about surface coverage of stereotypical stories such as Chinese New Year, immigrants, and educationally successful Asian children.

However, credit is given to the coverage advancing in certain areas, particularly in cities with large Asian American populations such as Seattle, San Francisco and Los Angeles. Some journalists even cited specific efforts, like news editors arranging meetings with Asian American community leaders, as positive steps in the right direction.

In summary, the respondents were fairly split between saying very little is being done right and some things are being done right in the media today in covering Asian Americans and issues facing Asian Americans, and about 7 percent said they were not sure of their answer to this question. A larger portion of television journalists said very little is being done right in coverage of Asian Americans, compared to print journalists. Many respondents said there is too much lip-service coverage paid to standard articles such as Chinese New Year, and success stories of Asian immigrants. Many respondents also said that newspapers covering cities with larger populations of Asian Americans do a better job of covering the minority group compared to newspapers with smaller Asian American populations.

**Statistical Analysis of the Responses to Question Four.** Survey question four asked respondents:

> In your opinion, what is being done wrong in the media
> today in covering Asian Americans and issues facing Asian
> Americans?

Since several types of answers could be given for this open-ended question, the responses were coded for overall complaints, as explained in Chapter Four, for the following categories: 1) too many stereotypes used in how Asian Americans are covered (hereafter, "stereotypes"), 2) too much negative coverage of Asian Americans (hereafter, "negative"), 3) nothing seriously wrong (hereafter "nothing serious"), and 4) not sure.

However, after reading these responses, one discovers that very few persons responded "nothing serious" or "not sure," and that other categories of answers seemed to be cropping up. Those other categories were: 1) not enough coverage of Asian Americans (hereafter, "not enough"), 2) too much ignorance in reporting on Asian Americans (hereafter, "ignorance"), 3) too much lumping together of all Asian Americans and not enough recognition of the differences between ethnic sub-groups of Asian Americans (hereafter, "lumping"), 4) Asian Americans are not included in stories on minority issues (hereafter, "not a valid minority"), and finally, 5) more Asian Americans need to be hired in newsrooms and broadcast stations (hereafter, "hire Asian Americans).

So, this second set of codes was added in the original coding process to give the reader a better understanding of how respondents answered this crucial open-ended question. In all, there was a choice of nine codes. A few answers still did not fall under these codes, and are not included in the totals. Multiple coding was permitted with this question, as was permited with survey questions one through three earlier. However, none of the answers to the first three survey questions fell into more than one coding category, but with the fourth question most respondents listed several complaints, which resulted in multiple codes.

For this question, we calculated frequencies for the number of respondents whose answers fell within each of the coding categories; we then further broke those answers down by the respondents' place of work. Table 74 gives the results to survey question four.

Table 74. Wrong Media Coverage of Asian Americans: Responses to Survey of Asian American Journalists

| Answer | Number of Answers | Percent of Total Repondents* |
|---|---|---|
| Not Enough | 70 | 71.4 % |
| Stereotypes | 48 | 49.0 % |
| Negative | 22 | 22.4 % |
| Hire Asian Americans | 19 | 19.4 % |
| Lumping | 14 | 14.3 % |

Continued on next page

| Table 74 continued | | |
|---|---|---|
| Not a Valid Minority | 6 | 6.1 % |
| Ignorance | 7 | 7.1 % |
| Nothing Serious | 1 | 1.0 % |
| Not Sure | 2 | 2.0 % |
| Total Respondents | 98 | |

* Total sums to more than 100 percent due to multiple responses.

Table 74 indicates that the biggest complaint about the media's coverage of Asian Americans and issues affecting Asian Americans is that there is not enough coverage, with 71.4 percent of the total ninety-eight respondents, or seventy, citing this problem. The second main complaint, cited by forty-eight of the respondents or 49 percent, was that coverage of Asian Americans tends to reinforce stereotypes. The next most cited complaint was that coverage is negative (twenty-two respondents, or 22.4 percent), followed by the criticism that more Asian Americans need to be hired in the media (nineteen respondents, 19.4 percent), then that Asian Americans are too often lumped as one whole rather than reported on as diverse ethnic sub-groups (fourteen, 14.3 percent).

Those complaints cited the least were two people who said they were "not sure" what problems, if any, there were in current media coverage of Asian Americans, one person who said nothing too serious was wrong in the coverage, seven persons who cited problems of ignorance in reporting on Asian Americans, and six people who said Asian Americans are not included often enough in coverage of minorities.

Some other comments that did not fit into the coding categories were that too often only festivals such as Chinese New Year, dragon dances, and Tet receive much coverage. Many people complained about the image portrayed in news stories that immigrants are a drain to the social system of the United States when, in fact, many Asian immigrants do not depend on welfare or other social assistance and contribute to thriving economies. One person complained that most news of Asian Americans only deals with Chinese Americans and Japanese Americans. Finally, a few of respondents said that the recent coverage of the O.J. Simpson trial painted race issues in the United States as merely black and white.

The Pease and Smith study on the impact of racial diversity at newspapers also offers some comparison to the results to this survey question (Pease and Smith 1991). Several comments from minority journalists about a lack of understanding of minority perspectives on news were offered in that monograph. For example, an Asian American photographer was cited as describing his frustrations with explaining the importance of covering minority issues to his white newsroom colleagues: "I talk about this often with co-workers in the newsroom (better coverage of minorities). Sometimes it feels like talking to a rock—they just don't understand what I'm saying. . . . We have a long way to go at this paper before the news really reflects what's happening in the community" (25-26). This comment, and comments in the Pease and Smith study from journalists of other minorities, are very similar to the complaints registered by Asian Americans in response to this survey question (see Appendix 12). Therefore, this book's results to this question closely mirror the results to a similar question in the Pease and Smith study. This represents a significant strengthening of the sparse scholarship in the area of how minority journalists, particularly Asian Americans, perceive minorities are being covered in the media.

**Qualitative Analysis of the Responses to Question Four.** In reading the numerous and lengthy answers to survey question four in Appendix 12, one immediately sees that most all respondents had passionate, angry and articulate opinions on what the media are doing wrong today in covering Asian Americans and issues affecting Asian Americans. One begins to get a sense from reading these comments that these Asian American journalists feel forgotten in today's news media, and much maligned by outmoded stereotypes, including the false concept that Asians are passive, smart, nerds, and that the men lack sex appeal or leadership abilities.

On the whole these answers were much longer than the answers to the first three survey questions, which indicates that respondents had a lot of opinions on what is wrong and how to improve the situation. Over and over again we see suggestions that one solution would be to hire more Asian Americans in the newsroom, and to hire interpreters to give accurate and proper coverage to Asian immigrants.

The Asian American journalists said that there is not enough coverage in the media today being devoted to Asian Americans and issues facing Asian Americans. The coverage that exists, many said, concentrates too much on articles which reinforce stereotypes of

Asian Americans, including articles on Asian Americans as being a "model minority." Often coverage of Asian Americans are lumped into coverage of other minorities, according to 14 percent of the respondents. Other problems in coverage, as seen by some of the respondents, were that too much news coverage about Asian Americans is negative, such as stories on Asian gang violence. Finally, about 7 percent of the respondents said too much of media coverage of Asian Americans, or lack of coverage, reflects ignorance on the part of editors and reporters concerning Asian Americans and issues facing Asian Americans. The responses to the fourth survey question were, overall, the longest and most passionate when compared to responses to the first three survey questions.

On a positive note, some respondents said newspapers in cities with large populations of Asian Americans are making more efforts to properly cover those communities. For example, reporters who speak native languages of Asian immigrants are being sent to cover stories on those immigrant groups. Overall, however, most media organizations in print, television, and radio are not doing enough to properly cover Asian Americans, an overwhelming majority of respondents said.

**Second Half of Research Question Six.** To restate, the second half of research question six asks:

> 6) How do editors of Asian American publications assess coverage (of Asian Americans)?

To answer this question, the responses from the survey sent to the editors of the twenty leading Asian American publications, as discussed in Chapters Two and Four, will be presented. The response from this segment of the book was a disappointing six letters, or 30 percent of those twenty editors contacted, making it the third worst response rate of any section of the book research (see Appendix 5 for the list of the twenty leading Asian American publications). Responses were received from *The Hawaiian Journal of History, Critical Mass: A Journal of Asian American Criticism, Filipinas Magazine, Northwest Asian Weekly, KoreAm Journal,* and the *International Examiner.*

Only two of the respondents answered the four survey questions, one of whom asked to remain anonymous. The other survey respondent was Dean Wong, editor of the International Examiner. This means the actual response rate on the survey portion of the twenty letters sent to the editors of leading Asian American publications had a 10 percent response rate. Both Wong's and the anonymous respondent's answers were incorporated into the larger survey responses of the five hundred Asian American journalists who were also sent the survey consisting of four questions. However, the content of those two survey responses can be found in Appendix 13 (Wong's responses) and in Appendix 14 (responses from the editor who asked to remain anonymous) so that these unique perspectives of two editors of leading Asian American publications can be considered separately from the other Asian American journalists surveyed.

Some of the other responses to the request for information about the publications were relatively short; therefore, the text of these letters will not be reprinted. None of the respondents was able to provide a comprehensive list of articles on Asian Americans and the media which had run in their publications. Appendix 15 gives a summary of the responses.

Since the response rate from the editors of the twenty leading Asian American publications to the four survey questions was so low, these responses were not be statisically analyzed separately since they would have no statistical significance. It would also be improper to translate the two survey responses received from editors of Asian American publications as applying to the entire group of leading editors, although they offer insight into the dissatisfaction these two editors see in media coverage of Asian Americans.

**Research Question Seven.** Research question seven asks:

> 7) How do Asian Americans working in the mainstream media feel about their jobs in terms of positive and negative experiences?

The answers to survey questions one and two will answer this research question. What follows are the responses to those two survey questions.

**Statistical Analysis of Responses to the Survey Question on Negative Job Experiences.** The first question of the survey asked:

> Have you ever had any negative experiences on the job that you feel were related to your ethnic status as an Asian American?

Table 75 gives the breakdown of responses to that question.

Table 75. Responses to Survey of Asian American Journalists About
Negative Job Experiences

| Had Negative Job Experience? | Number of Answers | Percent of Total |
|---|---|---|
| Yes | 70 | 71.4 % |
| No | 22 | 22.4 % |
| Not sure | 6 | 6.1 % |
| Total | 98 | |

The overall response was overwhelmingly "yes," with seventy persons answering "yes," or 71.4 percent of the total ninety-eight respondents, and twenty-two answering "no," or 22.4 percent of respondents, and only six persons answering "not sure" (6.1 percent). A chi square analysis was done for the answers "yes" and "no," but not for the answer "not sure" due to the small number of answers in that category. The chi square value at the 0.05 level for one degree of freedom is 3.84. The value of the first two answers is 23.877 is larger than 3.84. Therefore, the difference between the answers for "yes" and "no" is a real difference and did not occur by chance.

Table 76 gives the breakdown by media profession of respondents to the answers to survey question one.

Table 76. Responses by Media Profession to Survey Question About
Negative Job Experience

| Had Negative Job Experience? | No. Responding | Percent of Total in Each Media Profession |
|---|---|---|
| Print Journalists: | | |
| Yes | 40 | 70 % |
| No | 13 | 23 % |
| Not Sure | 4 | 7 % |
| Total Print | 57 | |
| Television Journalists: | | |
| Yes | 28 | 74 % |
| No | 9 | 24 % |
| Not Sure | 1 | 2 % |
| Total TV | 38 | |
| Radio Journalists: | | |
| Yes | 2 | 67 % |
| No | 0 | 0 % |
| Not Sure | 1 | 33 % |
| Total Radio | 3 | |

Since only three people employed in radio responded to the survey, any analysis of that medium lacks validity. In comparing respondents who work in print with those who work in television. We see little difference in the percentage of "yes" and "no" answers in each group. Again, the numbers in each category are too small to offer much significance.

The Pease and Smith study offers a context for comparison when studying the results of this research question (Pease and Smith 1991). As mentioned in Chapter Three of this book, that study found that of the 130 Asian Americans surveyed, nearly one-fifth of the men (19.3 percent), and 16.7 percent of the women cited race as the biggest obstacle to advancing in their careers as print journalists (20). While these results are approaching the question of negative job experiences from slightly different angle compared to this book's survey question, there does appear to be a significant percentage of the journalists in the Pease and Smith study who felt their race translated into a negative job experience in that race was the biggest obstacle they perceived in advancing on the job. A comparison of the results from this book with the Pease and Smith study shows that perceived racial discrimination against Asian Americans at newspapers is a key complaint of Asian American journalists.

It is worth mentioning here that several other important questions were asked of Asian American journalists in the Pease and Smith study concerning perceived problems of racial descrimination on the job. For example, in response to the survey question "do you think minority applicants for newsroom jobs at your paper receive preferential treatment?," of the 130 Asian American respondents, there were divided as follows among these answers: "yes" men - 46.8 percent, women - 67.6 percent; "no" men - 53.2 percent, women - 42.4 percent (29). When looking at the number of Asian Americans surveyed for this book's research who specifically cited they may have received preferential treatment due to their ethnicity in being hired as a journalist (which was cited as both a negative and positive job experience) we see a similarity with the responses to the Pease and Smith study (see Appendices 100 and 101 of this book for specific survey responses).

Along the same line of questioning, the Pease and Smith study also asked "do you think minority journalists are given as much opportunity as white journalists to succeed, less opportunity, or more opportunity" (29). Of the 130 Asian American respondents, the results were divided as follows between the three options presented in the question: "as much opportunity as whites" men - 31.7 percent, women - 30.8 percent; "less opportunity" men - 55.6 percent, women - 49.2 percent; and "more opportunity" men - 12.7 percent, women - 20 percent (29).

Again, we can draw comparisons with responses to survey question one in this book. There were many more respondents who cited negative roadblocks to newroom opportunity related to being Asian American compared to respondents who said they had more opportunity than whites in newsroom opportunities due to their ethnicity (see Appendices 16 and 17). In fact, one of the few positive aspects of being Asian American as it related to newsroom advancement given by this book's survey respondents was that they were promoted into beats covering Asian communities, often because the journalist spoke an Asian language. So, again, the similarities in results between this book and the Pease and Smith monograph, which had an overall response rate of 60.1 percent, are very important in building a body of scholarship on job perceptions and attitudes of Asian American journalists (Pease and Smith 1991, 8).

**Qualitative Analysis of Responses to the Survey Question About Negative Job Experiences.** When examining the actual written responses to survey question one (see Appendix 16) it becomes clear that there are some general categories of negative job-related experiences had by the journalists which they feel were related to their ethnic status as Asian Americans. Those categories are: 1) comments on affirmative action, 2) comments made out of ignorance or stemming from stereotypes of Asians, 3) intentional racial slurs, 4) experiences related to over sensitivity on the part of the Asian American journalist, 5) seeing Asians as all looking alike, 6) Asians not being considered a "real" minority, and, 7) other.

First, many respondents said colleagues or superiors had made comments implying, either directly or indirectly, that the respondent had only been hired to fill minority quotas, or due to preferential treatment given minorities.

Second, many respondents cited incidents where either colleagues, news sources or simply people they came into contact with in the course of covering a story made comments stemming from ignorance and/or stereotypes of Asians. For example, some respondents have routinely been asked, "Do you speak English?" There were numerous examples under this category, including the

Asian American woman who was asked in an interview for a media position, "Do you cook Chinese food?"

The third general category of negative experiences falls under intentional racial slurs. These stories were not only frightening, but sad. It includes those who are called "Japs," "gooks," "chinks" and other such racist and derogatory terms. Again, as one reads through Appendices 12 and 16, one finds there are numerous examples of these situations, some bordering on violence. For example, the Asian American journalist who was verbally attacked during a phone call from a viewer until a co-worker, concerned about the violent and angry nature of the caller's comments, told the Asian American to hang up the phone.

Fourth, there were several respondents who told of experiences they had which they suspected were racially motivated, but may have been misconstrued on their part due to over sensitivity. As one respondent explained, living in the United States as a member of a minority tends to make one overly sensitive to many comments and situations, for example, when jokes are cracked in the newsroom which have negative racial overtones.

Fifth, many respondents cited having colleagues and/or news sources mix them up with another Asian American who worked in the newsroom. Also under this category are all the complaints by women Asian American journalists who are called Connie Chung or told they look like Connie Chung. The stories of people who assume all Asian Americans are Chinese or Japanese may fall under this category, or under the category of statements due to ignorance.

Sixth, a few respondents cited incidents where they were not considered a legitimate minority. For example, one respondent recalled an occasion when a sports editor recommended him for a position that needed to be filled by a minority. The managing editor to whom the recommendation was being made replied, "no, a real minority."

Seventh, there were also many comments that did not fit into a general category, as was the case with numerous answers to the other three questions. This constitutes the "other" category.

In summary, on research question one nearly three-fourths of the Asian American journalists said they had had negative experiences on the job that they felt related to their ethnicity, and nearly one-fourth said they had not had any such ethnicity-related negative job experiences. Some of the key reasons for these negative job experiences included: 1) colleagues or superiors implying the respondents were hired only because they were Asian American to fill job quotas, 2) offensive racially motivated comments made by colleagues or persons interviews on news stories, 3) direct racial slurs made by colleagues, bosses, or news contacts, 4) subtle comments that the respondents were not sure were racially motivated or even insults against Asian Americans, 5) being confused with other Asian Americans in the workplace by colleagues or news sources, and, 6) not being considered a "legitimate" minority compared to African Americans and other larger minority groups in the United States. Finally, there were some reasons given for negative job experiences due to ethnicity of the respondents which did not fit into one of the six categories above. Those who said they had not had negative job experiences usually did not elaborate on their answer as much as those respondents with negative job experiences.

**Statistical Analysis of the Responses to Survey Question About Positive Job Experiences.** The second survey question asked:

> Have you ever had any positive experiences on the job that you feel were related to your ethnic status as an Asian American?

Table 77 gives the breakdown of responses to research question two.

Table 77. Responses to Survey of Asian American Journalists About Positive Job experiences

| Had Positive Job Experience? | Number of Answers | Percent of Total |
|---|---|---|
| Yes | 79 | 80.6 % |
| No | 15 | 15.3 % |
| Not sure | 4 | 4.1 % |
| Total | 98 | |

As Table 77 indicates, the answer to this question was an overwhelming "yes" with 80.6 percent of the respondents giving that answer, or seventy-nine persons. Conversely, only fifteen respondents, or 15.3 percent, said "no," and just four answered "not sure." A chi square analysis was done for the answers "yes" and "no," but not for the answer "not sure" due to the small number of answers in that category. The chi square value at the 0.05 level for one degree of freedom is 3.84. The value of the first two answers is 41.958, which is much larger than 3.84. Therefore, the difference between the answers for "yes" and "no" is a real difference and did not occur by chance.

Table 78 gives the breakdown by media profession of respondents to the answers to research question two.

Table 78. Responses by Media Profession to Survey Question About Positive Job Experiences

| Had Positive Job Experience? | No. Responding | Percent of Total in Each Media Profession |
|---|---|---|
| Print Journalists: | | |
| Yes | 44 | 77 % |
| No | 9 | 16 % |
| Not Sure | 4 | 7 % |
| Total Print | 57 | |
| Television Journalists: | | |
| Yes | 33 | 87 % |
| No | 5 | 13 % |
| Not Sure | 0 | 0 % |
| Total TV | 38 | |
| Radio Journalists: | | |
| Yes | 2 | 67 % |
| No | 1 | 33 % |
| Not Sure | 0 | 0 % |
| Total Radio | 3 | |

When looking at how the answers break down by media profession of the respondents, one sees a larger percentage of the television journalists, or 87 percent, answered "yes," compared to 77 percent of the print journalists. Again, these numbers are relatively small and carry little statistical significance.

**Qualitative Analysis of the Responses to Survey Question About Positive Job Experiences.** One of the first comments seen throughout these answers may be disturbing to some persons. Numerous respondents speculated that their ethnicity played a role in their getting a media job, either due to affirmative action policies or minority quota requirements in place (see Appendix 17). A few respondents, however, seemed to almost be reading an unintended implication into the question (i.e., did affirmative action play a role in your job status?) and stressed they did not get their job through any policies favoring hiring minorities. It must be pointed out quickly here that the newsroom percentages of Asian Americans and other minorities which were provided in the first section of this chapter support the need for many more Asian Americans in the newsrooms. In other words, even with affirmative action policies, the percentage of Asian Americans in the newsrooms that provided personnel data is lower than the nearly three percent of the U.S. population.

In summary, the majority of Asian American journalists responding to the survey, or 81 percent of the total ninety-eight respondents, said they had had positive experiences on the job which they felt were due to their ethnic status as Asian Americans. Many said they believed being an Asian American acutally helped them get a job in the media profession due to affirmative action policies.

So in response to research question seven it can be seen that the majority of Asian American journalists who responded to the book's survey, have had both negative and positive experiences on the job which they feel were related to their ethnic status. However, more passionate responses came from the journalists when describing the negative experiences they have had on the job due to being an Asian American. Certainly, more research needs to be conducted on the various problems discussed by these journalists concerning racial discrimination and other problems they have faced in the nation's media news organizations, which are ultimately responsible for the media images portrayed of Asian Americans.

## CENSUS AND SURVEY DATA

The results of research questions eight and ten will presented using U.S. Census data presented in Table 10 in Chapter Four. To answer research question eight, that census data will be analyzed with the total number of news articles for the year examined in the content analysis published by the newspapers for various cities. To answer research question ten, the census data will be analyzed with the data on the number of Asian Americans working in the newsrooms for which that information was provided. Finally, to answer research question nine, the information on the number of Asian Americans working in the staffs of the newspapers in the content analysis will be analyzed with the coverage of Asian Americans for the circulation areas of those newspapers. What follows are the results to research questions eight through nine.

**Research Question Eight.** Research question eight asks:

8) How does the percentage of Asian Americans living in a
city correlate with the amount of coverage of Asian
Americans?

To answer this question, Table 79 gives a breakdown of the
Asian American population (by number and percent of total city
population) of the major cities for the newspapers in the content
analysis compared to the total number of articles which ran in the
newspaper covering each city for the year studied in the content
analysis.   The newspapers which ran no articles on Asian
Americans, as well as the national newspapers (except for the *New
York Times*) are not included in the table.

Table 79.  Asian American population in the Cities of Selected
Newspapers and Volume of Coverage of Asian Americans, from
Feb. 28, 1994 to March 1, 1995

| City | Asian American Population/ Rank Order | Percent of Total City Pop. | Newspaper | Number of Articles |
|---|---|---|---|---|
| Seattle | 164,386 (6) | 6.4 % | Seattle Times | 215 |
| Los Angeles | 1,339,990 (1) | 9.2 % | Los Angeles Times | 73 |
| San Francisco | 928,026 (2) | 14.8 % | SF Chronicle | 70 |
| New York | 866,394 (3) | 4.8 % | New York Times | 54 |
| Boston | 119,949 (8) | 2.9 % | Boston Globe | 52 |
| Atlanta | 49,965(10) | 1.8 % | Atlanta J-C | 28 |
| Chicago | 255,621 (4) | 3.2 % | Chicago Tribune | 25 |
| Washington, D.C. | 201,502 (5) | 5.1 % | Washington Post | 20 |
| New Orleans | 20,976(13) | 1.7 % | Times-Picayune | 16 |
| Houston | 130,225 (7) | 3.5 % | Houston Post | 15 |
|  |  |  | Houston Chronicle | 12 |
| Denver | 42,279(11) | 2.3 % | Denver Post | 10 |
| Detroit | 67,886(9) | 1.5 % | Detroit News | 7 |
|  |  |  | Detroit N & FP | 1 |
| St. Louis | 22,808(12) | 0.9 % | St. Louis Post-Dispatch | 4 |

These  results  represent  a  .79  rank-order  correlation
(Spearman's rho) that the larger the percentage of Asian Americans
in the main city of a newspaper's circulation area, the more articles
published on Asian Americans. If the data on the *Seattle Times* are
removed from this table, the three cities with the largest populations of Asian Americans—Los Angeles, San Francisco, and New
York, respectively—also have the highest number of Asian
Americans, respectively.  It can also be seen, in general, that many

of the cities with the lowest populations of Asian Americans, such as New Orleans, St. Louis, Denver, and Atlanta, also have newspapers that have offered some of the smallest numbers of articles on Asian Americans during the year of the content analysis.

It is important to stress, however, that the relationship between the population and coverage is not simply that the presence of a population segment (in this case, Asian Americans) makes news or that members of that segment make news. What is more important is that the presence of that population segment creates what editors ought to recognize as the interest in news about that segment, whether it is local news, state news, or national news. So, in the case of Asian Americans, if the U.S. Congress is considering legislation to pay money to Japanese Americans interned during World War II, this news item should be covered by a newspaper if its readership has a segment of Japanese Americans, even if that newspaper is located in a small rural area that normally would not cover a specific piece of Congressional legislation over, say, a local 4-H fair. In other words, newspapers should have a responsibility to recognize the interests and news agendas of minority population segments within their circulation areas and the fact that majority readers need to know, for example, that their Japanese American neighbors may have suffered internment.

In summary, there is a pattern, with a rank-order correlation of .79, correlating the size of the Asian American population within a newspaper circulation area to the number of articles that run on Asian Americans. This gives a significant indication that some of the U.S. cities with the largest populations of Asian Americans have also seen stronger coverage of Asian Americans in local newspapers for those cities. This is particularly true in comparison to the cities with lower numbers of Asian Americans, which in some cases have also seen the newspapers for those cities offer relatively minuscule coverage of Asian Americans for a year's time frame.

**Research Question Nine.** Research question nine asks:

> 9) How does the percentage of Asian Americans working in a newsroom correlate with the coverage of Asian Americans?

Table 80 helps to present the answer to this question by comparing the number of Asian Americans who work at the newspapers in the content analysis which provided personnel figures with the total number of articles which ran in each newspaper during the year of the content analysis.

Table 80.  Asian Americans Who Work On Selected Newspapers and
          Volume of Coverage on Asian Americans, from
          Feb. 28, 1994 to March 1, 1995

| Newspaper | No. Asian Americans in News Operations | No. Articles on Asian Amers. in the Content Analysis Year/ Rank Order |
|---|---|---|
| Los Angeles Times | 53 | 73 (2) |
| San Francisco Chronicle | 29 | 70 (3) |
| Seattle Times | 24 | 215 (1) |
| Wall Street Journal | 23 | 8 (9) |
| Washington Post | 22 | 20 (7) |
| Boston Globe | 18 | 52 (4) |
| Chicago Tribune | 13 | 25 (6) |
| Atlanta J-C | 7 | 28 (5) |
| Houston Chronicle | 5 | 12 (8) |
| St. Louis Post-Dispatch | 5 | 4 (10) |

These results represent a .71 rank-order correlation (Spearman's rho), showing that the more Asian Americans employed in a newsroom the higher the volume of coverage of Asian Americans by that newspaper. Here it can be seen that the three newspapers with the most number of Asian Americans employed in their newsrooms—the *Los Angeles Times*, *San Francisco Chronicle*, and *Seattle Times*, respectively—also have the three highest numbers of articles on Asian Americans for the year of the content analysis. Overall, however, newspapers like the *Wall Street Journal* and the *Washington Post* break this pattern of the higher the number of Asian Americans employed in the news-room the higher the number of articles published on Asian Americans. The *Wall Street Journal* ranks fourth among the ten newspapers for the number of Asian Americans employed in the newsroom, but it is ninth for the number of articles which ran on Asian Americans during the year measured. Likewise, the *Washington Post* is ranked fifth for the number of Asian Americans employed in the newsroom, but comes in seventh for the number of articles it ran on Asian Americans.

The *Boston Globe* breaks this pattern from another angle, since it ranks sixth among the ten newspapers listed for the number of

Asian Americans employed in the newsroom, but it is fourth for the total number of articles which ran on Asian Americans during the year studied. There is also a pattern at the lower end, indicating that the fewer Asian Americans employed in a newsroom the fewer articles that will run on Asian Americans in that newspaper.

In summary, there is .71 rank-order correlation indicating the number of Asian Americans employed in a newsroom will reflect the amount of coverage on Asian Americans. However, it should be kept in mind that this correlation exists when measuring rank orders of ten newsrooms and the the volume of coverage of Asian Americans by those newsrooms. The pattern is strongest among the top three newspapers employing the most Asian Americans in their newsrooms—the *Los Angeles Times*, *San Francisco Chronicle*, and *Seattle Times*, respectively,—and among the lowest two newspapers employing the least number of Asian Americans in their newsrooms - the *Houston Chronicle* and St. Louis Post-Dispatch.

**Research Question Ten.** Finally, research question ten asks:

10) How does the percentage of Asian Americans living in
a city correlate with the percentage of Asian Americans
working in a newsroom of a newspaper covering that city?

Table 81 presents the results to this research question, by listing the population of Asian Americans, and percent of total population, for the major cities representing circulation areas of newspapers in the content analysis which provided newsroom personnel figures. The *Wall Street Journal* is not listed, even though that newspaper provided newsroom personnel information, since it has a national circulation and does not cater to a particular city.

Table 81. Asian American Population in Cities of Newspapers Reading
to the Survey, and Number of Asian Americans Employed in the
Newsrooms of Those Newspapers

| City | Asian American Population/ Rank Order | Percent of Total City Pop. | Newspaper | Asian Amers. in Newsroom |
|------|------|------|------|------|
| San Francisco | 928,026 (2) | 14.8 % | SF Chronicle | 70 |
| Los Angeles | 1,339,990 (1) | 9.2 % | Los Angeles Times | 53 |
| Seattle | 164,386 (5) | 6.4 % | Seattle Times | 24 |
| Washington, D.C. | 201,502 (4) | 5.1 % | Washington Post | 22 |
| Boston | 119,949 (6) | 2.9 % | Boston Globe | 18 |
| Chicago | 255,621 (3) | 3.2 % | Chicago Tribune | 13 |
| Atlanta | 49,965 (7) | 1.8 % | Atlanta J-C | 7 |
| St. Louis | 22,808 (8) | 0.9 % | St. Louis Post-Dispatch | 5 |

With these results we seen a strong rank-order correlation of
.81 (Spearman's rho) between the percent of Asian Americans in
the population of a city to the number of Asian Americans working in a newsroom of a newspaper serving that city. With the
exception of Chicago and Boston, the rankings (from most to least
percentage of Asian Americans) of the cities are identical to the
rankings, from most to least Asian Americans employed in newsrooms, for the newspapers serving those cities.

These data reveal a strong correlation of .81 between the percentage of Asian Americans in a city's population to the number of
Asian Americans employed in the newsroom of a newspaper covering that city. However, it is important to realize that this information only holds true for eight of the twenty newspapers in the
content analysis and should not be translated to all newspapers
throughout major cities in the United States.

## NOTES

[11] Style manuals sent to the author in response to these letters were the AP
Stylebook and Libel Manual, as well as specific style manuals from the following
newspapers: *Atlanta Journal-Constitution*, *Boston Globe*, *Chicago Tribune*, *Los
Angeles Times*, *New York Times*, *Wall Street Journal*, and *Washington Post*. The
*St. Louis Post-Dispatch* has its own style manual, which was not forwarded to
the author.

# CHAPTER 6

# SUMMARY AND CONCLUSIONS

"What is the correct strategy for organizing Asian
Americans?" It's ridiculous to think in terms of a
one-dimensional strategy. The sectarian says:
"Your heads are in a wrong place. You should be
into this, rather than that." There might be some
truth in what he says, but to try to make the
diverse reality of the Asian American experience fit
into a single, narrow mold of analysis is foolish,
and becomes destructive to achieving any kind of
real unity.

— "Asian Nation," *Gidra*

## OVERVIEW

The importance of the contribution to original knowledge offered
in this book is encapsulated, in many respects, in the following
excerpt from a letter sent to the author by a woman journalist in
a middle management position at a media organization in
Michigan, who asked not to be identified. In response to the book
survey of five hundred Asian American journalists, this woman
described her negative experiences as a journalist which she felt
were related to her ethnicity:

> When I used to cover stories for my place of employment,
> many people I interviewed failed to realize the ethnic desig-
> nation "Asian American" covers a broad spectrum of people
> including ethnic Chinese, Japanese, Pacific American, Arab,

Indian, etc. As a result, many people stereotypically assume that I personally know other Asians, all Asian languages, am familiar with martial arts and Asian foods and am proficient in the sciences and other intellectual pursuits. Also, when I was a general assignment reporter covering the labor or auto industry and foreign trade stories, many non-Asians I interviewed often questioned my loyalty as an American. Also, as an Asian American journalist, I am often forced to think against my desires to cover stories a certain way, in order to satisfy the white management's perception of how our viewers perceive the news. For example, some Asian people shun eating cow meat but will eat dog meat. I would be forced to cover this story as if it were inhumane based on Western thinking. In other words, I am often caught between two worlds. Being ethnic is a double-edged sword. The balancing act is often difficult.

Fortunately, unlike many other Asian Americans interviewed for this book's research, this woman has chosen to remain in journalism and has held her current position as a news producer for five years. But, as we have seen through the course of this book, Asian Americans are still sorely underrepresented at all levels of print and broadcast journalism, and most young Asian Americans are choosing to enter other professions for various reasons. Yet, we must stress the importance of Asian Americans to American society, both historically and currently, as Asian Americans are the fastest growing minority in the United States according to the 1990 U.S. Census, comprising nearly 3 percent of the U.S. population. That number has grown to nearly 4 percent of the U.S. population by 1999.

If the media are sluggish in recognizing the importance of this minority group, many other institutions are not. The telecommunications giant, MCI Corporation, for example, sees Asian Americans as a promising and profitable market as evidenced by a their Chinese-language magazine *MCI Lifestyles*. The magazine targets both an Asian market and Asian Americans living throughout the United States (*MCI Lifestyles* 1996). In the fourth edition of the magazine, it gave this message to its readers:

> *MCI Lifestyles* is written especially for you —our valuable Chinese customers who live inthe U.S. and around the world. We are the only telecommunications company that

provides the Chinese community with a magazine containing insightful informationon daily life in the U.S. (1).

It may, in fact, be the only telecommunications company to publish a specialized magazine for Chinese and Chinese Americans (note that the Chinese who live in the U.S. are mentioned first), but it certainly will not be the last telecommunications to target this market. Corporate America is recognizing both the importance of this fastest growing minority in the United States, as well as their links—often through relatives living abroad—to the thriving and growing Asian markets. Unfortunately, one of the broadest themes we have seen in this book's results is that the U.S. media, particularly mainstream newspapers, are failing to recognize the importance of Asian Americans as news consumers, news makers, and news professionals. Perhaps corporate America is filling a void that they see in mainstream media.

After all, most media outlets are for-profit institutions that constantly survey reader/viewer/listener interests with the hopes of a marriage between those interests and higher media consumption to result in profits. Much of the "civic journalism" craze of the past five years is based on the concept of going to the readers to find out what is news as opposed to turning to traditional news sources. Unfortunately, this book tells us few media outlets seem to be turning to Asian Americans to poll their news interests.

In the book Breaking the News, How the Media Undermine American Democracy, author James Fallows warns of such complacency and a skewed vision of what is news by the media (Fallows 1996). The lack of coverage devoted to Asian Americans not only smacks of racism—whether it is intentional or accidental—but is a threat to all of American society for the message it conveys concerning the importance of this minority. Out of a year's worth of coverage in twenty newspapers, we see only 635 articles, which would have dropped precipitously if Yo Yo Ma were not a concert cellist, or if *All American Girl* had not premiered on television, or if Chinese New Year and other Asian ethnic festivals were not celebrated in major cities throughout the United States. The most disturbing aspect of this low overall coverage of Asian Americans found in the book's content analysis, is that without the 215 articles which ran in the *Seattle Times*, the overall coverage of Asian Americans for one year's time would drop to a mere 436 articles. The editors of nineteen of the country's largest newspapers should be extremely concerned about this, and the editors and staff of the *Seattle Times* should be commended for demonstrating excellent coverage of Asian Americans.

With all this in mind, it is most important to clarify that coverage of Asian Americans and issues facing Asian Americans is not just for that minority or of value only to Asian Americans. Rather, accurate and fair coverage of Asian Americans is of great value to all of society and essential to many elements of American life, including politics, entertainment, and ongoing public discourse. The first step to the media's accurate reporting of Asian Americans is to know just who these people are. However, as was stressed in the first chapter of this book, the definition of just who is Asian American is still being debated and is far too broad in scope. Too often a newspaper feels it is "covering" Asian Americans if articles are run on one ethnic sub-group at the expense of other Asian Americans living in a circulation area. We saw this time and time again in the numerous tables showing minute detail of how Asian American coverage is spread over ethnic sub-groups.

Unfortunately, the findings of this book do not come as a real surprise to media scholars. As far back as 1947, the Hutchins Commission scolded the media for not offering fair and equal coverage to society's constituent groups, which included Asian Americans (Commission on the Freedom of the Press 1947). Just over twenty years later, in 1968, the Kerner Commission again admonished the media, in part, for failing in its social responsibility role in its "mission to inform and educate the whole of our society," particularly minority groups (The Report on the National Advisory Commission on Civil Disorders 1968, 208). In two more years it will have been thirty years since the landmark report of the Kerner Commission, and it appears that the need to bring together another commission to reexamine how well the media are meeting their social responsibility mission, particularly in coverage of minorities, is overdue. The findings of this book support the need for such a commission, specifically in relation to how well Asian Americans are covered in the media and are represented on the staffs of media operations throughout the country. Before further conclusions and discussion are offered on this and other points, we shall first recap key findings of the book, which follows in the next section of this chapter.

**Summary of Research Design.** The first methodological building block of this book was a content analysis of twenty of the largest newspapers in the United States, for a one-year period from March 1, 1994, to February 28, 1995, to see how much coverage was devoted to Asian Americans and issues facing Asian Americans, as well as to the type of coverage represented in that realm. The content analysis also examined how ethnic sub-groups of Asian Americans were covered during that time frame. The content analysis was based on studies in agenda setting and in stereotyping. Many of the newspapers with the largest circulations in the United States were used in the content analysis, which examined the following newspapers:

1) *Atlanta Constitution* (morning edition of the Journal)
   *Atlanta Journal* (evening edition of the *Constitution*)
   *Atlanta Journal-Constitution* (Sunday edition of the two newspapers)
2) *Boston Globe*
3) *Chicago Tribune*
4) *Christian Science Monitor*
5) *Denver Post*
6) *Detroit News*
7) *Detroit Free Press Detroit News* and *Free Press* (weekend edition of the *Detroit News* and *Detroit Free Press*)
8) *Houston Chronicle*
9) *Houston Post* (ceased publication in April 1996)
10) *Los Angeles Times*
11) *Michigan Chronicle* (Detroit)
12) *New York Times*
13) *San Francisco Chronicle*
14) *Seattle Times*
15) *St. Louis Dispatch*
16) *Times-Picayune* (New Orleans)
17) *USA Today*
18) *Wall Street Journal* (Eastern Edition)
19) *Washington Post*
20) *Washington Times*

All of these newspapers, with the exception of the *Seattle Times*, were searched via the computer data base "Newspaper Abstracts." The author has seen some research where the on-line contents do not match the actual content in the newspapers.

However, all 635 articles and article abstracts relating to Asian Americans found in this content analysis were carefully checked for any major differences in content which might have affected the coding of those articles and none were found.

The second building block of this book was a survey on job satisfaction as it relates to being Asian American, and on how respondents believe Asian Americans are being covered in the media. The survey was administered to two groups of Asian American journalists to hear their opinions on the state of reporting on Asian American issues in the United States today, and on their personal experiences on the job. The first group surveyed was five hundred Asian American journalists who work in print, radio, or television media to find out how Asian Americans working in the mainstream media assess coverage of Asian Americans and issues facing Asian Americans. The survey, based on studies in coorientation and communicator analysis, also sought to find out how Asian Americans working in the mainstream media feel about their jobs in terms of positive and negative experiences they have had due to their ethnicity. Journalists surveyed were selected from the 1,300-member Asian American Journalists Association, the largest organization of Asian American media employees in the United States. It brought a response rate of 19.5 percent.

The same survey of four questions was also sent to the editors of the twenty leading Asian American publications to seek their views and perspectives on the same issues. Some of those publications—which include newspapers, magazines, and journals—serve ethnic sub-groups of Asian Americans and others serve the Asian American community as a whole. Historical information on each of those publications was also sought in the survey cover letter and the information received was incorporated into Chapter Two, which discusses the history of Asian Americans and Asian American publications in the United States. Although the response to the survey from this smaller group of editors of the twenty leading Asian American publications was small, the few answers received were added to the results of the larger five-hundred-person survey.

The third and final section of the book was a survey of the executive editors or newsroom human resources managers of twenty newspapers used in the content analysis section of the book to find out how many Asian Americans were employed on those staffs, including editors, reporters, photographers, librarians, editorial aides, news aides, and copy aides. They were also asked for the total number of minorities working in the newsrooms, as well as for a full breakdown of those minorities and an historical record of minorities who had worked for their newspaper. Those figures were then compared with the number of Asian Americans living in the cities served within each newspaper's circulation area, as reported in the 1990 U.S. Census. Some of the most important findings of this book come from these comparisons. The newsroom minority personnel figures were also compared with recent annual surveys of minorities in newsrooms administered by the American Society of Newspaper Editors (ASNE). The ASNE data is the only comprehensive survey conducted nationally to track the number of minorities working on American newspaper staffs. This final methodological building block of the book's research is also based on the spiral of silence theory, and the theory of hegemony. All of the five theoretical basis of the book are explained at length in Chapter Three.

This survey of newspaper editors also asked what editorial policies, if any, the newspapers had on how to cover the Asian American communities in their readerships and issues facing Asian Americans in general. Also requested was a copy of each newspaper's style manual, if one other than the Associated Press Stylebook and Libel Manual was used. By examining various entries in the style manuals other conclusions on policies and style rules, as they applied to coverage of Asian Americans, could be made and are discussed in this final chapter.

The combined results of the two surveys unveiled many startling and poignant stories of Asian American journalists, including racist attitudes they have suffered in their media organizations, and positive experiences they have had on the job due to their ethnicity. Excerpts from some of those responses were presented at the beginning of Chapter One, and many more comments are presented in Appendices 11, 12, 16, and 17.

The survey results also gave a good picture of predictions Asian American journalists have on how Asian Americans and issues facing Asian Americans are currently covered in all U.S. media, including television, radio and print journalism. However, according to scores of social science publications and papers presented at academic conferences reviewed for this book, there has never been a content analysis done to look specifically on how

Asian Americans are portrayed in the U.S. news media. There have been a few studies conducted on how ethnic sub-groups, such as Japanese Americans, are portrayed in the media, but there has not been any study done on how the larger minority of all Asian Americans are portrayed.

This book does not attempt to draw any broader conclusions than the results offer, but clearly it can serve as a basis for future comparative research, for example how the volume of news on Asian Americans in this content analysis compares with news coverage of other minorities from the same time frame and in the same twenty newspapers. This book also only examined half of the agenda setting issue as it applies to newspaper coverage of Asian Americans. The content analysis provides rich information about the type and amount of news coverage on Asian Americans from the twenty newspapers, including thematic stereotypes presented in news articles on Asian Americans and ethnic subgroups of Asian Americans. However, whether that news agenda influences the perceived news agenda of Asian Americans or whether it is different from the perceived news agenda on Asian Americans as seen by Asian Americans cannot be determined by the research in this book. For that a large survey would need to be administered to Asian Americans in numerous regions of the United States. What follows are in-depth and comprehensive conclusions for each of the research areas of this book, as well as conclusions on what this book means to other related studies and the five theoretical foundations of the book. Recommendations on editorial policies and hiring practices at U.S. newspapers, based on the findings of the book results, are also offered. Finally, a critique of how this research could have been improved, as well as recommendations for future research to build on the findings here will be given.

## KEY FINDINGS

As just mentioned, some of the most important findings from this book came from the correlations found in the final three research questions. What follows is a discussion of each of those questions' results.

**Research Question Ten: Percent of Asian Americans in a City vs. Percent of Asian Americans in a Newsroom.** A strong rank-order correlation of .81 was found between the percentage of

Asian Americans who live in a city and the percentage of Asian Americans employed at a newspaper covering that city. This can be described as good news, in one sense, since it seems the larger a minority population is in a city, the more journalists who represent that minority are needed in a news operation covering the city for several reasons. First, as the actual comments from this book's survey indicate, as well as much of the research discussed in Chapter Three, having diverse views on the news—whether it mean minorities, women, handicapped persons, or other under-represented constituent groups—offers more depth and under-standing of what is news and of the people involved in news stories. Both the Hutchins Commission and the Kerner Commission emphasized the need for more diversity in newsrooms as a stan-dard to be achieved by the media in this country. Obviously, the First Amendment of the U.S. Constitution precludes any rules about what the press "must" cover.

Of course, as many of the Asian Americans have told us in this book, it is important that they not be utilized just as minority jour-nalists who cover minority beats. This is one area where newspa-pers and other media must make an effort to balance. In one sense, an Asian American reporter who has as a second language Vietnamese is a good candidate to cover issues in a Vietnamese immigrant neighborhood. However, that same reporter should also be given the opportunity to cover a variety of local, state, and national issues, if that reporter is interested and has the intellect for such beats. After all, as one Asian American surveyed for this book explained, "whites never have to worry about being cornered into a beat of covering whites just because of their race. Asian Americans always have to worry about that."

Some of the actual figures are not encouraging. For example, out of 665 total newsroom employees at the *Washington Post*, only sixteen Asian Americans work as part of the professional staff. At the *Chicago Tribune*, a newsroom of 590 professionals, there is one Asian American reporter and one Asian American supervisor, but five copy editors and four photographers who are Asian American. With few exceptions, such as the *San Francisco Chronicle* and the *Los Angeles Times*, most of the newspapers studied have low numbers of Asian Americans working in their newsrooms in all job categories. Again, it is not a huge surprise considering the results of the annual surveys conducted by the

American Society of Newspaper Editors, which indicate in 1995 Asian Americans comprise just one percent of the total newsroom workforce of newspapers in the United States (see Tables 65 and 66).

Once again, however, the *Seattle Times* stands head and shoulders above the other newspapers studied as it was the only newspaper with a higher percentage of Asian Americans on the total newsroom staff—8 percent—than the proportion of Asian Americans—6.4 percent—in the overall Seattle population. This may be one explanation for the impressive coverage the *Seattle Times* gives to the Asian American community in that city, as well as to state, national, and international news on Asian Americans. What this book does not answer, however, is precisely why the *Seattle Times* has such a higher volume of coverage on Asian Americans compared to the other newspapers. It may be that the larger percentage of Asian Americans in the newsroom resulted in Asian Americans finding more news about that minority in Seattle, but this book does not prove such a speculation. Since this study did not look at coverage of other minorities—e.g., African Americans, homosexuals—we do not know if the newspaper tries to cover many non-mainstream groups. It is important to the results of research question ten to note, however, that the *Seattle Times* is not only the newspaper with the highest volume coverage of Asian Americans, it is also the newspaper with the highest percentage of Asian Americans to total newsroom staff compared to the other newspapers.

So, while the results of research question ten were both instructive and, in part, positive, it is only one piece of a much larger puzzle about Asian Americans and their roles with the U.S. media. The results of the other two correlations in research questions seven and eight also represented key findings for this book.

**Research Question Eight: Percent of Asian Americans in a City vs. Coverage of Asian Americans.** The results of this research question found a strong rank-order correlation of .79 between the percent of Asian Americans who made up the total population of a city and the amount of coverage afforded Asian Americans by a newspaper covering that particular city. This was also a solid finding that represents some good news for Asian Americans and all media consumers. While this may seem like a logical and proper correlation, past research has shown the opposite to hold true.

One of the more relevant studies to relate directly to these results was a master's thesis written in 1994 which examined whether large German ethnic populations in cities resulted in higher volume coverage of events of particular interest to German readers (Maurer 1994). In fact, the study found the exact opposite to be true, and summarized: "Contrary to expectation, newspapers serving low German descended readerships had more coverage about Germany and more staff/correspondent created items" (Maurer 1994). That study differed from this book's research in that it was measuring the coverage of four key events in Germany: the fall of the Berlin Wall, the unification of Germany, and arson attacks on foreigners in Germany in 1992 and 1993. However, the premise of the research was similar to this book's research question eight, which sought to find a correlation between the percent of a minority in a city and the amount of coverage about that minority group—including international events—by a newspaper covering the same city population.

The question arises then, why is there a strong positive correlation between the percent of Asian Americans in a city and the amount of coverage in a newspaper covering that city, but not for the German ethnic minorities studied by Maurer? Unfortunately, this book's results offer no explanation. This certainly is fuel for further research on the relationship between ethnic minorities within a region and coverage of those minorities by media institutions. The answer may have to do with the visibility of a minority and/or the recency of a population's arrival in a city.

As mentioned above, Maurer also found that the number of staff-created (enterprise) news items relating to Germans was higher at newspapers with low populations of German immigrants and descendents in their readership areas compared to newspapers with high populations of German immigrants/descendents (38). This seems to fly in the face of logic and relates somewhat to this research question, as well as to the findings of research question nine which is discussed below. Unfortunately, this book did not examine staff-created news articles. If one recalls, in Chapter Four it was explained that in the planning stages of the content analysis some consideration was given to coding articles for bylines of reporters with "Asian sounding" names, and in fact this was done, and about one-sixth of the total 635 articles appeared to be written by reporters with "Asian sounding" names. However, as recognized in the Method Chapter, this was an experience in futility since Asian Americans have a variety of surnames and since it is somewhat racist to try and define the term "Asian sounding name."

In the case of the Maurer study, all staff-created news items were coded and counted using a valid method, but there was no attempt to seek out news that was created by reporters of German descent. It would be interesting, but extremely time consuming, to try and find out the amount and type of news articles being created by Asian American journalists, and this book certainly piques such an interest. In any event, the strong positive correlation between the percent of Asian Americans in a city and the amount of coverage on Asian Americans by a newspaper in that city is noteworthy and encouraging.

**Research Question Nine:    Percent of Asian Americans Working in a Newsroom vs. Coverage of Asian Americans.** The results of this research question also found a solid rank-order correlation of .71 between the percentage of Asian Americans in the overall population of a city and the amount of coverage a newspaper covering that city devotes to news about Asian Americans and issues affecting Asian Americans. Here, again, we see the significance of the Maurer study findings, as well as the significance of the high percentage of Asian Americans working at the *Seattle Times* and the extremely high volume of news on Asian Americans produced by that newspaper. Both of these points have already been discussed at length and will not be touched upon further in reference to the findings for this research question. However, this data, along with the other strong positive rank correlations, represent significant contributions to the body of knowledge on Asian Americans and media coverage of that minority. These correlations will no doubt be the basis of and fodder for future scholarship on Asian Americans and how they are covered by American media.

**Ethnicity of Asian Americans Covered in the Newspapers of the Content Analysis.** We also found a very strong rank-order correlation of .93 for the rankings of coverage, from most to least, for the sixteen categories of Asian American ethnic sub-groups (including the categories of "Well-Known Persons" and Asian Americans as a whole). Chinese Americans, the largest group, received the most coverage overall, followed, respectively, by

Japanese Americans, Vietnamese Americans, Korean Americans, Filipino Americans, Asian Indians, Hawaiian Americans, Pacific Islander Americans, Cambodian Americans, Hmong Americans, Pakistani Americans, Thai Americans, and Laotian Americans. Overall, articles which discussed Asian Americans as a whole group with no mention of ethnic sub-groups received the most coverage, followed by articles about Asian American personalities.

## OTHER IMPORTANT FINDINGS

**Content Analysis.** The most important finding from the content analysis is the incredibly high volume coverage of Asian Americans found in the *Seattle Times*. The quantum leap between the 215 articles found in the *Seattle Times* and the newspaper with the next highest volume coverage of Asian Americans—the *Los Angeles Times* with seventy-three articles, has to come as a shock to most people reading this. It is also important to note that the majority of stories on certain ethnic sub-groups of Asian Americans came in the *Seattle Times*. This is true of the following ethnic sub-groups (refer to Table 15): Laotian Americans, Pakistani Americans, Thai Americans, Hmong Americans, Hawaiian Americans, Pacific Islander Americans, Filipino Americans, Asian Indians, Korean Americans, Japanese Americans, and Chinese Americans. So of the fourteen ethnic sub-groups represented (including other Asian Americans), eleven, or nearly three-fourths, had a significant amount of the total coverage in all newspapers which came from the *Seattle Times*. For some groups the percentage of total coverage coming from the *Seattle Times* is startling. For example, five-sixths of the coverage of both Pakistani Americans and Thai Americans came from the *Seattle Times*.

So the significance of the amount of coverage afforded Asian Americans by the *Seattle Times*, as learned from this content analysis, should not be understated. The numbers for all types of comparisons between the twenty newspapers of the content analysis become very skewed with the inclusion of the 215 articles in the *Seattle Times*.

Beyond the importance of the coverage in the *Seattle Times*, as well as the correlation already mentioned concerning ethnic sub-groups of Asian Americans which received the most coverage, there are also a few other important findings from this content analysis.

First, the Asian American journalists surveyed for this book offered many assumptions that the media give too much coverage to stereotypical articles on Asian Americans, especially on Asian Americans as the model minority, and on gang violence and Asian festivals. However, this book did not find extremely high percentages of the total 635 articles to fall under the thematic sub-topics coded to measure this accusation (refer to Table 59). In fact, 68.6 percent of all articles did not deal with a thematic sub-topic, or stereotype. The article type with the most stories was racism, which accounted for only 9.4 percent of the total articles. This lack of articles which perpetuate Asian American stereotypes is a significant finding of this book. Here we must commend the newspapers for not falling into patterns of covering only articles on the model minority image, or on Asian festivals. Again, when one examines the minute details of this coverage newspaper by newspaper, as seen in the numerous tables of Appendix 9, some glaring contradictions and imbalance of article type begin to appear.

Second, this book found that the coverage of certain Asian American ethnic sub-groups differs in type and tone from coverage of other ethnic sub-groups. For example, Vietnamese Americans have a higher percentage of crime articles compared to the other ethnic groups. What cannot be shown from this information is whether the articles properly reflect the amount of crime associated with Vietnamese Americans. For that, one would have to undertake a detailed study of crime statistics in the cities covered by the twenty newspapers and compare that information with the crimes reported in newspapers. We also found that most classic arts stories deal with Asian American personalities, and that Cambodian Americans and Vietnamese Americans have a higher percentage of human interest articles compared to other ethnic sub-groups.

Third, one disappointing finding of this study was that three newspapers —the *Detroit Free Press*, the *Michigan Chronicle*, and the *Washington Times*—had no articles on Asian Americans. It is uncomprehensible that any newspaper covering a major city in the United States could find no news on Asian Americans. All of these newspapers need to take a serious inventory of their editorial policies concerning how they cover not only Asian Americans and issues affecting Asian Americans, but also to seek ways to reach out to the Asian Americans in their circulation areas to ask how their opinion of what is news and how to better cover Asian Americans.

Fourth, it seems necessary to revisit the comment on the media having an "East Coast Lens" reported in Chapter One and made by Deann Borshay, executive director of the National Asian American Telecommunications Association. In making her comment, Borshay accused the East Coast media of lacking a depth of understanding about Asian Americans and issues affecting them, which, she said, was reflected in painting minority issues in terms of African Americans vs. whites with all other minorities falling into a gray area. What was not reported from that interview was that Borshay claimed that West Coast media does a much more thorough job of covering Asian Americans since more Asian Americans live in the large cities of the West Coast than any other region of the country. The only credence this content analysis can offer to Borshay's comments are that the three newspapers with the most articles on Asian Americans are on the West Coast: the *Seattle Times*, the *Los Angeles Times*, and the *San Francisco Chronicle*. However, it is important to add that no effort was made in this book to define Borshay's term "East Coast media," or to answer whether there is a difference between West Coast newspapers vs. East Coast newspapers in volume and type of coverage on Asian Americans.

**Examples of Questionable Coverage of Asian Americans Found in the Content Analysis.** In Chapter One of the book, it was promised that some samples of questionable coverage of Asian Americans uncovered in the content analysis would be offered in this last chapter. What follows are a handful of articles from the *New York Times* which represent problems that continue to persist with coverage of Asian Americans. The *New York Times* was selected for a microscopic look at some articles on Asian Americans due to its strong national reputation and the amount of influence that newspaper has at swaying opinions and images of the news. Also, these few examples are offered in this summary to give the reader a brief glimpse of the various approaches to coverage on Asian Americans that result in skewed images and stereotypes. Even though this book has shown certain types of stereotypical articles are not as abundant as some might assume, stereotypes of Asian Americans can be buried in many other types of news articles. Articles falling into the subtle gray area that is difficult to judge if they represent responsible coverage or flawed coverage are perhaps the most damaging, as they readily present skewed images of the whole of Asian Americans. One such example is an article, which ran in the *New York Times* March 27, 1994, written by Jane Li with the headline "Neighborhood Report: Flushing; Asians Fear a Police Setback." While editors at the *New York Times* may have perceived the story as giving much needed coverage to the Asian American community, this is ultimately a story about difficult relations between that community and the police. In the grand scheme of coverage, it is one more crime-related story about the Asian American community.

Another example of a story which falls into this gray area of subtle negative coverage of Asian Americans is the Feb. 6, 1994 article by Nancy Malitz with the headline "Pop Music; Ethnic Voices Call the Tune in the Cities," published in the *New York Times*, which, while on the surface appears to give long overdue positive coverage to minority artists, it also includes the following passage:

> San Francisco may seem uniquely fortunate. Twenty-nine
> percent of its population is of Asian origin, a minority that
> is not only well educated and upwardly mobile, but also
> favorably predisposed toward European culture and classi-
> cal music in particular. But Asian-Americans have been
> slow to subscribe to these organizations and even slower to
> respond to fund-raising efforts. . . .Despite evidence of
> wealth in the Asian-American population, Peter Pastreich,
> the executive director of the San Francisco Symphony, said,
> "If we needed a big gift in a hurry, it is not the first place we
> would turn." (Malitz, *New York Times*, Feb. 6, 1994).

There are several problems here. First, no hard figures comparing contributions to the arts by Asian Americans compared to other minorities or whites are given to substantiate this claim. Second, if it is true, no cultural context is offered to explain why Asian Americans have been slow to give money to the arts. Considering the long history of excluding Asian Americans from the arts, which is still happening today, it may not be surprising that this minority group is reluctant to give to organizations. Third, no facts are presented on the number of Asian Americans in managerial positions at major arts institutions. Fourth, Asian Americans may give more support to the arts of the rest of the world outside of arts of European heritage. It is incorrect for the *New York Times* to assume that arts of European heritage are more valid than arts of other heritages, which is implied in this article. While there are many other criticisms to make of this reporting angle, it should finally be pointed out that if the *New York Times* were more informed about the Asian American community, it would not be a big surprise that these people have very broad cultural interests, just like mainstream whites, including being "favorably predisposed toward European culture and classical music in particular." This comment backhandedly perpetuates the image that Asian Americans are ignorant of mainstream culture, that they are negatively tied to their own heritage, and that they are different from the minority in the United States. Also, here the *New York Times* had the opportunity to educate its readers on the history of Asian Americans, but failed to do so. This same article also reported the following:

> Studying tax returns, Mr. Lee discovered that the favorite charitable cause (of Chinese Americans) was "the frail elderly, which fits into the Asian value system of respect for parents," he said. "Next comes hospitals and health care, then education and scholarship funds, then politics. Fifth is religion. Sixth is helping agencies on the China mainland, such as libraries and nursery schools. The Western arts are not at all high on the list." (Malitz, *New York Times*, Feb. 6, 1994).

The obvious question that arises here is, what's wrong with those priorities? It was buried in the article that Chinese Americans, as well as other Asian Americans, are very generous donors to the organizations they choose to support. So again, part of the key focus of a story has a negative spin, this time against Asian Americans who are slow in supporting the Western arts. However, the story fails to play up the overall generosity of Asian Americans in making charitable donations.

Another problem with how the media reports on Asian Americans comes from lumping all news of minorities into large sweeping stories. One example was the Jan. 18, 1994, article by Catherine S. Manegold with the headline "Fewer Men Earn Doctorates, Particularly Among Blacks," which ran in the *New*

*York Times*. Buried in the eighth paragraph of that story is the first reference to Asian Americans:

> Both Hispanic and Asian-American students had significant increases. Forty-one percent more Hispanic students won doctorates in 1992 than in 1982 as their number rose to 755 from 535. The number of Asian-Americans increased by 83 percent in the 10 years, to 828 from 452, while the number of American Indians almost doubled, to 148 from 77, and nearly half were women (Managold, *New York Times*, Jan. 8, 1994).

To add insult to injury, this was the only reference to any of these minorities in the entire article. So the first half of this article leads the reader to think that fewer Asian American men must also be earning fewer doctorates, particularly with the minority reference in the headline. Of course, the real point crying to be made is that there are two separate stories here. Why is it not worthy of a separate story to report that the number of doctorates earned by Asian Americans, Hispanics and Native Americans is skyrocketing, with Asian Americans demonstrating the largest leap in the past ten years? By not choosing to write such an article the *New York Times* is guilty of subtle racism, even if it is unintentional.

Another example of skewed reporting can been seen in the previously mentioned article published in the *New York Times* on March 27, 1994, with the headline "Neighborhood Report: Flushing; Asians Fear A Police Setback" and written by Jane Li. The article is about the police department's decision to move its Asian Crime Investigation Team out of a predominantly Asian American precinct. It begins by referring to the "cooperation of Asian-Americans in their fight against crime," but in the next paragraph, it reports, "Local Chinese, Korean and other Asian business owners say that moving the Asian crime team, which has three Chinese-speaking detectives and one Korean-speaking officer, will discourage Asian business owners from reporting extortion and robberies" (Li, *New York Times*, March 27, 1994). One of the problems here, of course, is rampant in news organizations across the country. There is no distinction made between Asian Americans and Asians who are legal citizens of another country but also legally living in the United States on extended visas. If this seems like a picky point, try to remember the last time an article was printed in any newspaper that mixed Nigerian store owners together with the term "African Americans." Distinctions between African Americans and Africans are always made in the media, so why aren't similar distinctions made between Asian Americans and Asians?

Just as many people question why books such as the controverseal book *The Bell Curve*, which masquerades as presenting "scientific" evidence that blacks inherently have a lower IQ than whites, are even published because of their racial content, so too some "news" items published or broadcast should be questioned because of their racial slant (Herrnstein 1994). Also, just as advertisers have long liked to portray the stereotype that women compete with other women (i.e. resenting each other) for the attention of men, so too has the stereotype that minorities are bigoted against other minorities been perpetuated in "surveys" and "news" such as this. But the more these false stereotypes are reported the more they are perpetuated. The true racist overtones of this article by Steven A. Holmes published in the *New York Times* on March 3, 1994, with the headline "Survey Finds Minorities Resent One Another almost as Much as they Do Whites," becomes quite clear, when in the ninth paragraph, well below the paragraph cited previously in this section of the book, this is reported:

> The survey, called Taking America's Pulse, did unearth evidence of positive views of America's big ethnic and racial groups. For example, more than 80 percent of those surveyed said they admired Asian Americans for "placing a high value on intellectual and professional achievement" and for "having strong family ties." A majority of all groups agreed that Hispanic Americans "take deep pride in their culture and work hard to achieve a better life." And big majorities said blacks, "have made a valuable contribution to American society and will work hard when given a chance" (Holmes, *New York Times*, March 3, 1994).

Also, the same article reported that 85 percent of Asian Americans, 72 percent of Hispanic Americans, 71 percent of blacks, and 66 percent of whites say they support "full integration," though the report does not say what is meant by that term. It appears that the report found more favorable attitudes among minorities than resentment, as reported in the headline. Obviously, the editors at the Times made a conscious decision to, first, report on this survey (in two separate articles) and, second, to portray the negative stereotype of minorities hating each other, rather than reporting that the largest majorities of those surveyed had positive feelings towards other minorities.

Another example of subtle racism against Asian Americans can be seen in the article by Karen De Witt with the headline "Suburban Expansion Fed by an Influx of Minorities," which ran in the *New York Times* August 15, 1994. The article, which ran on the front page, reported:

> The minority population has grown substantially in the nation's suburbs, the 1990 Census showed. From 1980 to 1990, the black population in the suburbs grew by 34.4 percent, the Hispanic population by 69.3 percent and the Asian population by 125.9 percent.By contrast, the white population in the suburbs increased by 9.2 percent (De Witt, *New York Times*, Aug. 15, 1994).

This was the only reference to Asian Americans in the entire article, which was quite long. There were examples of specific African American families and Hispanic families that had moved to the suburbs, including interviews with the families, but there was no other mention of Asian Americans or any interviews with Asian Americans. This seems particularly odd considering Asian Americans showed the highest exodus from urban areas into the suburbs. Many people would argue that a 125.9 percent increase in the number of Asian Americans living in the suburbs over the past ten years is worthy of a separate story, but the*New York Times* did not agree.

Of course, newspapers are not the only media organizations guilty of perpetuating racism against Asian Americans. A year-long study of news coverage across the nation of how minorities are covered in print, radio and television journalism was conducted by four minority journalism organizations last year. Those organizations were the Asian American Journalists Association, the National Association of Black Journalists, the National Association of Hispanic Journalists and the Native American Journalists Association. The result was a comprehensive report entitled "News Watch: A Critical Look at Coverage of Peoples of Color." It concluded that "the mainstream news media's coverage of people of color is riddled with old stereotypes, offensive terminology, biased reporting and a myopic interpretation of American society" (Glaberson, *New York Times*, Aug. 1, 1994).

One example cited in the study, as reported in the *New York Times*, was of an edition of the CBS television program "Eye to Eye" that focused on the issue of political correctness. The article by William Glaberson, headlined "The Media Business: Press; at a Meeting of Minority Journalists, Two Starting Points on Political Correctness," described this appalling incident:

> . . .Bernard Goldberg, the CBS correspondent, chuckled during the program and appeared incredulous when a critic of an Asian-American cartoon character took its creator to task for perpetrating 'the stereotype of Asian-Americans as slanty-eyed model minorities.' "What am I missing here?," Mr. Goldberg said on the air with a chuckle, "And that's bad?" (Glaberson, *New York Times*, Aug. 1, 1994).

In the study, Goldberg defended his actions and remarks by saying that, the article reported, "He chuckled because it was counterintuitive. If viewers approached his broadcast objectively, he said, 'you'll see a chuckle as a chuckle' " (Glaberson, *New York Times*, Aug. 1, 1994).

The same study gave another example of a negative stereotype of Asian Americans printed in a magazine article. It came in a *Vanity Fair* profile of Philip H. Knight, the co-founder and chairman of the athletic shoe company Nike Inc. The Times quoted the profile as saying people who had studied Mr. Knight, who has traveled extensively in Asia, "say that his immersion in Japan and other places Asian has more particularly influenced him in his ability to be inscrutable and manipulative" (Glaberson, *New York Times*, Aug. 1, 1994).

Of course, this perpetuates the false stereotype that Asians are inscrutable and manipulative, particularly in business. The study gave this as an example: "that journalism judgments today may be affected more by subtleties than ever before" (Glaberson, *New York Times*, Aug. 1, 1994). However, many people would argue that this was a rather obvious stereotype which should have been cut by an editor. The author of the profile, Frank Deford, defended his characterization of Knight in the study by saying his intent was to show how Knight had benefited from Asia. "I look at it as a positive that he (Knight) has been able to borrow from another culture," Deford was quoted as saying in the study (Glaberson,

*New York Times,* Aug. 1, 1994). So Deford sees the "positive" that was borrowed from Asian culture as how to be inscrutable and manipulative. Unfortunately, it appears Deford still does not see how this is an insulting and negative stereotype of Asians. It is not "negative" to be silent in Japanese culture, and it is important to point out here that stereotypes often started from a real basis and are over generalized.

These are just a few examples of subtle and not-so-subtle expressions of racism, stereotypes, biases, skewed reporting and poor news judgments in print, radio and television media against Asian Americans. There are also numerous positive images of Asian Americans and examples of responsible news coverage. However, it is the subtle stereotypes perpetuated in the examples cited here which have the potential to do far more damage for reasons already explained.

After looking at some of these examples, coupled with the other data collected from the content analysis, the value of this body of work becomes clear. As we shall see later in this chapter, the information on coverage of Asian Americans seen in these twenty newspapers offers a wealth of knowledge on which to build future research. Overall, the data of the content analysis offers one of the most comprehensive looks at the volume and type of coverage on Asian Americans and issues affecting Asian Americans in media scholarship. It is sure to serve as a reference to numerous other studies on Asian Americans and the media.

**Survey of Asian American Journalists.** Much of the impact and validity of the results from this survey is lost in the low response rate of 19.5 percent. One must question the value of many of the findings, and certainly none can be translated to all of Asian Americans working as media professionals.

However, with that in mind, it is disturbing to learn that 71.4 percent of the respondents to this survey said they have had negative experiences which they feel were due to their ethnicity. In reading the responses to this question the stories are sad, gripping, and at times very disturbing. We see examples of blatant racism against Asian Americans in the newsrooms across the country, and even more examples of subtle racism which the victims aren't sure how to interpret. Any person in a supervisory position at a media institution who reads this book should conclude the need for examining any possible problems of racist attitudes in his/or her media outlet, particularly against Asian Americans. The answers to this question were most likely enlightening to many non-Asian Americans, as problems of racism are often concentrated on white vs. African American tensions. The Pease and Smith study on job satisfaction and the impact of racial diversity in newsrooms offered a great deal of context to these findings. In that study, the Asian American journalists surveyed had many similar complaints of racial discrimination as one of the biggest obstacles to advancing on the job.

We also learn from this survey that a significant number of the respondents feel they got their current job or a job in the media business at one time due mainly to their status as an Asian American. Unfortunately, most respondents painted this as a "positive" job experience. While it is true that hiring more Asian Americans in a media organization is a positive, it is unfortunate if a journalist feels he or she received a job solely on ethnic status and not on intellect and ability. On the other hand, we found that 80.6 percent of those surveyed said they felt they had had positive experiences on the job due to their ethnicity. Some of the examples given included their ability to understand issues in Asian American communities, and to come up with relevant story ideas on Asian Americans that white colleagues had not considered. This was one of the most satisfying findings of the book, and the numerous personal stories given in the qualitative analysis are some of the strongest arguments found in all the related studies cited for the need to diversify newsrooms.

Those surveyed found far more things the media are doing wrong in covering Asian Americans compared to things being done right. Some of the problems cited included that the media are not giving enough coverage to Asian Americans, that there are too many stereotypes of Asian Americans perpetuated in articles, that Asian Americans are not treated as a valid minority in many news items, that they are often lumped together as one big minority with no in-depth coverage given to ethnic sub-groups, and that more Asian Americans need to be hired at all levels of media institutions. As was mentioned earlier in this chapter, some of these accusations were not proven true according to the findings of the content analysis. However, according to the theoretical foundations of corrientation and communicator analysis, these data tells us a great deal about the perceptions of Asian Americans about how the media cover that minority group. According to coorientation theory, the perception of coverage is an important barometer to measure against what is actually being covered in the news. Again we found similarities between these findings and the findings of the Pease and Smith study. That study also cited a high percentage of respondents having negative perceptions of how well their newspaper covered minorities and minority issues.

If the response rate on the survey of Asian American journalists had been higher it would have served as a good contextual framework against previous studies, such as the Pease and Smith monograph, as well against future studies on coorientation, communicator analysis and job satisfaction. Unfortunately, due to the low response rate, most of the findings from this section of the book can only be taken at face value and can not serve to validate other scholarship.

**Survey of Editors of the Twenty Newspapers.** Much valuable information came from this survey of the twenty editors of the newspapers used in the content analysis. The biggest drawback, however, was that only eleven of the editors responded to the request for the number of minorities working in their newsrooms. That data should be readily available at every newspaper and it should be available to the public, although no law requires such information to be made public (unlike broadcast media which are required by federal law to report similar data). Also, the response from the representative of the *New York Times* deserves criticism. That representative said the Times has a policy of not making the information on minority hiring in the newsroom public. Frankly, that policy seems hypocritical and just plain wrong, particularly for a company that routinely covers stories on affirmative action and the lack thereof in society's various institutions.

In general, however, those editors or representatives of editors who did respond to the survey supplied detailed information about the number of Asian Americans working in their newsrooms which served as a valuable contribution to the body of knowledge on Asian Americans and the media. Yet, from these figures, it becomes clear that nearly all the newspapers, with the exception of the *Seattle Times*, need to make much stronger efforts at recruiting Asian Americans for all types of professional positions. So this is one of the important recommendations of this book: that most newspapers, as seen by the American Society of Newspaper

Editors' annual newsroom surveys, need to implement detailed recruiting policies and plans to increase the number of Asian Americans (as well as other minorities) in their newsrooms. To do this, newsroom managers and senior editors should work closely with the Asian American Journalists Association to find out how to best recruit Asian American journalists. More efforts also need to be taken in recruiting Asian Americans graduating from journalism and other mass communication disciplines at universities and colleges throughout the country. Finally, managers at newspapers need to look to their own circulation areas for possible outstanding journalists in the Asian American communities they cover.

The strong positive correlation between the number of Asian Americans working in a newsroom and the amount of coverage afforded Asian Americans discussed earlier in this chapter further supports the positive results of aggressive recruiting and hiring of Asian Americans. Managers and other senior editors in the media should take a serious look at those results and use them as one argument for why it is necessary to have a good representation of Asian Americans in a news operation.

The survey of editors of the twenty newspapers also told us a great deal about the editorial policies at newspapers concerning coverage of Asian Americans. Much of that information came from examining relevant entries to Asian Americans and ethnic sub-groups of Asian Americans in the style manuals for the various newspapers. One glaring problem was that none of the manuals cited in this book had a reference to Asian Americans, but most had editorial policies for the proper way to address other minorities, such as African Americans. There were also no explanations offered in the style manuals on how to define Asian Americans. Most of the manuals had references to Chinese names, but proper style for other names of Asian origin was practically non-existent. This is an important problem uncovered in the book which top editors at news organizations need to address immediately. There needs to be clear editorial policies to offer consistency and correctness to various terms such as "Asian American," as well as to proper spellings of Asian terms, names, and historical facts. Some reporters and editors interviewed for this book did not know that the term "Oriental" is offensive, even though many of the style manuals had this particular entry with references to its negative connotations. The poem at the end of this book will further clarify why that term has gained pejorative status to many Asian Americans.

Most Asian scholars know that many Chinese people or people of Chinese descent list the last name first with the first name, which is hyphenated, listed last. Some people reverse this, just as some people keep the second name of the hyphenated name lower case while others write it upper case. While most style manuals had a reference to proper style of Chinese names, some did not. Also, none of the manuals explained the difference between Asian Americans and Asians in general. There are times when both these groups should be correctly labeled as part of an Asian community, and there are other instances when a distinction needs to be made.

This explanation of the style used for Chinese names by Chan in his book *Asian Americans, An Interpretive History* helps explain why some rules of style are needed by any decent style manual for publications, particularly newspapers.

> Rendering personal and place names in Chinese American history is especially vexatious because most of the early immigrants were Cantonese-speakers, and Cantonese pronunciation is quite different from putonghua (Mandarin), the official dialect that is usually transliterated in English-language writings on China. There is a standard transliteration for Cantonese designed by scholars at Yale University, but I choose to use the forms found in the available writings on Chinese Americans, inconsistent though they be, so that readers can identify the proper names in this book with those found in the existing literature. When the name first appears, I give the pinyin transliteration, then in parenthesis either the Wade-Giles transliteration for Mandarin names and words, or the old Post Office spellings commonly used before 1949, or the nonstandard (but accepted) transliteration for Cantonese ones (Chan 1991, xvi-xvii).

Westerners have struggled for so long with how to translate Asian languages that the series of changes discussed in this excerpt from the preface to Chan's book seem almost insulting. One must ask when the people publishing newspapers, books, magazines, and style manuals will agree on a proper style for Asian names and terms from Asian languages. It would seem as we approach the year 2000 this is not an overwhelming request.

Finally, the twelve "sensitivity tips" on covering and portraying Asian Americans offered by the Asian American Journalists Association (see Appendix 6) should be issued to every editor, reporter, supervisor, and photographer working in the news gathering business. It is unfortunate that most newrooms ignore such valuable advice from fellow journalists who have experienced the problems of insensitivity from the media first-hand.

While the response rate of the editors from the newspapers of the content analysis was disappointing, the yield from those responses was enlightening as to the number of Asian Americans working in many newsrooms. The survey responses also gave strong indications of the need for better recruitment and hiring practices in order to bring more Asian Americans into the profession of mass communication.

## THEORETICAL IMPICATIONS

Much has already been explained concerning the theoretical implications from this book's research, but we shall briefly touch on the main points. What follows are some principles that might hold true based on what was found in this book. As explained earlier in this book, the results here serve to answer only half of the agenda setting hypothesis: What is the news agenda being set by twenty leading newspapers in the United States concerning coverage of Asian Americans and issues affecting Asian Americans? We now know several aspects about this news agenda, which have already been discussed in great detail both in this chapter and in Chapter Five. What this book did not tell us was if that agenda matches the perceptions of the readers or if it actually affects the readers' news agenda about Asian Americans.

This book offers two new bits of scholarship on stereotyping as it applies as a theory base to coverage of Asian Americans. First, we learned that newspapers of the content analysis did have articles which fell into various thematic stereotypes of coverage on Asian Americans, but most of the coverage did not fall into those categories. However, we were also given a glimpse of subtle problems of stereotyping which is often buried in articles which would not be formally coded, according to the methodology of this book, as having a thematic stereotype. Finally, we learned that Asian Americans perceive there to be much more stereotypical coverage of Asian Americans than shown in the content analysis. They also discussed some personal experiences of stereotypes of Asian Americans held by colleagues, people encountered on story interviews, and with sources. This is an important link to both the spiral of silence theory and the theory of hegemony, as will be discussed later in this section. It is possible that the perception by Asian American journalists that too much coverage is being given to stereotypes of Asian Americans actually affects how they approach covering a story and story topics Asian Americans are proposing to cover at news operations.

If this is true, it is also possible then that Asian Americans buy into those false stereotypes and begin to propose articles which reflect stereotypical images of Asian Americans. As both the Hutchins Commission and the Kerner Commission reports pointed out, one of the reasons more representation of minorities is needed in news operations is so that different perceptions of what is news and how that news should be covered come into mainstream coverage. If the effects of stereotyping link to the spiral of silence theory with Asian American journalists, then it is possible that their perceptions of news about Asian Americans becomes a mere mimic of the white majority's perception of Asian Americans and how to cover news and issues on Asian Americans. If this is happening, there are serious ramifications to society as a whole, and it is up to media scholars need to see if such a phenomena is occurring. So the concept of stereotypes is still an important aspect of Asian Americans and media coverage which needs to be examined in future research.

Much has also been said already about the implications of the theoretical foundation of stereotyping from the book's results. We found similarities to the Pease and Smith study on perceptions of Asian Americans concerning how well the media cover Asian Americans and issues facing Asian Americans. The survey response showed clearly that Asian American journalists have strong perceptions of problems with coverage of that minority by the media. Overall, this book establishes the need for much more research on coorientation as it relates to minority perceptions of the news, and particularly to Asian Americans understanding of how they are covered in the media. Unfortunately, as we say in the related studies chapter of the book, there is not a strong body of scholarship in this area.

Some of the research in Chapter Two on the history of Asian Americans and specifically the recent growth of Asian ethnic media, offered some insight into the spiral of silence theory and the theory of hegemony as it relates to Asian Americans. Also, the results of the content analysis indicated that Asian Americans are sometimes portrayed in negative stereotypes which can contribute to the effects of the spiral of silence theory and the theory of hegemony. These two theories serve as powerful reminders that Asian Americans' perception of their own place within a society, and the value that society places on them as a minority, is greatly influenced by the media. Because of these two important theory bases, strong arguments can be made for the need for more in-depth research in the area of this book. Finally, media scholars should be curious about the sharp rise of Asian ethnic media in the United States in the past five years. It raises serious questions about the role of the spiral of silence theory on this trend. For example, many of those surveyed said they are considering leaving journalism altogether because their opinions are not validated in the newsroom and they are often discounted as only the "Asian reporter" by colleagues and news sources alike. Is the spiral of silence theory taking effect with these journalists? Are they starting to believe they are only as valuable as the low overall news coverage of Asian Americans tells them they are? Also, are these journalists starting to see the importance of being Asian American as only in terms of crime, festivals, and a few human interest articles? These are important questions which are not answered by this book, but which are certainly raised by the findings here. How Asian Americans are affected by the spiral of silence theory needs much more attention by media scholars, particularly in light of the results of the content analysis in this book. We now know that Asian Americans are receiving shockingly low coverage in large urban daily newspapers in all regions of the United States, and that only Asian Americans living in the Seattle area are given decent, broad-based coverage compared to twenty other of the nation's largest and most influential newspapers newspapers.

The effects of this coverage on Asian Americans' perceptions of their role in society and their own self-worth should be of grave concern to all persons since, ultimately, the perceptions of society's various constituent groups about their impact within a social structure directly determines the majority's perceptions of their role and the role of constituent groups. The spiral of silence theory proves that often these various perceptions are incorrect and have a serious negative impact on the values, principles, and ethics within a society.

Much has also already been said about the body of knowledge on communicator work satisfaction. The Pease and Smith study offered valuable context to the findings of this book in relation to these theories. We can conclude from the book's findings that there are some serious problems among the Asian Americans who responded to the survey concerning their job satisfaction as it relates to their ethnicity. Even though the response rate of the survey offers only weak confirmation to the results, they still should be considered somewhat of an alarm bell concerning unhappiness of minorities at white-dominated media institutions.

This book suggests that a hypothesis on work satisfaction needs to be tested. That hypothesis would state: Journalists who are a minority at a media institution will experience a higher level of work dissatisfaction than whites, and they will experience a higher level of alienation from the news agenda set by the media institution which employs them compared to whites, due to their minority status in the newsroom. The results from this book make a strong argument that there is a need among media scholars for more research on job statisfaction among minority groups at newspapers, radio stations, and television stations. The level of work satisfaction among minorities needs to be measured and tested for journalists in all stratum of the newsrooms, from senior editors to copy aides and secretaries. This book's research raises the question: Does the level of work satisfaction among minorities in newsrooms vary according to the percent of minorities within a particular level of job responsibility? In other words, do senior editors or producers who are minorities experience greater or lesser job satisfaction because they represent a much smaller minority percentage at that level of responsiblity when compared to secretaries or reporters who are minorities who make up a larger minority segment of the work pool at that level of responsibility? These are important questions and principles which need to be addressed in future research which builds on this book's findings.

Overall, these five areas offered a broad base of research necessary for the scope of this book. They also addressed other theories not formally used as foundations for this book. For example, the cultivation hypothesis would say that heavy media users would over estimate the Japanese American population for the United States and under estimate the Filipino American population due to the higher volume of coverage afforded Japanese Americans compared to Filipino Americans, even though Filipino Americans are the second largest ethnic sub-group of Asian Americans according to the 1990 U.S. Census. The skewed media representation of other Asian American ethnic sub-groups in relation to their proportion of the U.S. population, as seen from the content analysis research in this book, might translate to equally skewed perceptions of those ethnic sub-groups by media users according to the cultivation hypothesis. Also, the type of coverage given particular Asian American ethnic sub-groups, such as the higher volume of gang violence articles on Vietnamese Americans, might disproportionally, and thus incorrectly, affect media users' perception of Vietnamese Americans as being more involved in gang violence that is actually true. Again, to carry out this type of research on the cultivation hypothesis, building on this book's findings, researchers would have to examine crime records as well as test mainstream media users' perceptions and measure coverage of Vietnamese Americans. The findings from this book, however, do offer insight into the cultivation hypothesis.

The book's results suggest new theories, such as a "minority media effect," which would state that smaller urban West Coast cities are more attentive to minorities than larger West Coast urban areas, as reflected in media coverage of minorities. This comes from the extremely high volume coverage of Asian Americans in the *Seattle Times* compared to the coverage of Asian Americans in the *San Francisco Chronicle* and the *Los Angeles Times*. Such a proposed theory needs much more testing by future research. Yet, this book's findings indicate the possibility that this theory exists and the comments by Asian American journalists in the survey results indicate that these minority news persons suspected the existence of this theory prior to knowning the results of the content analysis.

## IMPLICATIONS FOR FUTURE RESEARCH

One of the most exciting aspects of this book's results are the many implications it holds for possible future research. Some possibilities for future research based on this book have already been mentioned. One area that should definitely be expanded upon is the content analysis. Now that we have the results of a year's worth of coverage on Asian Americans and issues affecting Asian Americans, the information will gather more meaning when given the context of coverage during other time frames. Now researchers can explore past coverage and future coverage of Asian Americans and have a point of reference from this content analysis. Questions such as, Has coverage increased or decreased from one time span to another? can now be answered simply by conducting a similar content analysis for another year's time using the same methodology. When one considers the serious lack of scholarship on media coverage of Asian Americans as a whole entity, as explained in the chapter on related studies, the value of this content analysis to future research becomes even more apparent.

The implications for future research from the survey of editors, as well as from the survey of Asian American journalists, have already been described in detail, so they will not be repeated here. In sum, however, these two segments of the book offered many questions to be pursued in the future. Certainly, there is a need to conduct a larger survey of editors and a larger survey of Asian American journalists with more questions on the entire area of how the media covers Asian Americans and perceptions of that coverage.

Possible theoretical foundations for future research are numerous. Two areas of psychology that could also serve as theoretical foundations for other research are: 1) ego psychology, which says humans pay more attention to messages that can be linked to their own experiences in life, and, 2) associationist psychology, which argues persuasive messages have impact on a person when he or she links those messages to goals and values that he or she determines to be important. It is the premise of this book that Asian Americans may, in fact, be more aware of what news appears in the mass media concerning Asian Americans because of these two psychological factors. Therefore, Asian Americans are excellent sources to seek out when determining perceptions of news coverage of Asian Americans.

In simpler terms, Caucasians or other non-Asians may tend to skip over, or ignore completely, some news items about the Asian American community because whites would not link those items closely to their own experience, or because whites may not link those articles with values they hold important.

In broader terms, there are several communication theories that explain the implications of this book's research, but which will not serve as a foundation for this research. They include the maximum effects theory, which says the media are powerful enough to sway ideology. So it would be interesting in future research to study if the media sways how media consumers construct ideology, such as prejudice, that formulates their perceptions of Asian Americans. Certainly the selectivity hypothesis, which says we tend to selectively interpret the media messages we encounter, could be examined in this book. For example, what media selections do majorities (i.e. Caucasians in the United States) make that might exclude news of minorities?

The minimalist theory of communication, which says people do things which are encouraged by the media because they were predisposed to do them anyway, could be considered in this book's research. For example, do acts of prejudice against Asian Americans arise from stereotypes of Asians encouraged in the media or from predisposed concepts that people had in their childhood before becoming adult media consumers?

The modified effects theory, which states humans share basic goals, social norms and customs, could also be examined at it relates to this book's research. Here the premise of this theory could be examined to see if Asian Americans share the same goals, social norms and customs of mainstream America. Finally, schema theory could examine the core beliefs of Asian Americans that shape how they interpret the world.

## CONCLUDING REMARKS

Understanding and knowledge are always the keys to enlightening a society on any issue or group of people within that society. Marjorie Li and Peter Li explained this in relation to Asian Americans by stating in the preface to their book *Understanding Asian Americans, A Curriculum Resource Guide* :

> Despite the 140-year history of Asians in America, Asians and Asian Americans are still not well understood in this country, and are often the victims of prejudice and discrimination. We believe that, by providing reliable information

and finding the proper channel for its dissemination, we can reduce conflicts between ethnic and racial groups (Li and Li 1990, viii).

The media should represent some of the most important institutions in society to offer proper channels of information dissemination. This book has shown areas where the media are doing that job well when in comes to news about Asian Americans. Unfortunately, this research has also indicated that most of the newspapers studied need to hire more Asian Americans in their newsrooms, and need to take a closer look at how this important minority is being covered. Clearer editorial policies need to be established concerning style and other issues of covering the numerous ethnic sub-groups of Asian Americans. This book has also shown the frustrations, experiences of racial discrimination, and positive experiences of Asian American journalists working at newspapers, television stations, and radio stations throughout the country. It is time for media institutions to listen more intently to the opinions of Asian Americans, especially those Asian Americans who are working media professionals.

It is sad, and somewhat ironic, that a month before this book was completed the longtime editor-in-chief of the *St. Louis Post-Dispatch*, William Woo, resigned his position. Woo had been editor at that newspaper for nearly ten years and he was one of the only Asian Americans in history to become editor of a leading American newspaper. His tenure at the *St. Louis Post-Dispatch* spanned thirty-four years. According to an article in Editor & Publisher, Woo, a Shanghai-born Chinese American, said, "I think the owners, with their eyes on the leadership of another century, were not sorry to see me go" (Fitzgerald, *Editor & Publisher*, Sept. 21, 1996). Woo has long been one of the leading skeptics in the newspaper business of public journalism and his successor and former editor of the *Virginia Pilot*, Cole Campbell, is a strong public journalism advocate.

Just days before the *St. Louis Post-Dispatch* announced Woo's resignation he spoke before the annual convention of the Asian American Journalists Association (AAJA) in Minneapolis in August. Woo encouraged the gathering of Asian American journalists to think if themselves as human beings first, and then journalists (Fitzgerald, Editor & Publisher, Sept. 21, 1996). He also had this to say about the daunting task of being an Asian American journalist in the mainstream media:

> Members of this organization [AAJA] have hinted to me that if only I had been a little less Asian, had only been a bit more assertive, all of this might not have come to pass . . . . In asking they are not suggesting anything so crude as racial discrimination. No they were referring, indirectly to that haunting question of whether Asians can ascend to and survive at the summit of a business that has few Asians above the timberline. . . . Of course, there is no answer to that question (Fitzgerald, Editor & Publisher, Sept. 21, 1996).

Woo represents one of the best of the hundreds of Asian Americans who work as journalists in print, radio, and television throughout the United States. There are even more young Asian Americans waiting in the wings to fill their shoes. But it is essential to ask, especially after reading this book, what kind of newsroom environment and world of news gathering awaits these future writers, editors, producers, and broadcasters?

Asian Americans represent a diverse, vibrant, and fascinating part of American society and its history. The research in this book on how this fastest growing minority in the United States is being treated in the media is not only valuable to enlighten society as a whole, but it is essential research which must be acknowledged for its importance by both media professionals and media scholars.

# APPENDICES

APPENDIX 1

# MEDIA USAGE OF ASIAN AMERICANS/ASIAN IMMIGRANTS AND HISPANICS, 1989

Reported responses of a survey of 104 Asian Americans/Asian immigrants and ninety-nine Hispanics in the New York metropolitan area on media use, conducted in 1989.

Table 82. Media Usage of Asian Americans, Asian Immigrants, and Hispanics in 1989

| Media Usage | Asians | | Hispanics | |
|---|---|---|---|---|
| | Number | Percent | Number | Percent |
| Television | 78 | 75.0 % | 75 | 75.8 % |
| Radio | 59 | 56.7 % | 69 | 69.7 % |
| Newspaper | 60 | 57.7 % | 53 | 53.5 % |
| Magazines | 34 | 32.7 % | 33 | 33.4 % |

SOURCE: Gall, Susan B. and Timothy L. Gall, eds. 1993. Statistical Record of Asian Americans. Detroit: Gale Research Inc., p. 33. Primary source: Delener, Nejdet and James P. Neelankauil. June/July 1990. Information Sources and Media Usage: A Comparison Between Asian and Hispanic Subcultures. Journal of Advertising Research 30:45. The sample consisted of personal interviews with 104 Asians and ninety-nine Hispanics in the New York Metropolitan area. Also in source: data on media preferences of the U.S. adult population.

APPENDIX 2

# MAGAZINE READERSHIP OF ASIAN AMERICANS/ASIAN IMMIGRANTS AND HISPANICS

Reported responses, in numbers, of a survey of 104 Asian Americans/Asian immigrants and ninety-nine Hispanics in the New York metropolitan area on readership of magazines by types, conducted in 1989.

## Table 83. Magazine Readership of Asian Americans, Asian Immigrants, and Hispanics, 1989

| Magazines | Asians | Hispanics |
|---|---|---|
| **Business/Trade** | | |
| Business Week | 39 | 26 |
| Economist | 11 | — |
| Forbes | 12 | 7 |
| Fortune | 23 | 11 |
| Money | 11 | — |
| Others | 4 | — |
| **Scientific** | | |
| Discover | 8 | 26 |
| Omni | 12 | 18 |
| Scientific American | 7 | 5 |
| **Men's** | | |
| GQ-Gentlemen's Quarterly | 21 | 13 |
| Playboy | 14 | 14 |
| **Women's** | | |
| Cosmopolitan | 14 | 19 |
| Glamour | 7 | 8 |
| Vogue | 18 | 23 |
| Others | 23 | 22 |
| **Sports□** | | |
| Body Builders | — | 12 |
| Car & Driver | 13 | 18 |
| Golf Digest | 15 | — |
| Sport | — | 16 |
| Sports Illustrated | 3 | 34 |
| Sports Today | — | 19 |
| **General Interest** | | |
| Life | 3 | 8 |
| Newsweek | 37 | 12 |
| People | 23 | 28 |
| Time | 39 | 26 |
| TV Guide | 5 | 4 |
| Others | 27 | 43 |
| **Ethnic: Chinese/Japanese and Hispanic** | | |
| Ef | 13 | — |
| Elle | 28 | — |
| With | 11 | — |
| Chromos | — | 4 |
| Lo Vanidad | — | 18 |
| Ola (Hola) | — | 25 |

SOURCE: Gall, Susan B. and Timothy L. Gall, eds. 1993. Statistical Record of Asian Americans. Detroit: Gale Research Inc., pp. 32-33. Primary source: Delener, Nejdet and James P. Neelankauil. June/July 1990. Information Sources and Media Usage: A Comparison Between Asian and Hispanic Subcultures. Journal of Advertising Research 30:45. The sample consisted of personal interviews with 104 Asians and ninety-nine Hispanics in the New York Metropolitan area. Also in source: data on media preferences of the U.S. adult population.

## APPENDIX 3

# ASIAN AMERICANS' INFORMATION SOURCES ON POLITICAL ISSUES

Reported results of a survey asking five thousand Asian Americans (1,149 respondents) the following quesiton: What is your major source of information about political issues?

Table 84. Asian Americans' Information Sources on Political Issues, 1992

| Ethnic Group | TV | Newspaper | Radio | Magazine | Friends |
|---|---|---|---|---|---|
| All | 39.3 % | 49.7 % | 4.4 % | 5.8 % | 0.3 % |
| Chinese | 34.1 % | 53.3 % | 4.15 % | 7.6 % | 0.4 % |
| Filipino | 50.8 % | 40.8 % | 1.7 % | 5.8 % | — |
| Japanese | 32.2 % | 59.6 % | 3.3 % | 4.9 % | — |
| Korean | 41.8 % | 43.0 % | 1.3 % | 13.9 % | — |
| Vietnamese | 46.4 % | 41.8 % | 8.2 % | 1.8 % | — |
| Asian Indian | 27.5 % | 61.3 % | 11.3 % | — | — |
| Others | 64.5 % | 28.0 % | 4.3 % | 1.1 % | 2.2 % |

SOURCE: Gall, Susan B. and Timothy L. Gall, eds. 1993. Statistical Record of Asian Americans. Detroit: Gale Research Inc., p. 24. Primary source: Republican National Committee, unpublished data. Results of an August 1992 survey of five thousand Asian American adults in California. Names were selected from membership directories of major Asian ethnic organizations and from an ethnic surname database of registered voters. The response rate was 27.9 % or 1,149 completed questionnaires. The ethnic composition of the response was: Chinese - 42 %, Filipino - 9 %, Japanese - 21.5 %, Korean - 17.5 %, Vietnamese - 24.4 %, Asian Indian - 32 %, and others - 15.5 %. The overall sample error was about 3 % at 95 % confidence level.

# APPENDIX 4

# PERIODICALS PUBLISHED IN THE PACIFIC ISLANDS LISTED BY COUNTRY/ISLAND GROUP, 1973 AND 1989

Table 85. Periodicals Published in the Pacific Islands, 1973 and 1989

| Island/Island Group | 1973 | 1989 |
|---|---|---|
| American Samoa | 3 | 3 |
| Solomon Islands | 2 | 8 |
| Cook Islands | 1 | 2 |
| Fiji | 15 | 22 |
| French Polynesia | 4 | 7 |
| Kiribati/Tuvalu | 3 | 4 |
| Guam | 2 | 15 |
| Johnston Island | - | 1 |
| Nauru | 1 | 2 |
| New Caledonia | 7 | 6 |
| Vanuatu | 5 | 3 |
| Niue | 1 | 1 |
| Norfolk Island | 1 | 1 |
| Papua New Guinea | 5 | 56 |
| Pitcairn Island | 1 | 1 |
| Tokelau Island | - | 1 |
| Tonga | 2 | 7 |
| TTPI | 6 | 9 |
| Wallis and Futuana | - | 1 |
| Western Samoa | 4 | 6 |

SOURCE: Layton, Suzanna. 1990. The Contemporary Pacific Islands Press. Paper presenteed at the 1990 annual conference of the Association for Education in Journalism and Mass Communication.

## APPENDIX 5

# TOP TWENTY LEADING JOURNALS, MAGAZINES, AND NEWSPAPERS SERVING ASIAN AMERICANS AND/OR ASIAN AMERICAN ETHNIC SUB-GROUPS IN THE UNITED STATES IN 1995 AT THE TIME OF THIS BOOK'S CONTENT ANALYSIS

## Academic Journals

*Asian America: Journal of Culture and the Arts*
Editorial Correspondence: Shirely Geok-lin Lim
Asian American Studies English Department
University of California
Santa Barbara, CA 93106
Tel. (805) 893-8584

*The Hawaiian Journal of History*
Editor: Helen G. Chapin
Hawaiian Historical Society
560 Kawaiahao Street
Honolulu, HI 96813-5023
Tel. (808) 537-6271

*Asian Pacific American Journal*
Co-editors: Juliana Koo and Soo Mee Kwon
The Asian American Writers' Workshop
37 St. Marks
New York, NY 10003-7801
Tel. (212) 228-6718

*Critical Mass: A Journal of Asian American Criticism*
Asian American Studies
516 Barrows Hall
University of California
Berkeley, CA 94720
Tel. (510) 642-6555

## Popular Magazines

*YOLK*
Editor: Larry Tazuma
P.O. Box 862130
Los Angeles, CA 90086-2130
Tel. (213) 223-7900
E-Mail: yolked@aom.com

*FACE*
Editor: Shi Kagy
Note: Published by Transpacific Media Inc.
31727 Pacific Coast Highway
Malibu, CA 90265
Tel. (310) 456-0790

*Transpacific*
Editor: Tom Kagy
Note: Published by Transpacific Media Inc.
31727 Pacific Coast Highway
Malibu, CA 90265
Tel. (310) 456-0790

*A Magazine*
Editor: Jeff Yang
270 Lafayette Street, Suite 404
New York, NY 10012-9657
Tel. (212) 925-2123
E-mail: amag@inch.com

*Special Edition: Philippine-American Quarterly*
Editor: Marites Aguilar-Carino
Special Edition Press, Inc.
104 East 40th Street
New York, NY 10016
Tel. (212) 682-6610 or 1-800-OK-PRESS

*Filipinas Magazine*
Editor: Rene P. Ciria-Cruz
Filipinas Publishing Inc.
655 Sutter Street, Suite 333
San Francisco, CA 94102
Tel. (415) 563-5878
E-mail: filmagazin@aol.com

## Newspapers

*Little India*
Editor: Achal Mehra
Little India Publications
1345 Richmond Street
Reading, PA 19604
Tel. (610) 352-8678
E-mail: litlindia@aol.com

*Hawaii Herald*
Editor:  Mark Santoki
P.O. Box 17430
917 Kokea Street
Honolulu, HI 96817
Tel. (805) 845-2255

*Rafu Shimpo*
Editor:  Micheal Komai
259 So. Los Angeles Street
Los Angeles, CA 90012
Tel. (213) 629-2231

*Northwest Asian Weekly*
Editor:  Demi Yamauchi Luna
414 Eighth Avenue South
Seattle, WA 98104
Tel. (206) 223-0623, 223-0626

*Hawaii Filipino Chronicle*
Editor:  Charlie Y. Sonido, M.D.
Hawaii-Filipino Chronicle, Inc.
1449 North King Street
Honolulu, HI 96817
Tel. (808) 847-6701, 847-6822

*Pacific Citizen*
Editor:  Richard Suenaga
2 Coral Circle, #204
Monterey Park, CA 91755
Tel. (213) 725-0083, 725-0064

*Korea Times*
Korea Times/Monthly English Edition
Editor:  Craig S. Coleman

P.O. Box 74517
141 N. Vermont Avene
Los Angeles, CA 90004-0517

*Asian Week*
Editor: James Carrol
811 Sacramento Street
San Francisco, CA 94108
Tel. (415) 397-0221
E-mail: awsf@aol.com

*KoreAm Journal*
Editor: Jung Shig Ryu
17813 S. Main St., #112
Gardena, CA 90248
Tel. (310) 769-4913

*International Examiner*
(The Journal of the Northwest's Asian American
Communities)
Editor: Dean Wong
622 S. Washington
Seattle, WA 98104
Tel. (206) 624-3925

*Asian New Yorker*
Editor: Sue Lee
Asian CineVision Inc.
32 East Broadway
New York, NY 10002
Tel. (212) 925-8127

\* This list does not contain one of the leading journals in Asian American studies, *Amerasia Journal*, since this journal was the subject of section F4 in Chapter Three of the book. *Amerasia Journal* is affiliated with the Asian American Studies Center of the University of California - Los Angeles, 2330 Campbell Hall, 405 Highland Ave., Los Angeles, CA 90024-1546. The current editor is Russell Leong.

NOTE: This list was compiled by Marjorie Lee, librarian of the UCLA Asian American Studies Center Reading Room. She selected these publications as the top twenty for Asian Americans based on the following criteria: 1) stability of circulation, 2) representation of the community/communities to which each publication is targeting, and, 3) coverage of topics and issues reflective of that targeted group/s.

## APPENDIX 6

## TWELVE TIPS ON COVERING AND PORTRAYING ASIAN AMERICANS, FROM THE ASIAN AMERICAN JOURNALISTS ASSOCIATION

1) Consider the Asian American community as a beat as much as real estate or sports. Become familiar with terms. Do research. Subscribe to community publications. Develop contacts.

2) Do not assume that "American" means "white" and that an Asian is a foreigner. Many persons of Chinese and Japanese descent, in particular, have been American citizens for generations. Asking about "your country" will confuse both you and your interview subject.

3) Recognize that not all Asians and Asian Americans are alike. Try to distinguish Americans of Asian descent from Asian nationals, as well as the different Asian nationalities from one another. Asians very widely in experience and culture among themselves and when compared with Asian Americans.

Realize also that stereotypes and reporting biased against one group of Asians—even a foreign nation—can affect all Asian Americans, because the general public often views all Asians and Asian Americans as alike.

4) Realize the difference between **immigrants** and **refugees**.

5) Avoid inflammatory combat terminology. The U.S. trade deficit with Japan (often referred to as part of a trade war) has resurrected some disturbing terms. A magazine article about Japanese dress designers, for example, was headlined "Tokyo's fashion invasion." Accompanying articles about German designers mentioned only hemlines and ruffles, with no references to warlike terms, even though Germany also was an enemy during World War II. Repeated references to Japan as if it still is an enemy are inflammatory and encourage violence against Asian Americans.

Reinforcing the concept of America as beachhead, some news media are now reporting that Koreans, Filipinos or Southeast

Asians are invading a particular city or neighborhood. These new Americans are not regarded as neighbors who can contribute to the development of a community, but as a foreign threat.

6) Recognize and avoid racial slurs. "Jap," "Chink," and "Chinaman" have all appeared in the media recently. The *New Republic* headlined a column "How to Gyp the Japs." When readers complained, the editor defended his use of the epithet by asserting that "Japs" is not an ethnic slur like "niggers," "kikes" or "slants." It is a national nickname, he argued, like "Yanks," "Brits" or, at worst, "Frogs."

Similarly, a cover of *The National Review*, devoted to an article entitled "The Underhandedness of Affirmative Action," showed a list that read, in part, "two (2) Jews, one (1) cripple, one (1) Hispanic, and one (1) Chink." Interestingly, the magazine, in its subsequent apology, also referred to "Chink" as a "nickname."

"Jap," "Chinaman," "chink," "gook," "nippers." These are not nicknames. They are slurs never to be used.

When a slur is used by a public official, try to get a reaction from a leader in the Asian American community or from the in the audience.

7) Avoid stereotypes, overgeneralizations and outdated terms. As it did during the 1940s, the press is again referring to Asians (in this case primarily Japanese and Koreans) as "clever" and "shrewd." Even complimentary adjectives like "industrious," when used to describe factory workers or students, can conjure up stereotypes of insect-like, mindless hordes.

Also omit references to "China doll" and "Dragon lady." *Why?* Because these terms do not take women seriously as individuals. They reinforce the feeling that younger Asian women are exotic and submissive, while older Asian women in authority, without such appeal, are threatening.

Also, avoid the word "Oriental." Just as "Negro" is no longer preferred by African Americans, Oriental is no longer preferred by most Asian Americans. Use it only to describe things, not people.

8) Portray Asian Americans from their perspectives, and with historical context. Make sure you interview Asian Americans on issues affecting them. And don't assume that your way of viewing a story is the only way. Put yourself in an Asian American's shoes.

For example, when doing a story about Asian gangs, interview some gang members. Try to understand why people join gangs. Often it is because of unemployment, discrimination or other problems.

When doing a story about tensions between Korean businesses and their African American customers, try to understand the frustrations and predicaments of both sides.

9) Avoid ethnocentricity and double standard when describing Asians and their cultures. For example, if you characterize a Chinese New Year's lion dance as "strange" or "exotic," make sure you also describe German Oktoberfests as exotic. If you say that an Asian speaks with a "a thick accent," make sure you say that a French movie director or Italian auto magnate also speak with thick accents.

10) Avoid making fun of Asian accents. "So solly, Cholly," "rots of ruck," and "flied lice" just encourage ridicule of those who are trying to communicate in English.

11) Interview people with accents. This helps shed the public perception that the majority of people on television who are important and make the news should be, and are, of Anglo-Saxon background. This point applies especially to the broadcast medium.

12) Include Asian Americans when you write about minorities. And be sure to use Asian Americans—as well as African Americans, Hispanics, and Native Americans—as sources in everyday stories and photos, not just in stories about minorities.

## Loaded words: Caution required

Certain stereotypes have become associated with certain groups. By force of habit, such "loaded words" often are then used to describe individuals of that group—*even when they don't fit*. That reinforces stereotypes and robs readers or viewers of an appreciation of people as individuals with their own uniqueness.

*Here are loaded words to be used with extreme caution when applied to Asians:*

Serene, quiet, shy, reserved, smiling.
Stocky, buck-toothed, myopic, delicate.

Obedient, passive, stolid, docile, unquestioning.
Servile, subservient, submissive, polite.
Mystical, inscrutable, philosophical, stoic.

SOURCE:    Asian American Journalists Association, Chicago
Chapter, National Conference of Christians and Jews, Chicago
and Northern Illinois Region. 1991. Asian American Handbook,
pp.4.1-4.4.

APPENDIX 7

## 193 KEY WORDS/SETS OF KEY WORDS USED IN COMPUTER DATABASE SEARCHES FOR THE CONTENT ANALYSIS

*Asian* and *American*
*Asian* and *Americans*
*Chinese* and *American*
*Chinese* and *Americans*
*Filipino* and *American*
*Filipino* and *Americans*
**Philipino** and *American*
**Philipino** and *Americans*
*Japanese* and *American*
*Japanese* and *Americans*
*Indian* and *American*
*Indian* and *Americans*
*Korean* and *American*
*Korean* and *Americans*
*Vietnamese* and *American*
*Vietnamese* and *Americans*
*Cambodian* and *American*
*Cambodian* and *Americans*
*Hmong*
*Hmong* and *American*
*Hmong* and *Americans*
*Laotian*
*Laotian* and *American*
*Laotian* and *Americans*
*Thai*
*Thai* and *American*
*Thai* and *Americans*
*Bangaldeshi*
*Bangaldeshi* and *American*
*Bangaldeshi* and *Americans*
*Bhutanese*
*Bhutanese* and *American*

*Okinawan*
*Okinawan* and *American*
*Okinawan* and *Americans*
**Okinawa**
*Pakistani*
*Pakistani* and *American*
*Pakistani* and *Americans*
     *Sikkim*
*Sikkim* and *Americans*
**Sik**
*Singaporan*
*Singaporan* and *American*
*Singaporan* and *Americans*
*Sri Lankan*
*Sri Lankan* and *American*
*Sri Lankan* and *Americans*
**Sri Lanka**
*Sumatran*
*Sumantran* and *American*
*Sumantran* and *Americans*
**Sumatra**
*Hawaiian*
*Hawaiian* and *American*
*Hawaiian* and *Americans*
*Samoan*
*Samoan* and *American*
*Samoan* and *Americans*
*Samoa*
*Guamanian*
*Guamanian* and *American*
*Guamanian* and *Americans*
     **Guam**

*Bhutanese* and *Americans*
**Bhutan**
*Borneo*
*Borneo* and *American*
*Borneo* and *Americans*
*Burmese*
*Burmese* and *American*
*Burmese* and *Americans*
**Burma**
*Celebesian*
*Celebesian* and *American*
*Celebesian* and *Americans*
**Celebes**
*Ceram*
*Ceram* and *American*
*Ceram* and *Americans*
**Seram**
*Indochinese*
*Indochinese* and *American*
*Indochinese* and *Americans*
*Indonesian*
*Indonesian* and *American*
*Indonesian* and *Americans*
*Iwo-Jiman*
*Iwo-Jiman* and *American*
*Iow-Jiman* and *Americans*
**Iwo-Jima**
*Javanese*
*Javanese* and *American*
*Javanese* and *Americans*
*American*
**Java**
*Malayan*
*Malayan* and *American*
*Malayan* and *Americans*
**Malaysian**
**Malaysian** and *American*
**Malaysian** and *Americans*
*Maldivian*
*Maldivian* and *American*

*Carolinian*
*Carolinian* and *American*
*Carolinian* and *Americans*
**Carolina Islands**

*Fijian*
*Fijian* and *American*
*Fijian* and *Americans*
**Fiji**
*Kosraen*
*Kosraen* and *American*
*Kosraen* and *Americans*
**Kosrae**
*Melanesian*
*Melanesian* and *American*
*Melanesian* and *Americans*
**Melanesia**
*Micronesian*
*Micronesian* and *American*
*Micronesian* and *Americans*
**Micronesia**
*Northern Mariana Islander*
**Mariana Islands**
*Palauan*
*Palauan* and *American*
*Palauan* and *Americans*
**Palau**
*Papua New Guinean*
*Papua New Guinean* and

*Papua New Guinean* and *Americans*
**Papua New Guinea**
*Yapese*
*Yapese* and *American*
*Yapese* and *Americans*
**Yap**
*Pacific Islander*
*Hong Kong* and *American*
*Hong Kong* and *Americans*

Maldivian and *Americans*
**Maldives**
Nepali
Nepali and *American*
Nepali and *Americans*
**Nepal**
Pohapean
Pohapean and *American*
Pohapean and *Americans*
**Ponapea**
Polynesian
Polynesian and *America*
Polynesian and *Americans*
**Polynesia**
Solomon Islander
Solomon Islander and *American*
Solomon Islander and *Americans*
**Solomon Islands**
Tahitian
Tahitian and *American*
Tahitian and *Americans*
Tahiti
Tarawa Islander
Tarawa Islander and *American*
Tarawa Islander and *Americans*
**Tarawa Islands**
Tokeluan
Tokeluan and *American*
Tokeluan and *Americans*
**Tokelua**
Tongan
Tongan and *American*
Togan and *Americans*
**Tonga**
Trukese
Chuukese
Trukese and *American*
Trukese and *Americans*
**Truk**

Manchurian
Manchurian and *American*
Manchurian and *Americans*
Mongolian
Mongolian and *American*
Mongolian and *Americans*
Taiwanese and *American*
Taiwanese and *Americans*
Tibetan
Tibetan and *American*
Tibetan and *Americans*
East Indian
East Indian and *American*
East Indian and *Americans*

## APPENDIX 8

## NAME KEY WORDS USED IN THE DATABASE SEARCH OF FAMOUS AND/OR PROMINENT ASIAN AMERICANS*

1) **Kyutaro Abiko**, editor of Nichi Bei Times and leader of the Japanese community of San Francisco,
2) **Peter Aduja**, first Filipino to be elected to the Hawaiian Territory prior to statehood,
3) **Chang-ho Ahn**, educator and social reformer,
4) **Philip Ahn**, actor and community leader,
5) **John Aiso**, first Nisei to be appointed to the Municipal Court of Los Angeles,
6) **Abraham Kahikina Akaka**, educational activist in Hawaii and chaplain of the Hawaiian Senate,
7) **Daniel K. Akaka**, U.S. senator from Hawaii,
8) **George Ariyoshi**, politician, business executive, and civic leader,
9) **Manuel Buaken**, novelist,
10) **Sudhindra Nath Bose**, teacher and scholar,
11) **Carlos Bulosan**, writer, labor organizer, and migrant farm worker,
12) **Jeffrey Paul Chan**, novelist,
13) **Subrahmanyan Chandrashekhar**, Nobel laureate, physicist, and scholar,
14) **In-Hwan Chang**, sugar plantation worker and activist,
15) **Michael Chang**, professional tennis player,
16) **William Shao Chang Chem**, major general in the U.S. Army as of December 1992,
17) **Anna Chennault**, Republican activist and widow of the head of the famous "Flying Tigers" air squadron of China,
18) **Frank Chin**, novelist,
19) **Hung Wo Chin**, businessman,
20) **Tiffany Chin**, ice skating champion,
21) **Paul Yukio Chinen**, brigadier general in the U.S. Army as of December 1992,

22) **Margaret Cho,** comedian and star of the TV series *All-American Girl,*
23) **Vernon Chong,** highest ranking officer (major general )in the U.S. Air Force as of December 1992,
24) **Herbert Y. Choy,** first Asian American appointed to a U.S. federal court,
25) **Louis Chu,** novelist,
26) **Constance Chung,** television news reporter,
27) **David Earl Kaleokaika Cooper,** brigadier general in the U.S. Army as of December 1992,
28) **Iva Ikuo Toguri D'Aquino,** World War II radio broadcaster better known as "Tokyo Rose,"
29) **Victoria Manalo Draves,** Olympic swimmer,
30) **Sugimoto Etsu [sic],** novelist,
31) **March Kong Fong Eu,** Secretary of State of California,
32) **Antonio Fagel,** leader of the Filipino Federation of Labor,
33) **Eni F.H. Faleomavaega,** U.S. congressional delegate from American Samoa,
34) **Hiram Leong Fong,** former U.S. senator from Hawaii,
35) **John Liu Fugh,** major general in the U.S. Army as of December 1992,
36) **Masajiro Furuya,** leading businessman in the Japanese community in Seattle,
37) **James Hattori,** foreign desk reporter for CBS-TV News
38) **Samuel Ichiye Hayakawa,** former U.S. senator from California,
39) **Sessue Hayakawa,** actor,
40) **Chinn Ho,** banker and chairman of the board of the Gannett Pacific Corporation,
41) **Harry Honda,** journalist and editor of The Pacific Citizen,
42) **William K. Hosokawa,** journalist,
43) **James Wong Howe,** photographer and cinematographer,
44) **Kim Huie,** novelist,
45) **Yamato Ichihashi,** scholar and educator,
46) **Lawson Fusao Inada,** novelist,
47) **Noguchi Isamu,** sculptor,
48) **New Il-Han,** novelist,
49) **Daniel Ken Inouye,** U.S. senator from Hawaii,
50) **Larry Dulay Itliong,** labor organizer,
51) **Ken Kashiwahara,** reporter for ABC-TV News,

52) **Har Gobind Khorana**, geneticist and Nobel laureate,
53) **Saburo Kido**, leader of the Japanese American Citizens League,
54) **Robert K.U. Kihune**, higest ranking (vice admiral) officer in the U.S. Navy as of December 1992,
55) **Charles Kim**, co-founder of the Kim Brothers Company,
56) **Harry Kim**, co-founder of the Kim Brothers Company,
57) **Warren Kim**, Korean American leader,
58) **Maxine Hong Kingston**, novelist,
59) **Harry H. L. Kitano**, sociologist,
60) **Tommy Kono**, Olympic gold medalist in weight lifting,
61) **Joseph Yoshisuke Kurihara**, famous Japanese American interned in World War II who renounced his citizenship,
62) **Michelle Kwan**, figure skating champion,
63) **Nancy Kwan**, actress,
64) **Abiko Kyutaro** [sic], leader in the Japanese community in San Francisco and former editor of Nichi Bei Times,
65) **Alfred Laureta**, first Filipino director of the Hawaiian Department of Labor and Industrial Relations,
66) **Taltic Sugiyama Lebra**, sociologist,
67) **Chin Yang Lee**, novelist,
68) **David Lee**, Korean American community leader,
69) **Rose Hum Lee**, teacher and writer,
70) **Sammy Lee**, Olympic gold medalist in swimming,
71) **Tsung-Dao Lee**, physicist and Nobel laureate,
72) **Maya Lin**, architect and designer of the Vietnam Veterans' Memorial in Washington, D.C.,
73) **Bette Bao Lord**, novelist,
74) **Pardee Low**, novelist,
75) **Yo Yo Ma**, cellist,
76) **Eduardo E. Malapit**, first Filipino to be elected mayor of an American city (Kauai, Hawaii),
77) **Pablo Manlapit**, labor leader,
78) **Mike Masaru Masaoka**, Japanese American Citizens League leader,
79) **Robert Takeo Matsui**, U.S. congressman from California,
80) **Spark Masayuke Matsunaga**, former U.S. seantor from Hawaii,
81) **Nobel McCarthy**, actress,

82) **Zubin Mehta,** conductor of the New York Philharmonic Orchestra,
83) **Benjamin Menor,** first Filipino appointed to the Hawaii Supreme Court,
84) **Norman Y. Mineta,** U.S. congressman from California,
85) **Patsy Takemoto Mink,** U.S. congresswoman from Hawaii,
86) **Yamasaki Minoru,** architect,
87) **Janice Mirikitani,** poet,
88) **Henry Dukso Moon,** medical researcher on hormones,
89) **Toshio Mori,** novelist,
90) **Makio Murayama,** award-winning researcher on sickle cell anemia,
91) **Yosuke W. Nakano,** architect,
92) **George Nakashima,** furniture designer,
93) **Inazo Nitobe,** novelist,
94) **Isamu Noguchi,** sculptor,
95) **John Okada,** writer,
96) **Ellison Onizuka,** astronaut who died in the space shuttle Challenger explosion,
97) **Yoko Ono Lennon,** artist and widow of slain musician John Lennon,
98) **Seiji Ozawa,** conductor and musician,
99) **Ieoh Ming Pei,** architect,
100) **Lee Yan Phou,** novelist,
101) **James Yoshinori Sakamoto,** prize fighter and journalist,
102) **Lazarus Eitaro Salii,** political leader of Micronesia,
103) **Masao Satow,** leader of the Japanese American Citizens League,
104) **Eric Ken Shinseki,** brigadier general in the U.S. Army as of December 1992,
105) **Dalip Singh Saund,** former U.S. congressman and first Indian American elected to Congress,
106) **Joe Shoong,** businessman and philanthropist,
107) **Monica Sone,** writer and clinical psychologist,
108) **Larry Taijiri,** editor of The Pacific Citizen,
109) **George Takei,** actor who played "Sulu" in the Star Trek series,
110) **Amy Tan,** novelist,
111) **Samuel Chao Chung Ting,** Nobel laureate in physics,

112) **Wilfred C. Tsukiyama,** Chief Justice of the Hawaii Supreme Court,
113) **An Wang,** computer expert,
114) **Taylor Wang,** astronaut,
115) **Wayne Wang,** movie director,
116) **Anna May Wong,** actress,
117) **Frederick Gamchoon Wong,** brigadier general in the U.S. Army as of December 1992,
118) **Jade Snow Wong,** novelist,
119) **Shawn Hsu Wong,** novelist,
120) **Kristi Tsuya Yamaguchi,** Olympic gold medalist in ice skating,
121) **Minoru Yamasaki,** architect,
122) **Chen-Ning Yang,** Nobel laureate in physics,
123) **Kang Younghill,** novelist.

* These names are of prominent and/or famous Asian Americans who died within the 1900s or were still alive at the time the content analysis of this book was conducted.

## APPENDIX 9

## BREAKDOWN BY TYPE OF ARTICLE AND ETHNIC SUB-GROUP, AND BY ARTICLE SUB-TOPIC AND ETHNIC SUB-GROUP FOR THE NEWSPAPERS IN THE CONTENT ANALYSIS

In all of the following tables, the abbreviation "WKP" stands for the coding category of Well-Known Persons. There are two tables for each newspaper, as defined above, and the newspapers are listed in alphabetical order. The information for the *Seattle Times* is listed in the text of Chapter Five. In tables 86 to 117 the initials stand for the following: AA - Asian Americans, AI - Asian Indians, CA - Chinese Americans, CAM - Cambodian Americans, FA - Filipino Americans, HAW - Hawaiian Americans, JA - Japanese Americans, KA - Korean Americans, LA - Laotian Americans, PA - Pakistani Americans, PIA - Pacific Islander Americans (other than Hawaiians), TA - Thai Americans, VA - Vietnamese Americans,

Other - Asian Americans of ethnic origins not listed above, and WKP stands for Well Known (Asian American) Persons.

Table 86. Type of Articles and Asian American Ethnic Sub-Groups in the *Atlanta Journal-Constitution*, 1994-1995

| Article Topic | AA | AI | CA | JA | KA | VA | WKP | Total |
|---|---|---|---|---|---|---|---|---|
| Classic Arts | 0 | 0 | 0 | 0 | 0 | 0 | 1 | 1 |
| Crime | 1 | 0 | 0 | 0 | 1 | 2 | 0 | 4 |
| Education | 0 | 0 | 0 | 1 | 0 | 0 | 0 | 1 |
| Entertainment | 1 | 0 | 0 | 0 | 0 | 1 | 3 | 5 |
| Human Interest | 5 | 1 | 0 | 0 | 0 | 1 | 1 | 7 |
| Moral | 3 | 0 | 0 | 0 | 2 | 0 | 0 | 5 |
| Health and Welfare | 0 | 0 | 0 | 0 | 1 | 0 | 0 | 1 |
| Politics | 0 | 0 | 1 | 1 | 2 | 0 | 0 | 4 |
| Totals | 10 | 1 | 1 | 2 | 6 | 4 | 4 | 28 |

Table 87. Article Sub-Topics and Asian American Ethnic Sub-Groups in the *Atlanta Journal-Constitution*, 1994-1995

| Sub-Topic | AA | AI | CA | JA | KA | VA | WKP | Total |
|---|---|---|---|---|---|---|---|---|
| All Am. Girl | 1 | 0 | 0 | 0 | 0 | 0 | 0 | 1 |
| Festivals | 1 | 0 | 0 | 0 | 0 | 0 | 0 | 1 |
| Gangs | 0 | 0 | 0 | 0 | 0 | 2 | 0 | 2 |
| Racism | 1 | 0 | 0 | 0 | 2 | 0 | 0 | 3 |
| Yo Yo Ma | 0 | 0 | 0 | 0 | 0 | 0 | 1 | 1 |
| None | 7 | 1 | 1 | 2 | 4 | 2 | 3 | 20 |
| Totals | 10 | 1 | 1 | 2 | 6 | 4 | 4 | 28 |

Table 88. Type of Articles and Asian American Ethnic Sub-Groups in the *Boston Globe*, 1994-1995

| Topic | AA | AI | CA | CAM | HAW | JA | KA | LA | VA | WKP | Tot. |
|---|---|---|---|---|---|---|---|---|---|---|---|
| C. Arts | 1 | 1 | 0 | 0 | 0 | 0 | 0 | 0 | 0 | 8 | 10 |
| Crime | 6 | 0 | 3 | 1 | 0 | 0 | 0 | 0 | 0 | 0 | 10 |
| Economic | 1 | 0 | 0 | 0 | 0 | 0 | 0 | 0 | 0 | 0 | 1 |
| Education | 0 | 0 | 0 | 0 | 0 | 0 | 0 | 1 | 0 | 0 | 1 |
| Entertain. | 1 | 0 | 3 | 0 | 1 | 1 | 0 | 0 | 0 | 1 | 7 |
| Human Int. | 3 | 1 | 0 | 2 | 0 | 0 | 2 | 0 | 1 | 0 | 9 |
| Moral | 4 | 0 | 1 | 0 | 0 | 0 | 0 | 0 | 0 | 0 | 5 |
| Health, Wel. | 1 | 0 | 0 | 1 | 0 | 0 | 0 | 0 | 0 | 0 | 1 |
| Politics | 5 | 0 | 1 | 0 | 0 | 0 | 0 | 0 | 0 | 0 | 2 |
| Other | 0 | 0 | 0 | 0 | 0 | 0 | 1 | 0 | 0 | 0 | 6 |
| Totals | 22 | 2 | 8 | 4 | 1 | 1 | 3 | 1 | 1 | 9 | 52 |

Table 89. Article Sub-Topics and Asian American Ethnic Sub-Groups in the *Boston Globe*, 1994-1995

| Sub-Topic | AA | AI | CA | CAM | HAW | JA | KA | LA | VA | WKP | Tot. |
|---|---|---|---|---|---|---|---|---|---|---|---|
| Festivals | 2 | 0 | 1 | 0 | 0 | 0 | 0 | 0 | 1 | 0 | 4 |
| Gangs | 1 | 0 | 2 | 0 | 0 | 0 | 0 | 0 | 0 | 0 | 3 |
| Model Min. | 1 | 1 | 0 | 1 | 0 | 0 | 1 | 1 | 0 | 0 | 5 |
| Racism | 5 | 0 | 0 | 0 | 0 | 0 | 0 | 0 | 0 | 0 | 5 |
| Yo Yo Ma | 0 | 0 | 0 | 0 | 0 | 0 | 0 | 0 | 0 | 1 | 1 |
| None | 13 | 1 | 5 | 3 | 1 | 1 | 2 | 0 | 0 | 8 | 34 |
| Totals | 22 | 2 | 8 | 4 | 1 | 1 | 3 | 1 | 1 | 9 | 52 |

Table 90. Type of Articles and Asian American Ethnic Sub-Groups in the *Chicago Tribune*, 1994-1995

| Article Topic | AA | HAW | JA | KA | VA | WKP | Total |
|---|---|---|---|---|---|---|---|
| Classic Arts | 0 | 0 | 1 | 0 | 1 | 7 | 9 |
| Crime | 2 | 0 | 0 | 0 | 1 | 0 | 3 |
| Economic | 1 | 0 | 0 | 1 | 0 | 0 | 2 |
| Education | 0 | 0 | 0 | 1 | 0 | 0 | 1 |
| Entertainment | 1 | 1 | 0 | 0 | 0 | 1 | 3 |
| Human Interest | 2 | 0 | 1 | 0 | 0 | 0 | 3 |
| Moral | 0 | 0 | 0 | 1 | 0 | 0 | 1 |
| Politics | 0 | 1 | 1 | 0 | 2 | 0 | 3 |
| Totals | 6 | 2 | 2 | 3 | 4 | 8 | 25 |

Table 91. Article Sub-Topics and Asian American Ethnic Sub-Groups in the *Chicago Tribune*, 1994-1995

| Sub-Topic | AA | HAW | JA | KA | VA | WKP | Total |
|---|---|---|---|---|---|---|---|
| All Am. Girl | 1 | 0 | 0 | 0 | 0 | 0 | 1 |
| Gangs | 1 | 0 | 0 | 0 | 1 | 0 | 1 |
| Model Minority | 1 | 0 | 0 | 1 | 0 | 0 | 2 |
| Racism | 1 | 0 | 0 | 1 | 1 | 0 | 3 |
| Yo Yo Ma | 0 | 0 | 0 | 0 | 0 | 6 | 6 |
| None | 2 | 2 | 2 | 1 | 3 | 2 | 12 |
| Totals | 6 | 2 | 2 | 3 | 4 | 8 | 25 |

Table 92.  Type of Articles and Asian American Ethnic Sub-Groups in the *Christian Science Monitor*, 1994-1995

| Article Topic | AA | KA | PA | WKP | Total |
|---|---|---|---|---|---|
| Crime | 1 | 1 | 0 | 0 | 2 |
| Education | 1 | 0 | 0 | 0 | 1 |
| Entertainment | 0 | 0 | 0 | 1 | 1 |
| Human Interest | 1 | 0 | 1 | 0 | 2 |
| Totals | 3 | 1 | 1 | 1 | 6 |

Table 93.  Article Sub-Topics and Asian American Ethnic Sub-Groups in the *Christian Science Monitor*, 1994-1995

| Sub-Topic | AA | KA | PA | WKP | Total |
|---|---|---|---|---|---|
| Gangs | 1 | 0 | 0 | 0 | 1 |
| None | 2 | 1 | 1 | 1 | 5 |
| Totals | 3 | 1 | 1 | 1 | 6 |

Table 94.  Type of Articles and Asian American Ethnic Sub-Groups in the *Denver Post*, 1994-1995

| Article Topic | AA | CAM | JA | KA | VA | Total |
|---|---|---|---|---|---|---|
| Crime | 1 | 0 | 0 | 1 | 2 | 4 |
| Defense | 0 | 0 | 1 | 0 | 0 | 1 |
| Human Interest | 1 | 1 | 0 | 1 | 1 | 4 |
| Politics | 0 | 0 | 1 | 0 | 0 | 1 |
| Totals | 2 | 1 | 2 | 2 | 3 | 10 |

Table 95.  Article Sub-Topics and Asian American Ethnic Sub-Groups in the *Denver Post*, 1994-1995

| Sub-Topic | AA | CAM | JA | KA | VA | Total |
|---|---|---|---|---|---|---|
| Gangs | 1 | 0 | 0 | 0 | 1 | 2 |
| Japanese Internment | 0 | 0 | 1 | 0 | 0 | 1 |
| None | 1 | 1 | 1 | 2 | 2 | 7 |
| Totals | 2 | 1 | 2 | 2 | 3 | 10 |

Table 96. Type of Articles and Asian American Ethnic Sub-Groups in the *Detroit News*, 1994-1995

| Article Topic | AA | AI | CA | Total |
|---|---|---|---|---|
| Crime | 1 | 0 | 0 | 1 |
| Entertainment | 3 | 0 | 0 | 3 |
| Human Interest | 1 | 1 | 1 | 3 |
| Totals | 5 | 1 | 1 | 7 |

Table 97. Article Sub-Topics and Asian American Ethnic Sub-Groups in the *Detroit News*, 1994-1995

| Sub-Topic | AA | AI | CA | Total |
|---|---|---|---|---|
| All American Girl | 2 | 0 | 0 | 2 |
| Festivals | 0 | 0 | 1 | 1 |
| None | 3 | 1 | 0 | 4 |
| Totals | 5 | 1 | 1 | 7 |

Table 98. Type of Articles and Asian American Ethnic Sub-Groups in the *Houston Chronicle*, 1994-1995

| Article Topic | AA | VA | WKP | Total |
|---|---|---|---|---|
| Entertainment | 1 | 2 | 1 | 4 |
| Human Interest | 2 | 0 | 0 | 2 |
| Moral | 2 | 0 | 0 | 2 |
| Health and Welfare | 2 | 0 | 0 | 2 |
| Politics | 2 | 0 | 0 | 2 |
| Totals | 9 | 2 | 1 | 12 |

Table 99. Article Sub-Topics and Asian American Ethnic Sub-Groups in the *Houston Chronicle*, 1994-1995

| Sub-Topic | AA | VA | WKP | Total |
|---|---|---|---|---|
| All American Girl | 1 | 0 | 0 | 1 |
| Festivals | 0 | 1 | 0 | 1 |
| Racism | 2 | 0 | 0 | 2 |
| None | 6 | 1 | 1 | 8 |
| Totals | 9 | 2 | 1 | 12 |

Table 100.  Type of Articles and Asian American Ethnic Sub-Groups in
the *Houston Post*, 1994-1995

| Article Topic | AA | KA | VA | Total |
|---|---|---|---|---|
| Crime | 1 | 0 | 0 | 1 |
| Entertainment | 3 | 0 | 0 | 3 |
| Human Interest | 3 | 3 | 0 | 6 |
| Moral | 1 | 0 | 0 | 1 |
| Health and Welfare | 0 | 0 | 1 | 1 |
| Politics | 2 | 0 | 1 | 3 |
| Totals | 10 | 3 | 2 | 15 |

Table 101.  Article Sub-Topics and Asian American Ethnic Sub-Groups
in the *Houston Post*, 1994-1995

| Sub-Topic | AA | KA | VA | Total |
|---|---|---|---|---|
| All American Girl | 1 | 0 | 0 | 1 |
| Racism | 1 | 0 | 0 | 1 |
| None | 8 | 3 | 2 | 13 |
| Totals | 10 | 3 | 2 | 15 |

Table 102.  Type of Articles and Asian American Ethnic Sub-Groups in
the *Los Angles Times*, 1994-1995

| Topic | AA | CA | CAM | HA | JA | KA | VA | WKP | Other* | Tot. |
|---|---|---|---|---|---|---|---|---|---|---|
| Accidents | 0 | 0 | 0 | 0 | 2 | 0 | 0 | 0 | 0 | 2 |
| C. Arts | 1 | 0 | 0 | 0 | 2 | 0 | 1 | 8 | 0 | 12 |
| Crime | 2 | 0 | 1 | 0 | 0 | 0 | 1 | 0 | 0 | 4 |
| Defense | 1 | 0 | 0 | 0 | 1 | 0 | 1 | 0 | 0 | 3 |
| Economic | 2 | 0 | 0 | 0 | 0 | 0 | 0 | 0 | 0 | 2 |
| Entertain. | 4 | 2 | 0 | 0 | 2 | 3 | 2 | 3 | 0 | 16 |
| Human Int. | 1 | 3 | 0 | 0 | 1 | 3 | 3 | 1 | 1 | 13 |
| Moral | 3 | 1 | 0 | 0 | 0 | 3 | 0 | 0 | 0 | 7 |
| Health, Wel. | 0 | 0 | 0 | 1 | 0 | 0 | 1 | 0 | 0 | 2 |
| Politics | 3 | 0 | 1 | 0 | 1 | 4 | 3 | 0 | 0 | 12 |
| Totals | 17 | 6 | 2 | 1 | 9 | 13 | 12 | 12 | 1 | 73 |

* Indonesian Americans.

Table 103. Article Sub-Topics and Asian American Ethnic Sub-Groups in the *Los Angeles Times*, 1994-1995

| Sub-Topic | AA | CA | CAM | HA | JA | KA | VA | WKP | Other* | Tot. |
|---|---|---|---|---|---|---|---|---|---|---|
| All Am. Girl | 2 | 0 | 0 | 0 | 0 | 0 | 0 | 0 | 0 | 2 |
| Festivals | 0 | 1 | 0 | 0 | 1 | 1 | 0 | 0 | 0 | 3 |
| Gangs | 1 | 0 | 1 | 0 | 0 | 0 | 1 | 0 | 0 | 3 |
| JA Intern. | 0 | 0 | 0 | 0 | 3 | 0 | 0 | 0 | 0 | 3 |
| Kobe | 0 | 0 | 0 | 0 | 2 | 0 | 0 | 0 | 0 | 2 |
| Model Min. | 0 | 1 | 0 | 0 | 0 | 0 | 1 | 0 | 0 | 2 |
| Racism | 4 | 0 | 0 | 0 | 0 | 0 | 0 | 0 | 0 | 4 |
| Yo Yo Ma | 0 | 0 | 0 | 0 | 0 | 0 | 0 | 3 | 0 | 3 |
| None | 10 | 4 | 1 | 1 | 3 | 12 | 10 | 9 | 1 | 51 |
| Totals | 17 | 6 | 2 | 1 | 9 | 13 | 12 | 12 | 1 | 73 |

* Indonesian Americans.

Table 104. Type of Articles and Asian American Ethnic Sub-Groups in the *New York Times*, 1994-1995

| Topic | AA | AI | CA | HA | HAW | JA | KA | PIA | VA | WKP | Tot. |
|---|---|---|---|---|---|---|---|---|---|---|---|
| Accidents | 0 | 0 | 0 | 0 | 0 | 3 | 0 | 0 | 0 | 0 | 3 |
| C. Arts | 0 | 0 | 0 | 0 | 0 | 0 | 0 | 0 | 0 | 12 | 12 |
| Crime | 6 | 0 | 0 | 1 | 0 | 0 | 0 | 0 | 0 | 0 | 7 |
| Defense | 0 | 0 | 0 | 0 | 0 | 1 | 0 | 0 | 0 | 0 | 1 |
| Economic | 0 | 0 | 0 | 0 | 1 | 0 | 0 | 0 | 1 | 0 | 2 |
| Education | 1 | 0 | 0 | 0 | 0 | 0 | 0 | 0 | 0 | 0 | 1 |
| Entertain. | 2 | 0 | 2 | 0 | 1 | 1 | 1 | 1 | 0 | 4 | 11 |
| Human Int. | 2 | 1 | 3 | 0 | 0 | 0 | 0 | 0 | 3 | 0 | 9 |
| Moral | 0 | 0 | 0 | 0 | 0 | 0 | 1 | 0 | 0 | 0 | 1 |
| Health, Wel. | 1 | 0 | 0 | 1 | 0 | 0 | 0 | 0 | 0 | 0 | 2 |
| Politics | 1 | 0 | 3 | 0 | 0 | 0 | 0 | 0 | 0 | 0 | 4 |
| Other | 0 | 0 | 0 | 0 | 0 | 0 | 0 | 0 | 0 | 1 | 1 |
| Totals | 13 | 1 | 8 | 2 | 2 | 4 | 2 | 1 | 4 | 17 | 54 |

Table 105. Article Sub-Topics and Asian American Ethnic Sub-Groups in the *New York Times*, 1994-1995

| Sub-Topic | AA | AI | CA | HA | HAW | JA | KA | PIA | VA | WKP | Tot. |
|---|---|---|---|---|---|---|---|---|---|---|---|
| All Am. Girl | 1 | 0 | 0 | 0 | 0 | 0 | 0 | 0 | 0 | 0 | 1 |
| Festivals | 1 | 0 | 0 | 0 | 0 | 0 | 0 | 0 | 1 | 0 | 2 |
| Gangs | 4 | 0 | 0 | 0 | 0 | 0 | 0 | 0 | 0 | 0 | 4 |
| JA Intern. | 0 | 0 | 0 | 0 | 0 | 1 | 0 | 0 | 0 | 0 | 1 |
| Kobe | 0 | 0 | 0 | 0 | 0 | 3 | 0 | 0 | 0 | 0 | 3 |
| Model Min. | 1 | 0 | 1 | 0 | 0 | 0 | 0 | 0 | 0 | 0 | 2 |
| Racism | 2 | 0 | 1 | 0 | 0 | 0 | 1 | 0 | 0 | 0 | 4 |
| Yo Yo Ma | 0 | 0 | 0 | 0 | 0 | 0 | 0 | 0 | 0 | 4 | 4 |
| None | 4 | 1 | 6 | 2 | 2 | 0 | 1 | 1 | 0 | 13 | 33 |
| Totals | 13 | 1 | 8 | 2 | 2 | 4 | 2 | 1 | 4 | 17 | 54 |

Table 106.  Type of Articles and Asian American Ethnic Sub-Groups in
the *San Francisco Chronicle*, 1994-1995

| Topic | AA | AI | CA | FA | JA | KA | VA | WKP | Other* | Tot. |
|---|---|---|---|---|---|---|---|---|---|---|
| Accidents | 0 | 0 | 0 | 0 | 1 | 0 | 0 | 0 | 0 | 1 |
| C. Arts | 0 | 0 | 0 | 0 | 0 | 0 | 0 | 4 | 0 | 4 |
| Crime | 0 | 0 | 2 | 0 | 0 | 0 | 0 | 0 | 1 | 3 |
| Economic | 0 | 0 | 0 | 1 | 0 | 0 | 0 | 0 | 0 | 1 |
| Educate | 1 | 0 | 1 | 0 | 0 | 0 | 0 | 0 | 0 | 2 |
| Entertain. | 7 | 0 | 1 | 3 | 1 | 1 | 0 | 1 | 0 | 14 |
| Human Int. | 10 | 1 | 1 | 2 | 3 | 0 | 0 | 0 | 0 | 17 |
| Moral | 2 | 0 | 2 | 2 | 3 | 0 | 0 | 0 | 0 | 9 |
| Health, Wel. | 9 | 0 | 1 | 0 | 0 | 0 | 1 | 0 | 0 | 11 |
| Politics | 2 | 0 | 3 | 1 | 0 | 1 | 0 | 1 | 0 | 8 |
| Totals | 31 | 1 | 11 | 9 | 8 | 2 | 1 | 6 | 1 | 70 |

* Indonesian Americans.

Table 107.  Article Sub-Topics and Asian American Ethnic Sub-Groups
in the *San Francisco Chronicle*, 1994-1995

| Sub-Topic | AA | AI | CA | FA | JA | KA | VA | WKP | Other* | Tot. |
|---|---|---|---|---|---|---|---|---|---|---|
| All Am. Girl | 4 | 0 | 0 | 0 | 0 | 0 | 0 | 0 | 0 | 4 |
| Festivals | 3 | 0 | 0 | 1 | 0 | 0 | 0 | 0 | 0 | 4 |
| JA Intern. | 0 | 0 | 0 | 0 | 2 | 0 | 0 | 0 | 0 | 2 |
| Kobe | 0 | 0 | 0 | 0 | 1 | 0 | 0 | 0 | 0 | 1 |
| Model Min. | 0 | 1 | 0 | 0 | 0 | 0 | 0 | 0 | 0 | 1 |
| Racism | 5 | 0 | 4 | 2 | 1 | 0 | 0 | 0 | 0 | 12 |
| Yo Yo Ma | 0 | 0 | 0 | 0 | 0 | 0 | 0 | 4 | 0 | 4 |
| None | 19 | 0 | 7 | 6 | 4 | 2 | 1 | 2 | 1 | 42 |
| Totals | 31 | 1 | 11 | 9 | 8 | 2 | 1 | 6 | 1 | 70 |

* Indonesian Americans.

Table 108.  Type of Articles and Asian American Ethnic Sub-Groups in
the *St. Louis Post-Dispatch*, 1994-1995

| Article Topic | AA | TA | VA | Total |
|---|---|---|---|---|
| Crime | 0 | 0 | 1 | 1 |
| Entertainment | 0 | 1 | 0 | 1 |
| Moral | 2 | 0 | 0 | 2 |
| Totals | 2 | 1 | 1 | 4 |

Table 109. Article Sub-Topics and Asian American Ethnic Sub-Groups in the *St. Louis Post-Dispatch*, 1994-1995

| Sub-Topic | AA | TA | VA | Total |
|-----------|----|----|----|-------|
| Gangs | 0 | 0 | 1 | 1 |
| Racism | 2 | 0 | 0 | 2 |
| None | 0 | 1 | 0 | 1 |
| Totals | 2 | 1 | 1 | 4 |

Table 110. Type of Articles and Asian American Ethnic Sub-Groups in the *Times-Picayune*, 1994-1995

| Article Topic | AA | VA | Total |
|---------------|----|----|-------|
| Crime | 0 | 2 | 2 |
| Entertainment | 1 | 1 | 2 |
| Human Interest | 3 | 6 | 9 |
| Moral | 1 | 1 | 2 |
| Other | 0 | 1 | 1 |
| Totals | 5 | 11 | 16 |

Table 111. Article Sub-Topics and Asian American Ethnic Sub-Groups in the *Times-Picayune*, 1994-1995

| Sub-Topic | AA | VA | Total |
|-----------|----|----|-------|
| All American Girl | 1 | 0 | 1 |
| Festivals | 1 | 3 | 4 |
| Gangs | 0 | 1 | 1 |
| Racism | 1 | 2 | 3 |
| None | 2 | 5 | 7 |
| Totals | 5 | 11 | 16 |

Table 112. Type of Articles and Asian American Ethnic Sub-Groups in *USA Today*, 1994-1995

| Article Topic | AA | JA | VA | WKP | Total |
|---------------|----|----|----|-----|-------|
| Accidents | 0 | 1 | 0 | 0 | 1 |
| Classic Arts | 0 | 0 | 0 | 2 | 2 |
| Educate | 0 | 0 | 1 | 0 | 1 |
| Entertainment | 9 | 0 | 0 | 4 | 13 |
| Human Interest | 0 | 0 | 1 | 0 | 1 |
| Other | 1 | 0 | 0 | 0 | 1 |
| Totals | 10 | 1 | 2 | 6 | 19 |

Table 113.  Article Sub-Topics and Asian American Ethnic Sub-Groups in *USA Today*, 1994-1995

| Sub-Topic | AA | JA | VA | WKP | Total |
|---|---|---|---|---|---|
| All American Girl | 8 | 0 | 0 | 0 | 8 |
| Kobe | 0 | 1 | 0 | 0 | 1 |
| Model Minority | 0 | 0 | 1 | 0 | 1 |
| Yo Yo Ma | 0 | 0 | 0 | 2 | 2 |
| None | 2 | 0 | 1 | 4 | 7 |
| Totals | 10 | 1 | 2 | 6 | 19 |

Table 114.  Type of Articles and Asian American Ethnic Sub-Groups in the *Wall Street Journal*, 1994-1995

| Article Topic | AA | AI | CA | CAM | WKP | Total |
|---|---|---|---|---|---|---|
| Classic Arts | 0 | 0 | 0 | 0 | 1 | 1 |
| Entertainment | 1 | 1 | 0 | 0 | 2 | 4 |
| Human Interest | 1 | 0 | 1 | 1 | 0 | 3 |
| Totals | 2 | 1 | 1 | 1 | 3 | 8 |

Table 115.  Article Sub-Topics and Asian American Ethnic Sub-Groups in the *Wall Street Journal*, 1994-1995

| Article Topic | AA | AI | CA | CAM | WKP | Total |
|---|---|---|---|---|---|---|
| All American Girl | 1 | 0 | 0 | 0 | 0 | 1 |
| Yo Yo Ma | 0 | 0 | 0 | 0 | 1 | 1 |
| None | 1 | 1 | 1 | 1 | 2 | 6 |
| Totals | 2 | 1 | 1 | 1 | 3 | 8 |

Table 116.  Type of Articles and Asian American Ethnic Sub-Groups in the *Washington Post*, 1994-1995

| Article Topic | AA | CAM | FA | JA | KA | PIA | WKP | Total |
|---|---|---|---|---|---|---|---|---|
| Classic Arts | 0 | 0 | 0 | 0 | 1 | 0 | 0 | 1 |
| Crime | 2 | 0 | 0 | 0 | 0 | 0 | 0 | 2 |
| Defense | 0 | 0 | 0 | 1 | 0 | 0 | 0 | 1 |
| Entertainment | 4 | 0 | 0 | 2 | 0 | 0 | 1 | 7 |
| Human Interest | 2 | 0 | 0 | 0 | 0 | 0 | 0 | 2 |
| Moral | 0 | 0 | 1 | 1 | 0 | 0 | 0 | 2 |
| Health and Welfare | 0 | 1 | 0 | 0 | 0 | 0 | 0 | 1 |
| Politics | 1 | 0 | 0 | 0 | 1 | 1 | 0 | 3 |
| Science | 1 | 0 | 0 | 0 | 0 | 0 | 0 | 1 |
| Totals | 10 | 1 | 1 | 4 | 2 | 1 | 1 | 20 |

Table 117.  Article Sub-Topics and Asian American Ethnic Sub-Groups
in the *Washington Post*, 1994-1995

| Sub-Topic | AA | CAM | FA | JA | KA | PIA | WKP | Total |
|---|---|---|---|---|---|---|---|---|
| All American Girl | 2 | 0 | 0 | 0 | 0 | 0 | 0 | 2 |
| Model Minority | 1 | 0 | 0 | 0 | 0 | 0 | 0 | 1 |
| Racism | 0 | 0 | 0 | 2 | 0 | 0 | 0 | 2 |
| None | 7 | 1 | 1 | 2 | 2 | 1 | 1 | 15 |
| Totals | 10 | 1 | 1 | 4 | 2 | 1 | 1 | 20 |

APPENDIX 10

# SEX, OCCUPATION, AND STATE OF EMPLOYMENT OF THOSE PERSONS WHO RESPONDED TO THE SURVEY WITH A LETTER, BUT WHO DID NOT ANSWER THE SURVEY QUESTIONS

Table 118.  Sex and Occupation of Persons Who Responded to the
Survey With a Letter But Who Did Not Answer the Survey

| Sex | | Number | Percent Total |
|---|---|---|---|
| Men: | | 10 | 55.6 % |
| | Print: | 5 | |
| | Television: | 5 | |
| | Radio: | 0 | |
| Women: | | 8 | 44.4 % |
| | Print: | 3 | |
| | Television: | 4 | |
| | Radio: | 1 | |

Table 119.  Media Occupation of Persons Who Responded to the Survey
        With a Letter But Who Did Not Answer the Survey

| Media Occupation | Number | Percent of Total |
|---|---|---|
| Print | 8 | 44.4 % |
| Television | 9 | 50.0 % |
| Radio | 1 | 5.6 % |
| Total | 18 | |

Table 120.  States Where Persons Who Responded to the Survey With a
        Letter But Who Did Not Answer the Survey Worked

| State | Number of Respondents Who Work There |
|---|---|
| California | 4 |
| Connecticut | 1 |
| Florida | 1 |
| Massachusetts | 1 |
| Nevada | 1 |
| New Jersey | 1 |
| New York | 2 |
| N. Carolina | 1 |
| Oregon | 1 |
| Texas | 1 |
| Virginia | 1 |
| Washington | 1 |
| Washington, DC | 1 |
| Wisconsin | 1 |
| Total | 18 |

## APPENDIX 11

# SELECTED RESPONSES TO SURVEY QUESTION THREE

The following are responses taken nearly verbatim from the journalists' written answers to survey question three. The name of the reporter, and his or her place of employment, is given in bold type at the end of each response, if that person did not request anonymity. If the sex of a respondent is unclear from the person's name or the content of the text, Ms. or Mr. will be printed before the name for reader clarification. These are listed in no set order and not all responses are reprinted here. Many of those answers not reprinted were brief "yes" or "no" answers, and some were brief answers that repeated points already made by other respondents. Some editing was done to make the style, such as the term "Asian American" not being hyphenated, consistent throughout for reader ease. Also, the job titles are taken directly from what the respondents gave on the survey.

*Question 3: In your opinion, what is being done right in the media today in covering Asian Americans and issues affecting Asian Americans?*

Token coverage of Asian American issues and events and letting Asian American staff members cover Asian American issues and events, a sign of maturity on the part of editors to trust Asian American staff members to cover their own events and still be objective. **Joseph Lariosa, news editor, *Philippinetime*, Chicago, Illinois.**

Answer to questions 3 and 4. The media continue to pursue the model minority role of Asian Americans without exploring these issues deeper. The same issues are constantly popping up in headlines. Superficially, they are positive stories. But they perpetuate stereotypes that are ingrained into the general public without examining the dire consequences. I'm sick of reading the story of the Asian violin child prodigy. Or the Korean kid who scored the perfect 1600 on the SAT. Or how the Chinese tongs are heating up again in Chinatown. The media look at Asian Americans in extremes as they do everything else. There needs to be an examination of the middle ground issues in the Asian American community. More Asian Americans of varying backgrounds need to be hired to cover their respective communities. A Korean journalist is not capable of fully understanding the depth of the Cambodian community without speaking the language. The same goes for a Chinese journalist covering a story concerning Korean grocers. We cannot be treated the same despite the fact that we may look similar or simply fall under the umbrella of being Asian American. **Ken Kwok, photographer, *Press-Telegram*, Long Beach, California.**

The news media is working hard not to portray Asian Americans as the "model minority." There is an effort to portray the good and the bad, and the press has worked hard to recognize that the Asian American community is made up of various ethnicities. **Benjamin Seto, business reporter, *The Fresno Bee*, Fresno, California.**

Answer to questions 3 and 4. I group these two questions in one because they are too broad even though you're asking for my opinion. First, they deal with the media as a whole and I can't speak of the entire industry when I only have experience with print journalism. Even within print journalism I don't read more than a handful of newspapers, and I don't think I can give a fair evaluation of newspaper coverage of Asian Americans and issues affecting them without undertaking a research project myself.

I may, however, speak of my observations of *The Record's* coverage of Asian Americans and AA issues. But then Stockton, the county seat of San Joaquin County where our paper has served for the last 100 years, and the county seat itself reflect a rather unique community. For some reason, there has been a great number of Southeast Asian refugees making their home here since 1975. The paper has been very sensitive to their cultures and experiences, as it has been with other minorities including Japanese, Chinese and Latino Americans. Just recently the local chapter of the National Association for the Advancement of Colored People met with our editorial staff and local law enforcement officials during a working lunch to voice their concerns and establish a communication channel for better understanding. The newly elected officials of a new Vietnamese American organization in San Joaquin County have learned (from a media guide prepared by the Asian American

Journalists Association that I gave them) how to promote their activities. *The Record* has sent a reporter to cover their election and later the swearing-in ceremony of the elected officials. Ms. Thai Nguyen Strom, columnist and chief librarian, *The Record,* San Joaquin County, California.

Answer to questions 3 and 4. I occasionally hear or see mistakes or misconceptions about Asian Americans in the news, but I do not believe that the majority of them are intentional or malicious. I think the obvious remedy for these mistakes is the continued education by all members of the media of the diverse cultures we cover. This will be helped by hiring more members of these cultures. (Not that hiring minorities is the cure-all for our gaffes. We, as journalists, should be able to accurately and fairly cover people outside of our own cultures.) **Archie Tse, graphics editor, The** ***New York Times*, New York City.**

They're aren't enough articles on Asian Americans for me to be able to tell what they are doing right. **Ms. Pueng Vongs, reporter, *Money* magazine, New York City.**

When it comes to what is being done right in covering Asian Americans and issues affecting Asian Americans, I think there are two maxims: (a) The West is best, and (b) If you want something done right, do it yourself. Because of the larger and more long-standing Asian population in western states such as California, Oregon, Washington, and Hawaii, the media coverage there is much more reflective of Asian diversity and covers a wider range of issues. Publications run by Asian Americans, such as *A. Magazine* in New York, are also effective because the people who are targeted and the people doing the targeting have the same backgrounds. **Amy Wang, copy editor, *The Philadelphia Inquirer*, Philadelphia, Pennsylvania.**

It's not doing enough. Either it's too specialized and it becomes ethnic, so you are, even though. . . I find we are much more culturally conscious than when I was back in India. When I was in India, America was a state of mind, but I came over here and I felt there was a need to identify myself with the Indian community. Something is wrong and it's almost like leading two lives. If you talk to immigrants like me who have been here tow years, at some point you have to choose which culture you are going to embrace.

The media only focuses on the stereotypes, like the language. . . .We are never shown on television in big houses or having good jobs. I think even Indian media in the United States is not doing what it could; it's clinging to the past too much. It is mostly reporting rehashed news going on in India. **Ms. Jyothi Kiran, staff writer, *India Currents* magazine, San Jose, California.**

There is the recognition, however belated, of the valuable contributions that Asian Americans have made in various fields—from the arts to the sciences.

There is, likewise, an effort on the part of some writers in the mainstream media to put issues affecting Asian Americans into perspective, taking into account the unique cultures of each ethnic Asian American group. **Ms. Marites Sison-Paez, editor, *Special Edition Press*, New York City.**

I believe the U.S. media is heading in the right direction by becoming increasingly open to uncovering and reporting on deeper issues that affect Asian Americans. However, I have found this to be true not in mainstream media, but in a much smaller niche, the Asian American presses of California and New York. New Asian American magazines and newspapers are reporting on a variety of largely untouched issues, including Asian Americas and homosexuality, identity issues (biculturalism), and hate crimes against Asian Americans. In addition, I have found that slowly, but surely, more Asian Americans are coming into the spotlight. I don't ever recall there being a sitcom with only Asian Americans until I saw *All-American Girl* on television. What's more, on the big screen, movies such as *The Joy Luck Club* and "Heaven and Earth" have been successful in introducing more realistic portrayals of Asian and Asian American culture. **Ms. Putsata Reang cultural reporter, *Spokesman-Review*, Spokane, Washington.**

I see an attempt to overcome the dichotomy of the "model minority" vs. "yellow peril" extremes of past coverage. **Paul Hyun-Bong Shin, staff writer, *The Courier-News*, Bridgewater, New Jersey.**

I think in terms of what I've seen in covering Asian Americans all the initiatives come from Asian Americans. I do think that we are kind of a non-entity in the media; you can count on one had the Asian Americans on television. People think we're better represented than we are because we have the occasional woman anchor, but there are hardly any (Asian American) males on television. It's like the harpist in the orchestra. You stand out. **Pamela SooHoo, associate producer for public television (media organization withheld upon request).**

Many news organizations today hire Asian Americans, as well as other ethnic groups, to give more input and participation in their news coverage. **Ms. Trinh Le, reporter, *Sun Newspapers*, Houston, Texas.**

I'm proud that one organization with which I worked depicted the wrongs/rights of an Asian politician as just that—the wrongs and rights of a politician, excluding ethnicity. I think it's also becoming increasingly common to see, on many national news magazines and bigger market news, Asian people, in general, whether it be a man-on-the-street response, main interview, victim, witness, etc. **Victoria Lim, reporter, WWMT-TV News, Kalamazoo, Michigan.**

I don't believe the media is doing much in the way of covering Asian Americans period. Real issues affecting the Asian American community are not covered at all. **Eric Chu, assistant picture editor, *Chicago Tribune*, Chicago, Illinois.**

Not much. There are a few reporters and anchors here and there on the networks. And, there's a television sitcom that was canceled [*All American Girl*]. And, there are some Asian characters that don't have accents on TV shows. But in the large part, I consistently feel they are tokens. They're there to appease the Asian American masses for awhile. Now, what should be done? I don't know the answer. I guess there needs to be more people like me behind the scenes making decisions. **Ms. Michile Kim-Gray, producer, KWTX-TV, Waco, Texas.**

In larger cities like New York (where I'm from) and Los Angeles, Asian Americans are part of the community and are covered well. In my market, there are so few of them and those which exist are so assimilated into the community that their concerns are really mainstream concerns. **Rose Tibayan, anchor/reporter, WINK-TV, Fort Myers, Florida.**

I think the media is correct to leave race out of most stories (whether they're about Asian Americans, African Americans or any other race) unless it is of issue. for instance, we would not include the race of gang members in a story on an incidence of gang violence. But it would be appropriate to discuss race in, for example, a story on the difficulty of going after Asian gangs (where factors may include a language barrier and a suspicion of authority among victims if they are recent immigrants from communist Asian countries). **Ms. Yuki Spellman, news writer, WGN News, Chicago, Illinois.**

I believe of all the minorities, Asians are still years behind in terms of broadcast television's perception of mature, professional on-air talent. True, many more Asian women apply and serve as reporters, producers, etc., yet the Asian male is still perceived as a scientist, doctor or accountant. If you include all aspects of television beyond broadcast journalism, only recently have Asian males been portrayed as confident, competent and even sex symbols in Hollywood. Dogging the gender for ages have been countless media references to martial arts, i.e., shedding what some call "the kung-fu curse."

My experience at the recent AAJA convention showed the tide seems to be turning for the positive in that many news directors were attracted to the fact I was an Asian male reporter with good experience, etc. They spoke of the "rarity" of Asian male reporters versus the numbers of Asian female reporters. Again, despite what the hiring trends in broadcast journalism on-air talent may show, being an Asian male reporter is a good thing right now. In what could be considered a "racist" remark, one news director mentioned that being Asian is not all a bad thing for the "IQ" factor. Meaning, viewers tend to trust Asian reporters on science, health and money stories because Joe Public thinks all Asians to be generally intelligent. Racist? Maybe. Prejudicial? Yes. Beneficial, again yes. **Robert Goozee, news assignment desk, KNBC NBC 4, Los Angeles, California.**

At least newspapers now see issues among other groups than white and blacks. **Ronald Patel, Sunday editor, *Philadelphia Inquirer*, Philadelphia, Pennsylvania.**

Increasingly, Asian Americans are being used as sources and examples, as are women, African Americans, Native Americans and Hispanic Americans. I'm glad to see this, just because their faces and their voices reflect what the world is like today. **Lisa Lee Daniels, reporter, *The Oregonian*, Portland, Oregon.**

I am happy to see that mainstream media has hired a few Asian and non-Asian journalists that have a good grasp or an awareness of the Asian American community. We definitely need more of these journalists, but we are doing better than before. **Connie Riu, manager, diversity and outreach services, Newspaper Association of America, Reston, Virginia.**

Efforts are being made to reach the [Asian American] community. People are willing to listen. **Ms. Anu Mannar, life copy desk chief, *News and Record*, Greensboro, North Carolina.**

I believe that there has been an increase in attempts to cover both sides, if there are only two sides, to the Asian American community. Perhaps we should say that there has been improvement in providing a broader view of the "Asian American" community. So much better that if a story appears that is clearly lacking in exploring an issues thoroughly, the lack if noticed. **Ms. Gimmy Park Li, manager, public affairs, KNBR AM - KFOG FM, San Francisco, California.**

There is more awareness, particularly at large organizations, of changing communities, changing readership, and the need to produce information that addresses that change. More Asian Americans are employed as editors, helping make coverage decisions—but we are far from where we need to be. **Ms. Mei-Mei Chan, executive editor, *Post Record*, Idaho Falls, Idaho.**

There is not enough coverage in the media today on the Asian American community or its issues. **George Kiriyama, desk assistant, KCAL-TV Channel 9 News, Los Angeles, California.**

I think there's a conscious effort to have more Asian Americans on television and in the newspapers. Asians are becoming a more dominant force and are being used as experts. **Mary Tan, news reporter, WMTV-TV, Madison, Wisconsin.**

Done right—speaking narrowly (in Phoenix's situation), the local press/media have done a fair job in covering Asian issues. The Henry Wu and U.S.-Sino relations coverage go without saying. The Arizona Republic/Phoenix Gazette, for instance, recently ran a Sunday package about the influence Intel Corporation has had in Chandler—the valley city that the computer giant made its headquarters' home—and touched on the influx of Asians and other nationalities. As part of the package, a sidebar was devoted to how one Asian family is trying to assimilate to U.S. culture without sacrificing too much of its own. The newspapers also ran stories during the 25th anniversary of the fall of Saigon, writing of local Vietnamese Americans who have chosen to return to their homeland and start businesses. It must be noted that the coverage is due largely to a longtime reporter, Paul Brinkley-Rogers, who covered the Vietnam War at one point for *Newsweek* and has great interest about that country. The electronic media do considerably less, but still manage to be fair and thorough (given their limited format) to cover spot news involving Asian issues, such as the racist graffiti that was sprayed on an Asian church in Chandler a couple of years ago. **Abraham Kwok, reporter, *The Arizona Republic/The Phoenix Gazette*, Phoenix, Arizona.**

The fact that more media companies are recognizing and respecting the reality of diversity has helped put faces of color in the news is a positive development. Asian Americans are being included in more reports; in bigger markets Asian Americans are more likely to be mainstreamed into a story, rather than the subject of a story—i.e., talking with an Asian American about the future of the city, versus, talking with an Asian American about Chinese New Year. **Janice Gin, executive producer/1996 Atlanta Olympics, Gannett Broadcasting, Atlanta, Georgia.**

What's right: Increasing understanding, especially on the West Coast, of the diversity within the Asian American community and the various contributions made by those communities. The increase in number of Asian American journalists is making a difference. But there's still much more to do. **Peter Bhatia, managing editor, *The Oregonian*, Portland, Oregon.**

I don't believe anything is being done right because I don't believe that the media recognized that something needs to be done. I see little things like, perhaps, more local Asian news anchors, but only in areas with high Asian residents (e.g., Los Angeles). Asian actors are starting to get more roles that aren't so stereotypical, but that's a rare thing. Certainly the book and magazine publishing industries don't see the need to diversity; diversification and racial equality aren't even discussed. As for newspaper publishing, well, I see more Asians getting printed, but still, overall the numbers are low. **Ms. Soomie Ahn, employee of Ellen Ryder Communications, New York City.**

A good example of what is being done right in the media today in covering Asian Americans and issues affecting them is reflected in a story that appeared in the November 6 (1995) edition of *USA Today*. The story explained how U.S. and Japanese business people have difficulty communicating because of sharp cultural differences. By including an explanation of cultural differences it helps readers understand where people are coming from when they make particular decisions that affect the entire world.

I think the media gradually are going beyond the bashing of races and beginning to examine cultures and attitudes. some papers, such as the *Detroit Free Press*, have devoted special sections to extensively study the lifestyle and relationship between the United States and another country. Unfortunately, it took incidents like Japan-bashing and people like Rodney King to bring out that type of "discussion" in the papers and in the community. **Henry Yuen, assistant features editor, *Star-Gazette*, Elmira, New York.**

The fact that Asian Americans are even covered at all is a tremendous step forward. There was a lot of coverage of the contributions of the Japanese American soldiers of the 442nd Combat Infantry Battalion and the Military Intelligence Service during this 50th anniversary [of the end of World War II] year. the stories of Chinese people being smuggled into our country and held hostage by members of crime rings and of Thai workers freed from slave conditions in California also add to our visibility. I wish more had been done when Congressman Norm Mineta announced he was leaving government service. Asian Americans are losing a big advocate in the Congress, yet our political loss wasn't explored by the general media. I see more inclusion of Asian Americans in general news coverage. It's good to see Asian Americans as part of the "American Scene"—a person on the street, doctor, janitor, teacher, student and business person. **Lori Matsukawa, anchor, KING TV, Seattle, Washington.**

Due to the increased presence of Asian Americans working in the media, I believe coverage of Asians, Asian Americans and Asian American issues have improved over the years. This includes being sensitive to the different nationalities, cultures, beliefs and social and political singularities within various Asian groups. I think I see a definite effort by most media organizations to distinguish each Asian culture (i.e., referring to Thai, Filipino, Korean, Vietnamese, Chinese, Taiwanese as opposed to just grouping everyone as indistinguishable, unidentifiable "Asians"). **Ms. Jinah Kim, producer - 11 p.m. news, KCCN-TV, Monterey, California.**

The best place for coverage of Asians and Asian American issues is undoubtedly the minority press. In Seattle, the *Northwest*

*Asian Weekly* and *International Examiner* play this role. In the mainstream press, I occasionally see features on the Indian community or Chinese New Year, but overall, I still don't see a lot of positive coverage of Asian American issues, just the tragedies like immigrant kidnapping rings. I do see an increased coverage of Asian American bands, playwrights, directors and authors, and I believe this does encourage other Asian Americans to pursue these less traditional careers. some media outlets are making an effort to interview an Asian as part of their stories, but it happens much less than I would like. I feel it's important for media outlets to make a good effort to try and convey a range of opinions from a diverse pool of voices, and hearing from an Asian American who is articulate helps bring down the stereotype all Asians are "F.O.B." (a derogatory term for new immigrants, meaning "fresh off the boat") and devoid of emotion, opinion or linguistic ability. **Susan Han, producer, DCTS TV, Seattle, Washington.**

"Diversifying" the newsroom! I believe I am the first on-air [Asian American] reporter at Newschannel Four. I see more and more Asian Americans on air. It's great! Not only does it help us destroy the stereotypes of Asians, it helps them have a voice, and many times they will be more open to talk with us in an on-camera interview.

The other positive aspect is that I see more news directors slowly giving Asians jobs as broadcast anchors—and I am seeing more Asians becoming managers in the broadcast media, ones that would be willing to diversify the newsroom by hiring prospective Asian journalists and taking them under their wings and becoming mentors to them. **Stephanie Nishikawa, TV news reporter, WDAF-TV, Kansas City, Missouri.**

I don't think enough is being done. I don't even think other Asian reporters are doing enough. Why? Because most Asian reporters have adapted to the "white" culture. It is exactly why they have been selected as broadcast reporters and while they have the sensitivities for the Asian community, most have little in common with them. Those who do have strong ties are perceived by management as "too" ethnic to appeal to the audience. **Alan Wang, reporter, KDFW-TV, Fresno, California.**

Newspapers are hireing more people of color. this will be harder to do as more papers close or downsize, but I firmly belive that a newspaper should reflect its readership. Otherwise, it becomes elitist. When I first came to the Daily News seven years ago, there was only one Asian American on staff to cover New York. Now ther are at least seven, including one in management. And we're not just pigeonholed into covering immigration and Chinatown. We're all over the city, writing about baseball, food, lifestyle, and the arts. **Wayman Wong, reporter for the New York *Daily News*, New York City.**

NOTE: The following responses are from Asian American journalists who requested anonymity. Therefore, if a respondent gave information referring to his or her name, or other identifying factors, that information is appropriately changed and in italics. If a respondent clearly identified his or her Asian American ethnic subgroup status, such as Japanese American, either in the text of the answers or on the permission/consent form, then that identification is given.

I feel there is very little coverage of Asian American issues in mainstream media, and when there is coverage, it is usually the type that reinforces stereotypes: Asian gangs, model minorities. I feel that the only way that coverage can be improved is for more Asian Americans to get into decision-making jobs in the media, and for the Asian American community to become more vocal consumers of news, that is, to explain about coverage or the lack thereof. **Female television journalist in New York City.**

I'm proud that one organization with which I worked depicted the wrongs/right of an Asian politician as just that—the wrongs and rights of a politician, excluding ethnicity. I think it's also becoming increasingly common to see, on many national news magazines and bigger market news, Asian people, in general, whether it be a man-on-the-street response, main interview, victim, witness, etc. **Female television journalist from Michigan.**

As far as what is being done right in the media, the most visible improvement is the addition of Asian reporters to news staffs. It is more reflective of the demographics in showing that there is an Asian population out there. The only problem is that I know of no station that has more than one Asian "on-air." (Tough for those of us who wanted to get into one of those stations.)

I feel Asian issues are covered as much as any other specific group. Basically, if there is an "event" then the topic is covered.

As news goes, it can sometimes be a negative story, such as Asian gangs. **Female television reporter from Vermont.**

Here at *name of newspaper*, Asian American reporters in Metro and editors in National and Foreign have heightened everyone's awareness and sensitivity to our numerous ethnic issues. It's still not enough—not enough coverage of less world-power countries. **Female newspaper journalist from New York.**

There is so little coverage of Asian Americans that I can't give a good answer to either of these questions [three and four of the survey]. I rarely see Asian people in newspapers or TV. I guess I'm too lazy to think about this. I think change will come when there are more Asian Americans in management positions. **Female newspaper journalist from Virginia.**

There are more efforts to cover the community from a multifaceted perspective, but that's mostly confined to areas with large Asian American populations—the West Coast and New York. **Male newspaper journalist from Kentucky.**

I guess many newspapers are trying a technique called mainstreaming; here at the *name of newspaper* it usually means getting quotes from blacks and Indians and weaving them into stories so even unsuspecting rednecks will suddenly find themselves reading about the views of people they would rather not associate with.

I guess people like Chinese Americans and Asian Indians are being quoted in many stories on business and investment. This kind of thing is okay.

Also, letters, indignant or explanatory, written by Asian Americans and others get published fairly regularly, I guess, in newspapers and magazines around the country. (I really can't say what is going on in TV and radio; I know even less about these two media.)

As a result of conferences, publications, and surveys there is more awareness now, I think, of the need to hire people with diverse backgrounds—racial, ethnic, cultural. This process doesn't show any sign of being reversed, but it must be speeded up. Your average Joe or Tom or Mike—five foot eight, great baseball fan, loves to barbecue, spend time with the wife and kids and is white, middle-class and Protestant—now dominates newsrooms.

I think the American media can benefit from having, say, Kim or Ravi or Arif in the newsroom. These people may not look all-

American (whatever that means) but the diversity of cultural experience they bring will be invaluable: the music they listen to, the authors they admire, the movements they endorse. Coverage will, inevitably, show the influence of their presence and personalities. **Male Asian Indian newspaper journalist from South Dakota.**

I think media are doing a better job of avoiding stereotypes and expanding coverage beyond "cliché" stories (cherry blossom festivals, etc.).

I also think media are doing a slightly better job including Asians in everyday coverage (or "mainstreaming," to use a Gannett term). For example, my paper is more likely these days to quote an Asian stock broker in a local story about the rising stock market. The broker's ethnic status is not the focus of the story, his or her expertise is. More media are realizing that coverage of Asians need not be limited "Asian" stories. **Male newspaper journalist from California.**

In the Midwest, I see little to no coverage of issues affecting Asian Americans. I also saw it as non-existent in the South. **Male newspaper journalist from Ohio.**

I really don't think there's much coverage of Asian Americans at all. They're getting better with a lot of things, for example, you hear a lot about debates between the black community and the white community and you really don't hear about Latinos and Asians and the white community. It's really like a non-community and the media really does have something to do with that. The news you do see is really immigrant oriented and it still gives out this perception that Asians can't communicate or speak English well and that they're just off the boat. I think it's changing a little bit, but it's slow.

For me personally, I would like to see Asian Americans portrayed just the way other Americans are portrayed and the news media panders to the perceptions of the American public. **Male magazine journalist from Washington, D.C.**

There are a few things I think are being done right in covering Asians and Asian American issues. First, I think more urban newspapers are hiring Asians to better represent the demographic areas they cover. There is a feeling in the two metropolitan newsrooms I've worked in, that there is a need to better understand the growing Asian population. And by management's push to hire more people that understand the language, customs, and culture of various Asian groups, they're enabling readers to get a better understanding of the diversity among Asians: that we're not all the same, but are in fact very unique and separate entities, each group sharing similarities but far more incongruities.

Media coverage may be helping some people learn that say, for example, the new year's customs for Chinese are quite different from those celebrated by Cambodians. That many Vietnamese living in the United States are well-educated or came from wealthy or privileged backgrounds. Or that Fijian immigrants are not the same as Taiwanese nationals. The *Boston Globe* did a series, I think, in 1990 that was titled "Faces of the North" which focused on the Vietnamese and Cambodian population explosion in Lowell, Lawrence, and Andover, which is a fine example of helping people understand the various Asian groups.

Another thing I think the media is doing right is they're taking a proactive approach to Asian community coverage. Instead of waiting to get story ideas, newspapers seem to be actively enterprising stories that have an Asian bent. Admittedly, coverage is still sporadic, but my feeling is they're trying. To me, management is on the right track by actively pursuing the few important stories happening in the Asian communities. **Male newspaper journalist from Massachusetts.**

I can see some conscious effort on the network news level to cover more Asian issues. However, it is sporadic and rare. There needs to be more inclusion of Asians in the news media and mainstream media. The few Asians we do see in the media are forced into positions of being role models, sometimes reluctantly, because there is no one else. **Female television journalist from Michigan.**

Hmmm, tough question. (Question four is easier.) In the past few years, I've seen many more Asian faces in broadcast journalism, as well as a growing interest in the field from Asian American students. So that seems to be a positive trend. Such an increase in Asian American journalists can only bode well for future coverage of Asian American issues. **Male newspaper journalist from New York.**

There is more coverage of Asian Americans and issues affecting them, as the public and the media recognize the continuing influx of non-whites into the U.S. and the growing importance of issues relating to these new Americans. As America's complexion changes, the issues we cover should reflect that. Immigration, mulitculturalism, English-only issues are all reflective of the demographic changes we're experiencing now and need to be explored. **Female magazine journalist from Washington, D.C.**

We're seeing stories—many stories—about these [Asian American] communities. I see more Asians being quoted as experts or included in a story as any other person, not specifically because they are Asian or the subject matter relates to Asians. In other words, Asian sources are entering the mainstream of media coverage. **Female newspaper journalist from Pennsylvania.**

Not much. There is a minute growth in covering some neglected Asian Americans, such as Hmong and East Indians, for example. **Female newspaper journalist from Oregon.**

It's hard to gauge what is being done well and what is not across the industry because there is such a wide range of coverage quality. What is being done right is that the media are finally recognizing that Asians are a diverse lot, not all just the chemistry and computer whiz kids we were once thought to be. And many media are making a concerted effort to understand the cultural context from which Asians and Asian issues develop. **Female newspaper journalist from Oregon.**

At least Asian American faces are being written about and photographed, not just for Asian gang stories and hard luck new immigrants, but also as successful business people and outstanding students. **Female newspaper journalist from Washington.**

I think many of my colleagues at the Asian American Journalists Association are doing a wonderful job covering the Asian American community. I only wish there were more of us. **Female newspaper journalist from Kansas.**

I think some media companies are making real conscious efforts to broaden news coverage to include Asian Americans and their issues. Coverage of cultural/festival type things has improved in the past five years with more space being devoted to such things as Indian dance, Chinese New Year, etc. Chinatowns, in a few markets at least, are being seen less as exotic places where you can buy lizard toe and lotus root and more as strong components of a community's overall economy. The economic success of Vietnamese and other recent Southeast Asian immigrants is getting good play.

Occasionally, reporters will delve thoughtfully into issues such as the psychological influences of Asian gangs. Political leaders who happen to be Asian American are in the news more for the fact that they're political leaders, with the "Asian" aspect of them occasionally highlighted.

Though insensitivity still runs incredibly rampant, I think we're starting to see editors and reporters thinking about what they're trying to say and whether the particular phrase might unnecessarily offend people. Overall, I think the fact that more Asian Americans are working in newsrooms and are beginning to gain the critical mass of journeyman experience needed is helping to spur a desire to really explain what certain traditions, rituals, ways of life, etc. are about. **Female newspaper journalist from Washington.**

The media are trying to hire more Asian Americans and encourage more Asian Americans to go into journalism. Media corporations also are supportive of Asian American Journalists Association functions.

However, Asian Americans are largely the forgotten minority. In stories, when the intent is to broaden the population pool, reporters refer to Latinos and African Americans, but rarely to Asian Americans. Also, before Judge [Lance] Ito gained prominence, I'm sure most of America would be hard pressed to name an Asian American of prominence.

The media does fine on the obvious stories—the World War II internment camp stories, etc.—but rarely probes beyond that and needs to be constantly encouraged to do so. **Female newspaper journalist from California.**

I believe more coverage is now being done towards exposing the discriminations towards Asian Americans. **Female newspaper journalist from Pennsylvania.**

I'm glad that newspapers are hiring more Asian American reporters and editors. This is a quick and effective way to have the Asian voice reflected in newspapers. However, I am distressed by the broadcast media's penchant for hiring beautiful Asian women, based largely on their supposed sexual appeal to white males. **Female newspaper journalist from Hawaii.**

I can't think of anything that's being done right in the media in covering Asian Americans and issues affecting that segment of the population. **Female newspaper journalist from Washington, D.C.**

There is significantly more coverage and awareness of Asian Americans and Asian American issues than in the late 1970s, when

I started in journalism. **Female newspaper journalist from Massachusetts.**

There's increased effort at coverage, quantitatively speaking. **Female newspaper journalist from Washington.**

This is a hard question for me to answer because I don't feel that much media coverage is given to issues affecting Asian Americans. It seems to me stories are written about political issues in Asian countries with a few takeouts here and there on say, Koreans in New York or Los Angeles. I found a piece on the trend of Asian women dating white men that was published in the *San Francisco Examiner* magazine a few years ago a step in the right direction toward discussing modern issues affecting Asians, but many people didn't like the stereotypes they felt the story perpetuated. I don't like the fact that there are white men out there with fetishes for passive Asian women, but its out there and I thought it was fair game to bring it up in a story. **Female newspaper journalist from California.**

I think that there is a better effort—among some newspapers at least—to understand Asian American communities. The problem is, we tend to clump them all together as if they were a single, unified ethnic group. The very title itself, "Asian American," implies a sameness that doesn't really exist. To be sure, Asian Americans share some common experiences, but the Chinese American community is different from the Japanese American community which is different from the Korean American community which is different from the Vietnamese American community and so on. **Male newspaper journalist from California.**

Asian Americans have been on the news—TV and newspaper—quite often lately and I find that the coverage of Asian Americans has been increased during the past year. **Male newspaper journalist from Louisiana.**

We are giving more coverage to Asian American issues, but much of it is crime related. **Male newspaper journalist from Texas.**

Well, I think some things are being done right in the media today in covering Asian American issues, but I still think more could be done. There is still this stereotype that Asian men are meek and quiet or that all Asians are either engineers, doctors, or lawyers. I am none of those. However, I do think that the O.J. Simpson trial has thrust Judge Lance Ito into the spotlight because now everyone knows who he is and I think he did a very good job considering all of the media coverage. **Male newspaper journalist from Nevada.**

Newspapers in cities with large Asian American populations seem to try to carry positive stories about Asian American lifestyles, activities, etc. However, especially in the New England area, these stories seem to be one-shot efforts. After it appears, there is nothing until the next Chinese New Year or similar event. We can't blame the newspapers totally, because the Asian American community tends to be isolated, partly through choice and partly through circumstance.

There have been efforts to mainstream stories about Asian Americans. The house featured in the "Living" section belongs to an Asian American, the economist quoted in an Asian American at MIT, etc., but once this is done, there is not effort to continue. Also, more Asian Americans are entering the field [of journalism]. **Female television journalist from Massachusetts.**

I notice more reporting of Asian Americans as ordinary citizens, in "man on the street" type interviews, although I feel there ought to be much more. I think this is extremely important if Asian Americans are to be seen as Americans. **Female television journalist from Washington, D.C.**

There's a growing awareness that Asian Americans are a diverse group, in part due to the infusion of Asian American journalists. **Female television journalist from Pennsylvania.**

I can't think of too much right, unfortunately. More Asian Americans are appearing on the air and many more are now behind the scenes. It's a combination of management willing to hire and the pool of available Asian Americans growing. But many on-air Asian Americans are still female and precious few are male.

In parts of the country where the Asian population is large, there is a great deal more coverage, but from where I sit, with a still small, less vocal Asian population, coverage is still difficult— [Chinese] New Year and the lion dance and Chinese babies being adopted and looking cute are still about all the coverage we see. **Female television journalist from Illinois.**

Not much is done in regards to Asian American issues in this market. Many issues are overlooked or not considered newsworthy. Once again I think it's due to a lack of understanding of the culture and the quiet path that most Asian Americans operate by.

On the commercial market more Asian Americans are used in advertising. It's a start. **Male television journalist from New York.**

Very little is being done right, because very little is done at all. As a journalist, I understand why. Unless there's a heinous crime or extraordinary controversy involved, Asian Americans remain a largely invisible constituency. How many Asian Americans have highly visible roles on television, or in print? Again, it's partly cultural. As a group, my parents' generation is not inclined to social activism or being outspoken. The Asian American story is not an easy one to tell. We're perceived as the so-called "model minority" because our education and income levels are relatively comfortable. However, the coverage is getting better. Now, on occasion, Asian Americans can be seen as having social problems, or being subject of the same glass ceiling as other minority strivers. Increasingly (though still rarely) Asian, African, Hispanic, and Native Americans are being used as "expert sources," (or "sound bites" in TV vernacular) for stories other than those dealing with minority issues. However, I think it will be some time before we're represented in proportion to our growing presence in U.S. society. **Male television journalist from New York.**

Asian American issues are more widely covered now and I think the news media is finally catching wind of the fact that we make up a large portion of the population. On the local level, I have noticed many papers and local stations are making a conscious effort to cover Asian happenings and special events. **Female television journalist from Georgia.**

I think we're fair in covering Asian American stories, but they're not stories that shed good light on us. **Female television journalist from Washington.**

Interestingly, the success of Asians in this country makes the coverage of Asians less interesting to the media. We are more of a "quiet" community, hard working, we believe in education, family, and taking care of our elders.

All these issues that come to focus in the general public are not "problems" in the Asian community. Therefore, we don't get the positive exposure that is deserved. **Female television journalist from California.**

The best stories I've seen about the Asian American community have been generated by staff members of Asian American descent. At least in my last two stations, management has seemed open to suggestions to stories pertaining to the Asian American community. **Male television journalist from California.**

I think the media has a long way to go before I can even give it credit for covering Asian Americans. The only media outlet doing a good job reporting about Asian Americans are the many magazines that have come out in recent years exploring issues in the community and giving praise to Asian Americans who deserve it, but who are often overlooked by mainstream media. I think many broadcast stations feel they are doing the community a favor by having an Asian reporter or anchor, but I haven't seen this translate into greater coverage of Asian American issues. **Female radio journalist from California.**

Locally, there's been some focus on the new immigrant population: who they are, what kind of problems they face here. A lot was done about the Japanese internment and redress issues some years back. The exposure is good because it reminds people we're here too; that we are part of a multiculural society. **Female radio journalist from California.**

# APPENDIX 12

## SELECTED RESPONSES TO SURVEY QUESTION FOUR

The following are responses taken nearly verbatim from the journalists' written answers to survey question four. The name of the reporter, and his or her place of employment, is given in bold type at the end of each response, if the respondent did not request anonymity. If the sex of a respondent is unclear from the person's name or the content of the text, *Ms.* or *Mr.* will be printed before the name for reader clarification. These are listed in no set order and not all responses are reprinted here. Many of those answers not reprinted were brief "yes" or "no" answers, and some were brief answers that repeated points already made by other respondents. Some editing was done to make the style, such as the term "Asian American" not being hyphenated, consistent throughout for reader ease. Also, the job titles are taken directly from what the respondents gave on the survey.

*Question 4: In your opinion, what is being done wrong in the media today in covering Asian Americans and issues affecting Asian Americans? How could this be improved?*

I believe there is not enough coverage of Asian Americans and issues of importance to them in areas other than the West Coast United States. However, this may be because Asian American communities are not as established or cohesive in cities such as Atlanta or Boston in comparison with Honolulu or Seattle. In the latter, the media coverage of Asian Americans is excellent. In addition, Asian Americans are often viewed as a "quiet or silent minority" who, as a whole, do not tend to attract much "mainstream" attention. **Stephanie Kanno-Wegner, video journalist, CNN, Atlanta, Georgia.**

Very few Asian Americans are being hired in the newsroom, although there is a big percentage of Asian Americans as direct consumers as readers or audience. This can be improved by an honest-to-goodness recruitment of Asian Americans in the newsrooms.

The affluent U.S. media should also extend support, including legal or financial, to individuals or industry-related groups, espousing causes that protect assault on personal and press freedom. For instance, in my case, when I was slapped by a subject of my news story. Nobody was around to extend me a helping hand. My publications, *Philippine* TIME, a monthly based in the Chicago suburbs, and *Filipino Reporter*, a weekly based in New York, are both mom-and-pop operations which could not afford to help me financially or provide me any legal assistance.

When I turned to industry-related organizations, like the New York-based Committee to Protect Journalists, the San Francisco-based Asian American Journalists Association, and Chicago's chapter of the Society of Professional Journalists, they do not have a support system, extending legal or financial aid to their indigent brothers in the profession who are being harassed while in the performance of their duties as journalists. . . **Joseph Lariosa, news editor, *Philippine Time*, Chicago, Illinois.**

As race becomes a major issue in today's society, the media continues to focus on the black-white issue, neglecting the concerns of Asians as well as Hispanics and Native American Indians. Asian Americans can be a force in the race relations issue, but aren't given the chance to voice their perspective on the situation. We're like the chorus in the backdrop. The media can improve this simply by remembering to include all minorities when discussing race relations and forcing the leaders who are pushing the debate to deal with the issues of mixed-minority race relations. **Benjamin Seto, business reporter, *The Fresno Bee*, Fresno, California.**

We need more articles on Asian America. Yet, I've had friends at newspapers who suggest articles all the time but are struck down by editors who feel the stories don't have enough mass appeal. Here at Time Warner there's a smattering of Asian editors and when I see an article profiling an Asian American I know they are responsible. There has to be a greater consensus among editors that Asian American stories need to be written, not just for the 10 percent of the population who are Asian, but for the whole population. **Ms. Pueng Vongs, reporter, *Money* magazine, New York City.**

As for what is being done wrong, the *Philadelphia Inquirer* is, unfortunately, a classic example. If alien beings were to scour the Inquirer for news about Asian Americans in Philadelphia, they would conclude that half of us were restaurateurs and grocers constantly preyed on by the other half, gangsters, and that we were all Buddhists who did lion dances and set off firecrackers on the street in late January or early February for our New Year, and that our young people all arrived in the Untied States as 8-year-old boat people and nevertheless became high school valedictorians 10 years later. The aliens would also conclude that we were all middle-class and college-educated professionals. The vast majority of the American media today still covers Asian America by stereotype; that is, the stories either fit the above stereotypes or they express shock when an Asian American breaks the stereotype by being poor or athletic or bad at math.

When Asian Americans aren't being forced into preconceived roles, they're just plain invisible. A good example is a recent project the Inquirer did on Philadelphia demographics: crime, education, city services, etc., and residents' perceptions. There was a bar graphic that gave a racial breakdown of Philadelphia residents living in poverty. The graphic included only blacks and Latinos. When I protested the absence of Asians, I was told that the graphic was meant as a comparison between blacks and Latinos and that its focus was on Latinos (indeed, the headline supported this argument). I was also given figures on Asians to prove that the reporters had done their homework. Nevertheless, I felt insulted that Asians were ignored, especially given their high rate of poverty in Philadelphia and I felt that I perpetuated the mistaken stereotype of Asian Americans as a uniformly successful group that no one needs to be particularly concerned about.

To improve this doesn't take a rocket scientist. Reporters could seek out more Asian Americans as sources in stories on any topic: home design, medicine, local history, college baseball— there are Asian Americans qualified as sources in any of these areas. Or photographers could include more Asian Americans in their candid feature shots, such as a mother a child playing in the park on a sunny day. Also, reporters and editors of Asian descent should be encouraged to promote the "Asian angle" in stories; for example, in a story about AIDS outreach, including a short section on how difficult it is to do outreach in Asian communities because of strict taboos against homosexuality and discussing sex or drugs in general. **Amy Wang, copy editor, the *Philadelphia Inquirer*, Philadelphia, Pennsylvania.**

When you say Asians there are a lot of groups. I really don't know how most people categorize Asian Indians. Most people say we [Asian Indians] are Asians, but when you take an Asian and an Indian we have nothing in common. So we are put into this big category and we have nothing in common. So they need to show that we are individual cultures and communities with our own issues and histories.

But media is a business, it's intended to sell. They are targeting the mainstream. I would like them to show the truth instead of just the old stereotypes. Most newspapers don't take time to spell Indian names correctly. I see that even in larger newspapers like the *San Jose Mercury News*, where they have spelled several Indian names incorrectly

If more Asians or Indians were hired at mainstream newspapers this might not happen as much. **Ms. Jyothi Kiran, staff writer, *India Currents* magazine, San Jose, California.**

I don't think Asian American issues are being covered enough by the mainstream media. I can count with my fingers the number of stories on Asian Americans that have appeared this year. Interest is limited to predictable topics such as food and language difficulties. There is also too much emphasis on the success stories of a few Asian Americans, when the truth of the matter is there are many who continue to be disadvantaged.

The scant coverage there is always devoted to either the Chinese Americans or Japanese Americans. Filipino Americans, for example, constitute the second largest ethnic group of Asian-Pacific descent, but it's as if they do not count. Another example would be the issue of race-related violence. While violence against Chinese Americans has, to a certain extent, been publicized in the mainstream media, this much can't be said regarding similar incidents involving Vietnamese Americans.

It has been a continuing dream of mine to be able to set up an Asian American news and features service (wire agency) where mainstream and suburban media could subscribe to it. **Ms. Marites Sison-Paez, editor, *Special Edition Press*, New York City.**

What's wrong with the media today in covering Asian Americans is something that has been in the media for decades and has not yet changed: Stereotyping. Today's media portrays Asian Americans as Orientals. Oriental is an image, a stereotype—one that media practitioners have consistently used to place Asian

Americans in a negative light. The most recent examples of the media stereotyping Asian Americans are Connie Chung and Lance Ito. During Connie Chung's episode with Newt Gingrich's mother, words and/or images that popped up in both print and broadcast media were: sly, sneaky, inscrutable, dishonest; and the list goes on. These stereotypes can be related to those found predominantly in print media during World War II; stereotypes of the sneaky, slanty-eyed Japanese enemies. Throughout the U.S. media's history, these stereotypes have prevailed, and recur again and again, however modified. As these stereotypes persist, it has become increasingly difficult for me to shape my own identity as an Asian American journalist. From television sitcoms such as *All-American Girl* to editorial cartoons in newspapers, the media has not taken any positive steps towards eliminating such negative stereotypes.

The answer to the problem seems simple enough; stop the stereotyping. If there is going to be a sitcom about Asian Americans, make the characters true, everyday people with problems. Everyday people deal with issues of drug use, sexual orientation, even mental illness. Television and film Asian American characters are constantly portrayed the same way: either submissive and hard working nerds, or exotic and sexually available beings.

In print journalism, reporters and editors alike need to pay closer attention to words used to describe Asian Americans. A very recent example is in one daily paper I read which compared Russian immigrants to Asian immigrants. Asian immigrants were described in the stereotypical manner of being industrious and obedient.

Another fault I find with the media is the tendency to lump all Asian Americans into one category when, in fact, a Vietnamese American is much different than a Japanese American. We are not all alike. We are as much separate individuals as any other American citizen.

We are human—something I tend to think the media at times consciously ignores. **Ms. Putsata Reang, cultural reporter, *Spokesman-Review*, Spokane, Washington.**

There is a tendency to overlook Asian American opinions and issues. Many polls you see still divide the respondents into white, black and Hispanic only. One simple way to improve the quality, accuracy and quantity of reporting on Asian American issues, of course, is to increase the presence of Asian Americans in the newsroom. **Paul Hyun-Bong Shin, staff writer, *The Courier-News*, Bridgewater, Connecticut.**

You see more Asian reporters than you see Asian Americans on television, but unless there's a problem between Korean grocers and African Americans in the community Asian Americans only seem to come into the news unless they involve another group.

As an Asian American, looking at the O.J. Simpson trial all the magazines are reporting it as black/white, black/white, you don't get a feeling as an Asian American that you exist and because racism is such a hot topic I think you feel people think you are honorarily white or black, or that your don't exist. It really bothers me because it's disconcerting that they don't seem to care about how Asian Americans feel. **Pamela SooHoo, associate producer for public television (media organization withheld upon request).**

I think that Asians are seen in one of three stereotypical ways: 1) victims or perpetrators of crime, 2) immigrant owners of Laundromats, restaurants or corner stores where the owners feud with the local black residents, or, 3) the braniac students, nerd doctors, engineers or hi-sci experts with pocket protectors. HELLO !!!???

Just as many are still learning about the black culture, many still have a lot to learn, or choose NOT to learn about Asians. Often, trouble with understanding someone's accent is considered a nail in the coffin and a reason NOT to include Asian news/stories. But doesn't the media hire interpreters for interviewees who do not speak English? I've seen it done. Why not in cases involving Asians as well?

Typically, they are a lot more meek, consider speaking out "stirring up trouble" or dishonorable. But that does not mean this part of the population should be ignored. As journalists, we should try to pus for these stories, but at the same time, the responsibility for these stories should not solely rest on Asian journalists' shoulders, but on ALL journalists looking for a story. Just a story. Not an Asian story. **Victoria Lim, reporter, WWMT-TV News, Kalamazoo, Michigan.**

We continue to cover Asian holidays and parades to satisfy the diluted objective of "diversity." We need to cover issues that affect the Asian American community as specific, but more importantly we need to include Asian Americans as well as all minorities in stories that affect all communities. When we cover politics, healthcare, crime, sports, weather, human interest stories, etc., virtually any story, there is no reason Asian Americans shouldn't be included. These need to be a balance in portraying Asian Americans in tight-knit communities with specific issues and needs alongside portraying Asian Americans as an integral part of mainstream America. Right now, the shallow coverage of "cultural events" serves only to reinforce stereotypes. **Eric Chu, assistant picture editor, Chicago Tribune, Chicago, Illinois.**

In my opinion, there is not much coverage of Asian Americans. I'm not sure if that's a good or bad thing. I think for the most part, by the third generation, most Asian Americans have assimilated and it's not uncommon to find Asians in most aspects of American life, at least in the states of California and Hawaii where I have lived. So there's no need to specifically single out a person's ethnicity when one does a story.

I think the grouping of Asian Americans is misleading, just as it is to group all whites and all Hispanics together. The grouping of Asian/Pacific Islander is just a census grouping and a political grouping because there is strength in numbers. The community is actually diverse and made up of ethnic groups with different cultures, physical appearances, and even prejudices against each other.

I think coverage of Asian immigrant communities is lacking. There are many stories in the Southeast Asian, immigrant Chinese, Samoan and Pacific Islander communities that are not being reported. I think Asians working in the media now should be taking the lead in seeking out these stories and they are, for the most par, not doing this. I think reporting on Samoans, for example, is filled with stereotyping. Samoans in the news are either criminal or football players. There is little coverage of the community other than that.

And while this is not an Asian American issue—I think there is interest in news from Asian among Asian Americans and whites. And both newspaper and television national news coverage tends to be Eurocentric. There are many stories in Asia, of interest to both Asians and whites, that are ignored. The reason is most national news originates out of New York and Washington which look east to Europe more than west to Asia. And because of East

Coast time, news in Asia happens while people in New York and Washington are asleep. Also, in terms of television, the cost of covering news in Asian cities is double or perhaps as much as six times as expensive as covering news in Europe.

I think Asian Americans in the media have a special responsibility to seek out stories about Asian groups whose stories are not being told. I thin there need to be more coverage of Pacific Rim issues. But until more people from the Pacific Rim get to decision-making positions in the East Coast, I don't think that will happen. **Craig Gima, producer, KHON-TV, Honolulu, Hawaii.**

First of all, whites have a huge misconception that Asian Americans are united because we are all clumped in the category of Asian Americans. But we are also sub-divided groups— Japanese, Vietnamese, Chinese, Korean, Taiwanese and so on— different countries and different cultures. Yes, we are united under that umbrella this country plays as Asian American, but we don't have that unity African Americans have or Hispanics have. So, when you see a Japanese reporter or Chinese actress on television, we know they are different, but whites see them as the same. Taiwanese want to see more of themselves on TV, Koreans want to see more Koreans on TV and so on.

I think the media stereotypes, but I also feel that society is the reason. We need to change the attitude around us first before we worry about television. Your workplace, your home and schools are real. Television is fiction. **Ms. Michile Kim-Gray, producer, KWTX-TV, Waco, Texas.**

Sometimes Asian slangs crop up, i.e., "Japs." Once in a while, you will also see cartoons featuring stereotyped characters. **Rose Tibayan, anchor/reporter, WINK-TV, Fort Myers, Florida.**

Occasionally you'll see a story that will identify an Asian American person or group as simply Asian American—without ever mentioning if the person or group is Japanese, Cambodian, Indian or whatever. This ignores the vast differences among the many different cultures included in the term Asian American. **Ms. Yuki Spellman, news writer, WGN News, Chicago, Illinois.**

Minorities and even those of Caucasian ancestry are constantly being tossed into a media-induced "plain-wrap" of culture and society. We see a black person on TV with an accent and assume he is black. But never it seems will the story call him a man who hails from Nigerian, or perhaps Sudanese ancestry. Despite the incredible numbers of Asian relative to world population, people tend to overlap Chinese with Japanese, and Korean with Filipino, etc. The media would just assume buy Chinese food, take Korean hapkido karate lessons, and drive in their Japanese sedan and say, "The Japanese affect us in many ways." At the same time the press makes an effort to promote a story on minorities, it blindly overlaps cultures and histories together as on Asian "gel." In some cases, as different as Caucasian is to black, so are the Japanese to the Vietnamese though outwardly both are clearly Asian.

Therefore, it is clear if one wants to report with a sense of "diversity" one must always look deeper. anyone can tell if someone is black, white, Latino, etc. But what gives the individual that much more depth is the race within so to speak. Accurate portrayals of the various Asian cultures in television and film must occur before the viewing public will have a basis to really know the difference between a John Doe Kim and a Rob Mayeda Goozee. **Robert Goozee, news assignment desk, KNBC NBC 4, Los Angeles, California.**

The closed nature of these [Asian] communities means that the more Asian journalists there are the more coverage is likely. **Ronald Patel, Sunday editor, *The Philadelphia Inquirer*, Philadelphia, Pennsylvania.**

It seems Asians are still stereotyped either as overachievers or loud-mouthed and obnoxious. **Brian Gee, special projects producer, Orange County Newschannel, Santa Ana, California.**

One problem in the coverage of Asian Americans afflicts stories about most ethnic groups, namely, ascribing the views of "Asian American leaders" to all members of the group. These leaders are usually the officers of some civic group, or perhaps politicians or academics, who espouse a predictable, liberal view of the world. In stories that I saw about admission policies at California's state universities, for example, the Asians quoted were solidly in favor of affirmative action. The reporters didn't bother to talk to students who were hurt by the policies. The range of opinion among Asians is much more varied and complex than presented in the media.

A second point is related to the first. "Asian Americans" are spoken of as a monolithic bloc, when in fact, the term encompasses everyone from Pakistanis to Filipinos to Koreans. (It's a narrower version of the problem that arises from a meaningless phrase like "people of color.") The world view and concerns of a third-generation Japanese person are quite different from those of a recent immigrant from Vietnam.

On the whole, I'm not impressed by mainstreaming efforts, which produce stories that have a *National Geographic* quality of foreignness. but in the short run, it's probably useful to have flexible quotas so that stories with Asians (or any other ethnic group) will lose that exotic flavor. Ultimately, I hope that editors and reporters will look for a wide variety of sources and topics, and will choose them simply because they're newsworthly. **Dean Inouye, assistant news editor, Knight-Rider Washington Bureau, Washington, D.C.**

Not enough Asian American issues are being covered. Some other races seem to have more coverage than us. **Darren Phan, news camerman, NBC-4, Burbank, California.**

Too many gee-whiz articles. As in "Gee whiz, it's Chinese New Year, and it's the Year of the DOG! Imagine that!" Overall, the media seems to "visit" the Asian American culture only on special occasions rather than covering their daily, yet significant, concerns.

And we still seem to promote stereotypes of Asian American kids; they are still mostly in the media when they've won science and math and academic competitions. It'd be nice to see them portrayed as regular kids—mall rats, jocks, cheerleaders—so that, over time, we can help society get accustomed to seeing them in print as well as in their communities. **Lisa Lee Daniels, reporter, *The Oregonian*, Portland, Oregon.**

The media does a poor job of explaining the events that take place in the Asian American community. Although there has been a slight increase in coverage of Asian Americans, there has been little in-depth reporting in those stories. For example, during the Los Angeles riots, a few Korean-American merchants were armed. Why? Asians have often been categorized as the model minority, what advantages do Asians have when they immigrate to the United States besides sheer will? And Asians are often portrayed as quiet, submissive and non-confrontational. Are these the characteristics of the first generation immigrants or second, third, fourth generation Asian Americans? **Connie Riu, manager, diversity and outreach services, Newspaper Association of America, Reston, Virginia.**

The group is largely invisible and overshadowed by others. Stereotypes are common and coverage largely relates to ethnicity. There is very little understanding of the community. Gangs and immigration become hot topics. **Ms. Anu Mannar, life copy desk chief, *News* and *Record*, Greensboro, North Carolina.**

Sometimes mainstream media still lumps Asian Americans into one category when they really need to be more ethnic specific. In San Francisco and the Bay area there are not just Chinese and Japanese and Koreans, there are in fact inter-ethnic groups that observe different traditions and culture and language. People from Shanghai, Guangzhou (Canton) and Beijing may all be Chinese, many may all speak Mandarin, but they also have their own languages within their own groups. People from Southeast Asian don't speak "Southeast Asian;" they speak Laotian, Hmong, Vietnamese, etc.

How can it be improved: This country is not a melting pot and the "playing field has not been leveled," as anti affirmative action proponents would have us believe. There continues to be a need for broadcast media and communications personnel to be from many different ethnic groups as possible, in order to be able to present as broad a picture as possible. There really needs to be a respect for individual ethnic differences; Filipinos speaking Tagalog should not be made to cease using their own languages when it doesn't interfere with their work duties.

Just because 100,000 people sign an anti-affirmative action petition doesn't mean that it's necessarily a good idea. Reporters need to talk to others who have a sense of history about a particular issue, to understand that affirmative action has an historical basis and that immigrants were kept out of entering this country legally based upon whatever political beliefs were in vogue at a particular time in history, etc. We need to understand that not all immigrants are illegal, that they are not ALL a drain on American society, that the majority of people who immigrate to the United States are eager to earn their own way and become self-supporting. **Ms. Gimmy Park Li, manager, public affairs, KNBR AM - KFOG FM, San Francisco, California.**

Coverage still is too shallow and token: gangs, high achievers, Chinese New Year, JACL suits. What we ought to be doing is "mainstreaming," incorporating Asian Americans into all coverage, as sources, pictures, features. While some issues are specific to Asian Americans, many issues are common among all Americans or other ethnic groups. The media is recognizing how critical it is to focus on their communities—that includes reflecting all its diverse nuances, which likely are all interconnected. **Ms. Mei-Mei Chan, executive editor, *Post Register*, Idaho Falls, Idaho.**

I think there are still some members of the media who feel that the Asian American community is immune to the problems which other communities experience. The so called "model minority" label has perhaps hurt and affect how Asian Americans are perceived by the media and society.

There are many issues facing the Asian American community today. Issues like the glass ceiling, gang violence, welfare, and hate crimes against Asian Americans should be addressed.

I think it's obvious that more Asian Americans should consider a career in the news industry, not just as reporters, but in positions of power.

But even if there are a sizable amount of Asian Americans in the media, the greater Asian American community must apply more pressure and assume more responsibility in making sure the broadcast and print industries are aware about its concerns and issues. **George Kiriyama, desk assistant, KCAL-TV Channel 9 News, Los Angeles, California.**

The media still lacks Asian representation or minority representation, especially in the Midwest where I'm from. I'm one of four or five Asian television reporters in the entire state of Wisconsin! This could be improved by recruiting and introducing Asian children to the journalism field. **Mary Tan, news reporter, WMTV-TV, Madison, Wisconsin.**

Still lots of stories/segments about Asian festivals, the Chinese New Year dragons, and other superficial, stereotypical aspects of Asian cultures. We need, for instance, to write about the upstart with Asian gangs, long a problem in places such as Los Angeles and Houston. We need to write stores that dispel some myths: Asians run only restaurants, dry cleaning, and liquor stores and markets, that they're all well-educated and have high upper-income earnings. More than anything, papers, TV stations and radio can stand to see more Asian voices and faces into regular stories, be it cuts in social services, the reaction/fascination with Princess Diana (isn't Hong Kong, and therefore its current and former citizens still British and British influenced?), President

Clinton's foreign policy (China, Bosnia, Ireland, whatever), or the rise and fall of gasoline prices. The goal is to make them Asian Americans, not Asians. **Abraham Kwok, reporter, *The Arizona Republic/The Phoenix Gazette*, Phoenix, Arizona.**

The appearances of Asian Americans as sources in stories is not as numerous as I would like. I believe that as journalists, we are obligated to "go the extra mile" to ensure that all voices are heard. News coverage must go beyond the traditional stories of Chinese New Year, Tet, and similar cultural activities. As far as issues are concerned, I think coverage is lacking, primarily because we (the media) do not understand the issues in the Asian community. Resources in the community have to be better cultivated, and media gatekeepers need to be willing to commit the time and then support the efforts to do it.

Developing Asian American media managers is a process that is still in its infancy. Organizations like the Asian American Journalists Association (AAJA) and the Radio Television News Directors Association (RTNDA) recognize the need for having minority managers in positions to affect media coverage. While these people of color do not guarantee improved coverage, it is a step in the right direction. **Janice Gin, executive producer/1996 Atlanta Olympics, Gannett Broadcasting, Atlanta, Georgia.**

Still much too much stereotyping (all Asians hard-working, etc.) and lack of depth in reporting on the multiple Asian communities. Newspapers need to do a much better job of explaining the values, culture of Asian Americans and how that influences perception. All that said, Asians still have it better in the media than blacks or Latinos. **Peter Bhatia, managing editor, *The Oregonian*, Portland, Oregon.**

What is being done wrong is that the media, especially national, is still perpetuating the Asian stereotypes. I went to school in Canada where multi-cultural awareness is basically forced on society. No one blinks an eye when an interracial couple walks down the street in Toronto. Yet in America, the big "melting pot," interracial relationships still make the front page. And because the dominant focus is on black-white relations, Asian American issues are simply pushed aside. Asian Americans will look like immigrants and who's interested in immigrants? The big problem here is that there are no Asians in management positions at media conglomerates like ABC or Time Warner or Hachette Filappachi.

Until Asian Americans get into decision-making positions behind the camera or behind the editor's desk, there won't be much focus on Asian issues at all. **Ms. Soomie Ahn, employed at Ellen Ryder Communications, New York City.**

I can say that for my paper, the *Star-Gazette* makes a greater effort to include African Americans in stories since they are the largest "minority" group in our area, but it fails miserably to have Asians represented. The reasoning behind it appears that because we're small in number in the Twin Tiers, we don't need to focus on this ethnic group.

The result is some journalists are unaware of the problem of stereotypes. **Henry Yuen, assistant features editor, *Star-Gazette*, Elmira, New York.**

Media need to do a better job of including Asian Americans in their everyday coverage. It's nice to do ethnic-specific stories (martial arts, bonsai and Miss Chinatown contests, for example), but how about including Asian Americans going about their lives being Americans, or talking about topics other than race or ethnicity?

The banker who happens to be Asian American—the teacher who happens to be Asian American—the barber or mechanics who happens to be Asian American—they should all be part of our daily news coverage. AS it turns out, "issues" for Asian Americans are often "issues" for all Americans!

KING TV has half-yearly community forums with various ethnic groups. These forums provide community leaders a chance to bring their concerns ("issues") to the news mangers. We learn what's happening in various communities and which events are most important to our forum members. We may not do actual stories on the topics, but at least we're listening. This is another help to improve coverage of Asian Americans. **Lori Matsukawa, anchor, KING TV, Seattle, Washington.**

The Asian American Journalists Association, to which I belong, has a committee called "Project Zinger" which keeps an eye out for blatant insensitivities and/or prejudiced portrayals of Asian Americans in the media. thus far, (in the past five years or so) I don't think I've heard of many major qualms they've had with any print or broadcast report. I myself don't have any fingers to point at anyone and to tell you the truth, can't really think of anything off the top of my head that I am completely dissatisfied with.

I am a believer in the idea that coverage of Asian Americans and Asian American related issues must inevitably improve with time and gradually increase exposure to Asian American related stories. Hopefully, the sheer number of reports by and about Asian Americans in time will allow the thinking public to understand those who have always been looked upon as the quiet ones. Asian Americans must continually speak out and tell their stories, and help journalists provide more than just brief news agenda bleeps about them. We need more in-depth analyses of Asian Americans and their issues as a means of educating the public. **Ms. Jinah Kim, producer 11 p.m. news, DCCN-TV, Monterey, California.**

I think it is unfortunate Asians tend to get classified as one voice, when the reality is there are many kinds of ethnic groups under the "Asian" category. Reporters seldom do a good job of seeking out such diverse voices, and applying the same stereotypes to Chinese, Laotians and Japanese is sloppy reporting. I think individuals working in the media need to work harder to cultivate sources in the Asian community so they will be able to report more accurately, and gain access to the various Asian communities when the need arises. It is not an overstatement that some Asian communities are very protective and some do fear retaliation within their own community for talking to the press. One thing our station does is invite community groups to speak at quarterly meetings, and to tell us what they want to see more coverage of. More media outlets can choose to be more pro-active in gathering story ideas. Also, media outlets who complain they cannot gain access to the various Asian communities because of a language barrier should consider being willing to spend the money to hire an interpreter or hire producers/reporters who are multi-lingual. And finally, when covering immigration issues, media outlets should take a stronger role in dispelling untrue but popularly-held notions that immigrants are a drain on the system. Many Asian immigrants I know take a lot of pride in being self-sufficient, and would be ashamed to depend on public welfare. **Susan Han, producer, KCTS TV, Seattle, Washington.**

In my opinion, not nearly enough is being done right in media to cover Asian Americans. There are occasional features on the "success" stories in print media, emphasizing business aspects. There are occasional "problem" stories on social or educational issues, feature Korean-black conflict, specialized schools, etc. But nothing really on an ongoing basis to help Americans understand Asian people better. Stereotypical treatment still reigns. Television is worst. There are many issues that should be covered that are not being covered—beyond the traditional litany of discrimination stories. Asian Americans, especially the younger generation, are either lost or looking for linkages with their heritage. Some are finding these linkages with their native countries through the arts, some through business. The press/media is way behind the times on these. These are greatly positive stories. Most are not even being touched! **Ms. Vyryan Tenorio, editor,** *Asia Environmental Business Journal***, San Diego, California.**

The first is letting Connie Chung go. She was someone I looked up to when I was in high school. I am from San Francisco, California—I remember watching Connie Chung anchor the CBS network weekend news, and after that I would see Wendy Tokuda anchor the nightly news on our CBS affiliate. These are women that I and thousands of other Asian Americans look up to. I wanted to become a TV journalist after watching Connie break that barrier where no other Asian American has gone. These are role models for us young, aspiring journalists.

Now on the network we can only look up to a few reporters who normally have very few minutes of air time.

If I lived in a small town I would not see an Asian American. It would not give me the courage or hope to become a journalist on TV. Many times new directors who are in small markets will pick and choose their reporters based on demographics. That's why it took so long for me to get a job on air. I had to more 3,000 miles away to get on air—in Guam!

I think being a member of AAJA (Asian American Journalists Association) has helped me. I have mentors who are "in" the business—made it to the top by working in the top ten markets—they helped me. Now it's my turn to become a mentor to an aspiring Asian American journalist and show him/her the ropes of the business, critique their tapes, and help them become professional journalists. Maybe even a Connie Chung one day. **Stephanie Nishikawa, TV news reporter, WDAF-TV, Kansas City, Missouri.**

Well, there aren't enough Asian Americans in management, for one. We're seen as good, hard-working people, but not as leaders, so we tend to hit the glass ceiling. And is it any wonder? Films and TV have long portrayed Asian American men, in particular, as only waiters, houseboys and other emasculated wimps. Is it any surprise that Asian American men are nearly nonexistent as news anchors? That's because we're not seen as authority figures. As for Asian American women, they're seen as desirable, subservient, non-threatening china dolls and geishas. Thanks to the legacy of "Madame Butterfly," they're often paired with older white male anchors. But with new role models for the '90s, like the gutsy comic Margaret Cho and sex symbol Russell Wong, let's hope the media's perception of Asians starts to change. **Wayman Wong, reporter for the New York** *Daily News*, **New York City.**

NOTE: The following responses are from Asian American journalists who requested anonymity. Therefore, if a respondent gave information referring to his or her name, or other identifying factors, that information is appropriately changed and in italics. If a respondent clearly identified his or her Asian American ethnic subgroup status, such as Japanese American, either in the text of the answers or on the permission/consent form, then that identification is given.

I still think there's a perception that Asians are not "Americans." Kristi Yamaguchi, the gold medalist figure skater is the Japanese girl who won, not the American girl. I can't point to how the media reinforce this perception, but I suspect they/we play a role. Improvement will only come when multiculturalism is accepted and internalized by those who cover the isseus. **Female Japanese American television journalist from Texas.**

As far as what is being done wrong, I'm not sure I can cite any specific articles or television reports that I've felt were unfairly biased. But I do feel the most visible examples of reinforcing derogatory, stereotypical perceptions have been in political cartoons. **Female television journalist from Vermont.**

There's overkill of coverage relating to Japan and China and not enough about those in America. It's more glamorous/sexy to do foreign stories than about "model" immigrants in American, which is not very exciting nor new. Publications need to hire more Asian Americans from different national backgrounds—after all, a Korean American would not necessarily understand the cultural history of a Pakistani or a Malaysian. **Female newspaper journalist from New York.**

Too often Asian Americans only appear in stories dealing with the traditional topics—education, immigration, bilingualism. For example, there is a cluster of Vietnamese immigrants in one section of *name of town in Kentucky*, and there is never a mention of their interests or activities except when they are involved in a controversy, such as when a local official hinted immigrants should be spread out and not concentrated in his area. Better contacts with the community would make newspapers more award of the variety of issues that could be explored in connection with Asian communities. **Male newspaper journalist from Kentucky.**

Deep-rooted perceptions take time to change and sometimes I fear that well-meaning managers—or those who know they can gain by doing the politically correct thing—will attempt to bring about a sea of change in a few years. This is not realistic. It is going to take longer than that.

But the average American (who, of course, becomes your average reporter or editor) doesn't seem to be reaching out to other parts of the world. Look at coverage of Somalia, Haiti, Bosnia, or India; it's almost always crisis-oriented and people, including journalists, tend to switch off. So attitudes aren't easy to change.

I don't see any widespread or thorough attempt to broader journalists' intellectual and cultural horizons through international exchange programs, stints in academia, or even the type of coverage we have today. To repeat, most reporting is so darned crisis-oriented. How will we ever enlighten people about the richness of other societies and cultures if we don't have many more feature- and analysis-type pieces on the broader realities in countries and societies?

I suppose we can argue that PBS and Discovery [channel] do this kind of thing on TV. But then your average journalist is so busy rooting for his or her favorite football or baseball team he or she hardly is paying attention, I would think. And even if no big-league game is on, he or she may be out barbecuing or digging up the weeds.

Sometimes I think it's hopeless. **Male Asian Indian newspaper journalist from South Dakota.**

I think too many media are afraid of tackling negative stories because they fear backlash from the community. In other words, political correctness scares media away from tough questions.

For example, my paper might be too scared to investigate the growth of Asian gangs locally. Some editors probably would fear accusations of racism from the Asian community. (Why are you picking on us? Why not investigate Vietnamese gangs? etc.) The result: an important story is buried because of political correctness.

Another example: I've talked to many young Asians who think their parents are clannish and xenophobic. As the editor of my paper's weekly teen section, I think this is a legitimate story: How do these kids deal with their parents' attitudes? In what ways do kids think their parents are xenophobic? Does it seem hypocritical that their parents complain of racism while they too propagate stereotypes of other ethnic groups? do kids feel uncomfortable bringing white friends home? Have any of the kids confronted their parents, and how do parents respond?

It's an interesting issue, yet I know that such a story would be buried. Editors are too scared of angering "marginalized" groups—too scared of political correctness, especially on racial issues. **Male newspaper journalist from California.**

Few newspapers are actively recruiting Asian American reporters and editors, which would reflect the growth of Asian Americans in the demographics. With more Asian Americans on your staff, who are in touch with their communities, that translates into better coverage. Few newspapers are also making the contacts and outreach in the Asian American community. We cover the suburbs and zone our coverage, but we don't assign beats to issues affecting Asian Americans. When I worked at a Gannett newspaper in California, a major emphasis was mainstreaming. But that seemed to apply only to getting more blacks, Hispanics, and women in our stories as sources and as mug shots. There was no effort to add Asian Americans to that list.

Recruitment drives are aimed more at bring blacks to the staffs, which is fine. But the Asian American population is also rising. Our newsrooms need to reflect that. **Male newspaper journalist from Ohio.**

The media are starting to change. I've seen photos, for example, of Asian Americans in magazines and newspapers, the *Los Angeles Times* in particular does a good job, but they have a large Asian American community. I think it really has to do with that thing that you need people in the newsroom that reflect diversity in society. It would be nice to see it at least in our newsroom. If you want better coverage of what's going on in the world and what's going on in the public then you need to know about issues that are affecting everybody. Everybody is trying to push diversity in the media business, but in reality it's not really happening. There are certain concerns that Asian Americans have and that editors look at and say that their readers aren't interested in that. **Male magazine journalist from Washington, D.C.**

What the media are doing wrong in terms of covering Asian Americans and issues relating to Asians, I think, is that the coverage is too geared toward helping the greater population understand Asians. Not enough is being done to produce copy that is important to Asian groups themselves. When was the last time you read a story pertaining to Asians that didn't put them under a microscope? The stories being covered do little to inform or help the Asians themselves unless, of course, they appear in a non-English format.

Papers like the *Boston Chinese News, Sampan, etc.* do the best job they can to inform Asians with their limited budgets, staff, and readership. They are local newspapers that give back information to Asians that they can actually use.

Wrapped into this problem is that the number of Asians that do read newspapers have hit a saturation point. Those that read now will continue reading, but there's not much to make those who don't want to read. I think many newspapers believe that a large or growing Asian population represents future readership, but I don't think they realize that day-to-day news just doesn't seem that important to the majority of Asians. And of those that are interested, they are more likely to flick on the TV to get their news in quick, digested, and often skewed tidbits.

I believe that because Asians tend to be isolated and keep to themselves to a greater degree than other ethnicities, they are not well represented in the media. Because many Asian cultures have gone through centuries of chaos or civil strife in their own countries, they choose the quiet route and do not advocate for themselves politically or otherwise here. But that's no excuse either. Asians are as much to blame for the coverage or lack of coverage they receive in the media. Asians, as well as other ethnic groups, must begin speaking up for themselves and begin acting like they are an integral part of society, before media coverage of them will

change significantly unless our country can fix the seemingly growing separatist rift. **Male newspaper journalist from Massachusetts.**

Movies still seem to treat Asians and Asian issues as if they
were mysterious, magical, and exotic. This is not necessarily
always bad. Sometimes simple exposure to other cultures in itself
can be positive. I do not believe the mainstream media are consciously or conspiratorially doing something wrong to cast Asians
in this light. Part of it is ignorance and an inability to accept an
idea or practice, i.e., some people automatically believe acupunc-
ture and herbology do not work. We need more education to
reach people about diversity and the need to respect that. **Female
television journalist from Michigan.**

There's little to no coverage on a national basis of Asian
American issues. Worse than that, much of the coverage that does
exist tends to rely heavily on stereotype approaches: the model
minority, etc. There seems to be little regard or understanding
about Asian American issues, and unfortunately, there's not much
impetus to change that situation. I don't know of a single reporter,
broadcast or print, assigned solely to cover Asian issues. I'd love
to see stories about the problems of second-generation Asian
Americans, Asian American literature and art, the growing influence of the Asian cinema, etc. But aside from pieces in niche publications, such coverage is rare. **Male newspaper journalist from
New York.**

The coverage often does not adequately include the perspective of Asian Americans or other ethnic Americans—since so much
journalism here is still written or produced by white Americans.
Since most editors and managers are white, their viewpoints natu-
rally tend to dominate the media. That can lead to sensationalized
coverage and create stereotyped or negative images of ethnic
Americans that can be harmful to the public debate. An example:
the portrait of the immigrant usually as an illegal entrant who is
very foreign and different from most Americans—someone who
snuck across the border to have a U.S.-born child or to take advantage of U.S. public services in some way, or a sweat-shop slave too
victimized to be seen as human. That can color the public's perception of immigrants—both legal and illegal—as undesirable,
unwashed, inhuman. A more representative portrayal of the life of
immigrants here, including legal ones, would help balance out the
picture. And often, reporters with ties to such communities have

a better fell for that and can do a better job of it. **Female Chinese American magazine journalist from Washington, D.C.**

While any story about Asians is an improvement over the lack of coverage in the past, I find that most of these stories deal with crime against Asians, gangs, or ethnic festivals on the waterfront. It would be nice to see more stories about issues pertinent to the Asian community. Also, Asians is a very broad label and often stories fail to explore the nuances and outright differences among the various ethnic groups that make up Asians. I also think newspapers need to make a greater commitment to ethnic coverage. The *name of newspaper* has not appointed anyone to cover ethnic issues for years. Often religion writers neglect religions other than Christianity and Judaism. Other beats also fail to cover aspects that relate to Asians. I don't think this is intentional by any means; it's simply ignorance. **Female newspaper journalist from Pennsylvania.**

Most of the stories I read on Asians reinforce two major stereotypes. One, Asians are smarter (e.g., the affirmative action debate at Berkeley), and Asians are gang members (e.g., Asian gangs prey on Chinatown restaurant owners). Another common story theme: **Asians don't vote. Female newspaper journalist from Rhode Island.**

Too often Asian Americans aren't considered [in coverage], and this applied to Native Americans as well. Pool results will often cite what Caucasians, African Americans, and maybe Latinos think about an issues—say the O.J. Simpson verdict—but too often Asians Americans and Native Americans are left out. This is especially troubling when the issue revolves around race matters, civil rights, or affirmative action. Often the researchers respond that the sampling size is too small. Well, maybe it should be included and noted how small the sample is, so people can get some ideas about what these communities think and understand that the results aren't as strong for some groups as for other groups.

Too often, I believe, it's a reflection of how many see diversity only in terms of black and white. the problems of Asian Americans in the media are shared by other ethnic groups, that they are restricted to the stereotypes—the story about the scholarship winner, expert scientist, etc. But what about Asian American movie stars, alternative musicians? The answer is for more Asian

Americans to get jobs in the media—management and throughout operations—for Asian American groups to push harder for coverage of issues and for other journalists to become better informed and concerned about Asian American issues. **Female newspaper journalist from Oregon.**

What is being done poorly is that Americans and many members of the press still fail to see that the various Asian nations are as different as the European nations, each with its own culture, ideas, and divides. We would not use Latvian and Spanish interchangeably. But to many, Korean is the same as Chinese is the same as Filipino.

Also, Asians are being under-represented in the news. They are rarely included in general stories and are seldom featured as centerpieces barring extraordinary circumstances.

A final failing of the media is their continued presentation of Asians as an exotic, backwards people. Men, if they are not computer geeks stealing your son's job, are in an Asian Mafia or gang. Women are gentle, servile flowers on the surface, but sex kittens underneath. And all of us are dog-eating communists at heart. Newspapers and magazines are not nearly as bad as, say, the movie industry, but these stereotypes still creep in once in a while. **Female newspaper journalist from Oregon.**

Asian Americans need to push for more stories on Asian Americans. Otherwise it won't happen. **Female newspaper journalist from New York.**

There are so many identity issues that are specific to Asian Americans. The issues are not addressed by mainstream press. Ethnic community press try to bring these to the surface, but it never reaches a broad audience. **Female newspaper journalist from Washington.**

We cannot complain that we are treated badly by the media, so much as we are ignored by it. I think it is a lack of coverage more than negative coverage that bothers me. **Female newspaper journalist from Kansas.**

There's a lot being done wrong. That's a research paper in and of itself. Many of the things that I mentioned above [to other survey questions] are occurring in spotty ways. Reporters still don't go to Chinatown to find out what "ordinary, Joe Blow Americans" think about a particular issue. They go to a predominately white neighborhood instead. I think the tendency to lump Asian

Americans into one heterogeneous group is hurting significant coverage as well. Asian Americans comprise at least fifteen significant communities in Seattle and many more communities elsewhere. To run a story about a Vietnamese business and say you've fulfilled the "Asian quota" is stupid and wrong. Yet, it happens a lot. I think the media also tend to see the community as monolithic. Call up so and so and ask her/him what the Asian community thinks about a particular issue. You would never do that with whites. You want to know what can be done to improve that—there is no answer to that question. I can suggest hiring more reporters of different Asian descents, or bringing them into decision-making positions. But the fact of the matter is that newsrooms are conservative, white, male-dominated hierarchical corporations.

A newspaper might think it's liberal because it supported the civil rights movement in the 1960s or because it always endorses democrats or because it's got a good hiring record of people of color. But the corporate creed that ultimately shapes news coverage is still white, male, and largely conservative. Until that changes significantly—and change is quite radical in this respect because it means those in power are going to have to voluntarily give up their power—I don't really see significant change taking place. **Female newspaper journalist from Washington.**

I feel that there should be more coverage on Asian Americans. I feel there should be reporters with beats in that area. Female newspaper journalist from Pennsylvania.

Too many stereotypes. Reporters and editors need to be more sensitive and educated. **Female newspaper journalist from New York City.**

The solution is to hire more Asian males as on-camera talent, and more Asian women for behind-the-scenes and executive work. **Female newspaper journalist from Hawaii.**

What is being done wrong is that Asians are lumped together as one ethnic group; we're all characterized as poor, uneducated immigrants, or illegal aliens who take jobs away from full-fledged Americans. At the same time, there are a host of stories that characterize all Asian American students as the smartest in the class or as leaders and members of tough street gangs.

The point is Asian Americans are as diverse as other segments of the population and should be reflected that way in the media. **Female newspaper journalist from Washington, D.C.**

My biggest gripe against the media (and I'm talking generally; I'm not referring to *name of newspaper* because I never did see the immigration series) Asians are portrayed as "foreigners" even though a good chunk of the Asian population have been here for decades. Case in point: The O.J. thing again. Judge Lance Ito— his first name is Lance, but he's still a "foreigner"? Of course the media didn't present this image, but they did nothing to prevent it. Only in the Asian media did I see charges of racism directed at Ito. All the TV and song parodies of Judge Ito were blasted by the Asian American Journalists Association, but in the mainstream media it was never an issue. For one day, there was a controversy over the way Dennis Fung and the LAPD criminalist were treated by the defense lawyers who brought in fortune cookies to celebrate their cross-examination. While defense lawyers made such a big deal over how Mark Fuhrman was a racist against a black defendant, they managed to cover up their racism against an Asian witness.

An Asian American judge was at the helm of the biggest trial of our day, and still we haven't earned a "place" in this society. But you know what? It was really nice seeing an Asian face in that courtroom everyday. I think may of the Asians I know were very proud. It was a chance to show America that we aren't all doctors or gang members.

Oh, on a side note, just so you can see what Asians have to put up with in this country (by the way, I love American and I am very grateful to be here) I was at a mall in downtown St. Louis today with a friend who is Asian. He was born in Orange County, California, and neither of us have foreign accents. A researcher approached us and asked us some questions. He asked my friend how many languages he spoke. My friend answered: one. The man asked, "Oh really. Which one?" **Male newspaper journalist from Missouri.**

Asian Americans tend to be lumped together—mainly as Chinese—and not enough care is given to distinctions and particularities. **Female newspaper journalist from Washington.**

I'm tired of how the media only seems to write about the Japanese American community when it comes to internment.

Don't get me wrong, I think it's an extremely important topic. But I think the number of articles written on that topic gives the public the perception that Japanese Americans equal internment camps and possibly not much more. I'd like to see other types of stories written about Japanese Americans. Have they assimilated too well? Maybe census stories on how many there are and how they compare to Korean Americans. I think more profiles need to be done on other Asian groups besides Koreans and Japanese, which seem to grab the most media attention (except in Orange County [California] where Vietnamese get a good amount of coverage). **Female newspaper journalist from California.**

We also tend to cover ethnic communities as if we've just discovered they existed, as if we've stumbled across some exotic culture while traipsing in country in some foreign land. Efforts are being made to hire reporters with the knowledge and language skills to cover these communities, but much of our coverage still lacks the insight that shows just how these varied communities fit into the fabric of the American experience. And we still tend to dwell on the negative aspects of any ethnic community—gang violence, for instance—venturing in only when some tragic event piques our interest or compels us to do some exploring.

The movie and television industries still tend to rely on stereotypes in portraying Asians. Males tend to be demonized, while women tend to be romanticized as exotic creatures. I've been heartened by a few movies over the years—*Joy Luck Club* was great, I thought. But little has changed since I was a kid, when there was no one who looked like me or talked like me up on the big screen to idolize or emulate. And how come there are no Asian American male anchors? I was surprised to find none on television in Hawaii, where you'd think some breakthroughs could be made. **Male newspaper journalist from California.**

The media continue to negatively portray Asian Americans as store owners, restaurant owners, and dry cleaners. Not all Asians own businesses. Many have degrees in law, medicine, and journalism. This stereotype I often see on television sitcoms. Why can't the media treat the social economic status of Asian Americans the same as Americans? **Male newspaper journalist from Louisiana.**

We are still perpetuating negative Asian stereotypes. I was a co-chair of a media watch committee for the Asian American

Journalists Association and we get many calls about negative stereotypes in both print and broadcast fro papers as reputable as the *New York Times* and networks like CBS. Columnists and commentators still use jargon like Chinaman and we still write stories that bash one Asian ethnic group against another.

The only way to relieve these frustrating problems is by encouraging Asian American journalists to go into management and pursue positions where they can set policy and oversee coverage. It's one thing being a peer and saying this story is racist and we should reconsider it and it's another to say the same thing when you're the editor or publisher. When you're the editor or publisher, people listen. **Male newspaper journalist from Texas.**

The media still tend to stereotype both Asian males and females and I think a lot of that blame should go towards Hollywood. A lot of the movies and television shows depict Asians in a less than glamorous light. Only recently have there been more Asian male and female actors in leading roles and I think that's a good start to improving the face of Asian Americans. But, we shouldn't stop there. We need to continue to push forward. **Male television journalist from Nevada.**

Not enough Asian issues are covered. **Male television journalist from New York.**

I feel that stereotypes still need to be eradicated. Whether it's "positive" ones like the model minority myth, or the "negative" ones like the Asian gangs mystique, the media should portray Asian Americans as real people—from doctors to garbage collectors. Coverage can only be improved if journalists realize this fact. For example, we don't have to go to Chinatown only on Chinese New Year. We can go there and interview people about coping with snow, or welfare cuts. I try to do that, and I hope non-Asian journalists would try as well. **Female television journalist from Pennsylvania.**

Here's a small point, but one that constantly irritates me. Why do newspapers continue to hyphenate Asian American, Chinese American, or Japanese American? I know they do it to the African Americans too. But none of our groups do it, not even the journalists' organizations for the different groups.

On the East coast race is only a black and white issue. Whenever I read any stories about race relations, racial statistics, or diversity, the only groups covered are whites and African

Americans, and sometimes Latinos. Never are Asian Americans mentioned.

When race is identified in a story, blacks are always referred to as African Americans and not just Africans because that would mean something quite different. They why is it that the majority press seems to feel Asian and Asian American are interchangeable?

On the whole, I feel that Asian American coverage is still on a patronizing level. We do it because we must and we want to show everyone how liberal we are.

The best way to improve this is to have more Asian Americans employed on all levels of information delivery. In the thirteen years I've lived on the East coast, I've see an improvement. I see more and more story and photo bylines with Asian American names. We have an Asian American reporter and anchor on almost every major television news broadcast. When I first moved here we had one reporter. But still the numbers are small and most are not in decision-making positions.

When I went to college Asian American women were usually enrolled in the School of Education studying to be teachers. The men were in the sciences or engineering departments. There were three of us in the School of Journalism. I think things have changed quite a bit since the 1960s. **Female television journalist from Massachusetts.**

The dearth of coverage of the Asian American community remains a problem. When the media address race relations, they often limit the discussion to black/white relations. I would also like to see more Asian Americans interviewed as experts—not as Asian experts—but as experts in economics, medicine, etc. Asian Americans are in every field and the media need to try harder to reflect that. **Female television journalist from Washington, D.C.**

One of the pet issues of AAJA [Asian American Journalists Association] members that we surveyed is that beyond colorful holidays, costumes, food, and cute babies, Asians are not real people. One of my own concerns is that when a lawyer, or doctor, or economist, or any other kind of expert is needed for a story, Asians are rarely asked.

Language deficiencies and accents are still assumed to be prevalent and a problem, even if an Asian speaks English fluently.

My sense of this problem is clearly a Midwest reaction. The East and West coasts pay much more attention to Asian issues because the Asian population is larger, has a stronger voice, and Pacific rim issues affect their economics and population a great deal.

Asians also probably share a frustration with Hispanics: a belief by others that we are all one within our ethnic group, i.e., Koreans, Thai, Chinese, Japanese, etc. all look the same and agree on everything. **Female television journalist from Illinois.**

Improvement in coverage. My basic instincts tell me that unless we get more Asians in management and in the reporting side, we won't get deserved coverage. People in the business of media are people after all, with ideas of their own. Unless we get inside the business and voice our ideas and do the stories it won't get done. **Female television journalist from California.**

Often, coverage of Asian American issues are too broad and many sweeping generalizations are made. I think it is imperative that Asians take a prominent role in the newsroom as producers and news directors. If the newscast is to reflect the audience, then the newsroom should too. **Female Vietnamese American television journalist from Georgia.**

I don't think Asian Americans are covered enough in the media. Part of the reason seems to be the Asian American communities are not as "media savvy" as say, the black community.

If there's a great injustice being done to an Asian American, the community doesn't rally around that person and call all the media the way other groups might. Press releases would help the Asian American community more, as a stepping stone to getting better coverage. **Female television journalist from Massachusetts.**

There are not enough stories about Asian Americans, unless it's about Asian gangs in San Francisco or Silicon Valley. Usually, stories about "home invasion robberies" are tagged with "police are looking for four Asian males." That doesn't tell me much, nor do I think the race of the suspects is germane. Would we, for example, say "police are looking for four white males"? There seems to be interest in covering Asian issues as they relate to illegal immigration and gangs. I believe there's more to the community than that. But our newsroom provides no time to find that out. **Female radio journalist from California.**

Asian Americans' "coverage" is too often lumped into ambiguous stories about "minorities," when, in fact, it's African and Hispanic Americans who are being addressed. Because Asian

Americans are a relatively small population, they are often over-looked as having discrete problems or issues of concern.   Of course, most of the issues facing Asian Americans are the same issues facing most of the rest of Americans, yet we are being marginalized.   We're worried about individual success and achieving the American Dream, but somehow don't fit in the Andrew Wyeth vision of it.   Improving it can be as simple as making an effort to seek out a diversity of voices in stories.   Improving it can be as simple as not always characterizing Asian men as "inscrutable" or "sneaky," and Asian women as "sexy" and "exotic."   Improving it can be as simple as casting Asians in commercials as print ads.   Improving it can be as simple as hiring an Asian American op ed columnist.

On a more philosophical level, the media can be improved by more inclusion and more outreach.  The world according to middle aged white male managers works pretty well, but especially if you're middle aged, white, and male.  Obviously, that's not a true reflection of the society in which we live.  To become more responsible, responsive, and economically viable, the media must become more like the constituency they serve, and no longer view the world from a singular perspective or life experience.  **Male television journalist from New York.**

Asian Americans are often excluded from stories directly affecting them.  The world is made up of more than just blacks and whites.  But you wouldn't know it watching news coverage.

In California, there are several major issues at the forefront of political debate in this state affecting Asian Americans—proposition 187, affirmative action, and English as an official language are just a few of them.  Yet, proposition 187 and the English language debate are often seen only as impacting Hispanics.   Affirmative action continues to be framed as a black and white issue.

This will continue until stations decide the community is important enough to assign reporters to cover the Asian American community as a beat.  This is the only way stories about the community can be generated and news sources can be made.

Until then, the majority of the stories about the Asian American community will continue to be gang shootings and Chinese New Year.  While such stories are newsworthy, they are only a small snapshot of a very diverse, growing, and economically powerful community in this country. **Male television journalist from California.**

There are many problems with coverage by local television stations. Much of it has to do with the ignorance of reporters and producers. Some of these problems can be alleviated by Asian American reporters and, more importantly, Asian American management-level personnel (news directors, executive producers, etc.). These are the decision-makers in the newsroom. They decide what stories are covered, who covers them, and how they're covered. This is one area where improvement can be made. From there, the trickle-down effect will take place. **Male television journalist from Virginia.**

Offhand, I can't think of any recent stories that I like (or dislike) regarding Asians. Part of the problem is I'm out touch with community issues. For the last two years I've lived in towns where I was one of a handful of Asians. I can go months without seeing another Asian. I stare at other Asians like they're UFOs. The other part is, I'm fourth generation American so my family doesn't really have any problems regarding assimilation or anything. I just don't know if there's a story that needs to be covered but isn't.

I will talk about other forms of media, however. I feel pop culture does not give Asians enough attention. We are a huge and growing segment of America. We aren't treated like it.

It upsets me that magazines, movies, and TV shows do not give Asians prominence. It was incredibly rare to find an Asian in anything mainstream up until the last several years. If you did, it was a stereotyped role (the nerd, the karate expert). I remember growing up, if we saw an Asian on TV we'd yell and everyone would come running to the set. I'm tired of seeing people who do not look like me. It makes me feel like we don't count as part of American society if we aren't represented in it.

The positive thing is, this decade I've been noticing Asians are given more and better roles and more modeling jobs. I feel Asians are still decades behind where blacks and Latinos stand, but I do feel the 90s have seen a small progress. **Female television journalist from New Jersey.**

On those few occasions that I've caught Asian American stories on local news, I've been disappointed at the shallow treatment given to the stories. Many times, I feel the news will only show problems I the community such as gang violence, labor problems, illegal immigration—things that the mainstream public "expects" to see about Chinatown or Asians. I would like to see someday where events in the Asian American community are covered as the newsworthy events that they are, and not isolated for their "Asianess."

I feel the only way coverage can be improved is a change in the mentality in the newsroom, a willingness by the assignment editors, news directors to say we are going to cover the community— whether it be Asian, African American, Hispanic—we will look at what's going on in our community and cover it. These are the people in the community and news, especially local coverage should try to broaden issues to reflect the concerns of these people. This means moving away from isolating each community and talking stories that come only when something big in the community happens (i.e., Thai workers are released from sweatshop). **Female radio journalist from California.**

# APPENDIX 13

## SURVEY RESPONSES FROM DEAN WONG, EDITOR OF THE *INTERNATIONAL EXAMINER*

*Question 1: Have you ever had any negative experiences on the job that you feel were related to your ethnic status as an Asian American?*

I once worked in television news as a production assistant. This was an entry level position, considered the very bottom of the news room hierarchy. There were two other Asian Americans who were production assistants. Often times, members of the news room would get confused and call us by the wrong name. It's that you all look the same mentally. They found it amusing, when I worked with a young Vietnamese news photographer. We became known as the "Oriental crew."

As far as being a community journalist, there have not been many experiences that I felt were negative. There have been situations where not being a member of the mainstream media gave me the feeling that they didn't respect me in the field, but that's not necessarily based on race. But then it is, a little.

When the soldiers began returning from the Persian Gulf War, I followed an Asian American family to McChord Air Force Base to greet a relative. I tried to break away from the crowds of family members and move into a roped off area in front of the crowd to get a better angle on their faces. The guards would not let me in this one gate, although they would let White camera crews in freely. I joined them and walked in. It may have been a racial thing, or it may not have been. This is the kind of "paranoia" that people of color feel in some situations.

*Question 2: Have you ever had any positive experiences on the job that you feel were related to your ethnic status as an Asian American?*

As a community journalists for the last 15 years, who is Asian American and has chosen to work in his own community where he was born and raised, who I am is determining what I do.
Covering the issues of importance to this community and sharing the experiences of other people through the stories we print, is a positive result of my ethnicity.

*Question 3: In your opinion, what is being done right in the media today in covering Asian Americans and issues affecting Asian Americans?*

The *Seattle Times*, with some culturally sensitive reporters of color have covered a good number of stories on Asian Pacific Americans. This is due to the presence of these reporters, who are willing and interested in pursuing these stories. This is also due in part to Seattle's active Asian Pacific Islander community and the region's proximity to the Pacific Rim.
The *Seattle Times* is the exception. Most other mainstream media does little to cover issues of importance to Asians.

*Question 4: In your opinion, what is being done wrong in the media toady in covering Asian Americans and issues facing Asian Americans? How can this be improved?*

The mainstream media does not cover enough stories on Asian Americans. when they do cover stories, it is because they see an advantage to it. such as in sensational gang violence or murders. They come into the community with few contacts. Often times they come to the community press to find out who to talk to. Once the big story is gone, they leave also. they leave behind the more common everyday concerns of this community. Concerns such as immigration, welfare reform, racial violence and how it affects this community are ignored.

NOTE: At the time of this study, Dean Wong was the Editor of the International Examiner, the journal of the Northwest United States' Asian American communities. The editorial headquarters of that journal are located at: 622 South Washington, Seattle, Washington 98104. The telephone is (206) 624-3925.

# APPENDIX 14

## SURVEY RESPONSE FROM AN EDITOR OF ONE OF THE TWENTY LEADING ASIAN AMERICAN PUBLICATIONS, WHO ASKED TO REMAIN ANONYMOUS

*Question 1: Have you ever had any negative experiences on the job that you feel were related to your ethnic status as an Asian American?*

Yes, it was hard getting a job in mainstream media.

*Question 2: Have you ever had any positive experiences on the job that you feel were related to your ethnic status as an Asian American?*

N/A. I've worked mainly in community/ethnic media.

*Question 3: In your opinion, what is being done right in the media today in covering Asian Americans and issues affecting Asian Americans?*

There's increased effort at coverage, quantitatively speaking.

*Question 4: In your opinion, what is being done wrong in the media today in covering Asian Americans and issues facing Asian Americans?*

Asian Americans tend to be lumped together—mainly as Chinese—and not enough care is given to distinctions and particularities.

# APPENDIX 15

## SUMMARY OF RESPONSES FROM THE EDITORS OF THE TWENTY LEADING ASIAN AMERICAN PUBLICATIONS

*Hawaiian Journal of History.* Helen Chapin, editor of the *Hawaiian Journal of History*, explained that it is "a scholarly publication available in many libraries" and that it is "an annual that includes historical material on Hawaii and the Pacific" (Chapin 1995, Letter to the author).

*Critical Mass: A Journal of Asian American Criticism.* Sau-ling Wong, associate professor of Asian American studies and ethnic studies at the University of California, Berkeley, explained that *Critical Mass: A Journal of Asian American Cultural Criticism* " is actually an academic journal featuring critical essays written by mostly graduate students" with some faculty and undergraduate student contributors (Wong 1995, Letter to author). Wong felt the journal did not really fit into the topic of this book and declined, with regrets, to respond to the survey.

*Filipinas Magazine.* Rene Ciria-Cruz, editor of *Filipinas Magazine*, was most helpful in explaining the mission of that publication and providing a recent issue of the magazine (Ciria-Cruz 1995, Letter to author). Much of the information from the letter and sample magazine was incorporated into the history chapter of this book.

*Northwest Asian Weekly.* Also incorporated into this book's history chapter was much of the information sent by Deni Yamauchi Luna, editor of *Northwest Asian Weekly* (Luna 1995, Letter to author). Luna forwarded copies of the magazine which had articles that were pertinent to the history of Asian American publications. Those articles were cited in the history chapter.

*KoreAm Journal.* Jung Shig Ryu, editor of *KoreAm Journal*, gave a brief description of that publication and explained its mission to cover news of interest to Koreans and Korean Americans living in the United States, as well as explained that back issues are available to the public for a fee of $3 per issue (Ryu 1995, Letter to author).

***International Examiner.*** *International Examiner* editor Dean Wong offered lengthy responses to the four survey questions (see Appendix 94). Wong's responses were added to and calculated as part of the total number of respondents to the survey of five hundred Asian American journalists. Wong did not offer any historical or other information about the publication *International Examiner.* However, that journal, with headquarters in Seattle, Washington, officially calls itself the journal of the Northwest United States' Asian American communities and covers news from that region.

## APPENDIX 16

### SELECTED RESPONSES TO SURVEY QUESTION ONE

The following are responses taken nearly verbatim from the journalists' written answers to survey question one. The name of the reporter, and his or her place of employment, is given in bold type at the end of each response, if that person did not request anonymity. If the sex of a respondent is unclear from the person's name or the content of the text, *Ms.* or *Mr.* will be printed before the name for reader clarification. These are listed in no set order and not all responses are reprinted here. Many of those answers not reprinted were brief "yes" or "no" answers, and some were brief answers that repeated points already made by other respondents. Some editing was done to make the style, such as the term "Asian American" not being hyphenated, consistent throughout for reader ease.

*Question 1: Have you ever had any negative experiences on the job that you feel were related to your ethnic status as an Asian American?*

Several negative things I have experienced as an Asian American journalist rank worthy of note. The usual stereotyping of an Asian American male carrying cameras has punctuated my career as a photojournalist. When I worked in Ann Arbor, Michigan, while covering the threat of auto plants closing down supposedly due to Japanese competition, I was met with discern from my editors. My picture editor feared that because of my Asian descent I would not be able to cover the story objectively. He also feared for my safety. As a Chinese American, I did not share these concerns. Nevertheless, I was not allowed to cover the story. **Ken Kwok, photographer, *Press-Telegram*, Long Beach, California.**

I don't recall any negative experiences on the job as an Asian American. Why, I'm not sure. Maybe because I am a woman and an individual who has certain life experiences that command certain respect, if not curiosity. I came from Saigon 20 years ago and had been an established fiction writer, journalist and publisher-editor of a daily newspaper, *Song Than (Tidal Waves)*, that fought corruption in the government and military in South Vietnam. Maybe because I'm always willing to learn, or maybe I'm just plain lucky. Speaking English with an accent does have some disadvantage on the job, but then that's another issue, as long as I don't apply for a reporter's job with a television or radio station, which is not my interest anyway. **Ms. Thai Nguyen Strom, columnist and chief librarian for** *The Record*, **San Joaquin County, California.**

In all the above venues (the writer listed several jobs before his current position), I can safely say I have had exactly one negative experience that I feel was related to my ethnic status. About a year and a half after I arrived at the (Philadelphia) Inquirer, I was promoted from rim editor to backup slot, to sit in for slot editors absent because of vacation, illness, etc. Shortly after the promotion was made public, a white copy editor approached me and without saying so directly, got across the fact that she believed I had been promoted primarily because management wanted more minorities in higher positions. She quickly added that she considered me a good editor, but her point was clear: She believed that my race was the crucial factor. I believe I was truly the best candidate at the time, regardless of race.

Otherwise, I've been lucky. **Amy Wang, copy editor, the** *Philadelphia Inquirer*, **Philadelphia, Pennsylvania.**

I was not specifically targeted out, but it's not easy to go ahead and be a part of the mainstream job market. First of all, you have to have your name, that itself sets you apart, most people don't take the time to learn how to pronounce it, but the reaction is normally that it's not worth it. Most people I talk to think the name is Judy. I've been here for three years and after a while you just stop trying and just let them call you what they want to. I don't know if it's a negative thing, it's just an obstacle. It's more psychological and it's a question of your identity. In many cases, like when I was in school, most friends changed their name to something Americanized, like Lee, but I wanted to keep my name.

In small towns you just stand out. It's not as bad in big cities.

**Ms. Jyothi Kiran, staff writer, *India Currents* magazine, San Jose, California.**

When I began looking for a job shortly after I arrived here, I became aware of a certain bias regarding my educational background. It did not seem to matter that I had vast experience as a journalist, not just in Manila but in other countries as well. The bottom line, as far as come editors were concerned, was where I was educated, or at least, if I did master's studies in America. There were also certain doubts as to how much English I knew even if I passed the language and grammar tests.

**Ms. Marites Sison-Paez, editor, *Special Edition Press*, New York City.**

This question calls to mind an incident that happened to me when I was interning for a small paper in Corvallis, Oregon. The paper rarely has had minority staff members, and when I came aboard I was the only Asian American reporter, and one of two Asian American staff members at the paper. Before I took the job, I was already beginning to wonder whether I was hired solely for affirmative action reasons. One assignment, while one of the paper's photographers and I waited to find our subject, the photographer began discussing affirmative action. He kept insisting he thought it was a good thing, but that newspapers should not hire reporters who are not qualified. He then said, in a very suggestive tone, that he knew of two instances that the paper hired reporters based on their minority status; one of which, he said, happened very recently. it was clear that he was talking about me. I won't soon forget that day, or the way I felt after contemplating the possibility of this actually happening. I began to feel worthless as a reporter; soon believing myself to be a young, female, Asian intern who had no skills in the journalism field. I've since come to realize how that is not true. Still, I think back on that intern and sometimes wonder if the photographer was telling the truth, or if indeed the paper did hire me because I am not white.

In even more subtle ways, my negative experiences on the job relate to story assignments. Looking back, I begin to notice trends in what stories I get assigned to do. For instance, when a group of international students from Japan came to Albany while I was interning in nearby Corvallis, the first person my editors went to was me. As an intern, I felt obligated to take every assignment and never say "no." This is only one of several examples of story assignments that automatically gets handed down to me because of my ethnic status. **Ms. Putsata Reang, cultural reporter for the *Spokesman-Review*, Spokane, Washington.**

Negative experiences: In some rural sections or urbanized areas where people have not had much contact with Asians, people tend to take a little time to warm up to you. However, I suspect this is the same for reporters of any race or ethnic background working in an unfamiliar neighborhood. **Paul Hyun-Bong Shin, staff writer for The Courier-News, Bridgewater, New Jersey.**

In terms of things that are very flagrant like ethnic slurs, I've never really had that sort of experience. I remember I was slightly annoyed the other week when I was running around very busy and somebody asked me why wasn't I at the minority training workshop. Besides that it's just like working in any other all-white environment, people tend to ignore your ethnicity most of the time and that's not necessarily good. You'll be in a room and people will assume that everyone is white. **Pamela SooHoo, associate producer for public television (media organzition withheld upon request).**

Many negative experiences I've had stem from people's ignorance, and perhaps previous run-ins with other Asians. For example, while covering Memorial Day/Veteran's Day/Pearl Harbor commemoration stories, I'm often confronted with hostile veterans, friends, family members and widows who see me only as someone who "looks like the enemy." I've been denied access to certain ceremonies, causing my photographer to go alone to get video. I've also been outright snubbed, verbally, because I'm an Asian.

Another experience is continually "fighting" about the importance of stories dealing with Asians. There's more than just Asian gangs and bath houses! There are a lot of other stories that center around Asians, and stories that happen to involved Asians. Considering in the various places where I've worked that Asians are time and time again the minority (more so than African Americans), stories involving Asians most times aren't even CONSIDERED, let alone deemed newsworthy. I understand the effort to diversity and make more people aware of "cultures," but as I mentioned, gangs, bath houses and Chinese New Year aren't the only things making news.

I'm often "mistaken" (if you can use that term LOOSELY) for Connie Chung, probably the most recognizable Asian female broadcast journalist. But that may be more pomposity and annoyance than actual "negativity." **Victoria Lim, reporter for WWMT-TV in Kalamazoo, Michigan.**

Yes, of course I have had negative experiences on the job that were related to my status as an Asian American. The same prejudice, stereotyping and ignorance that abounds in almost every community doesn't disappear because I'm a journalist, nor does it disappear in the newsroom. I would be very surprised if there were any Asian Americans who didn't have a negative experience on the job, let alone in life.

Anecdotes:

1) While covering the completion of an elaborate city playground as a photographer for *The Boca Raton News* (Fla.), an elderly white gentleman approached me and asked, "Do they build them like this in your country?"

"This is my country," I replied.

2) While working as a photo editor at the *Chicago Tribune*, a page designer asked me if I had a brother named so-and-so Wu or something to that effect living in Chicago.

Since my last name is not Wu I said, "What?"

The designer continued, "Are you related to him? That's your name isn't it?"

"No it's not," I stated. for some reason, even if my last name were Wu, this guy figures, among the three million or so people living in Chicago, I must be related to this guy.

3) After working at the *Chicago Tribune* for about a year, a reporter asked me how my first day went. she had confused me with another Asian male who had started that day. This guy is at least a foot taller than me, formally dressed, younger, didn't wear glasses at the time and otherwise looked completely different, sounded different and worked in a different department. I had gone on assignment with this reporter only a month previous, yet she still had me confused with a guy who'd only been there a day.

Also, and not surprisingly, throughout my time here, people consistently confuse me and the otehr Asian working on the picutre desk, Jim. People call Jim, Eric. People call me Jim. Again, we don't look alike or talk alide. I wear glasses, he doesn't. Jim has worked here about five times longer thatn I have. **Eric Chu, assistant picture editor for the *Chicago Tribune*, Chicago, Illinois.**

In this day and time, it's simple to point and blame another for a negative situation you've experiences. I could say, "I didn't get the promotion because my boss is a racist" and rest a little easier about myself. But, I've seen both sides of the track. I am part American and part Korean, and I am able to relate to the white theory that minorities are taking all the jobs and advance quicker, and I'm also able to understand how minorities feel about the job ladder. I've only been in "the business" for a little over a year, but I've seen a remarkable change in the way my superiors' hiring practices. I can't say I've "never" had a negative experience because of my ethnicity, but certain times I may have misunderstood, or taken too seriously, comments not directed toward me. I know people see me as me and they're not always on pins and needles while talking to me because I'm not defensive about my ethnicity. Sometimes co-workers will say "oriental" instead of Asian American, or will comment on Connie Chung as a "dingbat," but is this something I should feel strongly defensive toward? I choose to be patient toward people's ignorance and educate them so that the next minority that co-workers meet, he or she will not be stereotyped. **Ms. Michile Kim-Gray, producer for KWTX-TV in Waco, Texas.**

There is another Asian American female reporter on the staff and sometimes people in the community get us mixed up. I don't think we resemble each other, but because we are Asian, people sometimes assume we are the same person. It's hard to have an identity or to establish sources when obviously some people can't remember which reporter you are. **Rose Tibayan, anchor/reporter for WINK-TV in Fort Myers, Florida.**

When I was an intern at a radio station and applying for a job at a TV station, a reporter at the radio station told me I was lucky because as an Asian I would probably get a job easily. That's because many newsrooms actively seek minorities. But I resented the idea that anyone thought I would be hired on the basis of my race instead of my ability. **Ms. Yuki Spellman, newswriter for WGN News (TV) in Chicago, Illinois.**

No, which is not to say there were no "signs" of subtle racism in my current working environment. It seems there will always be jokes about Blacks, Latinos, Asians and the omnipresent "potluck" and such are figments of light humor. However, my experience has been "pampered" to some extent by the fact I work in the nation's number two market in a traditionally liberal occupation in a very racially mixed city. I sense in obtaining my first reporting job at a smaller market, even within the state of California, will be more likely to serve as an atmosphere for racist attitudes. Markets where there are no "diversity" classes or a compelling need to welcome a minority reporter to a market where 95 percent of the viewers are Caucasian. In summary, I have not been a victim of racism, yet as my career takes me into smaller, rural markets for my first reporting job, the chances are higher of something happening. **Robert Goozee, news assignment desk, KNBC NBC 4, Los Angeles, California.**

Only once in 1969 when a slot man gave me 20 shorts about India. **Ronald Patel, Sunday editor for the *Philadelphia Inquirer*, in Philadelphia, Pennsylvania.**

When I've been asked questions like this in the past, I've answered: "I don't know of any instances, but I ought to think about that." These days, I don't think it's worth the trouble to think about it.

If there have been any instances of discrimination for or against me they must have been awfully subtle. (In answer to questions one and two). **Dean Inouye, assistant news editor, Knight-Ridder Washington Bureau, Washington, D.C.**

I have had negative experiences on the job that I feel relate to my ethnicity, however they are always subtle, never overt. I question whether the negative experiences are based on my gender (female), ethnicity, age (appearance of being young) or all of the above. The negative experiences range from having my ideas ignored at meetings to "cute" comments about my appearance. **Connie Riu, manager of diversity and outreach services, Newspaper Association of America, Reston, Virginia.**

I have a very unusual position in media as I've been with the same station(s) since I was hired March 25, 1968. Throughout this period, I've had the opportunity to observe a variety of people, both within the company and in the community, which is where my work is focused. I produce public affairs programming, a type of radio that is slowing becoming less evident in broadcast media. A sheet of the programs and their broadcast times (not the best!) are enclosed.

The late 60s was the time when the Great Society and all things good for community and low income people was beginning to happen. It was a great time to be hired at the station, because it was my purpose to provide media access to people.

As to your question, it is difficult for me to find any specific "negative experiences," because San Francisco is a very supportive community for minority populations; if any of us has an issue, we can pretty much find a referral or someone to help us with our questions.

I have been told that shortly after I was hired, I was the first Chinese American woman to be hired at that time (the other being a union engineer who was hired well before I was, but whose skills were somewhat limited, so I don't think he ever was promoted). The word I got was that the non-minorities, upon hearing of my being hired, asked of my employer, "Does she speak English?" This shows the lack of exposure that many in our station might have had to Chinese, aside from perhaps having been served by a waiter at a Chinese restaurant, or having picked up laundry from the cleaners.

Indeed, my hiring employer responded, Gimmy does speak English; she is a native of San Francisco; she holds a BA in English Literature from San Francisco State, etc. **Gimmy Park Li, manager, public affairs, KNBR AM - KFOG FM, San Francisco, California.**

Only in confronting stereotypes. When I joined a large metro newspaper as an assistant city editor, I did not feel I got the support I needed from my supervisors. During a conversation with my boss, he said perhaps the staff expected someone less aggressive, more compliant. The implication is my heritage projected an image of passivity that was rudely shattered—and I was at fault somehow. Management needs to take an active role in dispelling any stereotypes and in supporting staff, especially new hires. **Ms. Mei-Mei Chan, executive editor, the *Post Register*, Idaho Falls, Idaho.**

No negative experiences at KCAL Channel 9. Being in the Los Angeles market (with a large Asian American population) may be a factor. **George Kiriyama, desk assistant, KCAL-TV Channel 9 News, Los Angeles, California.**

So far I have not had any negative experiences on the job related to my ethnic status. Being in the Midwest, I think that racism is more subtle in this part of the country. People would not show their true emotions if there were racist. **Mary Tan, news reporter, WMTV-TV, Madison, Wisconsin.**

Negative experiences—None from my colleagues or supervisors. I've on two or three occasions been harassed by people/sources in part because of my race. Once when I was covering a race melee (between Hispanics and African Americans) at a local high school—"get out of here, (expletive) chino"—and once as I was researching at the Superior Courts (Mariopa County) when a middle-aged (Anglo) woman harangued me for about 10 minutes, accusing me of being Japanese and telling me to "go back to your country." In the latter instance, upon telling her I am a newspaper reporter (she asked my profession), the woman said, "Why don't you write the truth? That your people are buying up our land and our banks and taking jobs from Americans! Why don't you ever print that?" She was later instructed by a couple of court clerks who know me as a reporter to leave me alone. Lastly, There have been a couple of cases in which people at police/fire scenes have yelled out "sayanara" (spelling?) and "gook." **Abraham Kwok, reporter for the *Arizona Republic/The Phoenix Gazette*, Phoenix, Arizona.**

Yes, I have had negative experiences on the job that were related to my ethnic status. The most hurtful was being accused of giving preferential treatment to an Asian American subordinate. A reporter reportedly claimed I was more harsh with her than with her Asian American counterpart when editing stories. I never confronted this reporter about her claim, in part because I learned of this third hand. Over time I demonstrated to her that I was even handed (equally hard, I suppose) with all reporters, including her. It took a while, but in the end I believe she was convinced that being a tough editor was also valuable to her own development.

Another negative instance also stands out. The first thing one General Manager said to me when I showed up for an interview, "Do you cook Chinese?" **Janice Gin, executive producer/1996 Atlanta Olympics, Gannett Broadcasting, Atlanta, Georgia.**

No, I have never experienced anything negative on the job. The only negative thing I might have experienced on the job as a result of my ethnicity is the feeling that the marketing director was trying to diversify the staff (I was one of two Asian minorities; there were a total of three minorities: 1 Korean, 1 Filipino, 1 Black). This was at *The Atlantic Monthly* in the marketing department. I quit shortly thereafter. **Ms. Soomie Ahn, employee at Ellen Ryder Communications, New York City.**

During my six years as a journalist, I don't recall any negative experiences on the job that were related to my ethnicity. Now you must realize that my career thus far has been spent in the newsroom on the editing desk. I don't have the daily direct contact with the communities our reporters do. If there were any unpleasant experiences I can clearly recall, however, it would more likely be a matter of ignorance on the reporter's part or editor's part (for example, referring to an Asian as an Oriental or neglecting to include Asian voices in stories in which other ethnic or racial groups are represented). **Henry K.P. Yeun, assistant features editor, the *Star-Gazette*, Elmira, New York.**

When I was quite new to the business and anchoring in Portland, Oregon, I received a phone call after a newscast on December 7, 1979. The caller was irate and abusive and said, "If I could carry a gun on the streets, I'd shoot all the Japs." I asked what was bothering him, and he answered that we "weren't telling the whole story about the bombing of Pearl Harbor." It sounded like he was also a bit drunk. I had never heard such racial rantings before and was almost mesmerized, unable to put the receiver down. An African American producer sitting nearby, asked, "Who IS that?" I described it and she said, "Just hang up!" It didn't occur to me to do so until she said that.

In 1991, on the 50th anniversary of the attack on Pearl Harbor, I was sent by my station and NBC Newschannel to cover the commemoration in Hawaii. I did several features on the servicemen and women, civilians and others who were affected by the bombing. I also did several live shots for affiliates across the country. Upon my return from Hawaii, I was told that KING received several dozen calls from viewers who were angry that "Jap" was out covering the Pearl Harbor story. My news director was angry and disturbed by the callers (he told off several of them) and told me, "They're just idiots."

The only other negative experience wasn't an experience at all. I was specifically not selected to cover a convention of white supremacists (Aryan Nation) at Hayden Lake, Idaho. The news director said the supremacists would only allow white reporters and camera people onto their campus. **Lori Matsukawa, anchor, KING TV, Seattle, Washington.**

Probably the most negative experience I've had on the job from a co-worker happened soon after I started working at my present station. A support staff in Word Processing commented to me how many of our co-workers were talking about the station's decision to hire three Asian Americans in a row as producers (including myself). She viewed the move as unusual, and felt the company may have been trying to fulfill a racial quota. I resented that, as all three of us have credible media backgrounds and did not believe we were "quota hires."

I guess dealing with assumptions is a bothersome part of my job. My station used to produce a show called "Asia Now" and everyone assumed I was the producer of that show because I'm Asian. Consequently, a lot of mail and calls for that show were directed to me. Ironically, the actual producer was Hispanic.

On the job, outside my workplace, the most negative experience was probably on a shoot with a well-known candy manufacturer in Washington. I was appalled when the Director of International Marketing/Sales made several ignorant statements in the interview, like "Asians like to hoard gold under their bed." At the time, I did not know how to react and have since regretted not correcting the guy.

Oh, one often-experienced phenomenon is being mistaken for Connie Chung when out on a shoot. For some reason, seeing an Asian woman with a camera crew brings out this odd assumption. We do not look anything alike, and I know many female Asian reporters encounter this syndrome. **Susan Han, producer, KCTS/9 TV, Seattle, Washington.**

Yes, many years ago, when I first started working in the U.S., I was with a small architectural firm (may not count) and a small publishing firm that produced a community newspaper, working pretty much the same time or concurrently. People at the architectural firm openly criticized me for difficulties in communication and treated me somewhat condescendingly. I sensed there was a similar attitude at the community newspaper where I was associate editor. I came in contact with contributors who could not readily accept editorial changes or copyedit changes because there was an implicit attitude that I wasn't really "good enough" or qualified enough to do that job. **Ms. Vyryan Tenorio, editor of *Asia Environmental Business Journal* at Environmental Business International, San Diego, California.**

A few times. I have been in this business now for four years and I think some people deep down inside believe I got my past jobs, as well as this one here, because I'm an Asian female—or it was an EEO (equal employment opportunity) requirement. I like to think I am here today reporting because I have talent and I can do the job. **Stephanie Nishikawa, news reporter for WDAF-TV, Kansas City, Missouri.**

None that affected my job status. Mostly ignorance on the part of work mates. In Texas they would ask ignorant questions because few had ever known an Asian American. It didn't bother me much because ignorance is not intentional. **Alan Wang, reporter at KDFW-TV, Fresno, California.**

By and large, no. I beleive being an Asian American generally has been an advantage. Many of my colleagues are so considerate and sensitive that they often have asked me for my opinion about a story or headline involving Asians.

But I have run into racism on two occasions—and they are all the more distrubing because they invovled co-workers. In 1991, the Broadway musical "Miss Saigon" opened amid a casting controversy: Welsh actor Jonathan Pryce was chosen to play the lead "eurasian" character. I broke the story and quoted angry Asain American actors who were incensed over this. I also tried to reach Pryce for his reaction, but his agent told me that Pryce didn't want to speak to me and add fuel to the fire. So the story ran and I reported that the Welsh actor had no comment.

The next day, someone left a mysterious envelope at my desk and it was anonymous. Enclosed was a critique of my story that accused me of unfairly covering the story and carrying out a pro-Asian agenda. Because my last name was Wong, it was assumed I was automatically anti-Pryce.

Now, if my surname were Jewish and I had written a piece about Israel, would someone have left a note accusing me of being pro-Jewish? I really doubt it.

An ironic footnote: Months later at the Tony Awards, I introduced myself to Pryce and he flew into a rage: "Why didn't you ever talk to me?" I told him that I tried to, but his agent and the producers of "Miss Saigon" rebuffed me. (They were not, however, too busy to talk to the *New York Times*.) Anyway, Pryce said he and I would have to sit down sometime and have a long talk. I later wrote to remind him of this discussion, but I never heard from him again.

The other occasion invoved a phone call from a makeup person in the composition room. An older opinionated woman, she ws complaining to a copy editor about my work on the copy desk. Somehow she then sequed into a harangue about Asian men and "how small their dicks are." To add further insult, the copy editor who was hearing this harangue was herwself Asian American. But because they were on the phone and because the editor's las name was English-sounding (her parents are Chinese and European), the makeup person had no idea she was slurring Asians to an Asian. The copy editor and I told management that we were outranged at this, and the makeup woman was docked a week's pay and apologized to the copy editor (although never to me). Still, I was thrilled to know that my bosses would not tolerate such racism. **Wayman Wong, reporter for the New York *Daily News*, New York City.**

NOTE: The following responses are from Asian American journalists who requested anonymity. Therefore, if a respondent gave information referring to his or her name, or other identifying factors, that information is appropriately changed and in italics. If a respondent clearly identified his or her Asian American ethnic sub-group status, such as Japanese American, either in the text of the answers or on the permission/consent form, then that identification is given.

I have only been identifiably Japanese for two years of my career. I am half-Japanese, and grew up as *Caucasian sounding name*. My first reporting job was at radio station in city name, California, where the news director name told me I could be *Caucasian name* or *Japanese sounding name*, it didn't matter to him. It was common wisdom at the time that having the Asian name was fashionable and marketable, but I was "*Caucasian sounding name*" and short of a mentor or employer telling me to change, I would stay Caucasian sounding name. So. . .when I went to Seattle a year later and they wanted me to be *Japanese sounding name* and *Japanese sounding name* I became. With these now two years of experience with my new name (mother's maiden) I can say the only vaguely negative experience is what may only be an imagined resentment among my colleagues. I say imagined because I suspect it is more about my insecurity than their attitude. I have moved very fast, from *California city name* to *Texas city name* in two years. . .and I know my new name has helped.

So I worry I'm here in large part because of the political value of my [Japanese sounding] name as opposed to merit alone. On the other hand, I know I am doing a competent and sometimes even superior job, and ultimately wouldn't survive here if I couldn't cut the mustard.

The net negative result is that in addition to suffering the usual rookie, new-person jitters, I have an added pressure of proving that I'm not "just" a political hire. **Female Japanese American radio journalist from Texas.**

A big negative experience that stands out in my mind is the time a tape editor called me a "f- - king gook" to my face, inside her edit room. At the time, I was a lowly production assistant, new to the industry and to the job, and I was devastated by this blatant, angry display of bigotry. I told some people in the newsroom about the incident (but no managers) and they all told me that this editor was known as a bigot and racist, and just to avoid her. Unfortunately, no one advised me to report the incident to managers, and I decided at the time that it wasn't worth "bothering" anyone with a complaint.

This incident happened before the Anita Hill hearings. Later, as I watched the hearings, when the senators grilled Hill on why she never reported the alleged harassment to authorities, I remember identifying with Hill, recalling my own fears of "making waves" and what this editor might do to me if I reported the incident. A lot of it had to do with my own insecurity and my feelings that I was "only" a production assistant. Now, I would not hesitate a second to report such an incident.

Another unpleasant experience I had was when the Woody Allen scandal broke, and it came out that he was dating Mia Farrow's Korean-born adopted daughter, Soon-Yi. A very high profile anchorman yelled out the following joke across the newsrooms: "What does Woody Allen have in common with Kodak film? The answer: They both come in little yellow boxes." I was typing in a cubicle, hidden from others in the newsroom, when I heard this joke, and I remember being too embarrassed to come out for a long time after I heard people laughing. Being the only Asian American in the newsroom, and female, I remember just sitting in that cubicle, face flushed, hoping no one would see me there.

As far as how being an Asian American affected my career, I think I had to make more of an effort to show how aggressively I could go after stories and interview subjects, always aware that people may have a stereotype of me as being submissive and soft. **Female television journalist in New York City.**

I have to say my answer to your first two questions would have to be "no" on a professional level. I guess I've been lucky enough to be judged on my ability rather than my ethnic background. Personally, though, I know of at least one person who is prejudice against a variety of people, including those who are similar to me. (I feel you run into that everywhere.) This luckily has never affect our working relationship, and, in fact, has never become an issue. **Female Asian Indian television reporter from Vermont.**

During my employment at the name of major *New York City newspaper (dates she worked there)*, in both business and editorial departments, I was the only Asian for many years. Needless to say, I had to endure countless "Oriental" comments and innuendoes, re: "Suzy Wong" et al. I was cautioned about by English pronunciations on the phone with the public. Also, the personnel director commented that "you people are known to be passive—we need someone perky and outgoing!" (I became a full-time employee in two months!) **Female newspaper journalist from New York City.**

No. The first paper I worked for, the *Oakland Tribune*, was probably the most racially sensitive workplace a journalist could work in. My current paper, *name of major newspaper in Eastern Kentucky*, doesn't have a lot of racial minorities (and only one other Asian journalist), but I have not encountered any negative responses attributable to race. **Male newspaper journalist from Kentucky.**

I feel certain that my colleagues on the copy desk would more readily acknowledge my expertise in areas like headline writing and world news selection if I were white-skinned and spoke with an American accent instead of being brown-skinned and speaking with a mixed American-British accent.

(I am a native of India; I came to the United States in date to get a master's degree in journalism at *name of university in Illinois.* I joined this newspaper after I graduated in 1993. I am in the process of qualifying for permanent residency.)

I have also found that the average American's ignorance of other countries is profound. Journalists in the newsroom are no exception. Their lack of reading is usually reinforced by their failure to have traveled outside the U.S.

Example: I have surprised colleagues by stating that India, like most developing countries, has all the infrastructure you would associate with the developed West, only there also are problems of overcrowding and poverty. I suppose many Americans don't find it easy to believe that countries in Asian can actually have luxury hotels, skyscrapers and such.

Third, the usual stereotypes persist. Once my supervisor, only half in just, said, "I guess you can go back to Indian to the yogi beat." (Whatever that means.) It would be refreshing if people in every U.S. newsroom realize that the English-language press is thriving in almost every world capital and that even third world media use modern techniques of news gathering like beat reporting and telephones!

Finally, I think some Americans tend to think of you as being strange if you don't share their passion for football or baseball. The newsroom here is full of people who spend inordinate amounts of time following sports. Showing any irritation doesn't endear you to them; they don't understand, for instance, that other countries tend to be more devoted to other games (like cricket or soccer). Or that not everyone wants to hear the details of some (stupid) baseball game. Sports talk immediately sets up an all-American clique, and it helps me understand why so few people nowadays sound well-read or cultured. **Male Asian Indian newspaper journalists from South Dakota.**

As a copy editor and former business reporter, I have not had any negative experience on the job that were related to my ethnic status.

However, in previous marketing and public relations jobs and internships, I did have negative experiences. For example, at a Fortune 100 company, many high-ranking executives and members of the communications department were surprised at my English and writing skills—even though I was an honor student from the *name of top-ranked journalism school at a leading university.* They were surprised that I spoke without an accent and were shocked to learn that I can't speak Japanese. The underlying assumption was that because I looked Asian, I must be Asian (not American), and therefore my English skills were in doubt.

I have not noticed the same attitudes at the two newspapers for which I have worked. In both cases, the newspaper staffs were much more diverse than what I experienced in corporate America. **Male Japanese American newspaper journalist from California.**

Yes. As a columnist in a small Southern town, I wrote a column criticizing the editor of the town's weekly newspaper for serving on a council-appointed task force seeking to build a baseball stadium. In this editor's next two columns, he pointedly referred to me as the "Asian-American editor." My executive editor was outraged; he wanted to reply with a letter. But I didn't want to dignify it with a response.

Also, when I was interviewing for my position at the paper, one of the editors said, "you know, you're not going to have a social life in that town." At first, I was taken aback. But knowing the racial makeup of a small Southern town and the inherent prejudices, I laughed. I was born and raised in *name of major southern city*, and had also worked for a small Georgia daily in the northeast Georgia mountains. So, I shot back, "They have Chinese restaurants, don't they?" Ironically, I did become good friends with the owners of two Chinese restaurants in town and later became engaged to one of their daughters.

Also, I recall one time when my sports editor was called into the managing editor's office and told we needed a minority on our staff. I was told my sports editor pointed out to me, and said, "What about *his name*?" The managing editor told him, "No, a real minority." So, my sports editor hired another minority sports writer. Still, I felt the exchange was an insult to Asian Americans in our community, who were probably our largest minority population. **Male Chinese American newspaper journalist from Ohio.**

No, for me personally I've never had any [negative job experiences] because I'm an Asian American. If negative experiences come up they are not ever as a result of my race. **Male Japanese American news magazine journalist from Washington, D.C.**

I've never felt any bias against me because of my ethnic status from my employers. I have, however, had some interesting experiences while in the field reporting. I once interviewed a bookie in Ohio who was surprised that I had such an American-sounding name. (I had spoken to him on the phone first and then flown out to meet him. He obviously didn't realized that *person's name* was a Korean surname.) I've also driven into towns in the Deep South (Alabama, Georgia, Texas) where I clearly stood out. No comments were ever made, but I was often stared at and pointed to. Occasionally, people asked me if I spoke English. **Male Korean American who works at a major national magazine in New York City.**

I've had one such experience. After a successful two-year stint at a national business magazine and before my current eight-year stint at another such publication, I went to *USA Today*. To the outside world, the newspaper is touted as a paragon of a diverse workforce. But the heavy emphasis on hiring minorities has backfired, and many white managers seem to resent the presence of minority hirees. Some minority hirees are treated condescendingly as a result.

I was as or more qualified than most of the reporters I worked with at the newspaper. I had a B.A. from a well-respected college, and M.A. in international economics, and a successful tenure at my previous job (which I left because I needed to

stay in the D.C. area for my family). I knew what I was writing
about, yet I had a very rough time with a white female manager, then recently promoted. I thought her treatment of me was
irrational and motivated by resentment against someone who
was different and with whom she felt uncomfortable. I left the
paper and went on to my current position, where I have not
encountered that kind of bias and where I feel my work has been
valued. **Female magazine journalist from Washington, D.C.**

I haven't had any negative job experiences that I can directly attribute to racism/ethnicity. But as I grow older and less
naive—or more paranoid—I do think my ethnicity and the
stereotypes associated with Asians play a role in people's relationship to me.

I try very hard to find other reasons for situations that might
be considered negative. If, for example, I don't get a raise, I
attribute it to the quality of my work compared to others, rather
than to discrimination. Some people think that's an ostrich attitude, but I don't think everything should be filtered through
racism.

In general, I think people assume Asians are too nice for the
tough, hard-hitting stories. One Asian colleague has told me she
was discourage from entering journalism because she's "nice." I
have heard insensitive comments on the job—things such as
mocking Indian accents or indicating that Indians have an
accent as if Americans don't. Once an African American colleague called a snake charmer a swami, who is a religious man,
not a sidewalk entertainer, and laughed off the mistake.
Another time, jokes were made about those Third World people
who worship animals. **Female Asian Indian newspaper journalist from Pennsylvania.**

There have been isolated incidents I would characterize as
bigoted. In most of these cases, they occurred as a result of
interviews with older, white men, mostly veterans, who assumed
that I was Japanese. (I am a Chinese American.)

In one instance, the director of an airplane museum told one
of my colleagues that I must have a "problem with World War
II and airplanes" after I wrote an unflattering piece about the
museums' collection.

In another instance, I was conducting a telephone interview
with a World War II flying ace. He described his mission this

way: "That was my job, to go out and kill as many bastards as I could. My job was to kill the Japanese. Just like you go duck hunting, you go out looking for these guys." Because he could not distinguish my race, I would call this an example of indirect racial harassment.

Often I am mistakenly called Connie (as in Chung) or Kim (as in the common Korean surname). Another common negative experience: People who I believe were less than candid with me during interviews for fear of being portrayed as "politically incorrect."

In discussing race-related incidents, I often feel that the person I'm talking to is taking extra precautions to say the right thing. Perhaps this is a noble attempt to not offend me, but I often wonder if they would shoot their mouth off and be more transparent with my white colleagues. **Female Chinese American newspaper journalist from Rhode Island.**

I feel that negative experiences are not as tied to my particular ethnic identity, but just being a person of color. Success is questioned by some, others set standards for people of color higher than for white colleagues. There is also a lot of additional pressure—if you fail then that reflects on your ethnic group, how much do you hold yourself, and how much do people ask you to speak for, knowledgeable and accountable for the concerns of your ethnic group. **Female newspaper journalist from Oregon.**

I have not had any blatant discrimination against me, but there are times when I have felt uncomfortable. Most significant is the perception by some that I am less qualified than my white counterparts because they think I was hired to fill an unwritten minority quota in the newsroom. No one has said anything outright to this effect to me, but the feeling is there. (I have a friend who was confronted by a white person she beat out for an internship and told that she got the job only because she's Asian.)

I have also experienced occasional subtleties that remind me that my race is always salient. These include guarded talk about Asians, overemphasis on Asians when they are not relevant to the topic being discussed (Murphy Brown calls this a manifestation of the white liberal guilt, the "I'm not prejudice because I understand you and have friends like you" attitude), and questions about Asian nations that, as a Chinese American, I have no more knowledge of than many Americans have of Mexico.

Another issue of pigeonholing of Asian journalists to cover Asian stories, an issue that I am still trying to sort out in my head. While an Asian reporter does likely have a better understanding of the Asian community than non-Asians, no journalist should be required to cover certain topics or be denied certain topics because of her race. I have been on both sides. As an intern, I have been asked to cover Asians or Asian stories, which I did happily. As managing editor, I thought an Asian should not be singled out to cover the standoff between a college campus's Asian American group and the administration. Either way, there will be some readers who think that having an Asian cover an Asian issue skews the coverage and others who think the opposite. **Female Chinese American newspaper journalist from Oregon.**

I have experienced what I consider to be discrimination. In a prior position I was paid as much as a less experienced male. I cannot attribute it only to being Asian American, but also a female. **Female newspaper journalist from Washington.**

I've only had one major negative experience at work that was related to my ethnic status. A few Asian American friends and I were turned away from a bar because of our race. I wanted to do a story on it because it was such a racist and offensive incident. The editors felt I was too close to the story and did not want me to write it. The story they ended up running was very cautious and mainly focused on the fact that we filed a complaint with the state human rights commission about the incident. The bar ended up closing a few months later and the commission ended up closing the case because they could not find the owners, or figure out who the owners were, a year later when they (the commission) finally looked into it. In any case, I felt the story was watered down and buried because my editors at the time were scared of a controversy. **Male newspaper journalist from Kansas.**

I haven't had what I'd call "negative" experiences on the job because of my ethnicity. However, I have had annoying experiences.

For instance:

—A human relations recruiter at the name of major *California newspaper* covering the San Gabriel Valley, an area with a large percentage of recent Chinese immigrants, told a visitor that the newspaper did not have a Chinese reporter covering the community, however, the recruiter said the newspaper has had a Japanese reporter covering that community. The recruiter was referring to me.

One, I am not Japanese; I am an American of Japanese descent. Two, the statement implies that although a Chinese reporter has not covered San Gabriel, the paper found second best—someone from, by jove, the same continent.

—A reporter in her sixties once asked me a technical question about tai chi, assuming that I would know because of my ethnicity, as if all Asian Americans would know everything about the culture of Asia. **Female Japanese American newspaper journalist from California.**

Yes, I have had negative experiences related to my ethnicity. In Hawaii, Asians are perceived to be the "haves" while other nationalities, such as Polynesians, are perceived to be the "have nots." Therefore, fewer true minorities in Hawaii can relate to my columns and develop so-called trust in my opinions as a writer and editor. **Female newspaper journalist from Hawaii.**

The negative experiences that I've had on the job have more to do with the way people relate to me. I believe I am rarely taken seriously by the people I interview—until they get to know me and routinely see my work.

I think one of the main reasons for this problem is that I look like I'm still in high school. Although I am twenty-nine years old and have six years of solid hard-news reporting experience under my belt, the fact that I am petite and wear my black hair long (to my waist) seems to always work against me. However, I refuse to wear three-inch heels to work or cut my hair just to gain the instant respect that my colleagues routinely get. My long hair is so much a part of me and my traditional values that I cannot forego it just to assimilate myself into society. **Female newspaper reporter from Washington, D.C.**

There is a perception among editors and colleagues—an society at large—that Asians are quiet and docile. I believe that coworkers and bosses often have seen me as being "too nice," not tough enough, not feisty enough. At times throughout my career, this has hurt my chances of getting the plum beat, the high-profile story assignment, or the promotion I desired. They don't see us as assertive enough to be management material.

Asian Americans are betwixt and between. We often are not perceived as members of the white majority, yet neither are we considered a "real" minority. Asians often are invisible in the newsroom diversity efforts.

I once was passed over for a promotion in favor of an outside hire who was black. While I concede that it was arguable who was more qualified or a better fit for the job, the experience rankled me because I was told by management that the other person would diversity the ranks of editors. The clear implication was that I was less valuable as a minority, perhaps not even a minority in management's eyes.

On another occasion, I worked on a series of stories about race relations with two other reporters—one black, one white. The editor, a white male, clearly "bonded" with the white reporter (also a man) and constantly sought his input and gave him the "heavy lifting" reporting and writing duties. The editor also frequently sought out the opinion of the black reporter, who represented the "minority" viewpoint in the editor's eyes. I tried 100-plus percent to speak up frequently and firmly; otherwise I would have faded into the invisible minority role. **Female newspaper journalist from Massachusetts.**

The worst part about being the only Asian on the night shift is that it seems like no one knows how to deal with me when it comes to certain issues (such as the O.J. Simpson story). On a personal level, people are always asking me questions as if I can speak for all of my people. I know it's not meant to be offensive, but it's hard to be a 21-year-old watchdog for the media for everyone on the eastern half of the world. But there are the good points. The *name of newspaper* recently ran a series on immigration, especially in the growth of Vietnamese immigrants in the area. But after that, there hasn't been a story about any Asians since. It's been a couple of months. The only time Asians are mentioned in the paper is when there is some kind of festival. **Female Vietnamese American newspaper journalist from Missouri.**

Yes. It was a hard getting a job in mainstream media. **Female Filipino American magazine journalist from Washington.**

No, I don't believe being Asian has ever had a significantly negative effect on my work. The only thing I can think of is that because I'm little and look very young, people may not take me as seriously as say a tall white guy who is the same age as me. But I think this is a problem a lot of short women may experience and not just Asians. **Female newspaper journalist from California.**

Because I've spent my entire career at newspapers in California, I've encountered few of the "negative" experiences that others may have acquired elsewhere in the country. Maybe I was too dumb to know that I was having a negative experience. Certainly, no one has called me a "fat Jap," but that probably has more to do with my weight than with the enlightenment of the republic. **Male Japanese American newspaper journalist from California.**

None. The entire name of major television network is very helpful in every respect. I am very fortunate. **Male television photo/video journalist from California.**

Because of my ethnic status as an Asian American, I feel that it's difficult to be promoted. After working two years at *name of newspaper* as an editorial assistant, last summer I applied for a reporting internship but I was turned down because, I was told, I don't have enough experience. During that same summer, I had an opportunity to serve as a fellow at the *name of leading media research institute*. However, my company, at first, did not grant my leave of absence, citing it would not benefit the company if I left. But later, the publisher overrode the editors' decision and allowed me to go and come back with my job. In other words, the editors did not hire me as an intern, and when I got another offer elsewhere to gain experience, they were reluctant to let me go. So I guess they don't want me to do anything beyond what I'm doing now—answering phones and writing obituaries. **Male Vietnamese American newspaper journalist in Louisiana.**

I have experienced several negative experiences on the job that I feel were related to my ethnicity. I am constantly seen as someone who isn't assertive when I am actually very assertive.

People have the stereotype that Asians aren't assertive or aggressive. People have also questioned my judgment concerning race-related stories because they say I'm biased. **Male newspaper journalist in Texas.**

Yes, I have had some negative experiences on the job because I am an Asian American. For example, at my station I am the only reporter who is also a photographer, meaning I shoot my own stories. I have been at the station for over a year now and I have more seniority and experience than some of the newer people. In addition, I am also working the graveyard shift, so I don't get to report as much as I would like to. Most of what I end up covering are shootings, accidents, and fires. Unfortunately, I am not working for the same news director who originally hired me. Two weeks after I started, he was fired and a new news director was hired. Six months later he put me on overnights and told me it was because I'm not just as Asian American, but an Asian American male. There's a big difference. If I was a pretty Asian female, things might be different. **Male television journalist from Nevada.**

I have worked in San Francisco, New York, and in Munich, Germany, and never felt being Asian American was a hindrance. It wasn't until I moved to the Boston area that I felt it was a problem. I came to Boston with more than fifteen years of experience in public relations and newspaper work. I would apply for job after job and not even get called in for an interview. My husband finally convinced me to send out my resume under my married name, *English sounding name.* I did and the phone began to ring. In the interviews I would either make it to the finals or the interviewer would be so shocked to find me answering to *English sounding name* that it would be a waste of time.

The strange part of it all is when I did finally get a job, it was at a hospital forty-five minutes outside of metropolitan Boston where most people had never seen an Asian in person. I was fortunate that a management consultant friend of my husband's (for whom I did some freelance work) recommended me.

I got a clue to what the problem was when (again through my husband's contacts) I got an interview with one of the top PR agencies in Boston. I applied for a position as an account executive for health care clients. The president of the agency told me he already had someone in mind for that spot, but would I be interested in working with some of their Japanese clients? I asked him if he was aware of how a Japanese man would feel working with a woman, especially a Japanese American woman? Well, he said, he thought they might be more comfortable working with someone who spoke Japanese.

Two problems here. First he obviously does not understand the culture of his clients and how women are treated as second class citizens in the workplace in Japan. And second, he thinks I look Japanese, I must speak Japanese. He never asked me if I spoke the language, which I don't. My language is German. Would he make the same assumption about someone with an Italian last name, Swedish, Polish? Then I realized that is how the other perspective employers were viewing me, as someone whose first language was not English. If it were true, it could be a hindrance in the field of public relations where writing and language are your working tools.

The above incidents occurred in the years after I moved to Boston in 1983. More recently I've applied for other positions within the television station where I work. One I applied for at the encouragement of the people who would work under me, as well as the direct supervisor for the job. After being in the finals along with two outside people, I did not get it. The final decision was made by a vice president. The official reason I was told was because I did not have "national" experience (which is ridiculous since I've worked for *name of major international media conglomerate* which is more national than a PBS television station). The unofficial reason I heard through the office grapevine was because I was not "aggressive" enough. Again a label attached to me by someone who had never worked with me nor had an opportunity to see how I work. Instead he assumed I was the passive, quiet Asian woman. The person he did hire was a Jewish woman from New York City. How many stereotypes were operating here? **Female Japanese American television journalist from Massachusetts.**

The most negative aspect of being an Asian American woman in television news is that people constantly think I'm Connie Chung. I hear it all the time out in the field. It's annoying because I get the sense that people may not try to distinguish one Asian from another, and also because it clearly shows that there aren't enough prominent Asians. Only one seems to have the name recognition.

Sometimes as an Asian American reporter I get assigned to cover stories involving Asian Americans. I don't necessarily agree that Asians should cover Asians, whites should cover whites, and blacks should cover blacks. Not that I only cover stories involving Asians, but I get the distinct impression that management believes that I would have an "in" when that may not be the case. **Female television journalist from Pennsylvania.**

When I first tried to get into this business, way back in the '70s, there was a station with one opening. I was asked to audition. When I didn't get the position, I was told by the secretary who answered the phone that I wasn't "ethnic" enough. The point was, they wanted a black female. So the lesson I learned was that minorities, and especially minority women, were pitted against each other for one position. I think that picture has substantially changed over the years, at least in the major markets. I have not seen anything close to that recently.

Also in the 1970s, I knew of only a few other Asian Americans on television, and some of them chose not to cover stories about Asians, fearing they would be relegated to a "minority ghetto" when it came to stories. It was a subject of some controversy. I took the side that I definitely would cover stories about Asians, especially Chinese, because my knowledge of the language and culture could give additional insight into the subject, and that might provide more education or information for the audience.

I'd have to say over these twenty-one years in the broadcast business, I have encountered little prejudice from management and other reporters. I have heard of it for others, but experienced none myself. As for viewers, there have been occasional racist letters, but not many and I have always seen them as the rantings of crazy people. I have received many more simply crazy letters that all people, especially women, on television receive, regardless of the color of our skin. **Female television journalist from Illinois.**

No, I have not had any negative experiences related to my being Asian American. I feel that I've been treated fairly. **Female Chinese American television journalist from Washington, D.C.**

I don't feel I've had any negative experiences on the job. On the contrary, I feel positive about my work status and the opportunity I have had thus far. **Female television journalist from Washington.**

I've never experienced anything horrible because I'm Asian American during my time reporting or anchoring.

The one experience I recall that made me really aware that I was seen as an "Asian" and not a "good reporter" was when I ironically applied for a job at the station where I'm currently employed.

I was just out of graduate school and I interviewed at *name of television station.* The news director was lukewarm to me. He told me what I needed to work on and then he said, "There isn't a demand for Asian reporters around here." Perhaps it was true (the Asian population is small in this area), but his comment struck me as rude.

Ironically enough, the same news director came looking for me one and a half years later and hired me. **Female television journalist from Massachusetts.**

Regarding negative experience, I can't recall any overt negative remark or occurrence directed to me over my being Asian American. This does not mean that by implication or innuendo, some remark was made. Early in my career, I would politely "laugh" over some small remark. However, as I matured with my career, I would politely correct any infractions. Still, the often used term "Oriental" bothers me. I have made every effort not just to say, we prefer Asian American, but to explain why. (Interestingly, in Hawaii, where I grew up, "Oriental" among my parent's generation is more accepted. It is now less accepted among my peers.) I still feel that in the broadcast medium, Asian women are still seen as more of a commodity than anything else. We are still seen as hard workers and more "accepted" by the white audience, as opposed to Asian men on television. (FYI, I have been doing television since 1976. Previously to that, I was on the radio for four years.) I was encouraged at the last Asian American [Journalists Association annual] conference in Hawaii, one of the recruiters told me he was never interviewed as many qualified Asian men as he had at the conference! **Female television journalist from California.**

I have had few very negative experiences as an Asian broadcaster. The one that stands out in my mind is at my last place of employment. In a five-person newsroom, I was the only minority female. the rest were white males. When I first got there, the men (with the exception of my boss) constantly made cracks about how minority women could get jobs anywhere. They had been in news for the better part of the decade and insisted if they were black women they'd be in New York by now. None of my rebuttals worked; I'd say I might get a job because of my race (and gender), but I couldn't keep it if I couldn't prove myself. They would argue I was wrong.

After several months all but one man stopped this. I ended up having a terrible time at my job, because of the man who kept resenting me. I felt it had everything to do with my skin color (and sex) and not who I was as a person. This man picked many small fights, did his best to make me feel left out, and tired to actually sabotage me.

While I was on a story he went through my personal belongings, found a letter I was writing in which I complained about my station, him, and how much I was trying to find a new job. He Xeroxed this letter and sent it anonymously to the general manager. I knew it was him and when I confronted him, he blatantly admitted to it. It's unfortunate there are people who will blame you and your whole race for stealing "their" jobs. I now have a first-hand experience of such incredible prejudice.

Of course, talk to almost any Asian newswoman and you'll find she's been called Connie Chung at least once. While I am of mixed heritage, that doesn't come across to many non-Asians. It drives me nuts that people, mostly whites, are stupid enough to think we all look alike, even the "half-breeds." I get called Connie all the time, either in jest or in seriousness. I can't say this has hampered my news gathering because despite the Newt's-mom-affair, many people still respect her. But I'm getting mighty sick of it. **Female television journalist from New Jersey.**

Negative experience: Following what I call the "fall of Connie Chung," one of my sources accused me of pulling a "Connie Chung" on him when I printed his actual comment instead of just printing no comment. It seems that every Asian woman in this business is now compared to Connie Chung and her mistakes may have an affect on all of us.

I have not had any other negative experiences thus far as an Asian journalists. **Female television journalist from Georgia.**

Aside from the occasional, "You speak English very well," or, "What country are you from?," while out in the field, I must say I've not had many overtly negative experiences that I can attribute to being an Asian American. There's little doubt in my mind, however, that looking "foreign" has had a tangible affect on how I'm perceived and treated by people with whom I work or associate. A lot of it is stereotyping. I've had a (former) network executive tell me I look "intelligent" on the air. It was meant as a compliment, and I certainly wasn't offended. But the subtext is that somehow the reason Asians are acceptable on television is that they look intelligent. The unspoken characterization, I fear, is that Asians (especially males) are not thought to be ambitious, forceful, or charismatic—all prized attributes in this industry.

A lot of it is also cultural. I think that, as is often the case with non-white people attempting to succeed in establishment organizations, I was at first reluctant to assert myself. I did not feel particularly comfortable trying to fit an unfamiliar environment. Of course, the argument could be made that anyone, regardless of racial ethnicity, would be intimidated under similar circumstances. The difference is that there have been only a few Asian American network correspondents in the history of television news. As sophisticated as I'd like to think I am, that burden—that responsibility—does not go unshouldered. It was a seminal moment when, early in my tenure, I first complained about others getting a major story over me. The response was positive—like, "It's about time you spoke up," and I got the assignment I wanted. But I wondered why it was that I had to ask? Why were others automatically selected, yet I was automatically excluded?

In my opinion (and I've been given no reason to think otherwise) I was more than capable of carrying out the assignment, and could, perhaps, provide a more incisive approach to the story. I think, too often, managers make judgments based on superficial and often stereotypical assessments. The fact that because someone is from a different cultural experience—that they don't fit into the New York, fast-talking and schmoozing, rarefied environment of network news—puts them at a disadvantage. In my case, however, I think it will ultimately work to my advantage. **Male television journalist from New York.**

I haven't had any negative experiences on my current job, but my ethnic status has kept me from getting another job. I've been told on several occasions that the television market where I have applied for a position "is not ready for an Asian sports anchor." Obviously, the majority of television news directors and general managers believe that Asians can't anchor and report the sports news. How many Asian sports anchors/reporters can you name? Not many, because there aren't that many. I can go on and on about this topic. *Male television journalist from Virginia.*

Yes, during the course of my professional tenure I have come across a good deal of uncomfortable situations at work due to my race (Asian/Hispanic). I think a lot of it is due to a lack of exposure to other cultures and races while raised. Initially when I was younger and confronted negative experiences I didn't do much about it. Now if someone does or says something out of line I will tactfully and immediately let them know that I do not appreciate it. It's usually very effective. **Male television journalist from New York.**

Yes, one can feel extremely isolated being among the few Asian Americans, if not the only one, in the newsroom. I have been the only Asian American in two of the five television stations that I have been employed full time. I have been among only a handful of Asian Americans in the other three. It was only been recently that I have been able to turn to a mentor for guidance. This lack of support network has made my career in the newsroom a lonely one.

Compounding the problem is how others are perceiving me. The Asian American male is stereotyped as quiet, passive, and non-aggressive. These are not considered leadership qualities in the dominant white culture. as a news producer, I must often overcome how others perceive my "leadership" qualities. This has made it difficult for me to advance beyond being a line producer and into management.

My parents raised me to respect authority and not to embarrass others in front of their peers. They also taught me not to interrupt others and to speak when it is your tern.  In my Chinese American upbringing, the collective "we" is often more important than the individual "me." My value system, however, may conflict with others brought up in a different culture and environment.  For instance, European Americans may act in a way they consider assertive and entirely appropriate. I may look at them and consider them rude.  But it's the dominant culture that sets the rules in this society.  Thus, I am automatically at a disadvantage.

The examples I cite are very subtle forms of institutionalized racism.  Rarely do you see Klansmen dressed white robes any more.  But what we have in our newsrooms today is a much ore sophisticated form of racism.  I can say with 100 percent certainty that I have worked under at least one manager who harbored racist feelings towards me.  His actions set my career back severely.  It eventually led to my demotion and almost caused me to leave the business.  Only the support of my wife kept me from quitting.  **Male Chinese American television journalist from California.**

I don't recall encountering blatantly negative experiences in my reporter job or internships with various television stations because I'm Chinese American.  But I always felt that because I'm Asian, they assumed that I must be very smart, very capable, very docile—not a troublemaker intern.  this manifested itself in comments like, "You can do it, you're smart" coming from people who had no idea what my background is and people who had never worked with me before.  I also feel many times in an all-white newsroom I would get people who were very uncomfortable socializing with me.  They just didn't know what to say and chose to stay away.  At the same time, they would be very receptive and chummy with other interns who were non-Asian.  **Female Chinese American radio journalist from California.**

Yes, back in 1985 I had a negative experience.  At that time, I worked weekends at a San Francisco radio station doing hourly news briefs during talk shows.  A caller phoned the newsroom and asked what kind of name was *Asian sounding name*.  When the editor told her I was Chinese, the caller said, "Get that chink off the radio.  She has no business telling me the news."  I was wounded.  It took me back to the days when my sister and I were tormented at a predominately white high school in the city.   **Female Chinese American radio journalist from California.**

Racial issues in the newsroom can spring up when you least expect them to, and sometimes we are called upon to take a stand.  One such incident occurred last year, not long after the *name of newspaper* issued its controversial ethnic style guidelines.  A group of male staff members at the *name of county* edition had formed several touch football teams.  Members of one of one team decided to spoof the guidelines and named themselves "The Deaf Chinamen."  They even had T-shirts made up with the name printed across the front.  Their stupidity might have gone undiscovered by the rest of us except that a young reporter who is of Chinese descent happened to come across a photograph of someone wearing the T-shirt.  After several weeks of trying to decide what to do, the young staffer confided his feelings to me.  My initial reaction was one of incredulity.  How could anyone be so dumb as to print a racial epithet on a T-shirt, much less wear it in public?  this wasn't a group of card carrying members of the KKK.  This was racially mixed group of well-educated *name of newspaper* staffers, people I considered not only colleagues, but friends.

As then-deputy city editor, I felt it was my duty to confront the members of the team and explain the stupidity of their actions.  I realized from the outset that the T-shirt wasn't aimed at anyone in particular—it was merely meant as "a joke."  I was assured that, following discussion with the offended staff member, the team had discarded the T-shirts.  Most of the members seemed deeply remorseful and embarrassed.  I reported the situation to my supervisors.

. . . .There was this [other] incident, which occurred some years ago. . . .We had an intern who was assigned to the night shift.  He had just graduated from Harvard with honors.  He came from a wealthy, fairly prominent family in Boston.  He was well educated, well spoken, and he could even write.

On this particular late afternoon I asked him to check out an upcoming visit by a trade delegation from Japan.  He made a few phone calls and wrote up his member, which he slugged "Jap notes."  I called him over to the city desk.  I told him that "Jap" was a racial slur akin to "nigger."  "No, it isn't," he said.  The conversation went downhill from there.  We argued about the use of the word for what seemed like a very long time. At first I found it hard to believe that he, a white guy, would be telling me what was and was not offensive to my race. But then it made perfect sense. Of course he would take that view. No one ever called him "Jap."

Finally, being the caring, sensitive editor that I am, I told him, "Either you change the goddamn slug or I'm going to kick your ass." He seemed to understand that part of the argument well enough.

I suppose the point of both these anecdotes is this: There is a certain pervasive arrogance among those of us who practice journalism. We tend to believe we have an enlightened view of the world. In fact, our view is no more enlightened than anyone else's. In some cases it's a lot more myopic. It's no wonder that journalists are viewed by the public with such distrust. We operate from a cocoon, what we like to think of as our own privileged seat. Somehow we've managed to lose that connection with our readers, our viewers, who are rightly asking: Where's the relevance? **Male newspaper journalist from California.**

# APPENDIX 17

## SELECTED SURVEY RESPONSES TO SURVEY QUESTION TWO

The following are responses taken nearly verbatim from the journalists' written answers to survey question two. The name of the reporter, and his or her place of employment, is given in bold type at the end of each response, if that person did not request anonymity. If the sex of a respondent is unclear from the person's name or the content of the text, Ms. or Mr. will be printed before the name for reader clarification. These are listed in no set order and not all responses are reprinted here. Many of those answers not reprinted were brief "yes" or "no" answers, and some were brief answers that repeated points already made by other respondents. Some editing was done to make the style, such as the term "Asian American" not being hyphenated, consistent throughout for reader ease. Also, the job titles are taken directly from what the respondents gave on the survey.

*Question 2: Have you ever had any positive experiences on the job that you feel were related to your ethnic status as an Asian American?*

I can't help but think my being an Asian American was an asset in my pursuit of employment at CNN. It is a known fact CNN is actively recruiting minorities. **Stephanie Kanno-Wegner, video journalist, CNN, Atlanta, Georgia.**

The most positive experiences I have had as a journalist of Asian American descent have been when I was seen as a journalist by my subjects and not a person of color as is usually the case. Race seems to always have a way of sneaking into a conversation with a subject, even with the most educated of leaders. As an Asian journalist, people are so compelled to judge and stereotype before they even have the chance to talk to me. **Ken Kwok, photographer, *Press-Telegram*, Long Beach, California.**

Race plays no part in my current job as a business reporter, so there has been no time when my ethnicity has been a positive at work. However, it could be. For example, I speak Cantonese, which makes me an asset for any news organization interested in expanding their coverage of businesses in Chinatown or the changes in Hong Kong as 1997 approaches. Unfortunately, I don't work in an organization that currently finds those topics priorities. **Benjamin S.F. Seto, business reporter, *The Fresno Bee*, Fresno, California.**

I'm not sure whether being an Asian American has much to do with some of my positive experiences on the job. I remember my first real journalism job at a local newspaper in a Northern California town with mostly Caucasian residents I landed immediately after the interview without the usual formality of we'll-get-back-to-you-in-a-few-days. The editors took me in minutes after reviewing my writing test that followed the interview, which surprised me. I still don't know why they selected me that quick, as if they were afraid I might take another offer that paid more. That was four, five years ago. Again, I don't think being an Asian American has much to do with my being selected for the job. **Ms. Thai Nguyen Strom, columnist and chief librarian, *The Record*, San Joaquin County, California.**

Frankly, I don't think I would be here if I weren't Asian given the competitiveness of the industry, and the competitiveness of landing a job at Time Warner. This company actively pursues minorities for positions, and I was recruited at a job fair sponsored by the Asian American Journalists Association a year ago. **Ms. Pueng Vongs, reporter, *Money Magazine*, New York City.**

I have had positive job experiences that I feel were related to my ethnic status. While at the Utica paper, I was promoted from rim editor to assistant news editor, a middle-management job, one year after I was hired. I was 22, it was my first newspaper, and there were several people ahead of me in seniority who were equally good candidates. I later found out that the executive editor got a bonus every time she promoted a minority (this was a Gannett paper). In any event, it was an invaluable learning experience; also, I was able to participate in the company's special training program for managers.

Also, at the *(Philadelphia) Inquirer* I am a member of the company-wide committee that has been charged with choosing a new computer system. The Inquirer's concern about diversity definitely extends to the makeup of its committees, and I am sure that while my computer knowledge was a factor in my being tapped as a member, my race (and gender) were also considered. As a result of this committee's work, I have learned quite a bit about desktop publishing systems, about how a large company evaluates major, multi-year decisions and about how different departments do or don't work together. In addition, I've joined the subcommittee on staff training, which was formed in antici- pation of the new computers' arrival, which will also be an edu- cational and beneficial experience for me. **Amy Wang, copy edi- tor,** *Philadelphia Inquirer,* **Philadelphia, Pennsylvania.**

I'm not qualified to answer this question. I came here as a student. What happens is you can't target straight away into the mainstream newspapers. I could have changed my name, and in a way Americanized myself. In that way I would have had not problems. But that's a farce. **Ms. Jyothi Kiran, staff writer,** *India Currents* **magazine, San Jose, California.**

There is a lot of plus in being able to know not just English but another language as well. some people tend to think that you have achieved a certain advantage in that you are knowledgeable about cultures other than American.

The image that Asian Americans are generally hardworking and respectable is also very helpful. **Ms. Marites Sison-Paez, edi- tor,** *Special Edition Press,* **New York City.**

I have had many positive experiences on the job that have been related to my ethnic status. Looking back, almost all of them concern dealing with sources and how my ethnic status helped me get interviews, make better interviews, and make bet- ter stories. Culturally, speaking from the perspective of an Asian American, I feel safe to say that in general, Asian Americans are a very private people. I can count at least three instances when my "Asianness" helped me transcend the boundaries of privateness to get an interview and a story. In one instance, when I was writing a story about Asian refugees, two of my sources blatantly told me that they were glad I was conducting the interview because they didn't feel comfortable talking with American (Caucasian) reporters. In another instance, I used my own refugee status as an ice-breaker when doing a story about a Vietnamese folk per- former who continued to flee during the Vietnam War. **Ms. Putsata Reang, cultural reporter,** *Spokesman-Review,* **Spokane, Washington.**

Positive experiences: It has been my experience that Asians tend to be quite wary of the press, even more so than other minority ethnic communities. Therefore, it is an advantage to be a familiar face among them, to get them to express themselves more freely. **Paul Hyun-Bong Shin, staff writer, the *Courier-News*, Bridgewater, New Jersey.**

The few things, because Asians are such a non-entity at my station, my producer will ask me what I think if there's something on Asians; he'll ask me my opinion and I guess that's good. **Pamela SooHoo, associate producer, for public television (media organization withheld upon request).**

I have been consulted on my opinions as a minority and had opportunity to write about Asian American related issues. **Cynthia Szubzda, copy editor/lifestyles, *Lowell Sun*, North Billerica, Massachusetts.**

Positive experiences mostly come from people's curiosity. Perhaps, on the flip side, they also serve in the military and have fond memories of the people there, or I've run into parents who've adopted Asian/Amerasian children, or just met people who genuinely are interested in my background, my perception of a story/incident, what have you. And because in this part of the country, Asian journalists are rare, when I meet another one, there's almost this instant "bond," not just as professionals, but someone who shares in the "culture." **Victoria Lim, reporter, WWMT-TV, Kalamazoo, Michigan.**

Yes, I have had positive experience on the job related to my ethnicity. I believe I have done a more effective job of covering issues affecting minorities and recent immigrants because of my own racial identity. **Eric Chu, assistant picture editor, *Chicago Tribune*, Chicago, Illinois.**

I can say I have had opportunities open up for me, in part, because I am an ethnic minority. I think I would have had the same opportunities—for jobs, for mid-career education—had I been white. But because I was Asian, the people who decide these things recruited me. If I was white I would have had to seek those job opportunities on my own. but any job or honors I've received have been on my own merits, not because of my ethnic background.

And while its never happened to me, I have friends who have gotten plum travel assignments because they were Asian. They were chose to go to china over white reporters because they were Asian. **Craig Gima, producer, KHON-TV, Honolulu, Hawaii.**

I have always felt an advantage in this career, honestly, because of the road Connie Chung has paved for Asian American women in this business. She is not so much my role model, but a symbol that "we" can make it too. Living in Texas, and working with mostly Anglo-Saxons, I have always felt because I was different, I stuck out from the crowd. But at the first station I felt degraded, almost ashamed that I was a minority. Everyone in the newsroom was talking about changing their last name into an Hispanic last name. They thought this would help them get a job faster. They said this as if I were not in the room, but I know good and well that on the basis of just the color of your skin cannot get you to the top. If you are good and you're a minority, true, it will advance you. But, if you're white and good it will advance you too. Also, other factors play into it, such as the market you're trying to get into and what you look like, etc. **Ms. Michile Kim-Gray, producer, KWTX-TV, Waco, Texas.**

The response from Asian American members of the community is very positive. When I first began anchoring morning cut-ins, the station received some calls from Asians, mostly Filipinos, inquiring about my heritage. Our market is mostly Caucasian and I believe Asians here appreciate having a visible and capable representative in the media. **Rose Tibayan, anchor/reporter, WINK-TV, Fort Myers, Florida.**

The television station I work for now celebrated Asian American Heritage Month with several in-depth stories. I was given the opportunity to field produce and write a feature story. The station gave me substantial time away from my usual news writing routine to put a nice piece together. The experience was terrific. I was also included as a subject in a story on the station's Asian American employees. **Ms. Yuki Spellman, news writer, WGN News, Chicago, Illinois.**

Working in the nation's number two market has its benefits and, other than salary, hiring practices are among them where minority workers are concerned. call it quotas, guidelines, tokens, whatever, there is a guideline this station must meet in terms of the working staff's minority worker ratio to non-minorities. My hiring was based solely on my performance as an intern, which impressed people in high places. Yet my ethnicity didn't hurt me when a good portion of the news desk team are Caucasian. It was something I knew I could play up if I had to. But I was hired before I had to try resorting to that. **Robert Goozee, news assignment desk, KNBC NBC 4, Los Angeles, California.**

Yes. When doing stories in the Asian communities the people seem more comfortable with me than other cameramen. **Darren Phan, news cameraman, NBC-4, Burbank, California.**

Quite a few. Those times were when I was interviewing Asians. The newcomers to the country seemed to appreciate meeting someone of similar descent. They felt they could relate and I felt they opened up a little bit more as a result. **Lisa Lee Daniels, reporter, The Oregonian, Portland, Oregon.**

As an Asian American, I often receive favorable comments about characteristics which "all" Asian Americans seem to possess. I have received comments such as: "Asians are hardworking and successful," "Asians are thin and do not have to worry about their weight," "Asians are smart and good in school," and "Asians do not complain." **Connie Riu, manager, diversity and outreach services, Newspaper Association of America, Reston, Virginia.**

Yes, contributing to coverage of Asians. **Anu Mannar, life copy desk chief, News and Record, Greensboro, North Carolina.**

No recollection of any positive experiences based on my being Asian American. I'd like to believe that I'm very accessible, and most who approach me professionally have either had some prior need for radio services or have been referred by an associate who has said that I'm accessible to the public. **Ms. Gimmy Park Li, manager, public affairs, KNBR AM/KFOG FM, San Francisco, California.**

I was hired for my first job because I was an Asian woman. If I could spell, I was going to get the job as features reporter, said the assistant managing editor years later. Clearly, ethnicity can help give you the edge. That's unfair to your competitors. But it's unfair to you too because once you're in the door, you're held to higher standards.

(There is a whole other angle in studying Asian American men vs. women in the media!) **Ms. Mei-Mei Chan, executive editor, Post Register, Idaho Falls, Idaho.**

I feel that any positive experience on the job has *not* been related to my ethnic status as an Asian American. Our newsroom is diverse, and we all do our part in making the newscast a successful operation. I have been asked to undertake many projects with full confidence of my superiors. If there is a difference in treatment it is based on seniority and experience, not on race or ethnicity. **George Kiriyama, desk assistant, KCAL-TV Channel 9 News, Los Angeles, California.**

I have had some positive experiences. When covering stories of Asian Americans I think they feel more comfortable with me, so I get better soundbites. **Mary Tan, news reporter, WMTV-TV, Madison, Wisconsin.**

Positive experiences—Once or twice, my conversational skills in Cantonese helped me interview sources in police-related stories: one the employees of a store that was held up and had its cashier shot dead by the robbers, another suspects accused of buying food stamps (they ran a grocery store) from patrons at black market value. But I sense those incidents/experiences may have had more to do with bridging the language barrier than cultural ones. There's also been some instances when, I believe, people felt more comfortable talking to me because of my race, especially in cases of police insensitivity toward the poor and minorities, a festering problem here in Phoenix after the deaths of two minorities at the hands of the police during confrontations. But I cannot support that believe with any scientific data or empirical evidence. **Abraham Kwok, reporter, The Arizona Republic/The Phoenix Gazette, Phoenix, Arizona.**

Yes, I've had positive experiences too. The most rewarding situation was being successful at bridging issues of diversity in reporting to the forefront. I have always felt that my obvious minority status forced the staff to recognize that there are people of color in their community and their voices should not be overlooked or stereotyped. **Janice Gin, executive producer/1996 Atlanta Olympics, Gannett Broadcasting, Atlanta, Georgia.**

I have not had any particularly positive experiences either. The closest "positive" experience would be when I was interning at *Modern Bride* magazine and was proofing editorial for make-up tips. what the writer wrote for the Asian face was slightly not positive (through certain use of words) and when I brought this up, they changed the edit to a much more positive and neutral tone.   **Ms. Soomie Ahn, employed by Ellen Ryder Communications, New York City.**

My presence in the newsroom has resulted in additional news sources for the paper and more stories on Asians and the culture. Because some of the sources are also my friends, I believe I am able to easily secure interviews with them.  To my displeasure, though, we have come to rely on the same source, rather than make an effort to expand our minority lists.

Overall, I don't at all believe my ethnic status plays any role in my success or failure to hook a phone interview or land a special section project.  I still have difficulty trying to get some of my Asian friends to open up to a reporter.  but what I've given to the newsroom is another diversity voice.  **Henry Yuen, assistant features editor, *Star-Gazette*, Elmira, New York.**

The fact that I am an anchor in a top 15 market is due, in part, to my ethnicity and gender.  My experiences on the job are overwhelmingly positive because of my being Asian American. I'm someone people in the Asian American audience can identify with.  I help educate my non-Asian colleagues about the Asian community.  I am relied upon to identify and, often cover, stories important to the Asian and larger viewing audience.

I am called often to speak to various groups (students, women, Asian American, civil rights, journalists, etc.) because I am a journalist of color.  this is a positive experience.  It again shows that Asian Americans can be journalists and do well in media.

When I was a senior in high school, I "worked" as Miss Teenage America.  I logged thousands of miles touring the country and visiting Japan and Peru, giving speeches and representing youth of America.  Not once during my travels did I hear a rude or racist remark.  People from the smallest towns to the biggest cities, from the youngest kids to senior citizens, were kind and friendly.  Perhaps it was because I was from Hawaii—paradise! Perhaps I was seen as a Hawaiian rather than an Asian American or Japanese American.  who can be rude to a Hawaiian from paradise?  The judges later told me that it didn't matter that I was Asian American; they saw me as All American.  the only people who were confused by my ethnic background were the kids in Japan.  They couldn't believe I was Miss Teenage America because I wasn't blond and blue-eyed.  On the other hand, they figured I couldn't be Japanese because I didn't speak the language! **Lori Matsukawa, anchor, KING TV, Seattle, Washington.**

I think this is positive: Most of my co-workers at KTLA assumed, even before they met me, that I would be a trustworthy, hard working, book-smart person. And I have proven them correct. **Ms. Jinah Kim, producer - 11 p.m. News, KCCN-TV, Monterey, California.**

Small things come to mind, like being able to get a story because I was able to communicate with a reluctant subject in Mandarin or Cantonese, and persuade him/her to talk with us. Also, being able to draw from my Asian background and give a different perspective on issues. **Susan Han, producer, KCTS/9 TV, Seattle, Washington.**

My positive experiences are not nearly so colorful. Once I wrote an opinion piece blasting the Frank Capra film "It's a Wonderful Life" as overrated, sappy claptrap. Obviously, I expected some hate mail from readers defending their favorite film. What I did not expect were the racist letters that read: "Why don't you take a slow boat to China," "You are writing with chopsticks in your mouth," "Judging from your last name, you are not qualified to criticize American films." Now, if my last name were Smith, would I have gotten these letters? Of course not.

So I took these letters to my editor and we decided to run some of them. Why? Because I feel our readers need to know how some of their neighbors think. Happily, this inspired some letters from people who came to my defense and were appalled by such blatant racism. That's positive. **Wayman Wong, reporter for the New York *Daily News*, New York City.**

Yes, my current job as editor of an Asian environmental business newsletter was essentially due to my own experiences and qualifications in the region as a long-time foreign correspondent. But my employers basically saw me as a hard working professional in my field. Since then, they've associated Asian Americans with the "hard working" work ethic, and have hired quite a number of Asian Americans full-time. **Ms. Vyryan Tenorio, editor, *Asia Environmental Business Journal*, San Diego, California.**

Yes, definitely, especially during the auto trade dispute back in May of 1995—President Clinton was threatening to charge huge tariffs on the 13 Japanese luxury models sold in America—

and I feel as a Japanese American doing the story I could make it as fair as possible by interviewing the Japan Consul General on the government's feelings, and at the same time talk with American auto makers, and Japanese luxury car auto dealers. Many stories would have left the Japanese government out of it and let their side of the story be part of the story.

The same with the recent World War II 50th anniversary—Enola Gay display at the Smithsonian, and the bombing of Hiroshima/Nagasaki. I would sometimes wonder why I would be chosen to do these stories. but I choose to do them and I know my news department, as a rule, wants fair and accurate coverage in a positive light, or at least let them have a voice on the news. As an Asian American broadcast journalist in the Kansas City market I would hope the small Asian population here would trust me to do these stories. So far I have had much positive feedback from them wherever I go. **Stephanie Nishikawa, TV news reporter, WDAF-TV, Kansas City, Missouri.**

As a reporter I felt I could ask other minorities questions that would have been perceived as offensive if asked by anyone else (i.e., I could ask a black man a question that would have otherwise offended him if a white or even perhaps an Hispanic asked the question). Asians, in my opinion, are viewed as the neutral race. Not much in America is known about Asian culture, but what is know is positive. **Alan Wang, reporter, KDFW-TV, Fresno, California.**

NOTE: The following responses are from Asian American journalists who requested anonymity. Therefore, if a respondent gave information referring to his or her name, or other identifying factors, that information is appropriately changed and in italics. If a respondent clearly identified his or her Asian American ethnic sub-group status, such as Japanese American, either in the text of the answers or on the permission/consent form, then that identification is given.

Just the feeling that my presence makes the newsroom more sensitive when it comes to Asian issues. I'm their Asian issues conscience. **Female Japanese American radio journalist from Texas.**

Being Asian American helped me on certain story assignments, for example, when a black-led boycott of a Korean-owned grocery broke out in Brooklyn, being the only Korean-speaking broadcast reporter in New York City at that time, helped me to get a lot of information that others could not. Obviously, being a part of the Asian American community also helped me to get sources and scoops over the years.

I also feel that being Asian American helped me on the employment front in that I was an ethnic face on name of television station. But, I feel there was a definite "quota" mentality: I was not brought on to report until another Asian American quit the station (despite years of persistent trying), and when I left, the station hired another Korean American female reporter. This kind of reality makes it very tough for Asian American journalists to be generous about helping each other to get jobs: if there is only one, we are all fighting for that position or jealously guarding it. **Female Korean American television journalist in New York.**

The most memorable "positive" experience: when I was being interviewed during the 1960s, I was told that I had to overcome several "hurdles" over the next three months and at the end of that time, if I was successful, I would then be on a three-month trial period before the final honor of being put on staff. When asked why the name of newspaper would bother with someone who needed to go through such a long trial period, the response was, "We have to hire a minority for that job and you're the best of the minority candidates!"

During the past decade, several section editors have consulted me on various Asian problems, slants, and sensitivities and have followed through in publishing mostly positive, unbiased articles. **Female newspaper journalist from New York.**

Asian interviewees trust me more. **Female newspaper journalist from Virginia.**

I'm sure I have been asked to participate in several newsroom committees because of an interest in having racial diversity represented, if that qualifies. **Male newspaper journalist from Kentucky.**

People do try to include you in conversations by asking questions about food habits, festivals, etc. I realize that these are genuine, if somewhat awkward, attempts by people to establish a rapport and expand the range of conversation and experience. Occasionally, you meet someone who has actually traveled abroad or met someone from that country X or Y and when this happens it brings a spark into the conversation. **Male Asian Indian newspaper journalist from South Dakota.**

Yes. I have no doubt that my ethnic status is one of the critical reasons why I was recruited so heavily by Gannett. Yes, I graduated with excellent grades from one of the best journalism schools in the country. Yes, I packed those four years with internships and part-time journalism jobs. Yes, I impressed an influential Gannett editor during an internship. Yes, I'm extremely ambitious and, unlike many colleagues, I strive to enter the upper (and lower) echelons of management.

But let's fact it: being Asian sure didn't hurt. With Gannett's strong emphasis on diversity, my minority status was an important consideration.

I certainly don't expect my ethnicity to be a magic ticket to the top; I intend to work and earn my way up. Yet I would be ignorant not to acknowledge the relevance of my race. I see it as an important responsibility, a chance to prove to co-workers that I am intelligent, talented, and worthy of every promotion that I earn—not just a quota-filler.

Also, because of my Asian heritage, I think my comments about my paper's coverage of Asian Americans carries more weight. For example, when my paper covered the murder trial of three Asian me, I objected to the reporter's consistent referral to the defendants as "Asian gang members." I said that the racial description only furthered a growing stereotype: the young Asian thug. The description fueled the growing anti-immigrant sentiment in California, which affects not only immigrants but also citizens who appear to be immigrants (such as my parents, who both were born and raised in California).

I reasoned that a reporter never would write "Hispanic gang members" or "black gang members." I asked top editors, "How is 'Asian gang member' any different? How is race significant to the story?" I argued that the paper should follow the same policy that's used for all crime stories: race is not mentioned unless it's significant to the story or used as part of a detailed description of a suspect on the loose. I think my comments were taken more seriously by top (white) editors because I am Asian. In subsequent stories, the racial reference was dropped. **Male newspaper journalist from California.**

Few. Other than when I would work on a story where my Asian American heritage would help, such as a feature on an internment camp, or a story profiling the racial prejudice directed against Asian Americans during World War II. Then my heritage would gain me access. **Male newspaper journalist from Ohio.**

I think sometimes people might bend to you a little bit on issues that involved Asian Americans, within the newsroom they may ask for my input to see if they are being discriminatory with a particular cartoon or article that involved Asian Americans and that's kind of nice. It's mostly the copy desk people who are sensitive to these. **Male magazine journalist from Washington, D.C.**

I've had more positive than negative experiences on the job that I think are related to my being Asian American. Being Chinese, I find has helped me find a job more easily, and do my job more efficiently in some instances. I find that my ethnicity allows me to slide easily between white and black cultures.

When covering stories involving blacks, Latinos, or Asians, I've found that my ethnicity seems to give sources a certain degree of comfort that they might not have if I was a Caucasian reporter. I believe that because they consider me a minority too, that I must also come from a similar socio-economic background or have some special insight into their lives and problems. I believe this to be somewhat true.

When doing stories involving Caucasians, especially in the ethnocentric Irish neighborhoods in Boston, I've found my ethnic background to be more advantageous than if I were a black or Latino reporter. I think this may be the case because whites have a tendency to lump us into the same category as themselves and then they feel more comfortable with talking. Perhaps this is because whites tend to view Asians as demographically the same as themselves, i.e. upwardly mobile, educated. Whatever the case, my ethnic orientation seems to break down barriers.

In both cases, I believe my ethnicity seems to give me commonalties with people rather than differences. The more comfortable they feel, the more they'll say and the higher likelihood that I'll get the deep details I need to make the best story. I think being

Asian has only helped me do my job. **Male newspaper journalist from Massachusetts.**

Yes. However, the battles are hard fought and won. Often, any positive experience I feel is on a personal level on the job, not a professional one. It is difficult to go against the tide of the desires of white management and make them realize there are other realms of thinking, especially when covering stories. Occasionally, I will be able to cover a story on the plight of other Asians. However, there is often no follow up, because our audience does not care (I work in an area that is predominantly white with little tolerance for diversity). My small victories come in story meetings, when I am able to persuade someone that their comments are racist and/or sexist and we should not cover them. For example, a white manager was very upset that he was seeing more white female teenagers becoming attracted to young black males. He wanted to do a story on it. But I told him, yes, we should do a story on it, but only because it would be extraordinary that the young man would not be punished; the we should congratulate ourselves that these young people can see beyond color. **Female television journalist from Michigan.**

Because of my position in the mainstream media, I've had a somewhat higher profile than many Asian Americans. One of the nice consequences of that is that I've received numerous phone calls and pieces of mail from other Asian Americans. Many are just students looking for career advice. Some are older immigrants who simply call to congratulate me on my accomplishments. I've also been contacted many times by the Korean media. I've been interviewed close to a dozen times by Korean newspapers and television. And I've also been asked to write for Korean publications (which I've turned down).

As far as treatment from my employers, I've never felt any bias one way or another from them, although I do realize that as a minority at a predominantly white company, I'm most likely a valuable commodity. Of course, that's never been expressed to me. It's simply my (self-centered?) assumption. **Male newspaper journalist from New York.**

The positive experiences have more to do with personal satisfaction from covering issues involving race and ethnicity than with outside recognition that I may bring a valuable point of view to this kind of coverage. In my current beat, covering legal affairs,

I've written quite a bit about affirmative action and immigration this year. I've rally been challenged and absorbed by these topics and have loved covering them.

At times my editors may tacitly like the perspective I bring to these and related topics. But at other times, my views may not jive with theirs in part because of differences in our ethnic backgrounds. But that's just reflective of the tensions on these topics on a national level. And perhaps it's good that such differences in viewpoint exist within the newsroom. **Female magazine journalist from Washington, D.C.**

I am certain I was hired because I'm a minority—Asian American. In fact, the recruiter told me as much. I also was considered and won several internships during my college years because of my ethnicity. Sure, it also was because of my talent, but the deciding factor was the color of my skin. **Female newspaper journalist from Pennsylvania.**

I believe I was hired primarily because my newspaper is not racially diverse and seeks to add color to its almost all-white staff. I am currently one of three minority full-time reporters. (There's one black and one Hispanic reporter.)

I consider my hiring a positive experience because I would not have been hired with just five years of experience in the field if I was a white male. As a minority reporter, I have the opportunity to serve on the paper's diversity committee, which is working to broaden its coverage of minority groups. **Female Chinese American newspaper journalist from Rhode Island.**

I suppose some look at me positively just because of the stereotype of the model minority, but that too can be troublesome if you don't fit the stereotype or the higher standards that don't apply to others—overachieving, uncomplaining, etc. **Female newspaper journalist from Oregon.**

The most positive experience is a general one—that I now work in a newsroom where I feel very comfortable with being Asian. Other places I've worked have not been this way.

As a minority, I have been the beneficiary of scholarships, job fairs, and job opportunities that I would not have had if I were white. I am grateful for these chances to prove myself, but as I've said before, they come at the price of some people assuming that race is the only reason I am where I am today. **Female newspaper journalist from Oregon.**

I've met other Asian Americans on assignment and they comment it's nice to see me working here. **Female newspaper photojournalist from Washington.**

I think being Asian American has let me explore a lot of stories that I would not know about if I were not half Filipino and half Chinese. Many of my best stories come from those communities and are areas our newspaper would never know to explore. I think my ethnic background is a constant and permanent asset to my reporting skills. **Female newspaper journalist from Kansas.**

I can't point to "positive" experiences on the job that I could specifically relate to my ethnicity. I would assume, however, that my ethnicity played a part in my hiring at the *name of California newspaper* at the age of twenty-nine, when people with more experience than I had applied for the same job. Also, my involvement with the Asian American Journalists Association has gotten me paid time off to attend conventions. **Female newspaper journalist from California.**

I believe that the fact that I am Asian allowed me to be hired into the company. Before I joined *name of media company* I was recruited as an intern with the company's internship director. He was very much for diversity in the workplace (he managed to hire an Indian on his staff as an editor and wanted very much to continue the process but he left abruptly). He was the one who managed to push through for my eventual placement in the company. **Female newspaper journalist from Pennsylvania.**

Conversely, other Asians and Caucasians tend to view me in a more favorable light because of my ethnicity. Therefore, more of these readers call and write me to say they enjoy my work. **Female newspaper journalist from Hawaii.**

Every once in a while, I will meet someone who is genuinely interested in my background and enjoys learning about my experiences as a Burmese American. Actually, this happens most frequently during Asian American Journalists Association meetings.

As for people I cover, I find those who get to know me turn out to be the best sources. I suppose that applies to most journalists. But in this regard, I think my ethnicity gives me an advantage that few others have. Usually, the conversations I've had with people who are curious about my heritage have all been positive and engaging. **Female newspaper journalist from Washington, D.C.**

I think affirmative action probably helped me get a start in journalism. Yet I also think that for every position I have ever held (including my first job), I have been at least as qualified (through education and experience) as other candidates. Affirmative action may have helped me get in the door for the first job. However, I do not believe it has helped me much since then, and certainly not in climbing the ladder. I believe that any opportunities or advancement since then simply reflect the experience I've added to my resume and my lengthening tenure in the business. **Female newspaper journalist from Massachusetts.**

Yes, as a police reporter I think being Asian has definitely helped me. Police view Asians as model minorities and as a result I think they find it easy to trust me. (I also think being a woman helps, I think as a woman I'm able to be much pushier with cops than men can.) Thought I do much of my reporting over the phone, when I do go out in the field I find it easy to gain both the police and public's trust. I think one reason is that I'm Asian plus I'm also small, which makes me appear non-threatening. **Female newspaper journalist from California.**

I do feel that my being Japanese American probably has helped me get some jobs that I might no otherwise have gotten had I been a white male. I'd like to think I was awarded a job based purely on my skill, talent, and experience, but that would be naive—especially in this Age of Diversity. **Male Japanese American newspaper journalist from California.**

Many reporters and some editors have been treating me very nicely. They talked and greeted me almost everyday. Some ate lunch with me. No one has ever made any racial remark against me. **Male newspaper journalist from Louisiana.**

I have had much fewer positive experiences on the job that I can attribute to my ethnicity. **Male newspaper journalist from Texas.**

Yes, I have also had some positive experiences on the job because of my ethnic status as an Asian American. I have had students who are aspiring journalists come up to me at job conventions. Many of them have told me that there are a ton of Asian females who want to get into this business, but there are hardly any Asian males and that I am a role model for them. I have also had people come up to me on the street and comment to me that I am doing a good job. That makes it all worthwhile. **Male television journalist from Nevada.**

The most positive part of my work relating to being Asian American is that I have easier access to other Asian American professionals with whom I might work. When I was doing PR I knew all the Asian American newspaper, television, and radio reporters and staff. They always helped me get stories told properly. Conversely, if I had a hot breaking story, they knew they had a inside source in me. It's our version of the "Old Boys Network."

I probably have been able to withstand the last three layoffs here because the station is anxious to keep our EEO figures high.

In public relations it's important to be remembered. There are so few Asian Americans in this business that I would be the only one at conferences, meetings, etc. People always remember me. It made it difficult for me because I usually couldn't remember who they were. **Female television/public relations journalist from Massachusetts.**

Being that I speak Chinese conversationally, I can often help anchors with correct pronunciations, etc. I feel that my ethnicity is an asset to the newsroom in this way and others. **Female television journalist from Washington, D.C.**

Every once in a while I derive great satisfaction from influencing the way my station covers stories involving Asian issues. For example, when there's crime either committed or suffered by Asians there's often the erroneous assumption that it's Asian gang-related. There's a certain mystique to the whole Asian gangs thing and I try to correct it. Usually they listen to me. I often lobby against some other common occurrences, like lumping various Asian ethnicitites together. Would anyone say "white gangs" or "black gangs?" I think not. Also, the media like to use the word "invasion" when talking about Asian crimes. That's clearly a reference to the menacing Japanese World War II stereotype. And even when the race or ethnicity is totally irrelevant to the story, the media often dwell on it. But the same thing doesn't apply to blacks, whites, or Hispanics. As an Asian American and as a journalist, I point these things out.

I enjoy knowing that Asian American children can watch me on TV and realize that television news is a viable career option. For a long time, Asian Americans have shied away from the spotlight. Some of it certainly is cultural, but I believe to succeed in this country it's important to have a strong voice. And I think more Asian Americans should venture into the media, law, politics, etc. **Female television journalist from Pennsylvania.**

I truly believe the door to broadcast news was open an inch, enough for a foothold, when I began in 1974. The FCC was telling stations back then to hire women and minorities. If not for that, I don't believe I would have gotten in. Once in, I believed, like many, that I had to work harder and longer and better in order to get ahead. I think that is a feeling all successful broadcast people shared.

When I was first hired in Chicago in 1979, my soon-to-be-bosses told me their bosses in New York questioned why they would want to hire an Asian woman here. That a black woman was much more reasonable and needed for this market.

The man who was then news director replied that he thought I was talented and he wanted to hire me for the job. At the time, the Asian population in Chicago was not large enough to make a ratings point difference, even if every single one of them watched me. But, I was hired and because I was different I immediately drew a following.

The following year, the station also sent me back to China and I ended up doing a major special program and twelve special reports for my station. They promoted it quite a bit and we received a phenomenal response from all kinds of people. It seems a heavily ethnic community (Polish, Irish, Italian heritage) identified with someone who had been an immigrant, no matter the color of her skin. It was a marvelous experience. **Female Chinese American television journalist from Illinois.**

Being Asian American has certainly helped me in the past when I covered stories on the Vietnamese and Chinese communities. The people trusted me. **Female television journalist from Massachusetts.**

Yes, I work in the number one market in the country. I feel that my early opportunities here were offered because of affirmative action. I say this because at the time I was one of the youngest and least experienced new hires. **Male television journalist from New York City.**

My first television reporting job was in Spokane, Washington—about as middle America as you can get. At the time, I was the only non-white reporter at the station. I credit *name of person*, the news director, for picking me out of the crowd and giving me a job. But I never felt it was because of my ethnicity (although I'm not so naive as to think that wasn't a factor). *Name of news director* was supportive, nurturing, a good journalist, and a good guy. It was the best experience I could have had as an Asian American—being treated just like anyone else. **Male television reporter from New York City.**

I honestly feel like I have an advantage being an Asian woman in this business. I am perceived to be intelligent and educated. I feel like others in this business value my opinion and truly listen to what I have to say. I'm not sure, however, that these perceptions are shaped solely by the fact that I'm Asian. **Female television journalist from Georgia.**

I think I'm more at an advantage as an Asian. There are only seven [minority] people in the newsroom (out of seventy-five). The number is so small considering what we do. These are the positions—newswriter (me), photographer, off-air reporter, on-air reporter (two), editor, producer. I don't feel there are enough Asians in the broadcast (TV) industry. In that matter, there are not enough Asians in management—that's one area I hope Asians will have an opportunity to grow in. That's where I feel Asian Americans can make a difference on Asian American issues—that's where our voice will be heard. Right now we take orders from people like our supervisor on the assignment desk and we're not in a position to delegate tasks or issues. **Female television journalist from Washington.**

I have also said, I was "two for the price of one," a double minority if you will, a woman, and an Asian. What I felt twenty years ago when I got started, and what I feel now remains unchanged. Use the double minority issue to our advantage! Sometimes I do feel, in doing stories involving minorities (Asians, blacks, native Americans, Hispanics) that I was at an advantage since would could find some relating pint that we were minorities and that I understood some of the issues they feel are important. **Female television journalist from California.**

I haven't had any blatant positive experiences related to being Asian, but I do have some theories that my race helped me at my last two jobs.

Firstly, I think being a minority helped me get my current job. In this top fifty news market, I am the only Asian person on the air. (There's one minority on the air and she's black.) In my entire building I'm the only Asian. I am not even sure if there are Asian reporters working at the other media. I haven't seen any. I've been told Asians tread on neutral ground here; it neither helps nor hurts ratings. But I think in light of these statistics, a news director would think it certainly can't hurt to hire a token minority, especially if she's the only one of her kind in the market.

Secondly, I encountered the exact same situation at the last job. I learned later, my former news director knew he wanted to hire a minority female for the reporter job. Thanks to the consultants I went from reporter to anchor within a week of getting hired. (However, I also think being a woman had a great deal to do with this, since I broke the monotony of white male anchors at that station.) **Female television journalist from New Jersey.**

Fortunately, not ALL news directors are like the ones mentioned above [in the response to survey question one]. In all honestly, my ethnicity probably helped me in getting my current position. My news director made considerable efforts to diversity the newsroom, so he was willing to allow his viewers to decide if they wanted an Asian sports anchor/reporter—and so far, everything has worked out pretty well. I also have received many positive letter, phone calls, and comments by viewers about how glad they were to see an Asian doing the sports. **Male television journalist from Virginia.**

I can only think of one example where I can definitely say being an Asian American was an advantage. I applied for a prestigious training program. I was told before I applied that the program wanted Asian Americans to enter the program and if I applied, I would almost be guaranteed acceptance. Out of fifteen in this program, I was the only Asian American and only one of two minorities. the other was an Hispanic woman. **Male television journalist from California.**

I've had to cover stories in which I used Mandarin [Chinese] to communicate with the subjects of my story. I find this extremely rewarding because I'm getting a story that many of the other reporters cannot get, and I'm reporting on my community. **Female radio journalist from California.**

Yes.  Those experiences mainly stem from the pride other Asian feel when they meet me. It's like, "Oh, you're *person's name*, how wonderful to meet you.  I didn't know you were Chinese." Many older people in Chinatown, community leaders, are happy that one of their own is part of the all-news radio station in town because it has such dominance in the market. **Female radio journalist from California.**

# BIBLIOGRAPHY

## BOOKS

Aguilar-San Juan, Karin, ed. 1994. *The State of Asian America, Activism and Resistance in the 1990s.* Boston: South End Press.

Anderson, Ian. E., ed. 1994. *Editor & Publisher International Yearbook, 1994.* New York: Editor & Publisher.

Asante, Kete and William B. Gudykunst, eds. 1989. *Handbook of International and Intercultural Communication.* Newberry Park, Calif.: Sage Publications.

Babbie, Earl. 1995. *The Practice of Social Research, Seventh Edition.* Belmont, Calif.: Wadsworth Publishing Company.

Backus, Karen and Julia C. Furtaw. 1992. Asian Americans Information Directory: A Guide to Organizations, Agencies, Institutions, Programs, Publications, and Services Concerned With Asian American Nationalities and Ethnic Groups in the United States. Detroit: Gale Research, Inc.

Barkan, Elliott Robert. 1992. *Asian and Pacific Isander Migration to the United States, A Model of New Global Patterns.* Westport: Greenwood Press.

Barringer, Herbert R., Robert W. Gardner and Michael J. Levin. 1992. *Asians and Pacific Islanders in the United States..* New York: Russell Sage Foundation.

Bennett, Judith A. 1986. *Wealth of the Solomons, A History of a South Pacific Archipelago, 1800-1978.* Honolulu: University of Hawaii Press.

Canning, Paul, ed. 1995. *1995 Who's Who in America, 49th Edition.* Providence, N.J.: Reed Reference Publishing.

Carlson, Lewis H. and George A. Colburn. 1972. *In Their Place: White America Defines Her Minorities, 1850-1950*. New York: John Wiley & Sons, Inc.

Carter, Earl, ed. 1978. *How Blacks Use Television for Entertainment and Information*. Washington: Booker T. Washington Foundation-Cable Communications Resource Center-West.

Chan, Sucheng. 1991. *Asian Americans, An Interpretive History*. Boston: Twayne Publishers.

Cheung, King-kok. 1993. *Articulate Silences*. Ithaca: Cornell University Press.

Choy, Philip P., Lorraine Dong and Marlon K. Hom, eds. 1994. *Coming Man, 19th Century American Perceptions of the Chinese*. Seattle: University of Washington Press.

Chu, Bernice, ed. 1986. *Asian American Media Reference Guide*. New York: Asian CineVision, Inc.

Cohen, Bernard. 1963. *The Press and Foreign Policy*. Princeton: Princeton University Press.

Commission of Freedom of the Press. 1947. *A Free and Responsible Press*. Chicago: University of Chicago.

Cowan, Robert Ernest and Boutwell Dunlap. [1909] 1980. *Bibliography of the Chinese Question in the United States*. San Francisco: R and E Research Associates.

Daniels, Roger. 1988. *Asian America, Chinese and Japanese in the United States Since 1850*. Seattle: University of Washington Press.

Deutschmann, Paul J. 1959. *News-Page Content of Twelve Metropolitan Dailies*. Cincinnati: Scripps-Howard Research.

Dissanayake, Wimal, ed. 1988. *Communication Theory, the Asian Perspective*. Singapore: The Asian Mass Communication Research and Information Centre.

Dyer, Ester R., ed. 1978. *Cultural Pluralism and Children's Media*. Chicago: American Library Association.

Ebihara, Wataru, ed. 1995. *An Asian American Internet Guide*. Los Angeles: University of California.

Espiritu, Yen Le. 1992. *Asian American Panethnicity, Bridging Institutions and Identities*. Philadelphia: Temple University Press.

Fallows, James. 1996. *Breaking the News, How the Media Undermine American Democracy*. New York: Pantheon Books.

Faung Jean. 1992. *Asian Americans, Oral Histories of First to Fourth Generation Americans From China, the Philippines, Japan, India, the Pacific Isalnds, Vietnam and Cambodia*. New York: The New Press.

Foner, Philip S. and Daniel Rosenberg, eds. 1993. *Racism, Dissent, and Asian Americans from 1850 to the Present, A Documentary History.* Westport, Conn.: Greenwood Press.

Gall, Susan B. and Timothy L. Gall, eds. 1993. *Statistical Record of Asian Americans.* Detroit: Gale Research, Inc.
Gee, Emma, ed. 1976. *Counterpoint, Perspectives on Asian America.* Los Angeles: Asian American Studies Center.
Ghymn, Esther Mikyung. 1992. *The Shapes and Styles of Asian American Prose Fiction.* New York: Peter Lang Publishing, Inc.
Goldstein, Norm, ed. 1994. *The Associated Press Stylebook and Libel Manual.* New York: The Associated Press.
Gordon, Thomas F. 1978-1995. *Communication Abstracts.* New York: Sage Publications.

Hamamoto, Darrell. 1994. *Monitored Peril: Asian Americans and the Politics of TV Representation.* Minneapolis: University of Minnesota Press.
Herman, Masako, ed. 1974. *The Japanese in America 1843-1973.* Dobbs Ferry, N.Y.: Oceana Publications, Inc.
Herrnstein, Richard J. 1994. *The Bell Curve, Intelligence and Class Structure in American Life.* New York: Free Press.
Hezel, Francis X., S.J. 1983. *The First Taint of Civilization, A History of the Caroline and Marshall Islands in Pre-Colonial Days, 1521-1885.* Honoloulu: University of Hawaii Press.
Hongo, Garrett, ed. 1993. *The Open Boat, Poems From Asian America.* New York: Anchor Books, Doubleday.
Howe, Irving. 1976. *World of Our Fathers.* New York: Simon and Schuster.
Hundley Jr., Norris, ed. 1976, *The Asian American: The Historical Experience.* Santa Barbara, Calif.: Clio Books.

Jordan, Lewis, ed. 1976. *The New York Times Manual of Style and Usage, A Desk Book of Guidelines for Writers and Editors.* New York: The *New York Times* Co.

Kim, Elaine H. 1982. *Asian American Literature, An Introduction to the Writings and Their Social Context.* Philadelphia: Temple University Press.
Kim, Hyung-chan. 1992. *Asian Americans and the Supreme Court, A Documentary History.* New York: Greenwood Press.
Kim, Hyung-chan. 1986. *Dictionary of Asian American History.* New York:Greenwood Press.
Kincaid, D. Lawrence, ed. 1987. *Communication Theory, Eastern and Western Perspectives.* New York: Academic Press, Inc.

Kitano, Harry H. L. and Roger Daniels. 1988. *Asian Americans Emerging Minorities*. Englewood Cliffs: Prentice Hall.
Knoll, Tricia. 1982. *Becoming Americans, Asian Sojourners, Immigrants, and Refugees in the Western United States*. Portland, Ore.: Coast to Coast Books.

Lee, Joann Faung Jean. 1991. *Asian American Experience in the United States*. Jefferson, N.C.: McFarland & Company, Inc.
Leong, Frederick T.L. and James R. Whitfield, eds. 1992. *Asians in the United States: Abstracts of the Psychological and Behavioral Literature, 1967-1991*. Washington, D.C.: American Psychological Association.
Leong, Russell. 1991. *Moving the Image: Independent Asian American Media Arts*. Los Angeles: UCLA Asian American Studies Center.
Leong, Russell and James R. Whitfield, eds. 1992. *Asians in the United States, Abstracts of the Psychological and Behavioral Literature, 1967-1991*. Washington, D.C.: American Psychological Association.
Levine, Ellen. 1995. *A Fence Away From Freedom, Japanese Americans and World War II*. New York: G.P. Putnam's Sons.
Li, Marjorie H. and Peter Li, eds. 1990. *Understanding Asian Americans*. New York: Neal-Schuman Publishers.
Lim, Genny, ed. 1984. *The Chinese American Experience: Papers From the Second National Conference on Chinese American Studies (1980)*. San Francisco: The Chinese Historical Society of America and the Chinese Culture Foundation of San Francisco.
Lim, Shirley Geok-lin and Amy Ling, eds. 1992. *Reading the Literatures of Asian America*. Philadelphia: Temple University Press.
Lippman, Thomas W., ed. 1989. *The Washington Post Deskbook on Style*. New York: McGraw-Hill Publishing Company.
Liu, Kwang-ching. 1963. *Americans and Chinese, An Historical Essay and a Bibliography*. Cambridge: Harvard University Press.
Lo, Samuel E. 1971. *Asian Who? In America*. Roseland, N.J.: East-West Who? Inc., Publishers in cooperation with Seton Hall University Press.

MacKinnon, Stephen R. and Oris Friesen. 1987. *China Reporting: An Oral History of American Journalism in the 1930s and 1940s*. Berkeley: University of California Press.
Martindale, Carolyn. 1987. *The White Press and Black America. Contributions in Afro-American and African Studies*. No. 97. Westport, Conn.: Greenwood Press.
Matabane, Paula. 1989. *Strategies for Research on Black Women and Mass Communication*. Creedon, Pamela J., ed. Women in Mass Communication: Challenging Gender Values. Sage Focus Editions, No. 106. Newbury Park, Calif.: Sage Publications.

McCombs, Maxwell E. and David Weaver. 1985. Towards a Merger of Gratifications and Agenda Setting Research. In Rosengren, K.E., L.A. Wenner, and P. Palmgreen, eds., *Handbook of Political Communication*, 95-108. Newbury Park, Calif.: Sage.

Miller, R.M., ed. 1978. *Ethnic Images in American Film and Television*. Public Papers in the Humanities No. 1. Philadelphia: The Balch Institute.

Nakanishi, Don T. 1980 The National Asian-American Roster: 1978. In *Political Participation of Asian Americans: Problems and Strategies*, Jo, Yung-Hawan, ed., 197-210 No place cited: Pacific/Asian American Mental Health Research Center.

Nakanishi, Don T. and Bernice C. LaForteza. 1984. *The National Asian Pacific American Roster, 1984*. Los Angeles: UCLA Asian American Studies Center.

Nieva, Pepi, ed. 1994. *Filipina, Hawaii's Filipino Women*. Honolulu: Filipino Association of University Women Publications.

Niiya, Brian, ed. 1993. *Japanese American History*. New York: Facts on File, Inc.

Ng, Wendy L., Soo-Yong Chin, James S. Moy and Gary Y. Okihiro, eds. 1995. *ReViewing Asian America, Locating Diversity*. Pullman, Wash.: Washington State University Press.

Noelle-Neumann, Elizabeth. 1984. *The Spiral of Silence*. Chicago: University of Chicago Press.

Okamura, Jonathan Y. 1996. Historical Legacies,Contemporary Challenges andFuture Visions: The Filipino American Community in Late Twentieth Century Hawai'i. Okamura, Johnathan Y. and Roderick N. Labrador, eds. *Pagdiriwang 1996: Legacy and Vision of Hawaii's Filipino Americans*. Manoa, Hawaii: Center For Southeast Asian Studies, University of Hawaii at Manoa.

Okihiro, Gary Y. 1994. *Margins and Mainstreams, Asians in American History and Culture*. Seattle: University of Washington Press.

Okihiro, Gary Y., ed. 1989. *Ethnic Studies, Vol. I - Cross Cultural, Asian and Afro-American Studies*. New York: Markus Wiener Publishing, Inc.

Olszyk, E. 1940. *The Polish Press in America*. Milwaukee: Marquette University Press.

Ong, Paul, ed. 1994. *The State of Asian Pacific America: Economic Diversity, Issues and Policies*. Los Angeles: LEAP Asian Pacific American Public Policy Institute.

Overbeck, Wayne. 1994. *Major Principles of Media Law*. New York: Harcourt Brace College Publishers.

Palmer, Albert W. 1934. *Orientals in American Life*. New York: Friendship Press.

Pearce, W. Barnett and Keith R. Stamm. 1973. Coorientational States and Interpersonal Commuunication, pp. 177-202, in Clarke, Peter, ed., *New Models for Mass Communication Research*. Beverly Hills: Sage Publications.

Perlmutter, Philip. 1992. *Divided We Fall, A History of Ethnic, Religious, and Racial Prejudice in America.* Ames: Iowa State University Press.

Phou, Lee Yan. 1887. *When I Was a Boy in China.* Boston: D. Lothrop Co.

Pipes McAdoo, Harriette, ed. 1993. *Family Ethnicity Strength in Diversity.* New York: Sage Publications.

Revilla, Linda A. 1996. Filipino Americans: Issues of Identity in Hawaii. Okamura, Johnathan Y. and Roderick N. Labrador, eds. *Pagdiriwang 1996: Legacy and Vision of Hawaii's Filipino Americans.* Manoa, Hawaii: Center For Southeast Asian Studies, University of Hawaii at Manoa.

Revilla, Linda A., Gailm M. Nomura, Shawn Wong and Shirley Hune, eds. 1993. *Bearing Dreams, Shaping Visions, Asian Pacific American Perspectives.* Pullman, Wash.: Washington State University Press.

Scott, Virginia, ed. 1979. *American Born and Foreign, An Anthology of Asian American Poetry.* New York: Sunbury Press.

Shoemaker, P. and S. Reese. 1991. *Mediating the Message: Theories of Influence on Mass Media Content.* New York: Longman.

Simon, Rita J. and Susan H. Alexander. 1993. *The Ambivalent Welcome: Print Media, Public Opinion and Immigration.* Westport, Conn.: Greenwood.

Smith, William Carlson. 1937. *Americans In Process, A Study of Our Citizens of Oriental Ancestry.* Ann Arbor: Edwards Brothers, Inc.

Sone, Monica. 1953. *Nisei Daughter.* Boston: Little, Brown & Co.

Stempel III, Guido H. and Bruce H. Westley, eds. 1989. *Research Methods in Mass Communication.* Englewood Cliffs, N.J.: Prentice Hall.

Stewart Dyer, Carolyn and James Hamilton, eds. 1993. *The Iowa Guide.* Iowa City: School of Journalism and Mass Communication, University of Iowa.

Sue, Stanley and Nathaniel N. Wagner, eds. 1973. *Asian-Americans, Psychological Perspectives.* Ben Lomond, Calif.: Science and Behavior Books, Inc.

Sumida, Stephen H. 1991. *And the View From the Shore, Literary Traditions of Hawai'i.* Seattle: University of Washington Press.

Tachiki, Amy, Eddie Wong, Franklin Odo, eds. 1971. *Roots: An Asian American Reader.* Los Angeles: The Regents of the University of California.

Takaki, Ronald. 1990. *Iron Cages, Race and Culture in 19th-Century America.* New York: Oxford University Press.

Takaki, Ronald. 1989. *Strangers From a Different Shore, A History of Asian Americans.* Boston: Little, Brown and Company.

Taylor, Charles A. 1989. *1989 Guide to Multicultural Resources.* Madison, Wisc.: Praxis Publications, Inc.

Toji, Dean S. 1993. *The State of Asian Pacific America: A Public Policy Report, Policy Issues to the Year 2020.* Los Angeles: LEAP Asian-Pacific American Public Policy Institute and UCLA Asian American Studies Center.

Trueba, Henry T., Lila Jacobs and Elizabeth Kirton. 1990. *Cultural Conflict and Adaptation: The Case of Hmong Children in American Society.* New York: The Falmer Press.

Tsai, Henry Shih-shan. 1986. *The Chinese Experience in American.* Bloomington: Indiana University Press.

Tuchman, Gaye. 1978. Introduction: The Symbolic Annihilation of Women by the Mass Media. Tuchman, G. et al, eds. *Hearth and Home: Images of Women in the Mass Media.* New York: Oxford University Press.

Vanden Heuvel, Jon and Everette E. Dennis. 1993. *The Unfolding Lotus: East Asia's Changing Media.* New York: The Freedom Forum Media Studies Center.

Vivian, John. 1993. *The Media of Mass Communication.* Boston: Allyn and Bacon.

Weaver, David H. and G. Cleveland Wilhoit. 1986. *The American Journalists, A Portrait of U.S. News People and Their Work.* Bloomington, Ind.: Indiana University Press.

Wegars, Priscilla, ed. 1995. *Hidden Heritage, Historical Archaeology of the Overseas Chinese.* Amityville, NY: Baywood Publishing Company, Inc.

Wei, William. 1993. *The Asian American Movement.* Philadelphia: Temple University Press.

White-Parks, Annette, Deborah D. Buffton, Ursula Chiu, Catherine M. Currier, Cecilia G. Manrique and Marsha Momoi Piehl, eds. 1994. *A Gathering of Voices on the Asian American Experience.* Fort Atkinson, Wisc.: Highsmith Press.

Wong, Diane Yen-mei. 1983. *Dear Diane: Questions and Answers for Asian American Women.* Oakland: U.S. Department of Education.

Wong, Eugene Franklin. 1978. *On Visual Media Racism: Asians in the American Motion Pictures.* New York: Arno Press.

Wong, Nellie. 1977. *Dreams in Harrison Railroad Park.* Berkeley: Kelsey St. Press.

Wong, Sau-ling Cynthia. 1993. *Reading Asian American Literature.* Princeton: Princeton University Press.

Woodrow, Shirley A., ed. 1995 *1995 Congressional Directory, 104th Congress.* Washington, D.C.: U.S. Government Printing Office.

Zimmerman, Jovita Rodas, ed. 1993. *From Mabuhay to Aloha, The Filipinos in Hawaii.* Manila: Filipino Association of University Women Publications.

# PERIODICALS

## Journal and Magazine Articles:

Atkin, Charles K., Judee K. Burgoon and Michael Burgoon. 1983. How Journalists Perceive the Reading Audience. *Newspaper Research Journal* 4(2):51-63.

Allen, R.L. and D. E. Clarke. 1980. Ethnicity and Mass Media Behavior: A Study of Blacks and Latinos. *Journal of Broadcasting* 24(1):23-24.

Aufderheide, Patricia. 1994. Controversy and the Newspaper's Public: The Case of Tongues United. *Journalism Quarterly* 71(3):499-508.

Ayuyang, Rachelle Q. 1995. Filipino American Me. *Filipinas* 37(4):38-39, 74).

Benton, Mark and P. Jean Frazier. 1976. The Agenda Setting Function of the Mass Media at Three Levels of Information Holding. *Communication Research* 3(3):261-274.

Blood, R.W., G.J. Keir and N. Kang. 1983. Newspaper Use and Gratification in Hawaii. *Newspaper Research Journal* 4(4):43-52.

Bramlett-Solomon, S. 1993. Job Appeal and Job Satisfaction Among Hispanic and Black Journalists. *Mass Comm Review* 20(3/4):202-211.

Brislin, Tom. 1995. Weep Into Silence/Cries of Rage: Bitter Divisions in Hawaii's Japanese Press. *Journalism and Mass Communication Monographs* 154.

Brown, W.J. 1992. Culture and AIDS Education: Reaching High-Risk Heterosexuals in Asian-American Communities. *Journal of Applied Communication Research* 20(3):275-291.

Buddenbaum, Judith M. 1987. Predicting Religion Reporters' Use of a Denominational News Service. *Newspaper Research Journal* 8(3):59-70.

Chaffee, Steven H. and Jack M. McLeod. 1968. Sensitization in Panel Design: A Coorientation Experiment. *Journalism Quarterly* 45(4):661-669.

Chaffee, Steven H., Clifford I. Nass and Seung-Mock Yang. 1990. The Bridging Role of Television in Immigrant Political Socialization. *Human Communication Research* 17(2):266-288.

Chaffee, Steven H., Clifford I. Nass and Seung-Mock Yang. 1991. Trust in Government and News Among Korean Americans. *Journalism Quarterly* 68(1/2):111-119.

Chen, Stanford. 1993. It's a Matter of Visibility. *Quill*, 4:33-34.

Chiang, Oscar C.K. 1985. American News Meida and the Chinese. *Chinese American Forum, A Cultural Bridge* 1(4):3-6.

Chiang, Oscar C.K. 1988. Journalism as a Profession - A Personal Experience. *Chinese American Forum, A Cultural Bridge* 3(4):11-12.

Chiang, Oscar C.K., Chia Ting Chen, Frnak M. Cho, S. Yen Lee, Elizabeth Lu, T.C. Peng, Angela Wong, and Paul Wong, eds. May 1984-1993. *Chinese American Forum, A Cultural Bridge* 1(1)-8(4).

Chiasson, Lloyd. 1991. Japanese-American Relocation During World War II: A Study of California Editorial Reactions. *Journalism Quarterly* 68(1/2): 263-272.

Chiasson, Lloyd E. 1991. The Japanese-American Encampment: An Editorial Analysis of 27 West Coast Newspapers. *Newspaper Research Journal* 12(2):92-107.

Chin, Rocky, ed. 1973. *Amerasia Journal* 1(1), entire edition.

Coward, John M. 1994. Explaining the Little Bighorn: Race and Progress in the Native Press. *Journalism Quarterly* 71(3):540-549.

Culbertson, Hugh M. 1975. Gatekeeper Coorientation—A Viewpoint for Analysis of Popular Culture and Specialized Journalism. *Mass Comm Review* 3(1):3-7.

Culbertson, Hugh. M. 1981. Reporters and Editors—Some Differences in Perspective. *Newspaper Research Journal* 2(2):17-27.

Culbertson, Hugh M. 1983. Three Perspectives on American Journalism. *Journalism Monographs* 83, June.

Culbertson, Hugh M. 1989. Should Journalists Follow or Lead Their Audiences?: A Study of Student Beliefs. *Journal of Mass Media Ethics* 4(2):193-213.

Danielson, Wayne A., ed. 1963. *Journalism Abstracts, Vol. 1.* Chapel Hill: Association for Education in Journalism.

Danielson, Wayne A., ed. 1964. *Journalism Abstracts, Vol. 2.* Chapel Hill: Association for Education in Journalism.

Danielson, Wayne A., ed. 1965. *Journalism Abstracts, Vol. 3.* Chapel Hill: Association for Education in Journalism.

Danielson, Wayne A., ed. 1966. *Journalism Abstracts, Vol. 4.* Chapel Hill: Association for Education in Journalism.

Danielson, Wayne A., ed. 1967. *Journalism Abstracts, Vol. 5.* Chapel Hill: Association for Education in Journalism.

Danielson, Wayne A., ed. 1968. *Journalism Abstracts, Vol. 6.* Chapel Hill: Association for Education in Journalism.

Danielson, Wayne A., ed. 1969. *Journalism Abstracts, Vol. 7.* Chapel Hill: Association for Education in Journalism.

Danielson, Wayne A., ed. 1971. *Journalism Abstracts, Vol. 9.* Minneapolis: University of Minnesota, AEJ.

Downing, J.D.H. 1990. Ethnic Minority Radio in the United States. *Howard Journal of Communications* 2(2):135-148.

Delener, Nejdet and James P. Neelankavil. 1990. Informational Sources and Media Usage: A Comparison Between Asian and Hispanic Subcultures. *Journal of Advertising Research* 30(3):45-52.


Entman, Robert M. 1994. Representation and Reality in the Portrayal of Blacks on Network Television News. *Journalism Quarterly* 71(3):509-520.


Faber, R.J., T.C. O'Guinn, and T.P. Meyer. 1987. Televised Portrayals of Hispanics: A Comparison of Ethnic Perceptions. *International Journal of Intercultural Relations* 11(2):155-169.

Fan, Maureen. 1993. Asian Americans Are Still Victims in News Media. *Photograph*, 12:16.

Fitzgerald, Mark. 1996. A Time For Reflection. *Editor & Publisher* 129 (38):17,44.

Fowler, Gilbert L., ed. 1989. *Journalism Abstracts, Vol. 26.* Columbia, S.C.: University of South Carolina, Association for Education in Journalism and Mass Communication (AEJMC).

Fowler, Gilbert L., ed. 1990. *Journalism Abstracts, Vol. 27.* Columbia, S.C.: University of South Carolina, AEJMC.

Fowler, Gilbert L., ed. 1991. *Journalism Abstracts, Vol. 28.* Columbia, S.C.: University of South Carolina, AEJMC.

Fowler, Gilbert L., ed. 1992. *Journalism Abstracts, Vol. 29.* Columbia, S.C.: University of South Carolina, AEJMC.

Fowler, Gilbert L., ed. 1993. *Journalism Abstracts, Vol. 30.* Columbia, S.C.: University of South Carolina, AEJMC.

Fowler, Gilbert L., ed. 1994. *Journalism Abstracts, Vol. 31.* Columbia, S.C.: University of South Carolina, AEJMC.


Gist, M.E. 1990. Minorities in Media Imagery: A Social Cognitive Perspective on Journalistic Bias. *Newspaper Research Journal* 11(3):52-63.

Gitlin, Todd. 1979. Prime Time TV: The Hegemonic Process in TV Entertainment. *Social Problems* 26:251-266.

Gleick, Elizabeth. 1996. Read All About It, The Biggest Story in the Newspaper Industry These Days is About Downsizing, Cost Slashing and Cutthroat Competition. Will the Dailies Survive? *Time* 148(19): 66-69.

Gordon, Thomas F. March 1978-February 1995. *Communication Abstracts, Vols. 1 (1)-17 (1)*. London: Sage Publications.

Grainey, T.F., D.R. Pollack, D.R., and L.A. Kusmierek. 1984. How Three Chicago Newspapers Covered the Washington-Epton Campaign. *Journalism Quarterly* 61(2):352-363.

Greenberg, Bradley S., Carrier Heeter, Judee K. Burgoon, Michael Burgoon, and Filipe Korzenny. 1983. Local Newspaper Coverage of Mexican Americans.*Journalism Quarterly* 60(4):671-676.

Guimary, D.L. 1984. Ethnic Minorities in Newsrooms of Major Market Media in California. *Journalism Quarterly* 61(4):827-830.

Guitierrez, F.F. 1990. Advertising and the Growth of Minority Markets and Media. *Journal of Communication Inquiry* 14(1):6-16.

Hall, William E., ed. 1972. *Journalism Abstracts, Vol. 10*. Chapel Hill: Association for Education in Journalism.

Hall, William E., ed. 1973. *Journalism Abstracts, Vol. 11*. Chapel Hill: Association for Education in Journalism.

Hall, William E., ed. 1974. *Journalism Abstracts, Vol. 12*. Chapel Hill: Association for Education in Journalism.

Hall, William E., ed. 1975. *Journalism Abstracts, Vol. 13*. Chapel Hill: Association for Education in Journalism.

Hamamoto, Darrell. 1992. Kindred Spirits: The Contemporary Asian American Family on Television. *Amerasia Journal* 18(2):35-54.

Haws, Dick. 1991. Minorities in the Newsroom and Community: A Comparison. *Journalism Quarterly* 68(4):764-771.

Henningham, J.P. 1993. Multicultural Journalism: A Profile of Hawaii's News-People. *Journalism Quarterly* 70(3):550-557.

Hesse, Michael B. 1976. A Coorientation Study of Wisconsin State Senators and Their Constituents. *Journalism Quarterly* 53(4):626-633.

Heuterman, Thomas H. 1987. "We Have the Same Rights As Other Citizens": Coverage of Yakima Valley Japanese Americans in the "Missing Decades" of the 1920s and 1930s. *Journalism History* 14(4):94-103.

Ichioka, Yuji. 1986-87. A Study in Dualism: James Yoshinori Sakamoto and the *Japanese American Courier, 1928-1942*. *Amerasia Journal* 13(2):49-81.

Jaret, Charles. 1979. The Greek, Italian, and Jewish American Ethnic Press: A Comparative Analysis. *Journal of Ethnic Studies* 7(2): 47-49.

Jeffres, Leo W. and K. Kyoon Hur. 1980. The Forgotten Media Consumer—The American Ethnic. *Journalism Quarterly* 57(2):10-17.

Jones Ross, Felecia G. 1994. Preserving the Community: Cleveland Black Newspapers' Response to the Great Migration. *Journalism Quarterly* 71(3):531-539.

Keever, Beverly Ann Deepe. 1991. Wilbur Schramm, On Windwagons and Sky Bursters: Final Regrets of a Mass Communications Pioneer. *Mass Comm Review* 18(1, 2):3-26.

Kim, Eric. 1995. Have You Ever Met an Asian Man You Thought Was Sexy? *Glamour*, 3:92.

Kim, Y.Y. 1990. Communication and Adaption: The Case of Asian Pacific Refugees in the United States. *Journal of Asian Pacific Communication* 1(1):191-207.

Kim, Y.Y. 1977. Inter-ethnic and Intra-ethnic Communication: A Study of Korean Immigrants in Chicago. Jain, N.C., ed. *International and Intercultural Communication Annual.* Falls Church, Va.: Speech Communication Association, pp. 52-68.

King, Amber, ed. 1996. *MCI Lifestyles* 2(2). Arlington, Va.: MCI Telecommunications Corp.

Korzenny, Filipe, Kimberly Neuendorf, Michael Burgoon, Judee K. Burgoon, and Bradley S. Greenberg. 1983. Cultural Identification as Predictor of Content Preferences of Hispanics. *Journalism Quarterly* 60(4):677-685.

Lacy, Stephen and Karyn A. Ramsey. 1994. The Advertising Content of African-American Newspapers. *Journalism Quarterly* 71(3):521-530.

Lacey, Geoff. 1993. Females, Aborigines and Asians in Newspaper Photographs, 1950-1990. *AUSJ* 2:244-269.

Lee, M.L. and C.H. Cho. 1990. Women Watching Together: An Ethnographic Study of Korean Soap Opera Fans in the U.S. *Cultural Studies* 4(1):30-44.

Leong, Frederick. 1990. Occupational Stereotyping of Asian Americans. *Career Development Quarterly*, 12:143-154.

Licata, Jane W. and Abhijit Biswas. 1994. Representation, Roles, and Occupational Status of Black Models in Television Advertisements. *Journalism Quarterly* 70(4):868-882.

Lichter, S.R. and L.S. Lichter. 1988. Does Television Shape Ethnic Images? *Media and Values* 43:5-8.

Lum, C.M.K. 1991. Communication and Cultural Insularity: The Chinese Immigrant Experience. *Critical Studies in Mass Communication* 8(1):91-101.

Ma, J. and K. Hildebrandt. 1993. Canadian Press Coverage of the Ethnic Chinese Community: A Content Analysis of the *Toronto Star* and the *Vancouver Sun*, 1970-1990. *Canadian Journal of Communication* 18(4):479-496.

Mansfield, Harvey C. Jr. May 4, 1984. The Underhandedness of Affirmative Action. *The National Review* 36(8).

Martindale, Carolyn. 1990. Changes in Newspaper Images of Black Americans. *Newspaper Research Journal* 11(1):40-50.

Massand, Dilip. N., ed. September/October 1995. Twenty Minutes With Ashok Amritraj. *Masala* 1(10):9-13.

McCombs, Maxwell E. 1992. Explorers and Surveyors: Expanding Strategies for Agenda Setting Research. *Journalism Quarterly* 69:813-824.

McCombs, Maxwell E. and Donald L. Shaw. 1993. The Evolution of Agenda-Setting Research: Twenty-five Years in the Marketplace of Ideas. *Journal of Communication* 43(2):58-67.

McCombs, Maxwell E. and Donald L. Shaw. 1972. The Agenda-Setting Function of Mass Media. *Public Opinion Quarterly* 36:176-185.

Miller, John J. 1994. Immigration, the Press and the New Racism. *Media Studies Journal* 8(3):19-28.

Messaris, P. and J. Woo. 1991. Image vs. Reality in Korean-Americans' Responses to Mass-Mediated Depictions of the United States. *Critical Studies in Mass Communication* 8(1):74-90.

Nakayama, Thomas K. 1988. 'Model Minority' and the Media: Discourse on Asian America. *Journal of Communicaiton Inquiry* 12(1):65-73.

Newcomb, Theodore M. 1953. An Approach to the Study of Communication Acts. *Psychological Review* 343-404.

Ng, Mabel. 1992. Miss Saigon: Casting for Equality on an Unequal Stage. *Hastings Journal of Communications and Entertainment Law* 14 (3):451-473.

Ogden, M.R. and J.M. Hailey. 1988. International Broadcasting Services to Isolated Audiences: The Role of Radio Australia During the Fiji Crisis. *Media Asia* 15(1):22-25.

Okihiro, Gary Y. and Julie Sly. 1983. The Press, Japanese-Americans and the Concentration Camps. *Phylon* 44(1):66-83.

Pease, Edward C. 1989. Kerner Plus 20: Minority News Coverage in the *Columbus Dispatch*. *Newspaper Research Journal* 10(3):17-37.

Pease, Edward C. and J. Frazier Smith. 1991. The Newsroom Barometer, Job Satisfaction and the Impact of Racial Diversity at U.S. Daily Newspapers. *Ohio Journalism Monographs* (1). Athens, Ohio: Bush Research Center of the E.W. Scripps School of Journalism, Ohio University.

Pease, Edward C. and Guido H. Stempel III. 1990. Surviving to the Top: Views of Minority Newspaper Executives. *Newspaper Research Journal* 11(3):64-79.

Popovich, Mark, ed. 1976. *Journalism Abstracts, Vol. 14*. Chapel Hill, N.C.: University of North Carolina, Association for Education in Journalism (AEJ).

Popovich, Mark, ed. 1977. *Journalism Abstracts, Vol. 15*. Chapel Hill, N.C.: University of North Carolina, AEJ.

Popovich, Mark, ed. 1978. *Journalism Abstracts, Vol. 16*. Chapel Hill, N.C.: University of North Carolina, AEJ.

Popovich, Mark, ed. 1978. *Journalism Abstracts Cumulative Index, Volumes 1 to 15, 1963-1977*. Chapel Hill, NC: University of North Caroline, Association for Education in Journalism.

Popovich, Mark, ed. 1979. *Journalism Abstracts, Vol. 17*. Chapel Hill, N.C.: University of North Carolina, Association for Education in Journalism.

Popovich, Mark, ed. 1980. *Journalism Abstracts, Vol. 18*. Chapel Hill, N.C.: University of North Carolina, Association for Education in Journalism.

Popovich, Mark, ed. 1982. *Journalism Abstracts, Vol. 19*. Chapel Hill, N.C.: University of North Carolina, Association for Education in Journalism.

Porter, William C. and Flint Stephens. 1989. Estimating Readability: A Study of Utah Editors' Abilities. *Newspaper Research Journal* 10(2):87-96.

Raub, P. 1988. The *National Geographic* Magazine's Portrayal of Urban Ethnicity: The Celebration of Cultural Pluralism and the Promise of Social Mobility. Journal of Urban History 14(3):346-371.

Richstad, Jim A. 1970. The Press Under Martial Law: The Hawaiian Experience. *Journalism Monographs* 17.

Roh, Kil-Nam. 1983. Issues of Korean American Journalism. *Amerasia Journal* 10(2):89-102.

Rogers, E.M., J.W. Dearing, and D. Bregman. 1993. The Anatomy of Agenda-Setting Research. *Journal of Communication* 43(2):68-84.

Shafer, Richard. 1993. What Minority Journalists Identify as Constraints to Full Newsroom Equality. *Howard Journal of Communication* 4(3):195-208.

Shaw, Donald L., ed. 1970. *Journalism Abstracts, Vol. 8.* Chapel Hill: Association for Education in Journalism.

Sherman, Spencer A. 1994. Letter From Hawaii Where the Breeze is Soft and the Media are Mellow. *Columbia Journalism Review October 1994,* 31-33.

Shim, Jae Chul. 1995. The Rise of an Ethnic Newspaper, Emergence of an International Newsmaking Organization. *The Journal of International Communication* 2(1):134-154.

Shim, Jae Chul and Charles T. Salmon. 1990. Community Orientations and Newspaper Use Among Korean Newcomers. *Journalism Quarterly* 67(4):852-863.

Shiramizu, S. 1991. Ethnic Press and Its Society: A Case of Japanese Press in Hawaii. *KEIO Communication Review* 11:49-70.

Siddiqi, Mohammed A. 1987. Indian Ethnic Press in the United States and Its Functions in the Indian Ethnic Community of the U.S. *Gazette* 38(3):181-194.

Stempel, Guido H. III. 1955. Increasing Reliability in Content Analysis. *Journalism Quarterly* 32:449-455.

Stempel, Guido H. III. 1985. Gatekeeping: The Mix of Topics and the Selection of Stories. *Journalism Quarterly* 62(4):791, 815.

Stone, Vernon A. 1988. Trends in the Status of Minorities and Women in Broadcast News. *Journalism Quarterly* 65(2):288-293.

Tachibana, Judy. 1986. California's Asians: Power From a Growing Population. *California Journal,* November, 535-543.

Tan, Alexis S. 1978. Evaluation of Newspapers and Television by Blacks and Mexican Americans. *Journalism Quarterly* 55(4):673-681.

Tan, Alexis S. 1983. Media Use and Political Orientations of Ethnic Groups. *Journalism Quarterly* 60(1):126-132.

Thomas, R.M. 1980. The Rise and Decline of an Educational Technology: Televisioin in American Samoa. *Educational Communication and Technology* 28(3):155-167.

Tierney, J.D. 1979. Defining Ethnicity Through Measurement Constructs: A Cultural Perspective According to Harold B. Innis. *Gazette* 25(3):176-185.

Tillinghast, William A. 1983. Source Control and Evaluation of Newspaper Inaccuracies. *Newspaper Research Journal* 5(1):13-24.

Underwood, Doug and Keith Stamm. 1992. Balancing Business With Journalism: Newsroom Policies at 12 West Coast Newspapers. *Journalism Quarterly* 69(2):301-317.

Uyeda, Clifford I. 1978. The Pardoning of 'Tokyo Rose': A Report on the Restoration of American Citizenship to Iva Ikuko Toguri. *Amerasia Journal* 5(2):69-93.

Van Dijk, T.A. 1992. Discourse and the Denial of Racism. *Discourse and Society* 3(1):87-118.

Wang, Georgette and D. Lawrence Kincaid. 1982. News Interest of Immigrants in Hawaii. *Journalism Quarterly* 59(4):573-580.
Ward, David A. 1971. The Unending War of Iva Ikuko Toguri D'Aquino: The Trial and Conviction of 'Tokyo Rose.' *Amerasia Journal* 1(2):26-35.
Wilhoit, Frances Goins, ed. 1983. Journalism Abstracts, Vol. 20. Chapel Hill: Association for Education in Journalism and Mass Communication (AEJMC).

Wilhoit, Frances Goins, ed. 1984. *Journalism Abstracts, Vol. 21.* Chapel Hill: Association for Education in Journalism and Mass Communication.
Wilhoit, Frances Goins, ed. 1985. *Journalism Abstracts, Vol. 22.* Chapel Hill: Association for Education in Journalism and Mass Communication.
Wilhoit, Frances Goins, ed. 1986. *Journalism Abstracts, Vol. 23.* Chapel Hill: Association for Education in Journalism and Mass Communication.
Wilhoit, Frances Goins, ed. 1987. *Journalism Abstracts, Vol. 24.* Chapel Hill: Association for Education in Journalism and Mass Communication.
Wilhoit, Frances Goins, ed. 1988. *Journalism Abstracts, Vol. 25.* Chapel Hill: Association for Education in Journalism and Mass Communication.
Winkel, F.W. 1990. Crime Reporting in Newspapers: An Exploratory Study of the Effects of Ethnic References in Crime News. *Social Behavior* 5(2):87-101.
Won-Doornink, Myong Jin. 1988. Television Viewing and Acculturation of Korean Immigrants. *Amerasia Journal* 14(1):79-92.

Yoo, David. 1993. 'Read All About It': Race, Generation and the Japanese Press, 1925-41. *Amerasia Journal* 19(1):69-92.
Yum, June Ock. 1982. Communication Diversity and Information Acquisition Among Korean Immigrants in Hawaii. *Human Communication Research* 8(2):154-169.

Yum, June Ock. 1983. Social Network Patterns of Five Ethnic Groups in Hawaii. Bostrom, R.N. and Westley, B.H., eds. *Communications Yearbook 7* Beverly Hills: Sage Publications, pp. 574-591.

Yum, June Ock and H.W. Park. 1990. The Effects of Disconfirmin Information on Stereotype Change. *Howard Journal of Communications* 2(4):357-367.

Zumwalt, James. 1996. The Little-Known Story of the Courageous Japanese-American Heroes of World War II: Our Parents Told Us "This is Your Country." *Parade, The Sunday Newspaper Magazine.* New York: Parade Publications.

No author cited. 1994. *The Korean Press 1994.* Seoul: The Korean Press Institute.

## NEWSPAPERS

Associated Press. 1995. Asians Better Educated, Earn Less. *Centre Daily Times*, 10 December, final edition.

Bjorhus, Jennifer. 1994. Carriers See Big Dollars in Phone Calls to India. *San Francisco Chronicle*, 7 September, final edition.

Chin, Stephen A. 1994. Asian Americans are 'Hot Commodities.' *San Francisco Chronicle*, 25 September, final edition.

Cho, Cyril S. T., ed. and publisher. 1995. *The USAsians*, 31 October.

Colon, Aly. 1995. News Outside the Mainstream—Ethnic Papers in the Area Find a Loyal and Growing Following. *Seattle Times*, 26 February, final edition.

Critser, Greg. 1983. Readers Slip Away From Japanese-American Press. *Christian Science Monitor*, 27 April.

De Witt, Karen. 1994. Suburban Expansion Fed by an Influx of Minorities. *New York Times*, 15 August, final edition.

Doyle, Jim. 1994. Lawyers Decry Lack of Asian Judges. *San Francisco Chronicle*, 2 March, final edition.

Dunn, Ashley. 1994. Southeast Asians Highly Dependent on Welfare in U.S. *New York Times*, May 19, 1994, final edition.

Faison, Seth. 1994. Asian-American Lawsuit Tries to Make a Point: Caution. *New York Times*, 1 May, final edition.

Fay, Tim. 1994. Korean Church at Odds With Archdiocese. *Atlanta Constitution*, 13 October, final edition.

Galbraith, Jan. 1989. Asian American Actors Meet to Break Industry Stereotypes. *Variety*, 18 January.

Glaberson, William. 1994. The Media Business: Press; At a meeting of Minority Journalists, Two Starting Points on Political Correctness. *New York Times*, 1 August, final edition.

Graham, Jefferson. 1994. Actors' Chance to Part a Racial and Cultural Curtain. *USA Today*, 13 September, final edition.

Graham, Jefferson. 1994. Asians' 'All-American' Opportunity. *USA Today*, 13 September, final edition.

Holmes, Steven A. 1994. Someone to Look Down on: Minority Groups Feel Thwarted by Each Other. *New York Times*, 6 March, final edition.

Holmes, Steven A. 1994. Survey Finds Minorities Resent One Another as Much as They do Whites. *New York Times*, 3 March, final edition.

Honda, Harry K. 1996. Asian Stereotyping, Out of Focus, Out of Time, Out of Line. *Pacific Citizen*, 1-14 March.

Kernshaw, Sarah. 1996. A Disruptive Regents Meeting, But No Change in Bias Policy. *New York Times*, 19 January, final edition.

Li, Jane H. 1994. Neighborhood Report: Flushing; Asians Fear a Police Setback. *New York Times*, 27 March, final edition.

Li, Jane H. 1994. Neighborhood Report: Flusing; A Victory for Queens Asians. *New York Times*, 3 July, final edition.

Ludwig, Ann K. 1994. Picnics and Historic Sites on West's 'Ellis Island.' *New York Times*, 5 June, final edition.

Luna, Deni. 1995-1996. "Out of Focus," Wing Luke Provides Clear Look at Stereotyping. *Northwest Asian Weekly*, 30 December to 30 January.

Luna, Deni and Dean Wong. 1995-1996. Asian Papers, Emerging Community Activism, a Growing Asian Population and Stronger Pacific Rim Ties Fuel Increases of Asian Pacific Newspapers. *Northwest Asian Weekly*, 30 December to 30 January.

Malitz, Nancy. 1994. Pop Music; Ethnic Voices Call the Tune in the Cities. *New York Times*, 6 February, final edition.

Manegold, Catherine S. 1994. Fewer Men Earn Doctorates, Particularly Among Blacks. *New York Times*, 18 January, final edition.

McDowell, Edwin. 1996. Hospitality is Their Business, Indian-Americans' Rooms-to-Riches Success Story. *New York Times*, 21 March, final edition.

McQuiston, John T. 1994. Plan to Revamp Nassau Legislature to Create 2 Minority Districts. *New York Times*, 28 March, final edition.

Mydans, Seth. 1994. 9 Youths Shot at Party Near Los Angeles. *New York Times*, 7 June, final edition.

Ni, Ching-Ching. 1995. Shedding Their Shirts—And a Stereotype. *Los Angeles Times*, 23 February, final edition.
Norris, Kathleen. 1994. This is the Army, Mr. Ting. *The New York Times*, 20 February, final edition.

Park, Michael. 1996. K.W. Lee: Godfather of Asian American Journalism. *Northwest Asian Weekly*, 30 December to 30 January.
Pepper, Anne. Japanese Among the Early Colonists of Florida. *Japan Times*, October (exact date not available).
Perez-Pena, Richard. 1994. Adjusting the Numbers; Cities Win a Round in the Census Fight. *New York Times*, 14 August, final edition.
Polochanin, David. 1994. State's Fastest Growing Minority Group Seeks Larger Political Role. *Boston Globe*, 13 October, final edition.

Read, Katy. 1994. Avondale's White, Asian Families are Strangers in CloseQuarters. *Times-Picayune*, 18 September, final edition.

Weinraub, Bernard. 1993. 'I Didn't Want to do Another Chinese Movie'. *New York Times*, 5 September, final edition.

Zimmer, William. 1994. Art; The Asian-American Artist Clad in the Cloak of Invisibility. *New York Times*, 27 March, final edition.

No author cited. 1995. UW Law Dean to Lead Academic Group. *Seattle Times*, 13 January, final edition.
No author cited. 1994. Racial Slur Causes Political Turmoil for Democrats in Northwest. *New York Times*, 8 May, final edition.
No author cited. 1994. Mending Fences in Chinatown. *New York Times*, 22 May, final edition.
No author cited. 1994. First Interstate Program for Chinese Immigrants. *American Banker*, 16 September, final edition.

## INTERVIEWS AND PERSONAL COMMUNICATIONS

Askari, Emilia. 1995. Speech at AEJMC 1995 annual conference followed by interview by author. In person, 9 August. Washington, D.C.

Borshay, Deann. 1994. Interview by author. Telephone, 10 November. Athens, Ohio.
Broderick, Patricia. 1995. Letter to author, 1 December.

Chapin, Helen G. 1995. Letter to author, 28 November.

Chinn, Marianne. 1995. Letter to author, 11 October.

Chung, Lisa. 1995. Interview by author. Telephone, 18 August. University Park, Pa.

Chung, Lisa. 1995. Interview by author. Telephone, 4 August. University Park, Pa.

Chung, Lisa. 1995. Interview by author. Telephone, 19 July. Athens, Ohio.

Chung, Lisa. 1994. Interview by author. Telephone, 10 November. Athens, Ohio.

Ciria-Cruz, Rene P. 1995. Letter to author, 12 December.

Denley, Susan. 1995. Letter to author, 15 December.

Dovalina, Fernando. 1995. Letter to author, 8 December.

Gulla, Richard. 1996. Telephone interview with the author, 17 April.

Langford, George. 1995. Letter to author, 18 October.

Lee, Marjorie, 1995. Interview by author. Telephone, 3. August. University Park, Pa.

Lee, Marjorie. 1995. Interview by author. Telephone, 14 July. Athens, Ohio.

Long, Jana. 1995. Letter to author, 10 November.

Luna, Deni Yamauchi. 1995. Letter to author, 20 November.

Mallory, James. 1995. Letter to author via electronic mail, 22 December.

Massand, Dilip N. 1995. Interview by author. Telephone, 16 November. State College, Pa.

Mathers, Belinda. 1995. Letter to author sent via electronic mail, 7 December.

McGill, Jennifer. 1994. Interview by author. Telephone, 14 November. Athens, Ohio.

Phillips, Carolyn. 1996. Telephone interview with the author, 16 April.

Phillips, Carolyn. 1996. Letter to the author, 17 April.

Ryu, Jung Shig. 1995. Letter to author, 24 October.

Stern, Dennis. 1995. Letter to author, 16 October.

Williams, Louisa. 1995. Letter to author, 14 November.

Wong, Dean. 1995. Letter to author, 12 December.

Wong, Sau-ling C. 1995. Letter to author, 2 November.
Woo, William F. 1995. Letter to author, 1 December.

Anonymous female employee of the American Society of Newspaper Editors. 1994. Interview by author. Telephone, 11 November. Athens, Ohio.

## UNPUBLISHED MATERIAL

American Society of Newspaper Editors. 1994. *Minorities Make Up 10.49 Percent of Newroom Work*. Reston, Va.: American Society of Newspaper Editors.

American Society of Newspaper Editors. 1995. *Minority Newsroom Employment Shows Small Gain, 1995 ASNE Survey Finds*. Reston, Va.: American Society of Newspaper Editors.

American Society of Newspaper Editors. 1996. *Newsroom Diversity Continues Expansion, Though the Growth is Small, 1996 ASNE Report Shows*. Reston, Va.: American Society of Newspaper Editors.

Asian American Journalists Association. 1995. *A Journalist's to Middle Eastern Americans*. San Francisco: Asian American Journalists Association.

Asian American Journalists Association. 1994. *Minority Hiring in Media*. San Francisco: Asian American Journalists Association.

Asian American Journalists Association. 1993. *Project Zinger, A Critical Look at New Media Coverage of Asian Pacific Americans*. San Francisco: AAJA Center for Integration and Improvement of Journalism.

Asian American Journalists Association, National Association of Black Journalists, National Association of Hispanic Journalists, and Native American Journalists Association. 1994. *News Watch, A Critical Look at Coverage of People of Color*. San Francisco: AAJA Center for Integration and Improvement of Journalism.

Asian American Journalists Association, Chicago Chapter; National Conference of Christians and Jews, Chicago and Northern Illinois Region. 1991. *Asian American Handbook*. No location of publishing given.

Association for Education in Journalism and Mass Communication. 1989. *Official Program for the 72nd Annual Convention of the Association for Education in Journalism and Mass Communication*. Washington, D.C.: AEJMC.

Association for Education in Journalism and Mass Communication. *Official Program for the 73rd Annual Convention of the Association for Education in Journalsim and Mass Communication*. 1990. Minneapolis: AEJMC.

Association for Education in Journalism and Mass Communication. *Official Program for the 74th Annual Convention of the Association for Education in Journalsim and Mass Communication.* 1991. Boston: AEJMC.

Association for Education in Journalism and Mass Communication. *Official Program for the 75th Annual Convention of the Association for Education in Journalism and Mass Communication.* 1992. Montreal: AEJMC.

Association for Education in Journalism and Mass Communication. *Official Program for the 76th Annual Convention of the Association for Education in Journalism and Mass Communication.* 1993. Kansas City: AEJMC.

Association for Education in Journalism and Mass Communication. *Official Program for the 77th Annual Convention of the Asscoiation for Education in Journalism and Mass Communicaiton.* 1994. Atlanta: AEJMC.

Association for Education in Journalism and Mass Communication. *Official Program for the 78th Annual Convention of the Association for Education in Journalism and Mass Communication.* 1995. Washington, D.C.:AEJMC.

Atlanta Journal and Atlanta Constitution. 1995. *The AJC Stylebook.* Atlanta: Atlanta Journal and Atlanta Constitution.

Auman, Ann. 1995. *From "Celestial" to "Model Minority": The Portrayal of Chinese-Americans in the U.S. News Media.* Paper proposal for the Hawaii/Pacific/Northwest Joint Regional Conference Association for Asian American Studies. University of Hawaii Journalism Department.

Chicago Tribune. 1995. *Chicago Tribune Stylebook.* Chicago: Chicago Tribune.

Fong, Colleen Valerie Jin. 1989. *Tracing the Origins of a "Model Minority": A Study of the Depictions of Chinese Americans in Popular Magazines.* Doctoral Dissertation, Department of Sociology, Graduate School of the University of Oregon.

International Communication Association. *Official Program for the 39th Annual Conference of the International Communication Association.* 1989. San Francisco: ICA.

International Communication Association. *Official Program for the 40th Annual Conference of the International Communication Association.* 1990. Austin, Texas: ICA.

International Communication Association. *Official Program for the 41st Annual Conference of the International Communication Association* 1991. Chicago: ICA.

International Communication Association. *Official Program for the 42nd Annual Conference of the International Communication Association.* 1992. Maimi: ICA.

International Communication Association. *Official Program for the 43rd Annual Conference of the International Communication Association.* 1993. Washington, D.C.: ICA.

International Communication Association. *Official Program of the 44th Annual Conference of the Internatinoal Communication Association.* 1994. Sydney: ICA.

International Communication Association. *Official Program of the 45th Annual Conference of the International Communication Association.* 1995. Albuquerque: ICA.

International Communication Association new membership letter. 1995 (June). Austin, Texas: ICA.

Johnston, Judy D. 1996. *Does Ethnic Composition Affect Newspaper Content: A Study of International News Items in Six Metropolitan Newspapers—1990-1995.* Unpublished research paper.

Kato, Gerald and Beverly Ann Deepe Keever. 1996. *Did the U.S. Press Contribute to the World War II Internment of Japanese Residents?* Research paper presented at the Asian American Studies Association Regional Conference, Honolulu, 25 March.

Kyodo News information pamphlet. 1995. Tokyo: Kyodo News.

Layton, Suzanna. 1990. The Contemporary Pacific Islands Press. Paper presented at the 73rd Annual Convention of the Association for Education in Journalism and Mass Communication in Minneapolis.

Mansfield-Richardson, Virginia. 1995. Asian Americans and the U.S. Media: A Wake-Up Call. Paper presented at the 78th Annual Convention of the Association for Education in Journalism and Mass Communication. Washington, D.C.

Martindale, Carolyn. 1995. Only in Glimpses: Portrayal of America's Largest Minority Groups by the *New York Times*, 1934-1994. Paper presented at the 78th Annual Convention of the Association for Education in Journalism and Mass Communication. Washington, D.C.

Maurer, Gabriele. 1994. *Effect of European Ethnic Readership on Newspaper Content: A Content Analysis of Six American Newspapers.* Thesis, E.W. Scripps Shool of Journalism, Ohio University, Athens, Ohio.

*Nikkei Weekly* information flyer. 1995. New York: *Nikkei Weekly.*

Ong, Paul, ed. 1995. *The State of Asian Pacific America: A Public Policy Report.* Los Angeles: LEAP Asian Pacific American Public Policy Institute.

Tan, Alexis S. 1990. *Why Asian American Journalists Leave Journalism.* (Study commissioned by the Asian American Journalists Association.) San Francisco: Asian American Journalists Association.

## PUBLIC DOCUMENTS

U.S. Government, National Advisory Commission on Civil Disorders. 1968. *Report of the National Advisory Commission on Civil Disorders.* Washington, D.C.: U.S. Government Printing Office.

*U.S. Census, 1990.* 1992. Washington, D.C.: U.S. Department of Commerce, Economics and Statistics Administration, Bureau of the Census.

*U.S. Census, 1990: Social and Economic Characteristics.* 1992. Washington, D.C.: U.S. Department of Commerce, Economics and Statistics Administration, Bureau of the Census.

U.S. Civil Rights Commission. 1998. Transcript of the Dec. 5, 1997, hearing. Washington, D.C.: U.S. Goverment Printing Office.

## VIDEO RECORDINGS

*Slaying the Dragon.* 1988. Produced and directed by Deborah Gee. 60 min. New York: Women Make Movies, Inc. Videocassette.

*Who Killed Vincent Chen?* 1988. Produced by Renee Tajima, directed by Christine Choy. 82 min. New York: Filmmakers Library, Inc.

*Yellow-Tale Blues: Two American Families.* 1990. Produced by Renee Tajima, directed by Christine Choy. 30 min. New York: Filmmakers Library, Inc.

## MATERIAL OBTAINED THROUGH LOOSE-LEAF, COMPUTER, OR INFORMATIONAL SERVICES

*Index to Journals in Mass Communication - 1989.* 1990. Riverside, Calif.: Carpelan Publishing Co.

*Index to Journals in Mass Communication - 1990.* 1991. Riverside, Calif.: Carpelan Publishing Co.

*Index to Journals in Mass Communication - 1991.* 1992. Riverside, Calif.: Carpelan Publishing Co.

*Index to Journals In Mass Communication - 1992.* 1993. Riverside, Calif.: Carpelan Publishing Co.

*Index to Journals in Mass Communication - 1993.* 1994. Riverside, Calif.: Carpelan Publishing Co.

*Index to Journals in Mass Communication - 1994.* 1995. Riverside, Calif.: Carpelan Publishing Co.

# Index

## DATE DUE

| | | | |
|---|---|---|---|
| | | | |
| | | | |
| | | | |
| | | | |
| | | | |
| | | | |
| | | | |
| | | | |
| | | | |
| | | | |
| | | | |
| | | | |
| | | | |
| | | | |
| | | | |
| | | | |
| | | | |
| | | | |
| | | | Printed in USA |

HIGHSMITH #45230